Dead Giveaways

ESCRIVANODECABIL
DO
NOMBRADO·DESV·M
D

quilcaycamayoc

enos Hereyno   escriuano

Dead Giveaways

Indigenous Testaments of
Colonial Mesoamerica
and the Andes

Edited by Susan Kellogg

and Matthew Restall

THE UNIVERSITY OF UTAH PRESS

SALT LAKE CITY

Copyright © 1998 by the University of Utah Press
All rights reserved

Typography by WolfPack

Cover and frontispiece illustration by Felípe Guamán Poma de Ayala from
El primer nueva corónica y buen gobierno courtesy of Siglo Veintiuno
Editores.

Printed on acid-free paper.
Manufactured in the United States of America
03 02 01 00 99 98 6 5 4 3 2 1

Library of Congress Cataloging-in-Publication Data

Dead giveaways: indigenous testaments of Colonial Mesoamerica and the
    Andes / edited by Susan Kellogg and Matthew Restall.
        p.   cm.
    Includes bibliographical references and index.
    ISBN 0-87480-579-1 (alk. paper)
    1. Indians of Mexico—History—Sources. 2. Indians of South
America—Andes Region—History—Sources. 3. Wills—Mexico.
4. Wills—Andes Region. 5. Mexico—History—Spanish colony,
1540–1819—Sources. 6. Andes Region—History—Sources.
I. Kellogg, Susan. II. Restall, Matthew.
F1219.D43   1998
972'.00497—dc21   98-28466

Contents

Maps

Tables and Figures

Introduction

MATTHEW RESTALL AND SUSAN KELLOGG

The scene is not hard to imagine. Mortally ill, probably bedridden, an Andean woman or Maya man summons family members, close friends, perhaps business associates, and the principal men of the community— especially the notary, who then begins to write down the dictated final statement, the last will and testament. The time may be a few generations, or a few centuries, after Spaniards first walked into Tenochtitlan; the place may be the dry flatlands of the Yucatan Peninsula or the wet valleys of the Quito highlands; the words may be spoken and written in Nahuatl or Spanish, Mixtec, or Maya, but the ritual opens more or less the same way—"In the name of the father, the son, and the holy spirit. . . ."—and testators usually go on to dispose of their worldly goods.

Whether this wealth, often modest, occasionally impressive, was assigned to pay for posthumous masses, to settle debts, or to be distributed among family heirs, the lists of material items sandwiched between religious and legal formulas lend these documents the appearance of something straightforward and mundane. Perhaps that, as well as the fact that colonial Mesoamerican wills are mostly in native languages, helps to explain why these materials were so little studied for so long. In recent years, however, they have been brought to both light and life in varied and exciting ways. As this volume demonstrates, testaments may be mundane, but they are far from straightforward; as rich ethnohistorical sources, they are simply not "dead giveaways."[1]

The following chapters are devoted to describing and analyzing wills dictated by indigenous men and women in colonial Spanish America.[2] These documents constitute approximately half of the extant archival material written in Spanish America's indigenous languages during the colonial period. All surviving native-language testaments come from colonial Mesoamerica (or New Spain), but Spanish-language testaments by indigenous Andeans of western South America are among the most important ethnohistorical sources for that region; this volume's ten chapters thus range from central Mexico to Bolivia, together covering the period from the mid-sixteenth to the early nineteenth centuries.

Broad in geographic scope yet focused on one particular documentary genre, this volume has three goals. First, it introduces readers to the history of the production of such documents. Second, it examines the impact of testament writing on colonial societies, especially their indigenous inhabitants. Third, the book describes the contents of these documents and explores the opportunities thereby presented for the detailed analysis of indigenous cultures and societies in three regions: central Mexico, southern Mesoamerica (Oaxaca, Yucatan, and Guatemala), and the Andes.

The purpose of this introduction likewise is threefold: to outline the ways such testaments represent an unprecedented meeting of various elements on a number of levels (thus assessing their significance as a source); to suggest the place for analysis of this documentary genre within regional historiographies; and to summarize the chapters' major themes, which are briefly analyzed in the conclusion. Readers should note that each chapter also contains the transcription and English translation of one testament analyzed in that chapter.

Wills are among the richest types of documents available for the colonial ethnohistorian (see table I.1 on indigenous-language colonial wills). Through this single source genre of notarial document, textual elements meet to provide an in-depth picture of a particular individual or group. In colonial Latin America, most of the individual testators were themselves illiterate, but because of widespread access to what we will call "legal literacy,"[3] the voices of non-elites, so often sought by social historians, become available.

Many sets of elements come together in these texts, one of the most important being the individual and his or her relationship to society's institutions and its patterns of cultural beliefs. Wills represent the desires of individual testators for the posthumous state of their souls and the disposal of their material goods, yet these desires are not completely idiosyncratic. Wills from particular regions of colonial Latin America often show bequest patterns. These patterns changed over the course of the colonial period, reflecting family and kinship structures and mirroring the presence of other social institutions such as neighborhoods, work groups, and *cofradías* (religious brotherhoods). The testaments express piety and class

Table I.1

Published Indigenous-Language Testaments

Origin Community	Date	Language/ Number	Publication
Culhuacan, central Mexico	1577, 1581	Nahuatl/2	León-Portilla 1976[a]
Culhuacan, central Mexico	1572– 1606	Nahuatl/65	Cline & León-Portilla 1984
Culhuacan, central Mexico	1580, 1590	Nahuatl/2	Cline 1986
Tlatelolco, Central Mexico	1623	Nahuatl/1	Durand-Forest 1962
Various central Mexican communities	1566– 1795	Nahuatl/6	Anderson, Berdan & Lockhart 1976
Pochtlan, central Mexico	1695	Nahuatl/1	Lockhart 1992
Tepemaxalco, Central Mexico	1731–36	Nahuatl/3	Lockhart 1991[a]
San Estebán, Coahuila	1627–1776	Nahuatl/3	Offutt 1992
Ebtun & Cuncunul, Yucatan	1699– 1813	Yucatec Maya/10	Roys 1939
Ixil, Yucatan	1765–69	Yucatec Maya/68	Restall 1995b
Ixil, Yucatan	1766	Yucatec Maya/2	Restall 1997b[b]
Sacatepequez, Guatemala	1642– 1708	Cakchiquel Maya/3	Hill 1989
Teposcolula, Mixteca Alta	1672	Mixtec/1	Terraciano 1994

Note: Archival abbreviations used in text and tables can be found at the beginning of the bibliography.

[a]Both wills are also included in Cline and León-Portilla 1984. While the wills are not published, interested readers would find the analysis of twenty-two late-seventeenth and early-eighteenth-century Nahuatl testaments from inhabitants of Coyoacan relevant for many of the topics dealt with in this book (Namala 1995).

[b]Both wills are also included in Restall 1995b.

and gender conceptions as well as the cultural beliefs embedded within, and shaping, these various social relationships.

Another set of elements colliding in wills relates to the individual in time. While the act of dictating and writing the will generally took place at the end of a person's life, wills reflect not just that moment in time but the individual's life history as well. The idiosyncratic nature of long- and short-term personal relationships often influenced bequests. Family demography also molded bequests in that customary patterns of property transmission were frequently difficult or impossible to carry out due to the complex and ever-shifting disease and demographic patterns of colonial Spanish America.

Language and culture also meet in wills. While colonial wills were often written in indigenous languages, at least in Mesoamerica, the form and much of the terminology used reflected Spanish practices; Spanish friars originally introduced written testaments in most areas under colonial rule (Karttunen 1982; Restall 1994; Kellogg 1995a: 129–33). Indigenous wills, therefore, mirror Spanish testamentary practices yet diverge from them because of their varying expressive forms,[4] family and kinship structures, gender relations, and the broader cultural patterns that testators brought to their use of the genre. Likewise, wills represent a meeting of indigenous and Spanish languages, both in the broad sense—Spanish had a gradual impact and influence upon colonial-era indigenous languages[5]— and specifically, in that Spanish served as the language into which many wills were translated for legal purposes. Eventually colonial Mesoamerican wills came to be written in Spanish, as Andean wills were from the onset.

Just as testaments represent the intersection of the personal and the social, so do they portray the intersection of the domestic with the public. This is especially true with respect to the legal practices that came to play such an important role in native colonial life (Rappaport 1994b; Kellogg 1995a). Wills served as important legal documents for asserting property ownership before courts in situations of interpersonal conflict between indigenous litigants or between them and Spaniards. Pedigrees of ownership for both individuals (wills, bills of sale) and communities (*títulos*) had important political functions as mechanisms for claiming material resources, harassing others with whom a conflictual relationship existed, and/or resisting material or political encroachments (Kellogg 1995a; Lockhart 1982; Harvey 1986; Wood 1991b).

The conjunctions discussed here reveal why testaments are such rich historical sources, but these meetings also suggest how and why the genre can present problems of interpretation. Wills are not transparent documents;

their meanings are multiple, sometimes contradictory, and they cannot always be readily mined for the many different areas of inquiry stressed by contemporary ethnohistorians. Nevertheless, they represent, in aggregate, an irreplaceable inventory of types of property owned. These texts shed much light on indigenous categories of property ownership.[6] But these categories do not necessarily or solely represent pre-Hispanic categories of property ownership. The evaluation of the effects of acculturation, transculturation, or "interculturation" becomes still more complex when we turn from the material world to social relationships and cultural beliefs. Untangling personal choice, demographic influence, and cultural patternings of bequest options can be challenging because wills often do not provide the requisite details with the consistency and clarity that contemporary scholars would like.

The wealth of sociocultural information on material resources, class, gender, family, and ethnic identity that comes together in these documents makes them incredibly valuable. But the analysis of these elements and how they changed over time must be done with detailed ethnographic knowledge (in effect, another meeting takes place with the interdisciplinary conjunction of historical and anthropological theorizing and methodologies),[7] a sensitivity to temporal and regional variation (both ethnic and urban/rural), as well as an awareness of the intricate webs of power relationships that shaped the colonial-era indigenous individual's life history.

The contributors to this volume all believe that close, careful analysis of testaments provides a type of detailed information impossible to find in any other documentary genre. Just as testaments reflect the kinds of meetings already outlined, so too does this book's design consciously reflect further meetings of scholarship: as just indicated, different disciplines and kinds of ethnohistorical methodologies and approaches coexist here; a variety of indigenous languages are brought together; and analysis is offered of a documentary source that existed in both colonial Mesoamerica and the Andes, regions that tend to be treated separately in the historical literature. While not denying that the indigenous societies and colonial histories of these groups varied greatly, we believe there is much to be gained by a close and careful comparison of the themes and cultural changes embodied in this genre across colonial Spanish America.

What might the place of an analysis of this genre of documents be in relation to recent historiographies of these regions? The post-Gibsonian[8] historiography of central Mexico has gone in two directions, and these are not necessarily mutually exclusive. One direction consists of the New Philology studies of James Lockhart, his students, and other scholars.

These studies stress the intensive use of indigenous-language documents (primarily Nahuatl, but now also Yucatec Maya and Mixtec), of which testaments are one type. Such works fall into the category of social history, and they emphasize strong continuities between late-pre-Hispanic indigenous societies and the early-colonial indigenous world (Wood 1984; Cline 1986; Burkhart 1989; Haskett 1991; Schroeder 1991; Lockhart 1992; Terraciano 1994; Restall 1997b; Horn 1997b). Other studies, while making use of Nahuatl documentation, stress the ruptures caused by the conquest and Spanish colonial rule (Gruzinski 1988, 1992) and theorize that colonial political economy provides a context through which social and cultural change must be understood (Martin 1985; Kellogg 1995a).[9]

Testaments have been important sources for some of these studies, particularly the work of Sarah Cline (1986), Susan Kellogg (1986, 1995a), and Stephanie Wood (1991a, 1997a, 1997b), who share a strong interest in the daily lives of Nahua people and the social groups and cultural processes that shaped their lives. Their work suggests that while the complex cultural formations of the pre-Columbian era did not disappear overnight, on the individual level Spanish property and inheritance law, alphabetic writing, and demographic decline shaped responses to the new realities of the colonial era. At the same time, the testamentary genre shows how Nahuas brought significant cultural resources to the colonial encounter on both individual and community levels. Likewise, with respect to southern Mexico and Guatemala during colonial times, testaments have provided unique insights into various aspects of culture and community among the Ñudzahui or Mixtec (Terraciano 1994), the Yucatec Maya (Restall 1997b), and the Cakchiquel Maya (Hill 1989, 1992). The earlier, larger corpus of Nahuatl-based work has enabled Terraciano and Restall, in particular, to draw detailed comparisons between colonial Mexican regions and to suggest supraregional conclusions. Testaments are also proving to be important sources for younger scholars working on other Mesoamerican regions.[10]

Andean colonial ethnohistorical historiography, perhaps due to the critical importance of silver mining in the early-colonial period (Assadourian 1982), has been shaped by dependency theory to a greater extent than the writings on the areas already discussed.[11] The works of Karen Spalding (1984), Steve Stern (1988), Irene Silverblatt (1987), and Brooke Larson (1988) have proven to be of enduring significance and provide a very clear, empirically rooted picture of the interrelationships between institutions of extraction of labor and wealth and the laborers, communities, and social structures that fueled such extraction. While the value of notarial documents for social history was made clear in James Lockhart's seminal work (1968), the relative paucity of native-language documentary resources meant that Andean ethnohistorians de-emphasized the philological and social-historical approaches that characterize Mesoamerican colonial ethnohistory in favor of approaches emphasizing exchange, ethnicity, and demography (Powers 1995: 5–6; also see Saignes 1985; Glave 1989; Wightman 1990; Larson and Harris 1995; Zulawski 1994; and Ramírez 1996b).

Nevertheless, a number of ethnohistorical works based on notarial documents such as wills have provided detailed pictures of specific aspects of colonial Andean Indian life and, in particular, have focused on gender (Burkitt 1978; Salomon 1988; Zulawski 1990; Rappaport and Cummins 1994). This scholarship illustrates the richness of notarial sources for ethnohistory in this region; it also shows the complexity of Andean early-colonial ethnogenesis and provides evidence of the individual strategies used to cope with changing political, economic, and cultural contexts.[12]

The chapters that follow address a wide range of testament-related themes, and they bring a variety of approaches—both theoretical and methodological—to bear on the analysis of the body of colonial-era indigenous testaments. Although the chapters are grouped geographically and begin in the Valley of Mexico, where conquest and evangelization were earliest and, in some ways, had their most intense impact, each section is chronologically, thematically, and methodologically diverse.

In the first chapter, "Fray Alonso de Molina's Model Testament and Antecedents to Indigenous Wills in Spanish America," historian Sarah Cline discusses the religious roots of the Hispanic testamentary tradition. She also provides an overview of the only known sixteenth-century guide to testament writing, which contains a model will (written by fray Molina) to help native notaries in their task of writing testaments for dying Nahuas. Then, in chapter 2, "Indigenous Testaments of Early-Colonial Mexico City: Testifying to Gender Differences," anthropologist Susan Kellogg describes and analyzes the early wills of Mexico City's Nahua population. The chapter shows contrasts in patterns of testament writing over time (even within families) and captures gender-related changes in ways that Nahua men and women shaped yet were affected by Hispanic testament writing and legal traditions as these practices took hold in the Valley of Mexico. Historians Rebecca Horn and Stephanie Wood also analyze Nahua wills, with Horn concentrating on early-colonial Coyoacan, and Wood, the Valley of Toluca region. Horn's chapter, "Testaments and

Trade: Interethnic Ties among Petty Traders in Central Mexico (Coyoacan, 1550–1620)," delineates a range of informal Nahua-Spanish interactions, especially in the economic realm, and demonstrates the way testaments document the wide-ranging networks of interaction of early-colonial Nahua nobles and commoners. In chapter 4, "Testaments and Títulos: Conflict and Coincidence of Cacique and Community Interests," Wood not only paints a highly detailed picture of the relationship, even fusion, of the more individual-focused testament and the community-concerned título (property title) but also illustrates how the growing conflict between individual and group interests in resources resulted in the production of new documentary genres in the later sixteenth and throughout the seventeenth centuries, rooted in Nahua conceptualizations but responsive to changing colonial conditions.

Part 2 shifts in geographic focus to southern Mesoamerica and covers a diverse array of indigenous peoples. In chapter 5, "Native Expressions of Piety in Mixtec Testaments," historian Kevin Terraciano analyzes a section of colonial indigenous testaments that is often ignored, the religious opening in which the dying individual pronounces his or her faith. Rooted in a close reading of nearly two hundred Mixtec (Ñudzahui) colonial wills, Terraciano finds a dialogic interaction between Ñudzahui religious and political conceptualizations and the Catholic beliefs that the Dominican ecclesiastics of western Oaxaca hoped to substitute. "Interculturation and the Indigenous Testament in Colonial Yucatan," by historian Matthew Restall, focuses on three wills (from a much larger body of Maya-language testaments uncovered by Restall) from the seventeenth, eighteenth, and nineteenth centuries, arguing that such documents do not represent a linear process of change and Hispanization but rather a dialogical interaction among individuals, corporate communities, and cultural traditions. In "Land, Family, and Community in Highland Guatemala," anthropologist Robert Hill examines seventeenth-century Cakchiquel Maya testaments and argues that for Guatemala this genre represents a postconquest innovation, with the actual texts highly focused on bequests of land. This postconquest practice allowed seventeenth-century Cakchiquel Mayas to regularize the access of family-based corporate groups to land in a context of declining population and labor shortages. As landholding became subject to increasing pressure in the eighteenth century, a shift from the more individual testament to the community-based título took place.

Issues of continuity and change are also discussed in part 3, which treats the Andes, the third major area of indigenous Spanish America covered in this volume. Historian Karen Vieira Powers's chapter, "A Battle of Wills: Inventing Chiefly Legitimacy in the Colonial North Andes" shows a chiefly kin group, the Duchiselas of Ecuador, using testaments to assert their legitimacy as political leaders to create and protect a sizeable family estate. This estate maintained the vertical control common for Andean indigenous communities yet placed access and control over a formidable array of material resources in the hands of one family line and specific members of that family unit. But the Duchiselas were not merely privatizing their property ownership; there is evidence of the communal obligations and alliances that their holdings supported. In chapter 9, "Rich Man, Poor Man, Beggar Man, or Chief: Material Wealth as a Basis of Power in Sixteenth-Century Peru," historian Susan Ramírez analyzes changing indigenous conceptualizations of wealth and property through the sixteenth-century wills of three indigenous nobles. She finds a shift in conceptions of wealth; wealth defined in access to supporters and labor power to work in a variety of environments began to shift, by the late sixteenth century, toward definitions emphasizing the size and monetary value of goods owned, especially animals. Land had not yet begun to be commoditized, and Ramírez, like Powers, also finds considerable evidence of a persistent notion of mutual obligation between lord and subject. Finally, anthropologist Thomas Abercrombie, in "Tributes to Bad Conscience: Charity, Restitution, and Inheritance in Cacique and Encomendero Testaments of Sixteenth-Century Charcas," suggests that both indigenous and Spanish elite testators in the *audiencia* (subdivision of a viceroyalty) of Charcas (in modern-day Bolivia) shared similar goals. Arguing that the wills of both sets of elites shared basically similar concerns and responded to overlapping legal and social constraints, Abercrombie finds that the testamentary form—fusion of religious belief and legal procedure that it was—attempted to navigate the need of testators to transfer their property, both material and in terms of social position, in an orderly way and affirm the eternal existence of their souls.

The intricate, even paradoxical, purposes, textual structurings, and material arrangements that Abercrombie and other authors find in the indigenous testaments of colonial Spanish America illustrate the complex and changing legal, social, material, and cultural patterns embedded in these texts. But the testamentary genre itself changed over time, leading to the development of forms of native legal literacy that have far-reaching implications for native communities, not only of colonial Spanish America but for modern Latin America as well.

Notes

1. In addition to our thanks to Kevin Terraciano for allowing us to use a brilliant title of his invention, the editors would like to acknowledge those who contributed to the development of this book. We are grateful to all the contributors for their enthusiasm and dedication. We are also very grateful to Mick Duffy, former editor, and Dawn Marano, current editor, at the University of Utah Press, enthusiastic supporters of a complex project. Dawn Marano has been especially patient and helpful. Alexis Mills Noebels, copy editor *extraordinaria*, and the production staff at the University of Utah Press have also provided invaluable assistance. Matthew Restall thanks Susan Kellogg for her cheerfulness and tenacity, and Kellogg thanks Lorena García, History Department business manager at the University of Houston, who seems to make all things possible; Katie Harrison for bibliographic help; and Restall, whose insights and humor were evident every step of the way.

2. In addition to the studies presented in this volume, a rich new literature on testaments in Europe and the Americas is emerging. For works of the greatest relevance to scholars of Latin America, in addition to Eire's (1995) magnificent study of death and testamentary practices in sixteenth-century Spain, cited by several authors in this volume, Antonio Peñafiel Ramón (1987) examines numerous wills from eighteenth-century Murcia, and Robert I. Burns (1996) analyzes Jewish wills in medieval Spain. Sarah Cline's chapter in this volume also cites relevant works from other parts of Europe, especially France. Latin American scholars are also turning attention to this rich source. Besides pertinent works by Margarita Loera y Chávez (1977) and Mercedes del Río (1990b), the Centro de Investigaciones y Estudios Superiores en Antropología Social (CIESAS) in Mexico has undertaken a major project of cataloging, transcribing, translating, and analyzing Nahuatl-language wills from central Mexico. The project is headed by Teresa Rojas Rabiela and is called "La vida cotidiana indígena y su transformación en la época colonial a través de los testamentos."

3. By "legal literacy" we wish to suggest that while many of the individuals who left wills were not themselves literate in the modern sense, their knowledge of and belief about the importance and role of writing, especially the writing of legal documents, made them "quasi-literate" in a meaningful sense. Important studies of literacy's impact on traditional societies include Goody 1968, 1986, 1987; Goody and Watt 1963; Ong 1982; and Boone and Mignolo 1994.

4. For a discussion of the Nahua orality that shaped the written expressiveness of these documents, see Lockhart 1992: 367–72.

5. With respect to Nahuatl, see Karttunen and Lockhart 1976 and Lockhart 1992: chap. 7. On Yucatec Maya, see Karttunen 1985 and Restall 1997b: chap. 22. On Ñudzahui (Mixtec), see Terraciano 1994: 178–218.

6. See, for example, Cline 1984; Horn 1997b; and Restall 1995b, 1997b.

7. On methodological issues in the "borderlands" of history and anthropology, see Ohnuki-Tierney 1990; Kellogg 1991; Krech 1991; and Comaroff and Comaroff 1992.

8. We refer to Gibson's seminal work, *The Aztecs under Spanish Rule* (1964).

9. Also see Chance 1989 and Farriss 1984.

10. For example, Lisa Sousa (1998) studies sources in Zapotec and southern Mexican dialects of Nahuatl, and John Crider (forthcoming) is working with native-language and Spanish-language Otomí wills.

11. For a discussion of dependency theory and its relationship with colonial Latin American history (particularly in the Andes), see Stern 1988.

12. Karen Powers defines "ethnogenesis" as "the process by which distinct ethnic cultures are continually recreated over time, especially cultures that have experienced colonization" (1995: 183 n. 1). In addition to her important study, other recent Andean ethnohistorical studies emphasize close readings of local-level texts and are influenced by a wide variety of poststructural theorizing. See, for example, Rappaport 1990, 1994a; Ramírez 1996b; and Abercrombie 1998.

Map 1   New Spain and Colonial Peru

CHAPTER 1

Fray Alonso de Molina's Model Testament and Antecedents to Indigenous Wills in Spanish America

SARAH CLINE

Chance played no part in the sixteenth-century appearance of European-style testaments by Indian women and men in key parts of Spanish America.[1] Only a generation after their military conquest by Spaniards, Indians in central and southern Mexico and the highland Andean region began making last wills and testaments. In the "spiritual conquest" of the Spaniards' new territories, these Europeans transmitted to many Indians the basic tenets of Christian belief and practice. The creation of testaments was one such practice consciously introduced by Spanish religious personnel and quickly taken up by Indian elites in central areas of Mexico, later spreading both to other social strata and to a number of other indigenous groups in other parts of the Spanish empire.

As the chapters in this volume demonstrate, indigenous wills are a rich source for colonial history. It is worth exploring the European background to testament making and examining the 1569 model testament created by the Franciscan friar Alonso de Molina to guide religious personnel and Indian notaries in central Mexico in setting down the words of the dying. Placing indigenous testaments in a larger historical context shows their connections to an established European tradition and heightens our understanding of some of the thoroughly indigenous features of Indian wills.

In the European context, wills were Christian religious documents, formulated within cultural and legal frameworks of a given area, but

13

directed by imperatives of the Christian church. By the early modern period, a wide range of European men and women made wills. This period marks the high point of testament production and preservation, with some European archives holding tens of thousands of them.[2] Production of wills by Indians never reached such levels. Moreover, Indian testaments are found only in certain parts of the Spanish sphere (where populations were densely concentrated and had complex sociopolitical organization). But indigenous wills were not an isolated phenomenon either. They are a major genre of native-language document, made by large numbers of Indians who might not have left any other written trace of their existence.

European and New World archives have given scholars the evidence for studies of family and inheritance, which began appearing in the early 1970s with the development of interest in social history as well as cultural history specifically dealing with attitudes toward death.[3] For studies of Indian family structure and inheritance based on information in testaments, a number of published collections of wills and analyses are now available for comparison of patterns. The high point of production of Indian testaments coincides with that in Europe, enabling scholars to compare different types of Indian wills as well as contemporaneous European testaments.

The introduction of the last will and testament was part of the Spaniards' evangelization of Indians by mendicant orders, especially the Franciscans, Dominicans, and Augustinians.[4] The mendicants' first step was teaching Indians basic Christian concepts and the principal prayers, all preparing the way for their baptism. The process was by no means quick and proceeded unevenly, as early evidence from Nahuatl censuses indicates.[5] In general, Indians in central Mexico and highland Peru mounted no concerted resistance to the replacement of their religious structures and leaders. Indians in central areas accepted new Christian rituals and beliefs, blending them with their older practices.[6]

Indians in more peripheral areas, where there were fewer Spanish religious and civil personnel (such as Yucatan or Guatemala), could maintain non-Christian beliefs and practices.[7] Layering and blending of beliefs was standard operating procedure for many Indian groups in the New World, for there was a long history of interethnic conflict, often resulting in shifts in the religious sphere. It was equally standard for Christianity in the period prior to the Reformation to accommodate religious layering and blending, so long as the essential Christian message and ritual practices were absorbed and observed publicly.[8]

Not until Indians learned basic tenets of Christianity, and until some men became literate in Roman letters, could Indian notaries record testaments of Indians in their native towns. But as early as the 1530s, literate Nahuatl speakers in Mexico produced lengthy works at the local level, with the pace accelerating by the mid-sixteenth century.[9] The creation of wills was a long-standing Christian practice, one that took root quickly among the newly converted Indians. As colonial institutions were established in more peripheral areas of the Spanish empire, such as Central America, Indians began making testaments there as well. Spaniards settled in regions with the densest indigenous populations, and so, not surprisingly, European practices took hold most strongly in those regions. The largest numbers of indigenous testaments come from these areas, and the range of people making them is greater. In other areas, few non-elite Indians (either men or women) made testaments, and even those that are extant tend to be less elaborate than in the central regions.

By the time Europeans encountered the Americas in the late fifteenth century, the Christian church had been an established institution for more than a thousand years. Early church history provides important information about the development of testaments as religious documents. During Christianity's first three centuries, the faithful were persecuted not only by the Roman government, but also by their non-Christian kin. In those circumstances, the sect developed mechanisms to ensure aid to its needy members who could no longer count on relatives to do so. Christian widows, orphans, and the sick were helped by their coreligionists. As a pious act, Christian faithful began to leave one or more bequests to the needy. These charitable acts also had the effect of strengthening the sect as an entity, reinforcing ties among the faithful. However, since the church had no legal status until the fourth century, it could not easily accumulate wealth in its own right (Goody 1983; Fox 1986).

After the Roman emperor Constantine converted to Christianity in A.D. 312, the sect evolved into an institutional church, with the Roman emperor as its patron and moderator. Beginning in the fourth century, the Christian church as an institution began to accumulate wealth by gift, inheritance, and purchase, and at the same time it grappled with the moral and legal implications of that accumulation.[10]

In this context, testamentary bequests of money and property to the church by Christian men and women became more standard, but I must emphasize that wills were not a new genre of document. In the Roman empire, testaments were a well-established legal instrument of civil law for individuals to bequeath wealth to their chosen heirs. In Christian Europe, many basic procedures for testamentary law derived from the pre-Christian Roman code of Justinian, which set out two types of wills, oral (*testamentum nuncupatiuum*) and written (*testamentum inscriptus*). Roman law empowered all free adult men and women to make final wills (Markov 1983). During the Roman empire, wills were secular legal instruments. When Christians began making wills, the testaments served a religious function as well—and some would argue primarily a religious function—to guarantee a testator's salvation. According to Carlos Eire, in his study of attitudes toward death in sixteenth-century Madrid, the church could deny Christian burial to anyone dying intestate: "the church was making it clear that without a will there could be no salvation" (1995: 21). Religious invocations were the standard opening phrases, and religious concerns were an integral part of the document. Generally, the religious elements were virtually always formulaic and can be seen as the most impersonal part of the testament (Peñafiel Ramón 1987: 49). Testators usually affirmed their Christian beliefs, made arrangements for Christian burial and recitation of masses for the repose of their souls, and made bequests to the church and its personnel.

More important for the church, once it became an established institution, was that it gained control over testaments, and administration of estates came under canon not civil law, giving the church tremendous power. This administrative function was a key element in the church's accumulation of worldly wealth, which coupled with its monopoly in the spiritual sphere placed the church in a dominant position in many matters.

In Europe there were variations in who wrote down the testator's words, but even with these minor variations, wills were religious documents. In the Mediterranean region, the use of notaries predominated, while in England and some other northern European areas priests themselves recorded the statements (Swanson 1995). Both priests and notaries of the church were functionaries in a crucial position to influence men and women at their most vulnerable time—"on the verge of their death," as many a testator stated. As early as the sixth century, laws were passed attempting to keep priests from hovering around the residences of the dying, but to little effect (Goody 1983; Fox 1986).

Not surprisingly, but nevertheless significantly, a guide for making testaments was among the first materials prepared by European friars for their pastoral and sacramental roles with the New World indigenous peoples. The guide is found in the 1569 confessional manual prepared by fray Alonso de Molina, O.F.M., *Confesionario mayor en lengua mexicana y castellana*.[11] The Franciscan *Confesionario* is typical of the genre that

evolved in Europe in the thirteenth century, which outlined in the ver-
nacular how the priest was to query members of his flock about matters of
faith and sin, and instructed the priest how to perform his role in confession and assigning penance. In the wake of the Council of Trent
(1545–63), which set out Roman Catholic church policies calling for uni-
form practice in ritual and orthodoxy in doctrine, many more confessional manuals were created to guide both the clergy and laypeople in
matters of belief and practice. For many priests, these guides were
absolutely critical to their performance of their sacred duties, since standardized education of the clergy was not yet established (Nalle 1992). In
any case, the mendicant orders of the Franciscans and Dominicans,
founded at the beginning of the thirteenth century, were instrumental in
the development of these manuals (Delumeau 1990: 198–205). As the
regular clergy assumed duties usually reserved for parish priests, they took
on new responsibilities, serving as shepherds to flocks of parishioners and
performing the sacramental tasks of baptism, marriage, extreme unction,
and the Eucharist.[12] When the mendicant order took up evangelization in
Spanish America, they soon produced confessional manuals in Spanish
and indigenous languages, many of which survive today.

Molina's confessional manual was designed for mendicants in central
Mexico and has parallel columns of text in Nahuatl and Spanish. The
columns mirror each other in phrasing and meaning as much as any two
distinct languages can.[13] So far as we know, the manual contains the only
known sixteenth-century model testament for Indians.

The section on testaments in the *Confesionario* is distinct from other
parts of the manual. Sandwiched between a typical section of questions
for priests to direct to couples wishing to marry in the church and a section of questions dealing with the mortal sins of theft, adultery, sodomy,
and drunkenness, Molina's instructions on testamentary procedure are
incongruous in terms of subject matter. Unlike other sections that give
instructions to a priest about how to minister to his own flock, the section
on testaments is a set of instructions for a priest to give a notary recording
wills. The notary, not the priest, is to be the interlocutor with the dying
testator, which is consistent with Mediterranean testamentary practice.[14]
The use of Indian assistants in the spread of Christianity was standard in
the early-colonial period in Mexico. Making a will was a religious act, but
not a sacramental one,[15] so a notary could record it without the presence
of a priest. It is likely that a friar gave direct instructions to a given notary,
and that, after a period of supervision, the notary functioned fairly
autonomously. Scholars have already postulated that once literacy and

notarial practice were learned by a given notary, that notary taught another, creating a self-perpetuating tradition at the local level (Karttunen 1982). Since Molina's instructions on testaments are apparently unique, the diffusion of knowledge of testamentary practice to other areas and cultures likely happened more unevenly.

Although only European men could serve as Christian priests, notaries could be men of indigenous origin, and in Indian towns, they usually were.[16] In Mexico, Indians became literate in Roman letters for their own languages, with Spanish colonial and religious authorities encouraging the process. Thus Indian notaries became adept at keeping records in a variety of indigenous languages, leaving as their legacy numerous native-language documents scattered in archives. As several authors in this volume point out, testaments constitute a large percentage of documentation in indigenous languages.

Molina's instructions for priests to give to notaries have some important assumptions, revealing of Spanish attitudes toward Indians. Since the instructions are a conscious European effort to introduce the testament as a legal, religious, and cultural instrument, and since there are explicit guidelines for notaries in their dealings with Indian men and women making wills, it is worth while to examine the instructions for making a will as well as the model testament itself in detail.

The section on testaments is divided into two parts of equal length. The first is titled "Admonition for notaries who make testaments." The second is a model will, in the manual titled "Head, or beginning of the testament."[17] At the start of each of the two sections, there is a woodcut illustration, but neither seems to relate in any direct way to procedures for making wills or the model testament.[18] Most of the illustrations in the text are scenes from the life of Christ. One is repeatedly used in the manual (f.3r, 8r, 18r) and can be read as directly expressing the Franciscans' view of Mexican Indians. A barefoot friar stands pointing his right hand in a commanding or hortatory gesture toward six male figures who appear to be adult but are about three-quarters the size of the friar. It is unclear whether this size difference in the figures reflected the reality of physical size of a given European man with a group of Indian men; modern-day Mexican Indians are generally shorter than most western Europeans. However, a more likely reading is that symbolically the male European religious specialist is instructing his neophyte flock, whose men, by 1569 when the manual was written, were deemed incapable of being ordained Christian priests.[19] The repetition of this illustration in various parts of the text is a reminder to Franciscans of their relation to their Indian charges.

The instructions make no allusions whatsoever to a notary's racial or cultural status. The guidelines spell out the good notary's characteristics solely in terms of his qualities as a person and his ability to carry out his functions properly.[20] The instructions to the notary called on him to reflect on his own qualities. "Think thus now, in what I [the priest] tell you and examine yourself well, because you are obliged to do and complete all the things that I will say and tell you here" (f.58v). The notary was "obliged to carry out [his] office well and faithfully, with discretion and well advised of all the matters that [he was] obliged to do" (f.58r–58v). Not all notaries followed the guidelines. The collection of sixteenth-century Nahuatl testaments from the Nahua town of Culhuacan is very likely the result of a notary's hiding an entire book of testaments (Cline 1986).

The notary's obligations included ascertaining whether or not the invalid could speak well and understand the legal proceedings. If the dying man or woman had lost understanding or judgment, that person could not make a valid testament. "You [notary] . . . see if s/he speaks well and understands or if s/he raves and has lost judgement, because if s/he is delirious, and lost all sense, s/he cannot make a testament" (f.59r). Christianity as a religion obligates its believers to make reasoned decisions and to enter voluntarily into contracts,[21] thus the admonition to the notary about the testator's "good sense" and "volition . . . to make a testament" (f.59r). A will made by a person not in sound mind had no legal or spiritual force. Since the question of soundness of mind is addressed, clearly the physical health of the testator was an issue, especially since testators usually made their wills when death was imminent. Among colonial Nahuas, there was generally no expectation that someone in good health would make a will. In central Mexico, testators occasionally recovered their health, and some died midway through dictating the document.[22] Molina, however, presents a Spanish model in which previous testaments are revoked (f.63r). This model would be consistent with the Castilian practice of preparing a will in advance of death and periodically reviewing it (Eire 1995: 23). In this volume, Karen Powers gives an example from the Andean region of someone who recovered his health and made another will later. And codicils to wills are occasionally found in collections of elite family papers in Mexico.[23]

The notary's next duty is to summon "all those who are to be witnesses."[24] Here there are crucial instructions to the notary concerning categories of persons who could not serve as witnesses. They were not be "neighbors" of the dying person, nor kin. Rather, the witnesses were to be those who lived somewhat farther away from the testator. The number of witnesses was to be "six, eight, or ten." All were to be "mature men, not boys nor very old." Furthermore, "everyone who lives in the house of the testator is to be kept far from the testator's chamber so that they would not listen to or hear what the ill person says; only the witnesses are to hear it" (f.59r). This exclusion of the testator's relatives and co-residents was presumably designed to give the testator freedom to speak without pressure from prospective heirs.

In practice in central Mexico, witnesses to Indian testaments generally do not conform to the Spanish ideal. I have discussed elsewhere that the number of Nahua witnesses did conform to the six to ten prescribed by Molina's manual. However, significant numbers were relatives, and often the husband or wife of the testator, and therefore potential heirs.[25] Many witnesses to the Nahua wills from Culhuacan did, in fact, receive bequests. Those who did not receive anything had exerted the last pressure on the testator they could. The fact that the dying man or woman did not bequeath anything to a witness meant that the relative's or neighbor's non-inheritance was now a public fact, witnessed by many should it later be disputed. Clearly the much more public and familial nature of Nahua testaments was at considerable variance from the European ideal outlined in Molina's manual.

Another important Nahua variation from Spanish norms was women's equal standing as witnesses. In Spanish law, only adult males in their prime could serve as witnesses, and as Molina's manual indicates, men in their great old age were excluded. But there is evidence in central Mexico that Indian women often served as witnesses. Indeed, sometimes they were in the majority. Listed as a witness in a significant number of Nahua wills is the wife of the testator.[26]

Something the notary was not obliged to do was inform the priest of the testator's imminent death. There is no direct connection between the priest's sacramental function of administering the last rites (extreme unction) and the ordering of a testament. Making a confession prior to dying was considered a key factor in speeding a person's way to heaven rather than remaining in Purgatory. Eire (1995: 23) says that making a will included a penitential function, but this is not evident in the notary's tasks.

Molina's confessional manual then specifies that the notary is to address the testator directly saying, "My brother (and if a woman) lady" [Nicauhtizine [yntla ciuatl] ciuapille; Hermano mio (y si fuere muger) señora] (f.59r). The difference in terms of address for men and women is very interesting, showing a kind of equality and familiarity of the male notary with the male testator, and a discreet distancing of the notary from a female testator.

It is worth probing questions of gender in the context of the model (also see Kellogg, chap. 2, this volume). First of all, clearly both men and women are presumed to be candidates for making a will, and indeed, both men and women did, seemingly in equal numbers in the various collections of extant indigenous wills. In the model will, both men and women are to be asked what property they own; whether they owe or are owed money; and whether they have borrowed goods or others have borrowed from them. "Hast thou charge of someone else's property? Something like a house, or land, or money, or cotton mantles or cacao? Or some pigs?" (f.59v). Such information is crucial for the well-ordered administration of an estate and is outlined in the instructions to the notary, with examples given in the model will. The questions are gender-neutral and implicitly acknowledge that women could own property, contract debts and extend credit, and lend and keep goods. The late-sixteenth-century Nahuatl wills from Culhuacan give specific examples of women engaging in these activities (Cline and León-Portilla 1984; Cline 1986). Payment of debts was important according to the instructions to the notary for the testator. "It is good that thou ordereth [the debt] to be paid promptly, without any delay before thou diest, because if thou dost not repay it, thou wilt be unable to save thyself" (f.59v).

Although many questions are gender neutral, two are explicitly not and presume that the testator is male. One asks, "How large was the dowry of [his] wife when she was betrothed and married" (f.59v). The other question that assumes the testator is male is in the section discussing illegitimate children. In the Spanish text those children are further described as "hijos de sus mancebas" [children of his mistresses] (f.60r), with no presumption that women testators could have children in an equivalent position. The Duchisela family discussed in this volume (chap. 8) shows that, while it was unusual, women of substance could have natural children.

The instructions to notaries on estate division in Molina's manual are extremely important. In essence, the notary guides the testator in his or her choice of heirs. As many scholars note in this volume and elsewhere, we have virtually no idea about pre-Hispanic inheritance patterns. Even in central Mexico, where information about pre-Hispanic culture is most abundant and the earliest extant indigenous records are found, there is no written document spelling out rules or customs of inheritance. Francisco López de Gómara's (1943) account from early-sixteenth-century Mexico, that the older brother acted as guardian for his younger siblings until they came of age, is often cited since there are no other sources. We know there were rules for succession to the throne in the Nahua sphere, which stressed male lateral ties to brothers but in the descending generation also considered nephews possible candidates as well as sons. The overriding concern was fitness to rule amongst the male candidates. There is evidence of women rulers, but only in exceptional circumstances (Schroeder 1991).

Can we infer from rules for choosing a king or lord the ways non-elite men and women disposed of their property? I think that is less than clear, especially since the number of wills for any given area is small. The earliest extant native testaments are those of elite men, dealing with large estates, tied to questions of succession to rule and legitimacy in the eyes of their own communities and the Spanish colonial government. Women testators and women heirs are well represented in colonial indigenous testaments, suggesting that some form of pre-Hispanic inheritance patterns was being extended into the colonial period.

The concept of legitimacy to inherit or to rule is worth examining. When Christianity was introduced in the New World, its ideal concepts of family structure were well developed and articulated. By the twelfth century, marriage had been elevated to sacramental status, and the church regulated marriage. The church declared many long-term procreative unions illicit or immoral, and forbidden. Marriage of close kin, which kept property within kin networks, was one example. Another was a man having multiple wives (the practice of polygyny), whose offspring were full heirs. Divorce and remarriage were not options in the Christian concept of marriage. Widowed persons were discouraged from remarrying. And adoption of non-kin as heirs almost entirely ceased to be a legal option to provide an heir to those without any offspring. The total effect of implementing these Christian religious ideas about family arrangements created new categories of relationships in many newly Christianized societies and reclassified others out of existence.[27]

The church's view that marriage was a sacramental union to one partner meant that it deemed any other sexual relationship as illicit and resulting offspring "illegitimate." The status of concubine, which does not impart full rights of a wife but which in many cultures is a socially sanctioned relationship, was downgraded in Christianity to that of "mistress." This status had no social standing, although it was tolerated. However, mistresses or concubines had no sanctioned religious or legal standing whatsoever.[28] In terms of kinship and potential status as heirs, only children of the sacramental union were given full legal and social standing with the designation "legitimate." Those born of any other union were termed "illegitimate" and had more limited rights as heirs.

Molina's sixteenth-century confessional manual deals explicitly with the questions of legitimacy and heirs. Legitimate children (*hijos legítimos; teoyotica ipilhuan*) were distinguished from illegitimate (*no legítimos; amo teoyotica ypilhuan*). In the Nahuatl designation for this category of children, *teoyotica ypilhuan*, the key element is *teoyotica*, meaning "through divinity."[29] In colonial Nahuatl, this term, "through divinity," indicates Christian marriages sanctified by the church and children born of these marriages. In Latin and Spanish the categories licit/illicit and legitimate/illegitimate are formalized and have implications for many spheres. In colonial Nahuatl terminology, the religious or divine nature of children born of holy matrimony is more apparent than in Spanish, where they were merely "legitimate."

In the Spanish text of Molina, illegitimate children were further clarified to be "children of mistresses" [hijos de sus mancebas], indicating not only the status of the children but also that of the mother in Christian classification. In the Nahuatl text, the children are referred to as "y çan ymecapilhua" [just his concubine's children].[30] Molina's use of "çan" ("just, only") is a non-neutral modifier, perhaps the judgment of the Franciscan writer and not a reflection of Nahua views of a concubine's children's status.

If a man had no legitimate children, then the estate was to be divided between sons and daughters equally. But if the testator had both legitimate and illegitimate children, then the illegitimate children were to receive no more than a fifth of his goods, no matter how many were to share them (Molina 1984a: f.60). If the testator, who is presumed to be male, had no children at all, nor surviving parents or grandparents, then he could bequeath his property to whomever he wished. Leaving property to his wife was not mandated, but "he can very well do it." Significantly, if his wife were pregnant, the entire estate was to go to the child. The mother-to-be was to have charge of the estate, presumably until the child reached a certain (unspecified) age.

Molina's working assumption for estate division is that the line of inheritance is to be lineal kin—parents, children, and grandchildren, both male and female. Wives (but perhaps husbands as well) have no claim on the estate if there are children. Children born of a sacramental marriage have full rights to inherit, but children of less formal unions have variable rights, depending on the presence or absence of legitimate children. In the absence of any offspring, parents and grandparents (ascending lineal kin) have priority. In the absence of those, a testator can freely dispose of the estate. Pregnant wives gain special rights, which derive solely from the status as mother-to-be of a legitimate heir. A pregnant concubine, mistress, or lover has no such status. Molina's instructions about estate division are not descriptive of what Indians usually did of their own volition but are explicit directions to testators via the notary about what is allowable. A testator's disinheritance of legitimate children is not anticipated by the instructions.

Nowhere in Molina's discussion of heirs is the church mentioned as a recipient of testators' donations. This is noteworthy, especially since the church accumulated a great deal of wealth as a result of testamentary bequests. Perhaps piety and charity were so embedded in the ideals of Christian culture that Molina assumed that testators would make spontaneous religious donations and did not need to be guided by explicit questions from the notary. In Castile, according to Eire, wills were supposed to contain "the ordering of alms and pious bequests" and once done, heirs could arrange for a Christian burial (1995: 21–22). In Molina's model testament, a number of suggested actions would result in testators' resources going to the church, but no explicit instructions to the notary to require donations to the church. The fictional testator, called Francisco Gómez for a man or Juana Sánchez for a woman (f.61r), requests burial in the church building; a vigil and a mass are to be said. These requests require payment to the priest or a donation to the church. In addition to those requests, the fictional testator asks that money be given to purchase ornaments for the church or to provide "whatever is necessary for the sustenance of the ministers, etc. [*sic*]" (f.61v), plus "three pesos for the poor" and one peso for the hospital, so that those there "may be cured" (f.62v).[31] Since testaments are religious documents, these sample pious acts and charitable donations are consistent with the spiritual function of the will.

Testaments can provide an enormous amount of information on indigenous families and their property and, to a certain extent, political and institutional structures during the colonial period. But can testaments provide insight into Indians' religious beliefs and practices? Here I argue we are on unsure ground. As a start, virtually all testaments were written by notaries who had a repertoire of formulas to shape the testator's statement. In places far from concentrations of Hispanic or Hispanicized population, the opening religious formulas of Indian wills are often entirely absent.[32]

While there is the possibility that religious language at the head of the testament expresses the religious beliefs of individual men and women, I think that the religious language is far less revealing than cultural historians would hope. Variations in language might be indicative of belief, but I think that studies of testaments in the aggregate will show that elite men's and women's testaments show more variation than commoners'. It is probable that notaries gauged the amount of religious language to use in a will based on the status of the testator, knowing that many eyes would see an elite individual's will, and few that of a low-born person. Appropriate to elites' station would be a testament with all the religious accoutrements, just as their burials were usually in the church building, with many masses said for the repose of their souls.

Even if the number and elaborateness of religious formulas are not entirely the product of notarial practice, it is still likely that elite testators had considerable facility for using religious language, more so than commoners. It may be fruitful to compare religious language in men's and women's wills. Women were usually more diligent attendees of mass than men. However, elite males had the opportunity to serve in a formal position in the church (although not as priests),[33] bringing them into regular and close contact with religious phraseology. In all likelihood, these men and women could spontaneously use elaborate religious phrases on their deathbeds, having heard them frequently throughout their lives. However, notaries likely shaped testators' religious language. Michel Vovelle examined tens of thousands of French wills, initially concluding (1978) that religious formulas could be used as an index of changing belief; he has, however, subsequently revised his view (1990).

In general, the religious formulas appear to be just that—formulas—with the more important part of the testament being the dispersal of property. But why did very poor people make wills? Certainly the church's requirement for a will was a big factor. But I would argue that religious obligation was embraced by the poor as well as the rich since by fulfilling the religious requirement, the poor achieved a status equal to the rich. Historically Christianity appealed to the poor and the outcasts of society—in the ancient world to women and slaves especially. The language of the New Testament can be interpreted to support the economic and social status quo, but the promise of salvation is open to all, and the poor are exalted especially in the Gospels. On the verge of their deaths, both men and women, both rich and poor, prepared for the life in the hereafter on an equal footing.

Dying well became an important question for many Europeans in the early modern period, with the development of a whole genre of literature known as *ars moriendi* (how-to manuals for those needing guidance in dying well). Spanish versions of such manuals exist dating from the early sixteenth century,[34] but so far as I know, no such manual exists in any indigenous language for the guidance of Indians. The formulas in Molina's model testament hardly constitute a guide to Indians for dying well, but they did establish a straightforward template for Indian notaries to use in creating testaments as legal and religious documents.

Fray Alonso de Molina's Model Last Will and Testament
(Molina [1569] 1984a: facsimile f.61–63)

[f.61r] Ytzontecon ypeuhca yn testamento

—Y nica ytocatzin, y tetatzin, yuan tepiltzin, yuan spiritu sancto: nicpehualtia yn notestamento.

—Ma quimatican in ixquichtin quittazque ynin amatl, ca in nehuatl notoca Francisco gomez: (anoco yn niJuana Sanchez:) nican nochan Tetzcuco, ytech nipoui i perrochia yn itoca sancta Maria assumpcion: nicchiua notestamento. Auh maciui mococua nonacayo, ye ce in noyollo in nocializ i notlalnamiquiliz, in notlacaquia aquen ca, can pactica: auh nicchixtica in miquiztli, yn ayac vel yxpampa yeua, yn ayac vel quitlalcauia, ic nictlalia notestamento y ca atlatzaccan yca tlatzonco notlanequiliz, inic mochipa mopiyez ynic ayac quitlacoz, ca yehuantlin [*sic*] yzcatqui ye [f.61v] nicpehualtia.

Uei achto, yehuatl yn naniman, ymactzino nocontlalia yn totecuiyo Dios, ca oquimochiuili, yuan nicnotlatlauhtilia, ynic nechmotlaocololiz, nechmopopolihuiliz, yn notlatlacol, nechmohuiquiliz yn ichantzino yn ilhuacatlitic (yn iquac naniman oquitlalcaui nonacayo.) Auh yn nonacayo ytech nicpoua in tlalli ca ytech quiz ca tlalli ca oquitl: yhuan nicnequi can ce tilmatli ynic moquimiloz, ynic motocaz yhuan nicnequi, ompa motocaz yn toteopan sancto Antonio de padua, vmpa nechmomachiyotiliz yn teopixqui nosepultura, yn notecoch, yn notlatatac yhuan nicnequi, yn ipampa naniman ypaleuiloca, ynic amo vmpa vehcauaz Purgatorio ce vigilia yuan centetl missa, ynic motocaz nonacayo, auh yntlacamo velitiz yquac, ma quinimoztlayoc, auh quicahuazque ventli yn ompa teopan. Auh intla quinequi oc quezqui tetl ypan mitoz yn missa, quiteneuhtiaz yn quezqui pesos mocahuaz teopan, yn teotlatquitl ye mocouaz, anoco teopixque yntechmoequi yc mocouaz. tc.

[f.62r] Auh yzcatqui nictenehua yn uel noneyxcahuilaxca yn nixcoyan naxca, yn nocal nauhtetl, yn nomitl etetl, yn noteocuitl, yn nochalchiuh, yn vel naxca catca, yn iquac ninonamicti. Auh yzcatqui: nictenehua yn vel y yaxca nonamic, yn nochan tlacatl, yn iaxca ytlatqui valmochiuhtia in iquac titonamictique, mochi quicuiz. Auh yn ixquich ycotlapihuix, yn ixquich cauitl tonehuan otinenque, yeuatlin [sic] ye nican nictenehua, monequi quitoz yn quexquich, tlacoxelihuiz: centlamantli cecni quicuiz: auh yn centlamantli yz cecni: quicuizque yn nopilhuan.

Auh yzcatqui nictenehua yn teaxca nicpia. Macuillli pesos ma yciuhca maco yn axcaua, ytoca Juan perez Tlaxcallan monemitia, quiximati yn nonamic. Auh in Diego sanchez macoz ce peso yc onechtlatequipanilihui: ynic onechtlayecolti ce metztli: Yzcatqui naxca quipia, ytoca Pedro Garcia: chicome pesos: ma quimmaca yn quimmocuitlahuizque nopilhuan. Yhuan nicnequi: ey pesos macozque ym motolinia, yehica notech [f.62v] poliuhtica notech actica cequi teaxca: auh amo niquimiximati yn axcauaque, yuan nitlanauatitiuh, yntla oc centlamantli neiz, yn notech poliuhtica teaxca, mochi moxtlaua (yntla necizque testigos, yn aco notlacuilol) yuan nitlanahuatitiuh yniccahualotiuh ospital ce pesos, yntech monequiz yn ompa mopatia. Auh yzcatqui, niquinteneuhtiuh yn nopilhuan yn vel axcauaque, vel yehuantin quicuizque, yn ixquich naxca. Ynic ce ytoca Francisco, ynic ome ytoca Pedro. tc. [sic] In yehuantiny, quimoxeluizque yn ixquich naxca notlatqui: can neneuhqui, can cen yaz: can mochixixquich, ynic quimoxexelhuizque, mochintin yn oquichtin yhuan yn ciua. Yzcatqui nicquetztiuh nicteneuhtiuh, yn quimmocuitlahuiz nopilhua: yuan yn intlatqui: ytoca Alonso de Sancta Maria: yuan nicteneuhtiuh oc cetlacatl, quipalehuiz ytoca diego xuarez. Yn yehuantini, niquintlatlauhtitiuh ynic quimocuitlahuizque ynin notlatlalil, ynic mochi neltiz, ma ypaltzinco yn Dios quichiuazque, ma quitequipanozque [f.63r] yn yehuatl notestamento, anoco nocodicilio anoco notzonquez ca tlanequiliz (yn iuhca nauatilli, ym melaua ca tlatoli) ma cenca quimocuitlauizque, ynic yciuhca mochiuaz neltiz, yn izquitlamantli ipaquitlamantli ytech nictlalitiuh notestamento. Auh oc cepa niquimotlatlauhtilia yn Alonso de Sancta Maria, yuan yn Diego Xuarez ynic nopantlatozque, ynic yciuhca mochiuaz. Auh yntla yciuhca mochiuaz inic niquinnotlatlauhtilia: yehuatzin yn totecuiyo Dios, quimmotlaocoliliz ynic no yuh ympam mochiuaz, yn iquac miquizque. Auh yntla oc ce ytla oc centetl notestamento canapaneciz, nicpolhua, niman amotle ypampohuiz yuh quin atley: anoco ytla aca quipiya notlatol, yn aco nicnonotzniquilihui nictenehuili ynic ytla ytech nicpouhtiaz ynic ytla ytech nicauhtiaz, yn iquac nimiquiz, mochi nicpolohua can ye yyo nicnequi neltiz mochiuaz yn ipan in notestamento nictlalitiuh. Auh yntla ym ixpan neciz Alcaldesme, ma quimatican yn quimocuitlauia justicia in tetlatzontequiliani: ca [f.63v] yehuatlin, yn vel notestamento yn vel noyollocopa niccauhtiuh. Auh yn onicchiuh, nican Tetzcoco, ytocayocan sancta Maria assumpcion ym ixpan testigome, yn vel ypampa onotzaloque: ynic ce tlacatl ytoca Juan gomez: ynic ome ytoca Sancho garcia. tc. [*sic*] Y nauellacuiloua Andres perez, yhuan Juan gocales, ypampa oquifirmati Antonio fernandez (canno testigo) Auh yn nehuatl Goncalo mendez escriuano nican ciudad tetzcoco oniquicuilo, onechtlatlauhti, yn. N. (yn tlacpac omoteneuh) yuan omofirmati. Yuan niquitohua, ca niquiximati yn N. yn quichiuh testamento, nixpan, yuan niquimiximati in testigosme yn tlacpac omoteneuhque. tc.

❧

In the name of the Father, the son, and the Holy Spirit, I begin to make my testament.

Know all who see this document, this written word, that I, Francisco Gómez, (or I, Juana Sánchez), resident in the city of Texcoco, in the parish of St. Mary of the Assumption, I make and ordain my testament. Even though my body is ill, my heart and will, memory and understanding are well and happy. And I am awaiting death, which no one escapes, nor is one able to be free of it. And for this reason I made this, my testament, my last and final will, in order that it will always be kept, and no one is to go with another and it is that which here I begin to declare.

First, I commend and place my soul in the hands of our lord God, who made it, and I ask him for mercy. I beg him to keep my soul, and I desire that he pardon all my sins, and I wish that he carry me to his house in heaven, after my soul has left my body. And my said body I leave and commend to the earth, from which it came, because it is earth and mud. And I wish my body to be wrapped in a winding sheet for burial. And I desire that it be buried in our church of St. Anthony of Padua, where the priest indicated the tomb and burial place. And this is my will, for the aid of my soul, in order that it not stay much time in Purgatory. A vigil and a mass are to be said for me when my body is entombed. And if it is not possible to say it that day, it should be the next one. And the offering will be taken to the church. And if desirable some masses will be said. The money I have left to the church is in order to buy some ornaments, or so that what is necessary is given to the ministers [or church people] for their sustenance, etc.[35]

And I declare that the goods that are mine, belonging to my person are four houses, three inheritances of mine of gold and silver and precious stones; these I had and possessed before I married. And I also declare here, the estate of my wife and resident of my house, that which she brought with her when we were betrothed and wed, all of that she is to take.

And all that has increased in all the time that we have been together, that is what I will say here, it is suitable that I will declare all, it is to be divided into two parts, the first she will take, and the other my children will take.

And I also declare here that the property I hold for someone else, five pesos which should be given with all speed to the one whose they are, Juan Pérez, who lives in Tlaxcala. And my wife knows him. And to Diego Sánchez, one peso is to be given for a certain job that he did for me, for the service of one month. And the one who has some goods of mine is Pedro García, he has seven pesos. They are to be given to the one who has charge of my children. And I wish that three pesos be given to the poor, because I am in charge of some things of others. And I do not know the owners of them. And I order that if I am apparently in charge of some goods, it is all to be paid (if witnesses are necessary, for my statement). And I also leave ordering that one peso be given to the hospital in order that those in it be cured.

And I leave here named my children, my true heirs, they will take my estate. The first is named Francisco; the second, Pedro, etc. [*sic*] They are to divide all my estate equally among themselves. Some are not to take more than others, the men likewise as the women.

And here I name the one who will have charge of my children and of their estate, Alonso de Santa María. And I also name another who will help him, whose name is Diego Suárez. To these I implore before my death that they have charge of this, my testament, in a manner that it be executed. And for the love of our lord God, they are to do and complete this, my said testament, or codicil, of my last and final will (according to what is ordered in the law). They will have much care that with all speed they will do and complete entirely all the things I leave ordered in this my said testament.

And once again I beg of the said Alonso de Santa María and Diego Suárez that they will favor me with it being done with all due speed. And if they perform it all with complete diligence, I beg and implore our lord God will do for them, in order that the same be done with them when they die. And if some other testament of mine should appear some place, I give it to no one; it has no value of [legal] force, as if it didn't exist. And if some person has some written statement of mine in which I promise to leave him something when I die, I have given [no such statement] to anyone. It is my will that which I solely make and complete and leave in this my testament. And if [someone] appears before the alcalde, they should know that they are invested with justice, to judge and to sentence, that this is my true testament, that which with all my heart I order.

And I make [the testament] here in Texcoco, in Santa María Assumption, before the witnesses who are named. The first of them is named Juan Gómez, the second Sancho García, etc. [*sic*] And those that do not know how to write are Andrés Pérez and Juan González, and because of this Antonio Fernández, who is also a witness, signs in their name. And I, Gonzalo Méndez, notary of the city of Texcoco, write this at the request of [N.], name above, who signs his/her name. And I declare I know the above said N. who makes this testament before me. And I also know the witnesses named above, etc. [*sic*].

Notes

1. So far as we know, there are no extant wills of Brazilian Indians.

2. For Vovelle's 1978 study of piety and de-Christianization in eighteenth-century France, he read some twenty thousand testaments from Provence. Philippe Ariès (1982), in his study of European attitudes toward death, also uses testaments extensively. Chaunu (1978) also has extensive information based on Parisian wills. In Spain, Carlos N. M. Eire's 1995 work on sixteenth-century Spanish attitudes toward death based on a sample of 436 testaments is particularly relevant, as is Antonio Peñafiel Ramón's 1987 work, based on 400 wills from eighteenth-century Murcia. Studies of wills whose focus is more on the socioeconomic aspects of inheritance include a collection of case studies on family and inheritance edited by Jack Goody, Joan Thirsk, and E. P. Thompson (1976). In colonial Mexico, Lavrin and Couturier's 1979 study of Hispanic women's dowries and wills is an important contribution to the literature.

3. A number of works using indigenous testaments began appearing in the late 1970s and early 1980s. A study of native land tenure and inheritance for towns in the Toluca region of central Mexico made use of approximately 100 wills (Loera y Chávez 1977). Dissertations based on testaments from this period include Susan Kellogg's (1980, 1995a) study of Mexico City and my own on Culhuacan (Cline 1981, 1986), both dealing with central Mexico and published subsequently as monographs. Philip C. Thompson (1978) studied a region of eighteenth-century Yucatan, using a considerable number of testaments for his unpublished dissertation. Much of Thompson's information was incorporated in Nancy Farriss's 1984 study of the Yucatec Maya from the sixteenth through the eighteenth centuries. Matthew Restall has done fine work on the Yucatec Maya, drawing extensively on testaments (1997b) and publishing a collection of them (1995b). A major source for James Lockhart's 1992 synthesis on the Nahuas is last wills and testaments, drawing extensively on *The Testaments of Culhuacan* (Cline and León-Portilla 1984).

4. Ricard (1966), written in the 1930s and for many years the standard view of evangelization and conversion, presents the mendicants' own interpretation of their enterprise. Louise Burkhart's (1989) subtle and superb analysis adds depth and complexity to our understanding of the process.

5. Cline (1993a) analyzes the data on baptism and church marriage, which give an indication of the outward pace of conversions. Using indicators such as baptismal patterns, naming patterns, numbers of couples married in the church, and numbers of nominal Christian converts still living in polygynous situations, I

have drawn some conclusions about the pace and impact of Christianization in central Mexico in the first generation after the conquest.

6. Klor de Alva (1982) has created a typology of responses to Christianity. There were isolated cases of apostasy, converts turning against Christianity, the most spectacular of which was don Carlos Ometochtzin, lord of Texcoco, who was executed (Greenleaf 1961: 68–75).

7. Clendinnen (1987) discusses the difficulties of the Franciscans in sixteenth-century Yucatan.

8. There were a few vigorous campaigns by friars to extirpate indigenous reversion to their old religious ways, one of the most noteworthy being in Yucatan (Clendinnen 1987), where Franciscans reacted violently to the Mayas' apparent reversion to old rites.

9. The tribute records from the Cuernavaca region are the earliest-known local-level records in Nahuatl (Carrasco 1964, 1976; Hinz, Hatau, and Heimann-Koenen 1983; Cline 1993a, 1993b). They have important information about baptismal and church marriage patterns for six Nahua communities (Cline 1993b).

10. The early Christians eschewed the accumulation of wealth, and there are ample references in the gospels demonstrating Jesus's hostility to material wealth. Theologians began to argue that church wealth enabled the institution to further Christ's work in the world.

11. A facsimile was published in Mexico in 1984 by the Universidad Nacional Autónoma de México, with an introduction by Robert Moreno (Molina 1984a). An earlier 1565 version also exists and is cited elsewhere in this volume.

12. Ricard (1966) discusses this in detail.

13. Burkhart (1989) has done brilliant work on the phrasing of Christian concepts in Nahuatl.

14. In the Spanish text of Molina, this functionary is called an *escribano*, and this word was taken as a loan into Nahuatl. I have translated it as "notary," since this person did more than simply make a transcription of an oral statement. Rather, his expertise in laying out the format and shaping the content places him in a larger legal role.

15. The sacraments in Roman Catholicism are baptism; the Eucharist (communion); confirmation of faith; marriage; reconciliation of a penitent; extreme unction (last rites); and ordination of a priest.

16. Few Indian women held office of any kind in their communities, much less in the role of notary. There is no evidence to date that any colonial Indian woman in central Mexico was literate, even to the extent of signing her own name (Cline 1986: 115, 122).

17. It is numbered by folios, f.58r–63v, with the section on wills coming exactly in the middle of the 124 folios.

18. The illustration on f.58r appears in an earlier section of the manual, which deals with questions of blasphemy (f.25v). The illustration on f.61r of the Trinity is not replicated elsewhere in the manual, but it is unclear whether the illustration is meant to amplify the meaning of the text it accompanies.

19. The Franciscan Colegio de Santa Cruz Tlatelolco was originally founded to train Indian boys for the Christian priesthood, but by the mid-sixteenth century,

that function had ceased. For a time Indians were prohibited from ordination (Barnadas 1984: 523). Women are still barred from being ordained as Roman Catholic priests.

20. As with all instructions for the priests, the other person is addressed in the familiar for *tú*.

21. Infant baptism was not permitted in the early church because infants were below the age of reason. Later, when infant baptism became standard, confirmation in the faith was instituted as a sacrament to deal with this difficulty. In the case of marriage, the union was to be by agreement of the man and woman, if there were no impediments to marriage, such as close kin relationship or existing marriage. Objections by the couple's families were not a consideration by the church, which was the arbiter of rules once marriage became a sacrament. In theory, there were no forced conversions to Christianity. The *requerimiento* supposedly gave Indians free choice of whether or not to convert peaceably to Christianity.

22. Cline 1986: 19–20; Karttunen and Lockhart 1976: 164–65.

23. Papers relating to a Xochimilco, Mexico, *cacicazgo* (the entailed estate of a native lordship) can be found in AGN Vínculos 279. The collection as a whole is discussed in Cline 1991.

24. In Spanish, *testigos*; in the Nahuatl text the loanword *testigome* is used (f.58v).

25. Cline 1986; Lockhart (1992) also discusses witnesses.

26. Cline 1986: 30.

27. Goody 1983; Motolinía (1971) discusses the difficulties in extirpating polygyny and trying to limit men to a single wife. Polygyny still continues to have an underground existence in some modern Nahua communities (Nutini 1965). In the Cuernavaca censuses of the late 1530s or 1540s, there were many households with plural marriages, even where some partners were baptized and others not (see Cline 1993b).

28. Hernando Cortés's son from his relationship with doña Marina/Malinche for many years was the heir apparent to Cortés's title of Marqués del Valle de Oaxaca and the entailed estates that went with the title. However, when Cortés's son with his (second) Spanish wife was born, the natural son lost out in favor of the second but legitimate son.

29. Deriving from *teo(tl)*, "god, divinity"; and *yo(tl)*, "quality of" and *-tica*, "by means of."

30. *Meca(tl)* literally means "rope, cordage," and the extended meaning of it is "concubine." *Mecatl* is an element of the term to describe kin relations or lineage, *tlacamecayotl*, literally "human cordage." In Nahua pictorial genealogies, the linkages between kin are shown with thick cords (Cline 1986: 66–67).

31. Hospitals for the sick were a Christian European introduction to Mexico, and the Spanish word *hospital* was a loanword into Nahuatl.

32. See Restall's and Hill's chapters in this volume for examples; Terraciano's chapter suggests there was variation in this feature of native testaments.

33. Indians were banned from ordination for a key period in the sixteenth and early seventeenth centuries, but even when the ban was lifted, few Indian men were ever ordained.

34. Eire (1995: 23) cites Alexo Venegas, *Agonía del transito de la muerte, con avisos y consuelos que cerca della son provechosos* (1536) and Luis de Rebolledo, *Primera parte de cien oraciones funebras en que se considera la vida, y sus miserias: la muerte y sus provechos* (1600).

35. The loanword phrase *et cetera* appears in the earliest-known local-level Nahuatl documentation. In *The Testaments of Culhuacan* the notary used it several times to save time and energy writing formulaic language (Cline 1986).

PART 1

Central Mexico

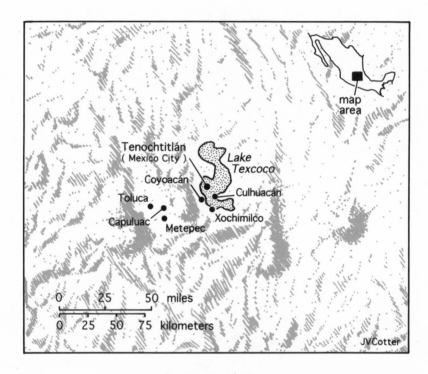

Map 2 Central Mexico

CHAPTER 2

Indigenous Testaments
of Early-Colonial Mexico City:
Testifying to Gender Differences

SUSAN KELLOGG

In 1606, in the barrio of San Sebastián Cuitlahualtongo in Mexico City, a Nahua woman named Magdalena Ramírez dictated a will describing her wishes for the distribution of her property at her death. In subtle ways, she commented on the nature of her familial and wider social ties. Ninety-three years later, in 1699, another indigenous woman in Mexico City, Melchora de Santiago, of the barrio of Santa María la Redonda Copolco, left a will that likewise expressed her desires for the distribution of her property and also commented on the nature of her significant relationships.

Indigenous testaments offer a valuable but sometimes neglected vista of the processes of cultural change. Such documents not only provide an inventory of the types and amounts of personal and real property that individuals owned and how ownership patterns shifted over time, but they also provide concrete evidence about changing gender and family relationships. The wills of Magdalena Ramírez and Melchora de Santiago are also of great interest because, in each woman's case, other relatives likewise left wills that have survived to today. In the case of Magdalena Ramírez, her grandfather and father also dictated testaments, as did the father of Melchora de Santiago. These five documents span the years from 1569 to 1693. They are part of a larger corpus of sixty-four extant testaments left by Nahua testators in the sixteenth and seventeenth centuries after the Spanish conquest of Tenochtitlan and Tlatelolco.

37

Most of these wills are embedded in the texts of lawsuits over property heard by local officials—sometimes native, sometimes Spanish—which were eventually appealed to higher-level Spanish officials and ultimately the final court of appeal, the *audiencia* (royal court) of Mexico.[1] The texts of these wills and the lawsuits in which they are often contained are found primarily in the *ramo Tierras* (Lands section) of the Archivo General de la Nación (AGN) (national archive) of Mexico. A few testaments come from a variety of other sections of the AGN as well as other libraries or collections. Tables 2.1 and 2.2 list these wills, describe their current location, and provide information about the languages of the texts (whether Nahuatl and/or Spanish). Thirty testaments exist for male testators (twelve from the sixteenth century, eighteen from the seventeenth), thirty-four for women (eighteen from the sixteenth century, sixteen from the seventeenth).

In this chapter I examine the wills of Magdalena Ramírez and Melchora de Santiago along with the wills of their male relatives in some detail. The issue at hand is how a new practice—ordering the writing of a will—introduced in a gender-neutral manner to both women and men, accompanied a general decline in Nahua women's status within indigenous communities during the colonial period. Given Spanish bilateral inheritance patterns, one might conclude that Hispanic women had a *relatively* higher status compared to their western European sisters.[2] But for Nahua women, the introduction of such codified European legal practices, like that of creating a written text to preserve their desires for the disposal of their earthly possessions, did not reinforce women's legal or social position and roles after the Spanish conquest (Kellogg 1995a: chap. 3).

I analyze this set of wills within the context of the larger Nahua testamentary corpus of early-colonial Mexico City in order to provide detailed examples of how such texts were constructed. The documents are then analyzed both as *written texts* whose wording and rhetoric contain some clues to the declining status of Nahua women compared to that of men, and as *property records* that indicate the shifting material basis that may have contributed to changes in gender roles. While several scholars have examined the effects of alphabetic writing on indigenous expressive forms,[3] few have sought to show how the introduction of codified legal practices, as well as new forms of writing and literacy, contributed to specific kinds of sociocultural change. However, before turning to issues of textuality and record keeping, I move first to a discussion of the particular texts examined here and focus on their organization and content. In addition, I try to

Table 2.1
Extant Wills by Nahua Men Resident in Mexico City,
Sixteenth and Seventeenth Centuries

Name	Source	Year	Language
Juan Tehuitzil	AGN-T 35-1	1548	Spanish
Martín Lázaro Pantecatl	AGN-T 20-1-3	1551	Nahuatl Spanish
Hernando de Tapia	AGN-T 37-2	1555	Spanish
Don Diego de Mendoza[a]	AGN-T 49-5	1555	Spanish
Diego Tlacochcalcatl	AGN-T 48-4	1566	Nahuatl Spanish
Antonio Quahuitencatl	AGN-T 1595-4	1569	Nahuatl Spanish
Francisco Hernández Quauhcequi	AGN-T 38-2	1576	Nahuatl Spanish
Francisco Xochpanecatl	AGN-BN 293-1	1576	Nahuatl
Martín Jacobo	AGN-T 39-2-1	1577	Nahuatl Spanish
Pedro Doçan	AGN-T 442-5	1587	Nahuatl
Pedro Jacobo	AGN-T 59-3	1588	Nahuatl Spanish
Joséph Ramírez	AGN-T 1595-4	1591	Nahuatl Spanish
Martín Xochitl	AGN-BN 1455-5	1604	Nahuatl
Antón Jacobo	AGN-T 95-8	1607	Spanish
Juan Matías	AGN-T 157-7	1615	Nahuatl Spanish
Don Melchor de Mendoza	AGN-T 1586-1	1618	Spanish
Gaspar de Mendoza	AGN-T 1592-1	1630	Spanish
Sebastián Francisco	AGN-T 1720-7	1632	Nahuatl Spanish
Baltasar Bautista	AGN-BN 339-8	1634	Nahuatl Spanish

Name	Source	Year	Language
Joséph Melchior	AGN-T 101-2	1642	Nahuatl Spanish
Don Matías Suarez	NL/Ayer 1481B-3b	1659	Nahuatl
Francisco Antonio	AGN-T 2776-18	1662	Nahuatl Spanish
Felipe de Santiago[a]	AGN-T 163-5	1672	Spanish
Felipe de la Cruz	AGN-T 165-4	1675	Nahuatl Spanish
Juan de la Cruz	NL/Ayer 1481B-3d	1679	Nahuatl
Francisco Agustín	AGN-T 163-2	1691	Nahuatl Spanish
Don Felipe de la Cruz	AGN-T 155-9	1692	Nahuatl Spanish
Don Francisco de San Pedro	AGN-C 592-1	1692	Nahuatl Spanish
Don Juan de Santiago	NL/Ayer 1481B-3l	1693	Nahuatl
Francisco de Luna[a]	AGN-C 1828-5	n.d.	Spanish

Note: Tables 2.1 and 2.2 draw on and modify Kellogg 1995a: tables 1, 2, 4, 5, 7, and 8. Note especially that two more seventeenth-century Nahua women's wills, those of Clara López and Nicolasa de los Angeles, are included here. One will by a male testator, don Gaspar de Buenaventura, which has certain features in common with *títulos* (see Stephanie Wood's chapter in this volume) and does not appear to be a genuine sixteenth-century testament, is not listed here. This document can be found at Tulane's Latin American Library, Gates Collection, box 1, folder 1. Also note that to conserve space, these tables use the following abbreviations: AGN, Archivo General de la Nación; BN, Bienes Nacionales; BNP, Bibliothèque National de Paris; C, Civil; NL/Ayer, Newberry Library, Ayer Collection; T, Tierras.

[a] Only a partial text is extant.

Table 2.2
Extant Wills by Nahua Women Resident in Mexico City,
Sixteenth and Seventeenth Centuries

Name	Source	Year	Language
Angelina Poqui	AGN-T 35-1	1546	Spanish
Francisca Tecuchu	AGN-T 42-5	1560	Spanish
Magdalena Tiacapan	AGN-T 22-1-5	1561	Spanish
Marina Tiacapan	AGN-T 2729-20	1561	Nahuatl
Ana Tiacapan	AGN-T 35-6	1566	Nahuatl Spanish
María Xocoyotl	AGN-T 35-6	1569	Nahuatl Spanish
Beatriz Papan	BNP 112	1570	Spanish
Juana Hernández	AGN-T 56-8	1574	Spanish
Francisca Tlaco	AGN-T 42-5	1576	Nahuatl Spanish
Juana Francisca	AGN-T 48-4	1576	Nahuatl Spanish
Juana de Santana	AGN-T 56-8	1576	Spanish
Angelina de la Cruz[a]	AGN-T 56-8	1579	Spanish
Angelina Martina	AGN-T 49-5	1580	Nahuatl Spanish
Elena Angelina	NL/Ayer 1481B-1a	1581	Nahuatl
Isabel Ana	AGN-T 54-5	1587	Nahuatl Spanish
Juana Hernández	AGN-T 56-8	1591	Spanish
Juana Antonia	AGN-T 59-3	1595	Nahuatl Spanish
Juana Mocel	AGN-T 70-4	1596	Nahuatl Spanish
Magdalena Ramírez	AGN-T 1595-4	1606	Spanish
Juana Agustina	AGN-T 128-2	1609	Nahuatl Spanish
Juana María	AGN-T 101-2	1616	Nahuatl Spanish

Name	Source	Year	Language
María Alonso[b]	BNP 299	1623	Nahuatl Spanish
Ana Melchiora	NL/Ayer 1481F-5	1642	Nahuatl
Clara López	AGN-BN 387-1	1650	Spanish
Juana Francisca	AGN-T 1594-4	1652	Nahuatl
Micaela Angelina	NL/Ayer 1481B-3e	1677	Nahuatl Spanish
Nicolasa de los Angeles	AGN-BN 1096-8	1679	Spanish
Diega Nicolasa	NL/Ayer 1481B-3f	1683	Nahuatl
Juana Micaela	NL/Ayer 1481F-9a	1685	Nahuatl
Juana de los Angeles	AGN-C 1763-2	1693	Nahuatl Spanish
Ana María	AGN-C 1828-5	1693	Nahuatl
Teresa de Jesús	AGN-C 592-1	1695	Nahuatl Spanish
Gerónima Verónica	NL/Ayer 1481B-3a	1697	Nahuatl
Melchora de Santiago	NL/Ayer 1481B-3l	1699	Nahuatl Spanish

[a]Only a partial text is extant.

[b]This will was transcribed and translated into French by Durand-Forest (1962).

allude to the experiences of Nahua men (at least the individuals under discussion here) in relation to changes in the roles and experiences of women.

Clearly, the small number of early-colonial Nahua testators of Mexico City whose wills are part of the historical record must be recognized.[4] Such testators undoubtedly are more representative of higher-status indigenous groupings in early-colonial Mexico City, though relatively poor individuals owning very little property are represented among testators and participants in colonial legal processes as well (Kellogg 1995a: 24–36). Nevertheless, these testaments, often in indigenous language, provide us with a wide array of information not otherwise available about individuals' lifetimes, their material possessions, and social experiences.[5]

The Colonial Wills of Two Nahua Families

Both the father and grandfather of Magdalena Ramírez left testaments, in Nahuatl with Spanish translations, that stated their wishes for the disposal of their goods. Magdalena's grandfather was named Antonio Quahuitencatl. In June of 1569, the alcaldes (local judicial officials) sent an *escribano* (notary) and an *alguacil* (constable) to his home upon hearing that he was ill and wished to make a will (AGN Tierras 1595-4: 13r–14r, 17r–18v).[6] Although no obvious status markers, such as the use of the term *don*, identify Quahuitencatl's class position, his real property ownership signifies that he was relatively well off, probably not of the nobility but perhaps ranking high among a middle group of property owners and citizens of the barrio (neighborhood). His house and its accompanying lot were large. The structure had seven rooms, two of which constituted an upper story,[7] a patio, and an accompanying plot of land measuring four by three *brazas* (Spanish unit of measurement, 1.67 m; f.13r). In addition to a substantial house site, Quahuitencatl also owned a number of pieces of land. He refers to three as *milpas* (*milli* in the Nahuatl text [f.17v]; perhaps cultivated fields [Cline 1986: 137]) ranging in size from forty by twenty brazas to twenty by twenty brazas. Five he calls *tierras* (*tlalli* in the Nahuatl text [f.18r]; perhaps uncultivated lands [Cline 1986: 137]). These were in the same size range as the fields identified as milpas (four were approximately twenty by twenty brazas and one was thirty by forty brazas [f.13v–14r]). This testator did not list any small items; thus his will consisted solely of substantial real property.

His chosen heirs were interesting as well. The house site was left largely to his wife, except for one room that he left to his son-in-law, Joséph Mahuito. But when he turns to the land, Antonio left his son-in-law the three milpas. Of the five other plots of land, two went to two women whose relationship to Quahuitencatl is not specified, one went to a grandson, and one went to his wife. Quahuitencatl closes his will by stating that according to "ancient custom" that "everyone knows," the passageway leading to the main doorway of the house should be for the common use of his descendants (f.14r).

In August of 1591, Joséph Mahuito (or Joséph Ramírez as he now referred to himself), dictated a will in which many of these same properties are discussed (AGN Tierras 1595-4: 15v, 16r–16v). Joséph Ramírez describes his house as having three rooms, two of which he left to his daughter, Magdalena Ramírez, and one which he gave to his son,

Andrés Ramírez. While the house structure was now referred to as having three rooms, it was clearly the same one referred to by Joséph's father-in-law because Joséph describes how he inherited it from his father- and mother-in-law (f.15v, 16v). Joséph gave the plot of land identified as lying in front of the house to one Juan Bautista whose relationship to himself he does not identify. He then describes three plots of land (*milli*; f.15v, 16v), which correspond in place name and measurement to one of the "milpas" and one of the "tierras" listed by his father-in-law, Antonio Quahuitencatl. The other plot cannot be matched but probably was one of the pieces left by Quahuitencatl. These he left to his son and daughter.

In 1606, Joséph Ramírez's daughter, Magdalena Ramírez, still resident in that same house, dictated her will, extant only in the Spanish language (AGN Tierras 1595-4: 14r–15r). Her text begins with a statement that her grandfather and grandmother left her the house in which she was currently residing. However, rather than immediately describing the structure of the house, as was normal practice, she refers to a doorway and passageway that she, like her father and grandfather, wanted to see used as a common area (f.14r–14v). She then describes the rooms, numbering five (one of which was a second-story room), four of which she left to her two children, Sebastián Miguel and María Pasquala. The additional room was to be sold, and the proceeds were to be used to pay for masses for her grandmother, her father and mother, her brothers, her uncle, and for her own soul as well (f.14v). She then lists a series of smaller items including money, household goods, religious objects (one of which was a figure of the Virgin Mary that Magdalena inherited from her grandfather), and some clothing. These were left to her children, with bequests of money given to a woman who had helped her, and to her *comadre* (godmother; f.15r). At the very end, Magdalena Ramírez's will lists three pieces of land, two of which came from Antonio and Joséph, with the third probably having been left to her by her grandmother. She bequeathed these plots to her children (f.15r–15v).

The next set of testators, don Juan de Santiago and his daughter Melchora de Santiago, dictated their testaments in the late seventeenth century, the father in 1693 and the daughter in 1699. Each will exists both in Nahuatl and in Spanish translation. Don Juan's testament speaks to his elite position through the title "don"; the high-ranking witnesses, including an *alguacil mayor* (a higher-status native official) of the church, an alguacil mayor of San Juan, and the *juez gobernador* (judge-governor), don Matías de los Angeles; his relatively substantial property holdings; and his concern with expressions of piety (NL/Ayer 1481B-31: 2r–3v, 3v–4v).

In addition to opening with a standard example of the statement of religious belief in the Holy Trinity as most colonial wills did, don Juan de Santiago's will returns to the theme of religious belief several times, explaining how he had married his first wife in a church marriage. He describes how he and his first wife had a son, Mateo de Santiago, but that he does not know where his son was. He also states that his daughter's marriage likewise had been in the church, and he describes how he was dying as a "true Christian" [nimiqui melahuaca xptiano] (f.2v).

After the expression of his devout piety, don Juan's will deals with more earthly matters. He describes his house of six rooms, giving three to his son Mateo and three to his daughter Melchora and her husband, Francisco Antonio. He adds that his daughter should care for her mother while she lives and that if his son Mateo does not return, his share should be sold and the money used to pay for masses. He also mentions land ("notlal") (f.3r) that he owned in San Juan Cochtocan, which he gives to his daughter and her husband.

Melchora de Santiago's will is structured quite similarly to that of her father (NL/Ayer 1481B-3l: 5r–6r; 6v–7v; 8v–9r). Her testament opens with an expression of her piety, including a description of how she prayed to all the saints, male and female, of heaven to help her ("in ixquichtintz-itzin Santos yhuan Santas in ilhuicac motemilticate nopam mehualtizque metlatoltizque" [f.5r]).[8] She then states that it was evident from her father's will that she inherited the house property she owned from him, that she loves her brother and prays that he will not force the child she raised as her own, Juliana de Santiago, to relinquish the house property that Melchora was leaving to her. Juliana, evidently not the biological daughter of Melchora (and referred to by her as "in piltzintli" [the child], never "nopiltzin" [my child]), was also to inherit the goods within the house, and Melchora asks Juliana to take special care of the saints' images ("tlaixiptlaiyotzitzintin"; f.5v).

Melchora de Santiago then mentions the lands in San Juan Cochtocan, which she refers to as "tlalli Cacicazgo" [cacique land] (f.5v). She orders these to be rented out, with part of the money going to pay for Melchora's burial costs (and in future years this bequest was to pay for masses) and part going to Juliana, her adopted daughter. Melchora then lists several items of jewelry adorning a statue of Our Lady of Purification (which was to periodically be brought to the local church), some other items of jewelry, and household goods. Some of these she ordered to be sold for masses, and some were to go to Juliana and Mateo. She ends her testament by appointing a guardian for Juliana and declaring her statements to be true.

All of these documents just discussed are composed of words describing property, the social relationships surrounding property, the statuses of the testators and others, and the familial and communal concerns these testators had as they tried to influence the course of events after their deaths. Gender is a useful analytical tool for analyzing these themes—not because the biological differences between testators determined behavioral or textual differences, but rather because the social and cultural environs of indigenous testators were becoming differentiated by gender in new ways in the colonial world. Some of these differences are reflected in these texts.

Wills as Texts

When did urban Nahuas begin turning to the written testament as a means of recording how they wished to dispose of their goods? Tables 2.1 and 2.2 suggest that the earliest wills written for Nahua individuals date from the 1540s, with two from that decade. Another three extant testaments date from the 1550s. During the next decade, the production of wills became more common, reaching its height in the last quarter of the sixteenth century. The practice continued throughout the seventeenth and eighteenth centuries.[9]

As urban indigenous testamentary production began and became more common, both women and men participated in the practice. The fascinating Nahuatl text of Alonso Molina (discussed in the preceding chapter by Sarah Cline) suggests that—at least according to Molina—priests were to encourage the practice for both men and women. Intended to help Nahua scribes follow proper procedure as they wrote down the last wishes of the dying (1565: f.58r–64r), Molina explicitly envisions testators as male *or* female. He chooses terms to illustrate for a notary how to address either a male or female testator and gives both male and female examples where names or gender identifications were to be used.[10] As Nahuas began to leave written testaments, both men and women frequently were testators (Loera y Chávez 1977; Kellogg 1986; Cline 1986; Wood 1991a, 1997b).

Several gender-related textual themes become apparent through a close reading of the testaments described at the beginning of this chapter and illustrate gender differences in the larger body of testamentary documents. One theme has to do with how testators identify themselves—i.e., their names. Antonio Quahuitencatl's name is an example of a common mid-sixteenth-century indigenous naming pattern, the use of a Spanish first name accompanied by a second Nahuatl name. Tables 2.1 and 2.2 show that both men's and women's names followed this common pattern. By the late sixteenth century, this naming pattern gave way to one where the second name was also Spanish, sometimes another first name, sometimes either a place name or name of religious significance (such as Melchora de Santiago), or occasionally this name was a Spanish patronymic (Lockhart 1992: 124–25, 127). This shift in names is captured nicely in these documents when Antonio Quahuitencatl refers to his son-in-law, Joséph, as "Joséph Mahuito," and Joséph refers to himself as "Joséph Ramírez." As this second naming transition was occurring, some gender differentiation can be detected. With this newer pattern establishing itself between the 1570s and 1650s, while the testatrices began to bear two Spanish names in the mid-1570s, as did testators, close to half of these men bore the second name that had religious or other significance (five of eleven, or 45 percent) whereas fewer than one-third of the women did (four of thirteen, or 31 percent).

Nahua women's first names underwent a further change as evidenced again by the testaments discussed here and as illustrated by the names "Magdalena" and "Melchora." Between 1585 and 1600, the names borne by indigenous women (both the first and second names they customarily used) began to change as an increasing percentage of women used "feminized masculine names" as opposed to the "gender-specific" names of the late-pre-Hispanic period (Lockhart 1992: 119; Cline 1986: 117) or the more clearly feminine Spanish names of the mid-sixteenth century. While names such as "Juana" and "Francisca" had been used by urban indigenous women in the decades after conquest (Cline 1986: 117; Horn 1997b), by 1600 women's names were becoming more varied. Among the new names appearing regularly in Mexico City's legal and parish records concerned with this population were "Diega," "Felipa" or "Felipiana," "Melchora," "Nicolasa," and "Tomasa." The source of these names was often a male saint, and the testaments, lawsuits, and birth records concerning the indigenous population all show this shift in women's naming patterns (Kellogg 1995a: 116–17). While changing naming patterns certainly demonstrate the increasing influence of Christian beliefs and practices— with parents, priests, and the Catholic ritual calendar all influencing naming (Taylor 1987: 16–19; Horn 1997b)—this shift also reflects the transition from the parallel women's and men's realms of the late-pre-Hispanic period to more hierarchically ranked masculine and feminine spheres (Kellogg 1997).

For men as well as women, second names with religious significance, such as "Santiago," or patronymics, such as "Ramírez," signified higher status (Cline 1986: 120–22; Lockhart 1992: 123). However, the passing of the second name in the lineal fashion that took place in both the families discussed in this chapter is unusual because many seventeenth-century urban residents, those whom Cope (1994: 55–66) has referred to as "plebian," used second names haphazardly and passed them to offspring in an inconsistent fashion. The transfer of these names from father to children thus reinforces a picture of higher social status for these particular testators. The second names used by the testators described here may therefore be seen as status markers for these individuals, both male and female.

Another status marker appearing in testaments and other legal documents was the use of the titles "don" and "doña." Neither Magdalena Ramírez nor Melchora de Santiago carried this title, which occurs in colonial documentation less often than the companion term, "don." Among the five individuals discussed here, only Melchora's father, don Juan de Santiago, did. Among Nahuas, the title "don" was less frequently inherited than among Spaniards, with the indigenous population reserving it for use with political offices that had been achieved (Cline 1986: 108–9, 118, 120–21; Lockhart 1992: 126; Horn 1997b). While Nahua wives or daughters might use the title "doña," they did so less frequently than their husbands and sons used "don." Tables 2.1 and 2.2 show that the use of the title "don" became more frequent after 1650 for male testators, while use of the title "doña" was never common among the testatrices. This pattern suggests that status may have been a less accessible and flexible social category for colonial indigenous women than it was for men, who through their monopolization of colonial political offices had access to political positions that indigenous women virtually never had.[11]

Another textual aspect of wills has to do with how testators organized these texts. Who shaped the structure of the written document, the testator or the notary? Are there any gender differences in the ways that testaments are structured or in the discussions of bequests?

In his model will, Molina lists property in the order of houses, lands, and movable goods (for which he provides the examples of gold and precious stones ["yn noteocuitl, yn nochalchiuh"; 1565: 62v]). While gold and precious stones were rarely listed among the many movable items listed in the wills, most testators—both male and female—followed the general order suggested by Molina. This format was followed into the seventeenth century, but around 1650, bequests of land become less frequent.

When land is cataloged in these later testaments, less land is listed and the descriptions are shorter and less complex. While the relative uniformity of the organization of these documents implies that notaries influenced how written testaments were structured, the wording of bequests themselves shows the important role that testators played in producing these documents. The strong emphasis on piety expressed in the religious formula so highly elaborated by Molina is lessened in the indigenous testaments of Mexico City, especially in those of the sixteenth century. In fact, the whole balance between Molina's lengthy spiritual opening and perfunctory listing of property is reversed by the Nahua testators, both male and female, whose spiritual concerns, while evident, were outweighed by the great emphasis testators placed on *what* they owned and *who* would inherit it after they died.

Some testators expressed a special concern over not just who would receive what but whether their wishes would indeed be carried out, and here a gender difference can be identified. Occasionally testators expressed anxiety about whether their wishes for their goods would occur in the way they directed. While there are examples of testators of both genders expressing this concern, the wills of male testators with such statements tended to be in the earlier period and can be found in wills written between the 1540s and 1580s.[12] Men's elaborate expressions of interest in the future of their bequests was expressed particularly when they emphasized that their wives should indeed inherit that property bequeathed to them.[13]

On the other hand, evidence of testatrices who worried about their ability to influence events after their deaths is found more frequently during the seventeenth century.[14] These wills express in subtle yet real ways fears about whether their wishes would be carried out. Such expressions can be found in Magdalena Ramírez's testament, and it is important to examine the actual organization of her document. The first issue her will deals with, after the obligatory opening statement of belief in the Holy Trinity, is that of the common entryway to the house. She states that she inherited this property from her grandfather and grandmother, identifying them both by name, that this had been stated in her grandfather's will, and that no one else could ever own it (AGN Tierras 1595-4: 14r).

Such an opening is an unusual way for an indigenous will to begin because most wills of the sixteenth and seventeenth centuries commence with fairly straightforward descriptions of property, usually house property, immediately after the opening statement of piety. While we can never know *why* Magdalena began in this way, it is reasonable to assume that she was referring to a deeply held concern over whether this property would continue to be treated by her family and neighbors as a commonly held area. Her grandfather, on the other hand, discussed this aspect of the house property at the end of his will, after other property—including land—had been listed. Antonio Quahuitencatl certainly attached importance to this directive, yet Magdalena's will could be interpreted as communicating a greater sense of concern by stating from whom she had inherited the property along with her grandfather's and her own wishes for the commonly held area.

An interest in having her wishes carried out was even more clearly stated by Melchora de Santiago. Melchora's testament begins with a long preamble attesting to her belief and piety. In the next part of her will, she discusses her real property, especially the house where she lived (NL/Ayer 1481B-3l: 5v). She prays that her brother will not force Juliana de Santiago, a child that Melchora was raising and evidently loved deeply, to relinquish the house. In fact, Melchora de Santiago left the bulk of her property to Juliana, including the house and a share of the rents from land she owned as well as clothing and valuable jewelry. Melchora left only two metates (grinding stones) to her brother Mateo (f.6r). Melchora de Santiago doubtless felt insecure about her wishes for several reasons: Juliana was not her biological daughter; she was leaving very little to her surviving brother; and legally, Mateo held a strong claim on the house because his father had left him a share in it.[15]

Melchora's text therefore communicates concern that her desired plans for property and people might not be carried out—or not in the way she envisioned. Her worry was rooted, at least partly, in this particular situation. But Cline has speculated that "there may have been a more general pattern of women's estates being vulnerable" (1986: 82). Property litigation involving early-colonial indigenous residents of Mexico City implies that this fear was rooted in reality. Women were involved in almost two-thirds of such lawsuits (forty-eight of seventy-three extant cases; 66 percent) as plaintiffs or defendants (Kellogg 1995a: 32). Both women's and men's wills—those discussed here and others—express feelings about family, property, and obligation, religious and social. Yet as time went on, Nahua testatrices expressed a higher level of concern about whether their wills would be executed as they ordered. Especially in the seventeenth century, they seem to have perceived that their customary and legal rights to inherit, manage, and bequeath property were more likely to be troubled.

Wills as Property Records

What about gendered patterns of ownership and bequests of property? Do these wills reveal a material basis for changing male/female gender roles or comparative status during the early-colonial period? Here we enter a murkier realm where the exegesis of textual themes must give way to analysis of both customary practices and practical constraints, both only partially reconstructible. Difficulties of reconstruction develop because early-colonial wills can offer only an incomplete picture of pre-Hispanic customary practices. This is so because the practice of ordering the writing of a will was itself new, because customary practices were shifting as individuals and families coped with changes wrought by the Spanish presence (Kellogg 1995a: chap. 5), and because wills often can be used to alter or subvert customary practice (Lewin 1992: 353).

Likewise, the practical constraints are difficult to reconstruct for two reasons. First, in any individual will, demographic reality plays a major role in shaping bequests by constraining which relatives (from among those one ideally would pick according to customary practices) can be chosen to receive bequests. But we generally can only partially reconstruct the genealogical structure of Nahua family and kin groups. Second, the emotional, social, and power aspects of human relationships also work as major constraints on testators, yet these qualities are often even less amenable to historical reconstruction. Magdalena Ramírez's and Melchora Santiago's wills certainly show that individual indigenous women held and maintained substantial property rights during the early-colonial period.

What do these two wills, in conjunction with those of their male family members, illustrate about changing Nahua patterns of property ownership during the sixteenth and seventeenth centuries? Turning first to the earliest will examined here, Antonio Quahuitencatl's, some typical mid-sixteenth-century Nahua testamentary practices can be discerned that perhaps offer some clues to patterns of gender differentiation. His closest living relatives were his wife and son-in-law. He left his rather large house site to his wife, Ana Teuhchon. Her inheritance of this house property differed from the more common pattern during most of the sixteenth century of inheritance by wives of use rights (as opposed to outright bequest) of specific rooms in houses. While Nahua women did sometimes inherit shares of house property from their husbands, these were generally small shares for use during their lifetimes (e.g., will of Martín Lázaro Pantecatl, AGN Tierras 20-1-3, 1551). A smaller number of wives inherited land (as opposed to rooms or houses); these, again, were usually small shares, most likely for the purpose of supporting them during their lifetimes (e.g., will of Martín Lázaro Pantecatl, 1551; will of Hernando de Tapia, AGN Tierras 37-2, 1555). In the case of Antonio Quahuitencatl's wife, Ana Teuhchon, her inheritance of land was probably related to the lack of a living child. However, when it came to the land, Quahuitencatl actually left the largest share of his landholdings to his son-in-law, Joséph.

There is some association of the female with the house site and the male with the land in this will. Not only do Antonio Quahuitencatl's bequests resonate with the association of female with household and male with extra-household activities and places (Burkhart 1997), but they also offer evidence of an association between women and households and men and land seen in other sixteenth-century testaments. While both men and women left shares in house compounds to spouses, children, and grandchildren, testatrices showed a small preference for female relatives—sisters, daughters, granddaughters—especially for bequests of space in house compounds. The male testators frequently left space in house sites for wives; testatrices did not do so for their husbands. Likewise, daughters, sisters, and granddaughters inherited rights to house property more often than sons, brothers, or grandsons.[16] Yet testatrices did not show this same preference with land, so that—when possible—they left larger shares of landed properties to male relatives (Kellogg 1995a: 137–44).

Another testament that shows this parallel structure is that of Angelina Martina from 1580 (AGN Tierras 49-5: 3r–6r, 7r–8r).[17] In this lengthy, complex document, in Nahuatl with a Spanish translation, Angelina Martina leaves most of the house in which she was living as her testament was written to her granddaughters, and other smaller house sites she gives to be shared between a granddaughter and two grandsons. This pattern was reversed with her substantial landholdings, which she primarily leaves to her grandsons. Her granddaughters were to inherit no lands other than those associated with the house sites she owned. The number and percentage of testatrices owning land to bequeath also decreased over time. During the sixteenth century, eight of eighteen testatrices (or 44 percent) owned land or *chinampas* (floating gardens). During the seventeenth century, four of sixteen testatrices owned land (25 percent).[18]

In comparison to the more parallel structuring of bequests for real property, Joséph Ramírez's 1591 will, on the other hand, follows a clearer bilateral bequest plan, with the house property and land being left in equal shares to his son and daughter. Magdalena Ramírez's will of 1606 also follows this bilateral pattern. But while female heirs maintained legal rights to inherit, their ability to use these rights actually came under new pressures.

Wills and other legal documents show that in comparison to the sixteenth century, seventeenth-century Nahua women bought and sold property less frequently and received fewer property grants (Kellogg 1995a: 111). In addition, urban indigenous women's labor may have become increasingly segregated in tasks that were menial and low paying, such as domestic service (Arrom 1985: 157–61). Their capacity generally to create wealth that could be passed on to others might therefore have been weakening.[19] The economic autonomy of a woman such as the testator Angelina Martina (AGN Tierras 49-5, 1580), who refers frequently to buying and selling land, is seen in neither Magdalena's nor Melchora's wills. Women's pathways to inheritance also may have been narrowing as they inherited more frequently as wives and daughters within the nuclear family. When women's ownership rights were challenged during the seventeenth century, they traced these rights through or to men more often than to or through women.[20] This pattern suggests that indigenous women's ability to use and bequeath property had, indeed, become more fragile.

The increasing legal importance of husbands further pressured women's property rights as sons-in-law increasingly represented women legally and shared women's inherited property rights. This is well illustrated by don Juan de Santiago's will, in which his long-absent son Mateo received an equal share in the house to that given to his sister Melchora, but Melchora's shares of property, both house and land, were left to her *and* her husband, Francisco Antonio. In this will, the son-in-law was not inheriting in place of a deceased or absent child; instead, he was inheriting as her *husband*, thereby undermining the autonomy, authority, and potential control over property that his wife might have. These pressures were reinforced in seventeenth-century courts when husbands increasingly became the legal intercessors for women, a role husbands (or, occasionally, other male relatives) had performed to a lesser degree during most of the sixteenth century.[21]

Conclusion

The testaments of early-colonial urban Nahuas offer a complex window onto a changing society. This chapter makes three points, first demonstrating the highly detailed information about individual people, property, and patterns of belief and behavior that wills make available. Second, it shows that these documents offer specific textual evidence of changing

gender relations. Naming patterns, status positions, and women's heightened concerns about their ability to bequeath property all are apparent
and illustrate some ways that the parallel gender structuring of indigenous
urban society declined over the first two centuries after the conquest.

Testaments also provide information about material and social relations. The Spanish bilateral inheritance practices so embedded in the way
that Catholic priests taught native scribes about how to write wills
ensured that indigenous women would retain theoretical rights to property ownership and also ensured that some indigenous women, especially
those of higher socioeconomic status, would inherit and bequeath property. The growing indigenous reliance upon Spanish testamentary practices also helps explain why writing had a dramatic impact on indigenous
culture and served as a major mode of transmission for specific Spanish
legal and cultural practices. Yet because other legal and social supports for
parallel gender roles decayed, the third argument articulated above is that
bilateral inheritance practices and will-making as a strategy for women to
maintain property rights could not alone support the parallel structuring
of Nahua gender roles during the colonial period.

Last Will and Testament of Joséph Ramírez, Mexico City (San Sebastián
Cuitlahualtongo), 1591
(AGN Tierras 1595-4: 16r)[22]

Ma moyecteneuhtzino yn itocatzin dios tetatzin dios tepiltzin dios Spu
sancto yei persuna yuh nicneltoca nicnocuitia yn nehuatl Joseph ramirez
nican nocha̅ san sebastian notlaxilacaltian Cuitlahuactonco Nictlalia
nomemoria yntla nechmopolhuiz yn tt°

Inic centlama̅tli niquitohua yn nehuatl Joseph ramirez ynin calli yn
oncan nihuetztoc ynic centetl çihuacalli tonatiuh ycallaquiyampa ytzticac
ynic ontetl xochmilcopa ytzticac caltepiton auh ynin nicmaca yn nochpoch mag^na ramirez auh yniquetetl calli tonatiuh yquiçayampa ytzticac
mixnamictimani yn çihuacalli ontequiztimani auh niquitohua nicmaca yn
nopiltzin andres ramirez ytechpouhqui

Inic ontlama̅tli niquitohua yn tlalmantli yn ixpan mani yn calli nicmaca
yn Ju° bautista oncan ytlatzin quimotlaliliz oncan qui[mo]pixtiaz yn itey-
ccahuan Canel iuhquin intatzin mochihua Yhuan yetetl chinamitl aço
ytlatzin onca̅ yc moyolalizque yehua̅ quimati

Auh yn huehuecalli Ca ynchan Caçan oniquinpieliaya yn quenin tla-
mani Caçan yuh yezque Ca ye yxquich yn niquitohua yn nehuatl Juseph
ramirez mahuitocas

Auh yn imixpan testigotin pablo marcos fran^{co} h̄r̄z̄ Jacobo xuarez pe^o
Jacobo

Axcan ypan cemilhuitl miercoles matlaquilhuitl Mani agusto 1591 años
Sebastian Miguel
Escr[iban]^o

[f.16v] Yhuan niquitohua omani milli tecpayocã yn calpolli²³ Calpilco
ompohualli ynic huiyac auh ynic patlahuac çempohualli auh nechmomaquilitiuh ynomõtatzin ant^o quahuitencatl auh yntechpouhqui yn
andres rramirez nopiltzin yhua ynochpo[ch] madalena ramirez

Ynic ocan mani çano ompa yn tepayocã acatliyacapan çempohualli çan
necoc yahualtic auh çanno nechmomaquilitiuh ynomõtatzin ant^o quahuitencatl auh çano yntech niccauhtiuh ynopilhuan andres ramirez yhuã
nochpoch madalena

Yn iqu[e]xcan mani oncã yn tlatzcantitlã ompohualli ynic huiyac auh
ynic patlah[. . .] çempohualli çano yntech ca ynopilhuã ye yxquich yn niquitohua notlatol²⁴

✕

May the name of God the Father, the Son, the Holy Spirit be praised,
three persons, thus I believe, I confess [are one]. I, Joséph Ramírez, a citizen of San Sebastián, Cuitlahualtongo being my district. I am making my
will so that our God will take me.

First, I say, I Joséph Ramírez, that this house where I have fallen ill,
that the first [room], the woman's room, faces west, the second small
room faces Xochmilcopa, this I give to my daughter Magdalena Ramírez;
and the third room faces east, it is across from the woman's room, I say
that I give this to my son Andrés Ramírez, it belongs to him.

Second, I say that the plot of land in front of the house, I give it to
Juan Bautista. There his honored uncle will put it in order for him, there
he will guard it, since he acts like a father to his younger brothers. And
about three chinampas to his honored uncle, there [with that] they will
content themselves. They know [about] it.

And the ancestral home, it is their home since I was only taking care of
them. So it happens, they will be thus. This is all I say, I Joséph Ramírez
Mahuitocas, in front of the witnesses, Pablo Marcos, Francisco
Hernández, Jacobo Xuarez, Pedro Jacobo. Now, today on Wednesday,
the tenth day of August, 1591.

Sebastián Miguel
Escribano

And I say, it is the plot of land [in] Tecpayocan, [of] the calpulli
Calpilco, forty in length and twenty in width. And my father-in-law,

Antonio Quahuitencatl, gave it to me, and it shall belong to Andrés Ramírez, my son, and my daughter, Magdalena Ramírez.

In the second place, also in Tecpayocan, in the place at the end of the reeds, twenty on both sides, likewise my father-in-law gave it to me, and likewise I leave it [to them], my children, Andrés Ramírez, and my daughter, Magdalena.

In the third place, it is there [at] Tlatzcantitlan, forty in length and twenty in width, likewise it is for my children. It is all I say, [these are] my words.

Notes

In addition to financial support from the Bunting Institute, NEH, and the University of Houston, I would like to acknowledge helpful suggestions from Sarah Cline, Susan Deeds, Frances Karttunen, and Matthew Restall. The responsibility for interpretations and translations remains mine.

1. See Borah 1983 and Kellogg 1995a for discussions of the Spanish legal system in New Spain, especially the central areas, and indigenous uses of that legal system.

2. See Lavrin and Couturier 1979; Arrom 1985: chap. 2; and Tutino 1983: 366–69 for this conceptualization. Also see Seed 1988, especially her concluding chapter, for a general discussion of patriarchy in Hispanic societies as compared to other parts of western Europe. For a general discussion of patterns of heirship, see Goody 1973; also see Goody, Thirsk, and Thompson 1976. On inheritance patterns in medieval and/or early modern Europe, see Kettle 1984 and Prior 1990 on England, and Birkett 1984 on France. On inheritance patterns in colonial North America, see Salmon 1986 and Ditz 1986. For a historical overview of inheritance patterns in the United States, see Shammas, Salmon, and Dahlin 1987.

3. On pre-Hispanic Mesoamerican writing systems, see Dibble 1971 and Marcus 1992. On the influence of alphabetic writing on human societies generally, see Goody 1986; in Mesoamerica, see, for example, Gruzinski 1992, 1993: 1–2, 54–55, 102; Lockhart 1992: chap. 8; and Mignolo 1994, 1995. For a discussion of legal documents, alphabetic writing, and changing Andean cultural practices, see Rappaport 1994b.

4. The corpus of testaments described in tables 2.1 and 2.2 and discussed in this chapter represent those currently known to exist. While the number of early-colonial wills for Mexico City is substantial in comparison to other areas (see, for example, Hill's contribution, this volume), sources such as *The Testaments of Culhuacan* (which includes sixty-five wills, fifty-two complete and thirteen fragments [Cline and León-Portilla 1984]), so ably analyzed by Cline (1986), have thus far not come to light.

5. Also see Salomon 1988: 327–28 for a discussion of the value of indigenous women's colonial testaments of Quito even when small in number.

6. The Nahuatl text of Antonio Quahuitencatl's testament is now severely damaged and unreadable in many places. The citations for this document refer to the Spanish translation except where noted.

7. In the late-pre-Hispanic era, two-story houses were generally owned by higher-status individuals (Sahagún 1950–82, 11:274).

8. See Wood 1991a: 264–65 for a description of invocations of saints in eighteenth-century testaments from the Toluca Valley.

9. For examples and analyses of eighteenth-century Nahua testaments, see Wood 1991a, 1997b; and Namala 1995.

10. In a later model will dating from 1611, Martín de León described only a male testator (f.138r–141r).

11. While there is some evidence that indigenous women continued to serve in low-level political roles, their roles in temples and the administration of markets disappeared as these institutions either vanished or were transformed. As the civil administrative apparatus for Indian towns and city barrios developed, there is little sign of women holding the associated offices to any significant degree, though they did play a noteworthy role in Indian colonial rebellions. On women in political offices during the pre-Hispanic period, see Kellogg 1995b. On political offices for Indian communities during the colonial period, see Gibson 1952, 1964; Haskett 1991; and Lockhart 1992: 48–52, 102–38; and on women and colonial rebellions in central Mexico, see Taylor 1979: 116, 124, 127; Cope 1994: 157–58; and Kellogg 1995a: 117–19. Barry Sell (n.d.), however, has found evidence of Nahua women serving as *cofradía* officers in Tula alongside of men during the seventeenth century.

12. The wills of Juan Tehuitzil (AGN Tierras 35-1, 1548), Hernando de Tapia (AGN Tierras 37-2, 1555), Diego Tlacochcalcatl (AGN Tierras 48-4, 1566), Martín Jacobo (AGN Tierras 39-2-1, 1577), and Pedro Doçan (AGN Tierras 442-5, 1587) all express such sentiments, though Doçan's special concern is the disinheriting of his daughter.

13. Note that while eight of thirty (26 percent) of testators stated such a concern, five of these eight were sixteenth-century male testators. During the seventeenth century, only three male testators evidenced much interest in whether their bequests would be carried out.

14. Eight of thirty-four (24 percent) testatrices expressed such worries. But three were among the earlier Nahua female testators, and five were among those of the seventeenth century.

15. Any potential claim that Mateo might make would have been strengthened by the fact that, according to the *Siete Partidas*, women did not have the right of formal adoption (*Partida* 4, *Título* 16, *Ley* 2). What the weight of an informal adoption—a seemingly common practice among Mexico City's early-colonial indigenous population (according to the texts of lawsuits)—might have been in a lawsuit over property is not clear.

16. For a discussion of land associated with houses, see Cline 1986: 135–36. For a similar pattern among the Yucatec Maya, see Restall 1997b: 125.

17. Angelina Martina was an indigenous woman with ties to merchants who probably herself functioned as a merchant. Through inheritance and her own

activities, she amassed a sizeable estate. Her will is contained in a 1585 lawsuit over property she left to two great-grandchildren.

18. The figures for the male testators are as follows. During the sixteenth century, eight of twelve owned landed property (75 percent); during the seventeenth century, seven of eighteen owned such property (39 percent). Also see Kanter 1995, which demonstrates the increasing fragility of rural indigenous women's landholdings in the late colonial and early national periods.

19. See Kellogg 1995a: 93–98 for a discussion of women's economic roles and relative autonomy in Tenochtitlan and Tlatelolco during the late-pre-Hispanic era. A late-seventeenth-century marriage register for San Sebastián (the same area and parish of Mexico City where Magdalena Ramírez and her relatives lived) contains some information about women's work that bears out this hypothesis about the changing nature of their work during the early-colonial period. The register for the years 1696 and 1697 includes occupations for most of the women who married and most female witnesses (which is highly unusual information for such records). Except for a cart driver (*carretera*), women's work was very low paying, and either relatively unskilled (for example, making mats [*petatera*]) or informal, raising tomatoes and probably selling them in local markets (*tomatera*), or making and selling tortillas (*tortillera*). These marriage entries come from a *Libro de Matrimonios* (*Indios*) for the parish of San Sebastián, GSU, Microfilm Manuscript Collection. This particular register is on roll 037421.

20. The short, patrifilial genealogy exemplified the way kinship relationships and genealogies were described by seventeenth-century urban Nahuas in order to justify property ownership. See, for example, AGN Tierras 183-4 (1607) and AGN Tierras 157-7 (1694). Also see Kellogg 1995a: 188–95.

21. For examples of seventeenth-century cases where men interceded for women, see AGN Tierras 183-4 (1607), AGN Tierras 128-2 (1682), and AGN Tierras 163-5 (1699).

22. Original punctuation and capitalization preserved.

23. This is one of the rare times the term *calpulli* appears in the Nahuatl documentation of Mexico City.

24. A final paragraph follows at the bottom of the page which reiterates that Joséph Ramírez inherited the passageway from his father- and mother-in-law. It is in a different hand, is placed at the bottom of the page apart from the rest of the text, and appears to have been added at a later point. Because of the way the page is bound into the volume, it cannot be completely transcribed and is therefore not included here.

CHAPTER 3

Testaments and Trade: Interethnic Ties among Petty Traders in Central Mexico (Coyoacan, 1550–1620)

REBECCA HORN

In his testament of 1573, don Juan de Guzmán, the Nahua ruler of the central Mexican province of Coyoacan, requested that the Spanish peddler Alonso de Yépez be paid the fifty or so pesos owed him. The actual amount was to be based solely on Yépez's testimony as it had never been recorded in writing "given that they were intimate friends, one to the other" (CDC II: 17). Don Juan de Guzmán's request illustrates that native rulers developed long-standing relationships with Spaniards other than the civil and ecclesiastical officials responsible for a rural Indian jurisdiction. And native rulers were not alone. Other Nahuas, nobles and commoners alike, formed ties with Spaniards living or working in the countryside. As with don Juan de Guzmán and Alonso de Yépez, these ties often involved loans, property, or outright commerce. Dispensing property and settling debts, Nahua testaments attest to the various commercial arrangements made between Nahuas and Spaniards, especially in the late sixteenth century as the basis of the economy shifted from the *encomienda* (grant of tribute and labor) to direct production by Spaniards.

Informal contact between individual Nahuas and individual Spaniards largely eludes documentation. On the one hand, few Spanish documents speak directly to informal Nahua-Spanish contact, especially when it involved Nahua commoners or small-scale commerce. One can hardly imagine a Spanish notarial document, our primary source for Spanish commercial dealings, recording the rental of a horse by a local Spanish landowner to a Nahua commoner to ply his fruit trade in neighboring towns. Some glimpses of petty traders do appear in the paper trail left by Spanish attempts to regulate them, but with humble buyers and sellers, and transactions of low value, much of the activity of petty traders, including their informal ties to Spaniards, escaped the gaze of Spanish authorities and, therefore, more official types of Spanish documentation. On the other hand, Nahuatl documents, which begin to appear in significant numbers around the 1540s, most immediately and directly bear on the internal affairs of Nahua communities. They form the basis of studies that explore aspects of Nahua society entirely missing from Spanish accounts and have transformed our understanding of postconquest Nahua society. Wills, in particular, have provided insight into such topics as household and sociopolitical organization, kinship, land tenure, gender, and religion.[1] In the context of this richness of source material and an appropriate concern for the broad features of postconquest Nahua culture, the references to informal Nahua-Spanish contact that do appear in Nahuatl documents have not been systematically studied. Indeed, recent studies based on Nahuatl documents largely treat Nahuas in isolation rather than in contact with local Spaniards.[2]

Nonetheless, Nahuatl documents are the most promising sources on informal Nahua-Spanish contact, and they clearly indicate that it was an important feature of postconquest Nahua life. In capturing the affairs of an individual Nahua at a particular moment in time, a Nahua testament can shed light on ties between Nahuas and Spaniards, especially when they involved commercial arrangements. A few are unusually rich, painting pictures of Nahua-Spanish interaction that are clear and detailed. Most, however, offer mere glimpses, making it difficult to construct a case study in any depth. These fleeting references are all the more valuable, however, when one considers that with the exception of native rulers such as don Juan de Guzmán and a handful of high nobles who carried distinctive names, it is impossible to track a single person through various documents over time; one must typically compile many discrete examples to discern broader patterns of Nahua behavior.[3] When supplemented with Spanish and Nahuatl sources, even oblique references to informal Nahua-Spanish contact found in Nahua testaments can paint a fuller picture, filling in the surrounding context or indicating the pervasiveness of a particular activity difficult to discern from other types of documents.

This article relies on the testaments of both Nahua nobles and commoners, supplemented by other types of Spanish and Nahuatl source material, to examine informal interethnic contact among Nahua and

Table 3.1
Testaments from Coyoacan, 1549–1748

Date	Testator	Source
1549	Don Pablo Çacancatl	CDC II: 12–1
1556	Don Luis Cortés	CDC II: 66–69
1567	Doña María Xalatlauhco	CDC II: 175–80
1573	Don Juan de Guzmán	CDC II: 16–25 (Spanish)
1576	Don Lorenzo de Guzmán	CDC II: 26–27 (Spanish)
1588	Doña Catalina de Sena	BC: 54–57
1590	Francisco Martín	AGN Bienes Nacionales 1453, 12:195r
1597	Mariana	AGN Bienes Nacionales 1453, 12:194v
1601	Juan Luis	AGN Hospital de Jesús 210, 57
1608	Bárbara Agustina	Karttunen and Lockhart 1976: 98–100
1609	Rodriguez Mateo	AGN Bienes Nacionales 1453, 12:195v
1617	Juan Fabián	BC: 58–63
1622	Don Juan de Guzmán	BC: 64–68
1627	Juan Miguel	AGN Hospital de Jesús 210, 1
1628	Baltasar Leonardo	AGN Civil 1037, 6:2r–3r
1628	Juana Susana	AGN Hospital de Jesús 210, 14
1631	Juana María	AGN Hospital de Jesús 210, 10
1638	Pedro de Santiago	AGN Hospital de Jesús 210, 65
1643	Juan Jacobo	AGN Tierras 1515, 1: 62r–62v
1658	Juana Catalina	AGN Hospital de Jesús 210, 12
1661	Agustina Juana	AGN Hospital de Jesús 210, 15
1661	Josef Francisco	AGN Hospital de Jesús 210, 18
1666	María Gerónima	AGN Hospital de Jesús 210, 4
1674	Lucía Cecilia	AGN Civil 1143, 6: 4r–v
1671	Juan Martín	AGN Hospital de Jesús 210, 7
1673	Ana María	AGN Hospital de Jesús 210, 8
1675	Juana Gerónima	AGN Hospital de Jesús 210, 2
1676	Roque	AGN Hospital de Jesús 210, 42
1676	Francisca María	AGN Hospital de Jesús 210, 54
1676	Baltasar Melchor	AGN Hospital de Jesús 210, 66
1677	Paula Juana	AGN Civil 1230, 8: 11r
1679	Catalina Isabel	AGN Hospital de Jesús 210, 13

1680	Mateo Juárez	AGN Hospital de Jesús 210, 6
1680	Diego Gaspar	AGN Hospital de Jesús 210, 53
1689	Sebastián	AGN Hospital de Jesús 210, 67
1691	María Pascuala	AGN Civil 1230, 9: 1r–v
1699	Tomás de Irolo	AGN Civil 1230, 8: 3r–v
1722	Diego de Santiago	AGN Civil 1213, 8: 2r–3r
1723	Sebastián de Dios	AGN Civil 1238, 2: 4r
1724	Sebastián Esteban	AGN Civil 1238, 2: 10r–11r
1734	José Gabriel	AGN Civil 1064, 1: 14r–v
1735	Jacinto Roque	AGN Hospital de Jesús 113, 21: 2r–3v
1737	Juana Anastasia	AGN Civil 1168, 8: 5r–6v
1737	Juan Diego	AGN Civil 1213, 10: 17r–18v
1740	Don Antonio Guillermo	AGN Civil 1142, 4: 1r–2r
1748	Doña Juana de la Trinidad	AGN Civil 1201, 9: 7r–9v

Spanish petty traders in the Spanish agricultural center of Coyoacan from the mid-sixteenth to the mid-seventeenth centuries. A substantial corpus of testaments from the Coyoacan region is extant, in part due to the region's central location and special jurisdictional status as part of Cortés's marquesado grant (see table 3.1).[4] A few Nahua testaments date as early as the middle decades of the sixteenth century, some concerning the Nahua rulers and nobles who, like don Juan de Guzmán, were so crucial to the operation of the encomienda and official Nahua-Spanish affairs. By the late sixteenth century, testaments by commoners became much more numerous, and they constitute the bulk of the corpus studied here, especially for the later periods, when associations between Nahuas and Spaniards became increasingly important as the economy shifted toward direct production by Spaniards.

Coyoacan and the Commercial Economy

In the immediate postconquest period Spaniards extracted goods and labor from Nahua commoners through the encomienda. The encomienda itself relied on indigenous traditions; the *altepetl*, or city-state, provided the contours of an encomienda jurisdiction, and the local ruler, or *tlatoani*, commanded Nahua commoners to pay tribute and to work on labor crews. Contact between the bulk of Nahua commoners and individual Spaniards remained limited; the tlatoani negotiated the terms of labor and tribute demands with the *encomendero* (an individual who held an encomienda grant) or his representatives. Over the course of the sixteenth century, however, Nahua-Spanish interaction broadened as the discovery of silver mines in the 1540s transformed the Spanish economy. Commerce quickened so as to supply the emerging urban and mining centers, Spanish immigration and the importation of African slaves accelerated, and the natural increase in the Spanish and mixed-race populations continued. The encomienda's indirect means of extracting goods and labor from Nahua communities could no longer support an expanding Spanish economy and population, and Spaniards moved directly into agriculture and livestock raising.

Early on, Spaniards in the colonial capital of Mexico City turned their attention toward the southwest, including the altepetl of Coyoacan, granted as an encomienda to Hernando Cortés along with the noble title of *marqués* shortly after the conquest.[5] They found Coyoacan attractive because of its proximity to the capital, its fertile soils, and its abundant fresh water. Low-lying areas offered lands suitable for the cultivation of wheat and European fruit trees; wooded highlands offered fuel, construction materials, and pasture for livestock. By the mid-sixteenth century, Spanish farms dotted the region, supplying Mexico City with fruits and vegetables as well as such staples as wheat and corn.[6] A mid-sixteenth-century contemporary traveler described Coyoacan as "a well endowed town [with] native and Spanish fruits [and] good forests" (Zavala 1984: 217).

Although Cortés and his heirs continued to collect tribute throughout the colonial period, private enterprises in the Coyoacan region quickly outstripped encomienda revenues in importance to the Spanish economy. By the late sixteenth century a complex network of commercial production and exchange had emerged as Coyoacan, the hinterland to the southwest, met some of the growing demand of the Mexico City market. With Mexico City unable to absorb them, Spanish immigrants and the growing number of racially mixed individuals increasingly moved to the countryside in search of livelihood. Simultaneously, the conversion of tribute from payment in kind to cash created a greater imperative for Nahuas to produce for the market, especially as the decline in the indigenous population increased the tribute burden on survivors. Although maize continued to be the primary crop, Nahua households diversified production in the face of the commercial economy, often adopting plants and animals introduced by Europeans.

The emerging enterprises in Coyoacan opened up a new arena of Nahua-Spanish contact that had little connection to the formal channels of the encomienda or the altepetl upon which it was based. With the shift to direct Spanish production and the diversification of Nahua household economies, the primary site of Nahua-Spanish interaction shifted from Nahua and Spanish officials in the central settlement of the altepetl to the myriad Spanish estates and enterprises throughout the countryside. Many of these newly emerging ties concerned land; some Nahuas sold plots of land to Spaniards, a few even working informally for buyers over time, helping them acquire parcel after parcel. Other ties concerned labor arrangements as Spanish landowners—frustrated with the inability of the *repartimiento* to supply adequate numbers of workers—increasingly turned to private agreements.[7] And, as Nahua testaments suggest, many ties between Spaniards and Nahuas also concerned commercial dealings.

In the middle decades of the sixteenth century, when Coyoacan's ruling family retained considerable prestige and authority, testaments point to close associations between Nahua elites and the petty traders, transporters, and farmers in the region, indicating that Spaniards trying to get a toehold in the local setting sought out local rulers. By the late sixteenth century, when the testaments of commoners become more numerous, one sees other patterns. Many Nahuas—drawing on preconquest traditions of merchants and marketplaces—sold the modest surplus from household production both locally and in Mexico City. Some traded on a larger scale, their fortunes often tied to local Spaniards who might provide credit, a mule, or some other advantage. These kinds of Nahua-Spanish relationships, prompted by the late-sixteenth-century economic transition from the encomienda to direct Spanish-controlled production, represent an important avenue of cultural transformation in the postconquest central Mexican countryside.

Nahua Rulers and Spanish Traders

In the early postconquest period, Nahua rulers were at the center of official Nahua-Spanish interaction and thus Spanish provincial life. In Coyoacan, don Juan de Guzmán Itztlolinqui held the title of tlatoani throughout the middle decades of the sixteenth century, the height of the postconquest ruling family. This influential and affluent lord enjoyed many of the traditional rights and perquisites of an indigenous ruler. He received tribute and labor service from Nahua commoners, market taxes from the central Coyoacan marketplace, and the produce from substantial landholdings scattered throughout the region and worked by dependent laborers. In keeping with preconquest patterns, Guzmán maintained a network of relations, including marriage alliances, with the ruling families of other central Mexican altepetl. His own marriage to doña Mencía de la Cruz, a member of a ruling lineage of Tetzcoco, united properties in Tetzcoco, Coyoacan, and neighboring Xochimilco.[8]

While his privileged position initially rested on indigenous traditions of rulership, Guzmán actively sought the confirmation and protection of rights associated with the rulership from Spanish authorities.[9] He called attention to the services rendered to the crown by his father and brother (both died around the time of the conquest) and petitioned the king for favors. Royal orders (*cédulas*) issued in 1534 and 1545 confirmed his landholdings as private property, creating a *cacicazgo*, or entailed estate. A royal cédula of 1551 granted him a coat of arms, and the viceroy authorized him to carry a sword "after the Spanish manner." In the 1550s Guzmán brought suit against Cortés for usurping land and demanding excessive labor and tribute; he complained to the king that Spaniards treated Coyoacan commoners as if they were slaves. And shortly before his death in 1569, don Juan, along with his wife, founded a *capellanía* (ecclesiastical endowment) at the local Dominican monastery.

Due to these efforts to protect the rights of the rulership and to acquire the appropriate Spanish symbols of authority, the Guzmán family stands out as one of the best-documented ruling families in all of central Mexico.[10] Much of the Spanish documentation originated in litigation in Spanish courts, but a significant corpus written in Nahuatl was generated at the local level. Most important is a group of mid-sixteenth-century Nahuatl documents that, while not including a testament per se, nonetheless list Guzmán's properties and perquisites, including landholdings and the tribute and services due him as tlatoani (among them, market taxes) (BC: 138–65). Two Spanish testaments (one a fragment) for two of his sons point to the difficulty the family had in trying to preserve these privileges over time; don Juan's oldest son complained in his testament of 1573 about the loss of cacicazgo lands and implored his heirs to recover them.[11] As a body, this material reflects the Guzmán family's deliberate attempts to preserve its position. It also sheds considerable light on Nahua-Spanish interaction.

After Guzmán's death in 1569, the rulership passed to his son and namesake (here distinguished as "the younger"), who died just a few years later, in 1573. The Spanish testament of don Juan de Guzmán the younger points to existing ties in the mid-sixteenth century between members of Coyoacan's ruling family and local Spaniards. At this time Spanish Coyoacan remained relatively humble. There were few permanent residents who carried the honorific titles of don and doña, and prominent landowners, including the highest provincial Spanish official (*corregidor*), typically resided in Mexico City, visiting the jurisdiction only periodically as circumstances demanded. The corregidor's deputy (*teniente*) and the resident Dominican friars constituted the core of local Spanish society headquartered in the jurisdiction's central settlement. Other professionals and artisans were virtually absent; Nahuas and Spaniards alike sought their services in Mexico City. Along with the Dominican friars and the teniente, some of the Spaniards who were involved in transport, petty trade, and other small-scale commercial or agricultural enterprises in the region also resided in the central settlement and constituted the elite of provincial Spanish society.[12]

The witnesses to the testament of don Juan de Guzmán the younger reflect the makeup of provincial Spanish society in Coyoacan. Several held formal positions, including the *vicario* of the Dominican monastery, three other friars, and the corregidor's deputy, Martín Pacheco (CDC II: 16–25). Local clerics rarely served as witnesses to Nahua testaments, "the whole proceedings taking place in the presence of Nahuas only" (Lockhart 1992: 535 n. 38), but the few exceptions involved the sixteenth-century rulers of Coyoacan and their close associates: two Dominican friars (along with don Felipe de Guzmán, the son and heir of don Juan de Guzmán the younger) witnessed the 1588 testament of the Coyoacan noblewoman doña Catalina de Sena (BC: 54–57), and one friar witnessed the 1622 testament of don Juan de Guzmán, a relative and namesake of the mid-sixteenth-century tlatoani (BC: 64–69). In addition to members of Coyoacan officialdom, witnesses to the testament of Guzmán the younger also included three local residents who had no official civil or ecclesiastical position but who, as participants in the local Spanish scene, sought out members of the Nahua ruling family with an eye to the economic advantages such associations might bestow.[13] At least two, Antón Gómez and Alonso de Yépez, were engaged in a variety of local economic enterprises and benefited substantially from their association with the Guzmán family.

Alonso de Yépez first appears in the Coyoacan documentation in 1553, when he was hired by the Nahua municipal council to cart wood belonging to the municipality to Mexico City. But Yépez's association with prominent Nahuas went far beyond the transport of wood. In 1559 he witnessed the title confirmation of some of don Juan de Guzmán's lands, and later lent money to don Juan de Guzmán the younger, leading to the instruction in don Juan's testament of 1573 to repay Yépez the fifty or so pesos owed him. Don Juan de Guzmán the younger had also sold Yépez a piece of land next to the plaza and marketplace of Coyoacan, for he requested in his testament that the sale be recognized as valid even though no bill of sale had been issued at the time. With this purchase and the neighboring property that he already owned, Yépez was physically as well as socially situated at the center of provincial life (CDC I: 205–6, 215, 233; II: 17, 22–24, 31, 137–38). Apparently he remained there for several more decades. In 1591 the viceroy confirmed the three repartimiento workers Yépez customarily received each week, and in 1595, still closely associated with local officials, Yépez witnessed the investiture of the new corregidor. Yépez (or possibly his namesake) was still alive in 1604, when he received a grant of one worker, two fewer than in the early 1590s, reflecting the repartimiento's declining fortunes (AGN Hospital de Jesús 278, 28:4r–4v; FHT III: 140; V: 233).

Another witness to don Juan de Guzmán the younger's testament was the Spaniard Antón Gómez, resident in Coyoacan at least as early as the 1570s. Although identified variously as a carter (*carretero*), peddler (*tratante*), and farmer (*labrador*), he was also involved with local Nahua and Spanish elites. Like Alonso de Yépez, Gómez was a frequent witness to local legal transactions. In 1573 he served as a witness along with Alonso de Yépez to the testament of Guzmán the younger. In 1574 he witnessed a loan made by Diego Pérez de Zamora (a Spaniard who was intimately involved in local affairs and occasionally served as teniente) to Julián Téllez, a member of a prominent Spanish landowning family. And in 1575 he witnessed a land transfer by a Nahua to the vicario of the local Dominican monastery (BC: 112–15; CDC II: 24, 163–64). Through his connections to Nahua elites, Antón Gómez also gained access to Nahua labor. Carters, who needed reliable workers but were unable to offer the professional training of the artisan, offered wages, which they sometimes paid in advance. In 1584 Antón Gómez advanced a local Nahua, Diego Sánchez, fifty pesos in exchange for his agreement to work in his carting business for the time it would take to repay the full amount at the rate of three and a half pesos a month.[14]

Gómez's prominent role in local municipal affairs is best illustrated, however, by his contested appointment as guardian to the children of don Juan de Guzmán the younger. He was appointed in 1574 by the teniente but was removed from the position because of the protests of don Juan's widow. She and witnesses testifying on her behalf claimed that as a labrador and tratante, Gómez had no experience in administering a tlatoani's estate. Furthermore, they charged he had attempted to buy lands that were part of don Juan's estate, thereby violating the trust placed in him as guardian.[15] A Spanish resident of Mexico City replaced Gómez (Diego Pérez de Zamora served as his guarantor). The newly appointed guardian apparently failed to carry out his responsibilities adequately, for a few months later Gómez was reappointed, only to request that he be relieved of his duties due to pressing concerns of his own. With the appointment of Pérez de Zamora in 1575, the matter was apparently settled (CDC II: 34–39, 56–60).

A member of an encomendero family, Diego Pérez de Zamora was a citizen (*vecino*) of Coyoacan and maintained his residence there, as did several of his relatives. He served as the corregidor's deputy at least in 1569 but undoubtedly also at many other times in the second half of the sixteenth century, and he was involved in diverse enterprises, including a substantial landholding.[16] Diego Pérez de Zamora was closely associated with generations of the Coyoacan ruling family. He served as witness to the possession of lands by don Juan de Guzmán sometime in the mid-sixteenth century, and he also witnessed the foundation of the capellanía at the Dominican monastery in Coyoacan by don Juan de Guzmán and his wife, doña Mencía de la Cruz, in 1569. He was named executor (*albacea*) for the estate of don Juan de Guzmán the younger in 1573, and two years later, after the dismissal of the Spaniard Antón Gómez, was appointed guardian of his property and minor heirs at the request of the widow doña María de Guzmán. As guardian, Diego Pérez de Zamora was involved in a number of affairs involving the cacicazgo, including the rental of lands belonging to don Felipe de Guzmán. He also represented don Felipe in a dispute with Spanish authorities over his rights as tlatoani to market taxes (CDC II: 24, 44–47, 59, 69–77, 118–22, 137–38).

With his close ties to the indigenous ruling family, Pérez de Zamora was positioned to further the interests of Spaniards with whom he was associated and who themselves were closely allied with the Guzmán family. The brothers Manuel Téllez Coronado and Cristóbal Téllez, members of a Spanish family that had built up considerable landholdings in the region, served as guarantors for Pérez de Zamora when he was appointed guardian of the minor don Felipe de Guzmán in 1575; in turn, as teniente, Pérez de Zamora may have used his position to their advantage.[17] In 1569 Pérez de Zamora granted Cristóbal Téllez possession of the property called Xoxocotlan sold by don Juan de Guzmán. And as executor for don Juan de Guzmán the younger, Pérez de Zamora received payment from Cristóbal Téllez for the redemption of a *censo,* or lien, on the property (CDC II: 59, 163–64; BL 84/116m: 171r–76r). Apparently, members of the Coyoacan ruling family sanctioned Diego

Pérez de Zamora's activities, aiding the Téllez family's acquisition of land before the Guzmán family itself suffered decline.

With the death of don Juan de Guzmán the younger in 1573 the eldest of his four children, don Felipe de Guzmán, inherited the rulership. As the contested appointment of a guardian indicates, don Felipe was still a minor at the time of his father's death and was unable to assume the responsibilities of the rulership. His uncles (the brothers of don Juan de Guzmán the younger) successively held the position of tlatoani in his place and for one, don Lorenzo de Guzmán, we have a fragment of a testament (in Spanish) dated 1576. Here too we find hints of the ongoing ties between the Guzmán ruling family and local European residents who shared the social type of petty traders, muleteers, and small growers, in this case a wheat farmer and innkeeper, Pedro Pérez de Portugal.

Portuguese settlers, like other Europeans whom Spaniards held in low regard, often moved into the Nahua countryside to engage in small commercial and agricultural enterprises (Lockhart 1976: 106, 112). Pedro Pérez de Portugal was active in Coyoacan in the second half of the sixteenth century and resided there at least as early as 1573, when he purchased a small piece of land near the border with Xochimilco from two Nahua noblemen. Apparently he cultivated wheat there, for in 1585 he received a grant for an inn next to his small wheat field located on the royal highway between Coyoacan and neighboring Xochimilco. Even Pérez de Portugal was at least marginally involved in municipal affairs, serving in 1576 as a witness to the testament of don Lorenzo de Guzmán, who served as tlatoani during the minority of his nephew, don Felipe (AGN Mercedes 13: 137r–137v; CDC II: 26–27; BC: 98–101).

Don Felipe succeeded his uncles to the position of tlatoani sometime after their deaths in the epidemic of 1576. When he became tlatoani, don Felipe had even fewer properties and laborers resident on his land than his father had had; moreover, he had also suffered the loss of the market taxes. Don Felipe's only son (named don Juan de Guzmán like his grandfather and great-grandfather) died in 1604 or 1605, leaving no direct heir to the Coyoacan rulership. Who served as tlatoani in the years between don Felipe's death, sometime in the early seventeenth century, and the 1680s, when the succession of the Coyoacan rulership was legally challenged in court, is not known (Horn 1997b: 54). The troubled succession of the Coyoacan rulership following the death of don Felipe's sole heir surely accounts for the scarcity of documentation (including testaments) concerning the direct tlatoani line in the late sixteenth and early seventeenth centuries. Nevertheless, two extant documents, one a testament and another testament-related (concerning members of the Guzmán family who were not themselves rulers), demonstrate that close ties between Nahua elites and provincial Spaniards persisted into the early seventeenth century.

The testament concerns don Juan de Guzmán, the relative and namesake of the mid-sixteenth-century tlatoani, but whose exact relationship to him is unknown (BC: 64–69). In 1576, decades before he wrote his own testament, don Juan intervened in the deathbed affairs of his sister, doña Juana de Guzmán (the feminized version of the same name), who had married a member of a ruling family of Xochimilco, neighboring Coyoacan to the southeast (Lockhart 1991a: 75–87).[18] Doña Juana's husband was already dead, and she had drawn up a testament that caused some concern in its neglect of his relatives. When don Juan arrived in Xochimilco to discuss matters with her (and in the end to see that her testament was altered), several Spanish women were in attendance. In 1622, when he wrote his own testament, don Juan was still heavily involved in family affairs. He made provisions for various family members and, perhaps because he had failed to do so at the time of her death, arranged to have masses said on behalf of his sister, doña Juana de Guzmán. He also settled a number of debts, and it is here we get hints of contact with local Hispanics: his deceased wife owed money to a Nahua woman whose husband was a Spaniard, and fifty pesos were to be collected from Juan de la Cruz, "Moorish silversmith." As mentioned above, a Spanish cleric served as a witness (BC: 66–67).

As Spaniards moved into the Nahua countryside in the early postconquest decades, they often established ties with Nahua elites for whatever advantages such associations might bestow. In Coyoacan provincial Spaniards such as petty traders, muleteers, and small growers may have continued to seek out members of the ruling family, but the advantages of such connections diminished over time. As the fortunes of the Guzmán family declined, and as Spanish production outstripped encomienda tribute in value, the ruling family became less central to the well-being of the local economy. Ties between provincial Spaniards and Nahua elites persisted after the sixteenth century, but they no longer reflected the importance of ruling families characteristic of the earlier period.[19]

Nahua Traders and Provincial Spaniards

Alongside the Spanish petty traders who sought out indigenous elites in provincial settings were the many Nahuas who pursued commercial opportunities in the expanding sixteenth-century economy. Drawing on a preconquest tradition of merchants and marketplaces and at times adopting Spanish goods and transportation, Nahuas were quick to participate in the market.[20] With access to both land and labor, nobles were initially the most advantageously positioned to do so, but they never held the stage alone. Faced with increasingly onerous tribute obligations in the context of population decline, commoners sold modest amounts of surplus household production to supplement income. Some found a viable livelihood in commerce, the most successful of whom established ties with local Spaniards, thereby gaining access to greater material or financial resources. The opportunity to create such ties increased over time as the primary site of Nahua-Spanish contact shifted from the Nahua and Spanish officials in the central settlement to the Nahua commoners and humble Hispanics living and working on the Spanish enterprises scattered across the countryside.

An extensive trade system existed in the preconquest period, with a developed network of local and provincial marketplaces, and well-traveled foreign trade routes. Long-distance merchants supplied exotic raw materials and the luxury goods desired by the status-conscious nobility. The markets of the major cities, especially the great Tlatelolco market serving Tenochtitlan, offered a wide range of both subsistence and luxury goods. Local markets, by contrast, generally offered basic, utilitarian goods such as food and household wares. These vendors, often women, sold the modest surplus from household production. Other individuals, including craftsmen, offered services in the marketplace. Professional merchants (*pochteca* or *oztomeca*) also plied the provincial markets, offering specialized wares or such items as salt and cotton, which were not available in all regions.[21]

Records from the Coyoacan market dating from about 1550 indicate both continuity and change in marketplace administration after the conquest (BC: 138–49). A Nahua judge still oversaw marketplace affairs, and the tlatoani continued to collect taxes levied on groups of sellers. Trade groups were organized by the two great halves of the Coyoacan altepetl, and their respective taxes were totaled separately. The oztomeca were still functioning as groups associated with particular altepetl subunits (*tlaxila-calli*), most from Coyoacan itself, although several groups of traders came from outside the area, including the Mexica boat people and the salt dealers and obsidian blade makers from Izquitecco. The luxury items so important in the preconquest period are not evident, as there was no longer a clientele for such items as lip plugs and warrior costumes. The bulk of the goods was utilitarian—native foodstuffs and household wares—and probably most items were sold by the producers themselves.

The carpenters for hire and the specialized products having to do with the supply and processing of wood reflected a regional specialty based on the forested hills of Coyoacan. Two important innovations were the use of Spanish coin (all taxes were assessed in *tomines*) and the sale of a small number of European items—one trade group sold candles, another European shirts and collars.[22]

Throughout the sixteenth century, producer-sellers also supplemented the massive tributes being sent to the capital (foodstuffs and other supplies, including construction materials) (Gibson 1964: 360). The earliest direct reference to this trade comes in the early 1550s, when a decline in indigenous agricultural productivity in the wake of the epidemics of 1545–48 brought about a crisis in the city's food supply. Spanish authorities ordered that all the Indian towns within a radius of twenty leagues bring their goods to sell in the city, even to the detriment of local markets. Around the same time the viceroy prohibited Indians from selling goods other than foodstuffs in the capital, in hopes of encouraging agricultural production (especially maize to feed the large urban Indian population) and drawing labor away from other, nonessential activities.[23] This must be the context for a set of Nahuatl annals from Mexico City. It mentions Coyoacan traders selling wood there in 1566 and reports that Mexica officers (or possibly Spanish authorities) arrested Coyoacan officers "because their people are coming selling and weighing wood in Mexico City, passing themselves off as Mexica residents and taking advantage of our people; Mexico City is just for Mexica and not for *tlacanechicoltin* [foreigners]" (MNAH-AH, Gómez de Orozco collection 14: 135).

The arrest of the officers responsible for Coyoacan residents selling wood in Mexico City suggests that at least some of the trade between province and capital was organized by the nobles who held office in Indian municipalities. Due to their close association with Spaniards, nobles were often the main conduit by which European goods, including plants and animals, initially entered indigenous communities, some of which became the basis of production for the market. The 1549 testament of don Pablo Çacancatl, a prominent noble closely associated with don Juan de Guzmán, mentions 440 sheep, while don Juan de Guzmán himself reportedly possessed 3,000. During an investigation into tribute and labor abuse in 1553, commoners testified that they cultivated wheat on various lands owned by don Juan de Guzmán; others worked the vineyards of don Toribio, the Nahua governor of Tacubaya (part of the Coyoacan jurisdiction), and don Pedro, another nobleman of Tacubaya

(CDC I: 25, 57, 113, 117; II: 12–16; Gibson 1964: 345). And some nobles organized their estates along Spanish lines; a 1577 land-sale document mentions the *mayordomo* of doña Mencía de la Cruz, using the Spanish term for an estate administrator (BL 84/116m: 70r). Nobles not only exploited their own properties for market production, but also used their authority to command the labor of commoners to channel goods to Spaniards in what essentially amounted to commercial exchange, although whether on their own behalf or that of the municipal corporation is not always clear. In the 1553 investigation, Nahuas complained that various nobles and municipal officials had ordered them to deliver charcoal and wood products to Spanish citizens of Mexico City and to cut wood, raise chickens, and transport grapes to the mines of Zultepec, all to sell to Spaniards (CDC I: 50, 60, 126, 206–16).

With Coyoacan so close to Mexico City, even small producer-sellers might participate in the urban market, and Coyoacan became known for certain specialties. Wood products have already been mentioned, but Coyoacan—a rich agricultural area where many European cultigens flourished—was also renowned for its orchards. Testaments and land-sale documents indicate that both nobles and commoners frequently possessed native and European fruit trees, including the (indigenous) avocado, zapote, and (American) cherry, and the (European) apple, apricot, peach, and quince.[24] For Nahuas, fruit trees not only supplied household needs but also represented an important investment, in terms of either potential crop sales or improved real estate; European species were cultivated alongside native ones throughout the lower-lying areas of the jurisdiction.[25] The orchards held by nobles could have supported relatively large-scale production for the market; a mid-sixteenth-century list of the properties associated with the tlatoani don Juan de Guzmán includes the renowned orchard at Chimalistac, which the Guzmán family eventually donated to the local Dominicans (BC: 160–61). Many commoners had only a few trees and sometimes used the fruit itself or income from its sale to meet tribute obligations, but a good deal also found its way to market, both locally and in Mexico City.[26] In the 1550s a viceregal order aimed at preventing price gouging by middlemen (*regatones*) specifically prohibited anyone from taking the fruit that Nahuas from Coyoacan brought to the capital to sell (Sarabia Viejo 1978: 422 n. 4).

The purchase and resale of Nahua goods by regatones was an ongoing problem to which Spanish authorities responded with a series of largely ineffectual regulations (Gibson 1964: 360; Hassig 1985: 228, 237, 238, 241). Whenever there was a potential for profit, Spaniards and others intervened, even if the product were a traditional indigenous one. Testaments and land-sale documents indicate that the inhabitants of Coyoacan widely cultivated the native maguey cactus for its honey (*miel de maguey*) and *pulque* (a fermented alcoholic beverage).[27] Within the region, producers sold pulque largely out of their own houses rather than in the marketplace. (It is not listed among the many items sold in the Coyoacan market in the mid-sixteenth century).[28] But small-scale producers from Valley of Mexico towns also sold products made from the maguey cactus in the markets of Mexico City (Gibson 1964: 150, 318, 329, 395–96). Traders included both men and women, most of whom were small-scale producers selling their own surplus, as is suggested by blanket viceregal permissions in 1595 and 1596 to any inhabitant of Tacubaya to sell as much as two or three *reales* in Mexico City. Some earned their tribute in this manner. Others complained of unfair competition from the Spaniards, mestizos, mulattoes, and blacks who also traded in maguey products; in some instances Nahuas accused Spanish officials of colluding with the competition by confiscating the official measures to weigh the maguey honey.[29]

Some producer-sellers operated on a larger scale than those individuals who sold a little fruit or pulque out of household resources, either because they had access to a pack animal or because they specialized in European goods. In the 1590s a small-scale female trader, Catalina Tiacapan of Tacubaya, sold candles (of European style) along with Coyoacan specialties: various kinds of fruit and the wood-related products identified as pine torches (*ocotl*) and ointment made of turpentine (*oxitl*).[30] And Bernardo Hernández, about whom we know little else, incurred the substantial debt of thirty-five pesos for the purchase of a mule, which after his death (around 1630) municipal officials intended to repay with the sale of his land (AN, unlabeled legajo: 289r–90r). A better sense of the commercial affairs of a small-scale trader comes from the 1608 testament of Bárbara Agustina, a commoner who raised small livestock to sell. She, too, possessed a mule, apparently to transport her turkeys and pigs. At the time of her death various people owed her money, most in amounts of a peso or less, although one debt totaled two hundred cacao beans, the commodity used as a medium of exchange in the preconquest period.[31] And don Juan de Guzmán (the namesake of the mid-sixteenth-century tlatoani) requested in his testament of 1622 that fifteen pesos be collected from Juan Tlaxcalchiuhqui on account of the mule, harness, and packsaddle of new cloth that he had had in his possession for six months (BC: 66–67). Tlaxcalchiuhqui literally means "baker"; Juan Tlaxcalchiuhqui may have used the mule to get his product to market, where Spaniards typically bought their staple wheat bread from indigenous sellers (Lockhart 1992: 188, 191).

Alongside the producer-sellers who sold in the urban marketplace were provincial merchants who operated in the tradition of the preconquest pochteca or oztomeca. Oztomeca are mentioned in the mid-sixteenth-century market records, and although the term does not appear in other sources, testaments suggest that in Coyoacan, as in other regions of central Mexico, Nahua provincial traders continued to operate well into the seventeenth century. They no longer traded in the luxury goods typical of the preconquest period nor operated over such long distances—enterprises that had been taken over by Spaniards if they remained viable at all—but they carried part of the trade between provinces and between province and capital. Beyond their connections to other regions, they were distinguished by the possession of mules or horses for transport.[32] Along with European transportation, some Nahua traders readily adopted European goods for trade, and some may have even specialized in them; in 1590 Bartolomé Ramírez and Pedro Hernández received viceregal licenses that permitted them to trade on condition that they pay the sales tax (*alcabala*) Indians were liable for when the transactions involved Spanish goods.[33]

The 1617 testament of Juan Fabián, a commoner from Coyoacan, provides unusual detail about the affairs of a provincial trader in the early seventeenth century. Moreover, it suggests that some Nahua traders benefited from ties with local Spaniards. Juan Fabián traded in the native zapote fruit (*tzapotl*), and his substantial landholdings included orchards. He hired local Nahuas to work for him, including carpenters to make poles. He had a horse and several mules, along with pack gear and sacks, to transport the fruit to market. His son (and namesake) and Diego Francisco, his son-in-law from the nearby town of San Mateo Churubusco, were also involved in the business, seeing the loaded pack trains to market. Some of the fruit must surely have been sold in San Mateo, where Diego Francisco's personal ties would have proven advantageous. In the end, however, the young men absconded with the goods—animals, pack gear, and cash—placed in their trust. In his testament Juan Fabián gave voice to his disappointment, calling his son an "evildoer" and demanding that "if his evilness ever diminishes, he is to pay me back." In addition, he appended a memorandum detailing the accounts of Diego Francisco. Here we discover that Juan Fabián borrowed and loaned money extensively with both Nahuas and Spaniards.

Aside from his land, Juan Fabián's most valuable possessions came from local Spaniards: the mule that Diego Francisco had lost belonged to Bartolomé Téllez, a member of a prominent local Spanish landowning family, and the horse he had killed, to the "Spaniard Fuente," possibly Antonio de Fuentes, the corregidor's deputy, who was also heavily involved in local land transactions.[34]

In postconquest central Mexico, traders operated at various levels ranging from the producer-seller who sold a modest amount of household surplus production in local and urban markets to the full-time specialist such as Juan Fabián who owned an orchard and pack train, hired employees, and maintained close ties to other regions. Producer-sellers clearly included women in both the pre- and postconquest periods, but traders along the lines of the pochteca/oztomeca all appear to have been men. Some market women might have participated in provincial trade in a small way—such as Bárbara Agustina, who owned a mule, or Catalina Tiacapan, who sold both regional specialties and the candles introduced by Europeans—but "the owners and conductors of packtrains always turn out to be men" (Lockhart 1992: 196). These provincial traders not only had access to transport animals and might have specialized in European goods, but some—perhaps the most successful—also enjoyed close ties to local Spaniards.

Conclusion

In the immediate postconquest period, Nahua-Spanish interaction was largely limited to official settings and personnel. Widespread contact between individual Nahuas and Spaniards outside the context of local government came slowly, increasing as the encomienda failed to meet the demands of a growing Spanish population and economy, and as more and more Hispanics moved into the Nahua countryside to grow wheat or to raise cattle. One of the sites where informal Nahua-Spanish interaction developed most quickly was the marketplace. Nahuas sold foodstuffs and other provisions in local markets as well as in Mexico City, much as they had in Tenochtitlan in the preconquest period. Nobles and municipal officials at times directed trade, either for their own benefit or that of the municipality, but many traders participated outside the direct supervision of indigenous authorities. Traders operated at various levels, ranging from the producer-sellers, many of whom were women, to the provincial traders, the heirs of the preconquest pochteca, who were, as far as we know, exclusively men. Spaniards were present in the markets from an early time, relying on them for daily needs, including such basic Spanish staples as wheat bread. Following a Spanish clientele and greater potential profits, mestizos, mulattoes, blacks, and even lower-class Spaniards participated in the marketplace; these petty traders employed Nahua commoners, bought their goods, and gave them competition. Some Spanish traders gained an initial foothold in the region through their close ties with the local ruling family, at least in the sixteenth century when Nahua rulers retained a certain prestige and authority.

By the early seventeenth century, Spanish enterprises, alongside an ongoing but shrinking Nahua subsistence agriculture, formed the basis of the provincial Coyoacan economy. Testaments indicate that Nahuas continued to cultivate maguey and fruit trees and sell the modest surplus in the markets of Coyoacan and Mexico City, but in Coyoacan as elsewhere in central Mexico, Nahua traders along the lines of the preconquest pochteca are harder to document after the early seventeenth century.[35] One author suggests that this reflects not their disappearance, but "rather that mules and especially horses—the two primary diagnostic signs—so decreased in value over the decades and centuries that they received less mention in testaments" (Lockhart 1992: 196). Nahua traders did face increased competition over time as the Spanish economy came to dominate interprovincial trade. By the late-colonial period, the lowest members of Hispanic society—humble Spaniards, mestizos, and mulattoes—dominated petty trade in the countryside. Yet Nahuas, too, retained a role, especially among the ruling elite, who, despite their overall fortunes having fallen since the sixteenth century, now found themselves engaged in economic enterprises alongside marginal members of Spanish society.[36]

As with the petty traders of Coyoacan, informal relationships between Nahuas and Spaniards formed an important part of life in the central Mexican countryside. Whether it was a Spaniard seeking the patronage of a local Nahua ruler or a Nahua commoner acquiring a mule from a nearby Spanish landowner, interethnic relationships were important to the provincial economy and an important avenue of cultural change among Nahuas. But the informal nature of such Nahua-Spanish relationships—with no direct association to the encomienda or the altepetl upon which it was based—makes them especially difficult to document. Nahua testaments are valuable precisely because they provide a window on the many aspects of Nahua life that held little interest for Spanish officials, including the small-scale economic activities and informal interethnic ties seen among the petty traders of Coyoacan.

Last Will and Testament of Agustina Juana, Coyoacan, 1661
(AGN Hospital de Jesús 210, 15: 1)

Jesus maᵃ y Juceph

v Yn ica ytocatzin yn dios tetatzin yn dios tepiltzin yn dios espirito
santo y sa ce huel neli dios teotl tlatohuani nohuiyan cm̄c ca nicnonelto-
quitia ȳ mochi quimoneltoquitia yn tonātzin sāta yglecia catolica de
romana niquitohua ȳ nehuatl agustina juguana notlaxilacalpā tlilac ca
notech oquimotlalili yn ijusticiatzi dios cocoliztli y notlalo y nosquiyo
huel etic: auh ȳ nanimātzi aque ca yntla nechmonequiltiz ȳ notlatocatzi
dios ca ycēmactzinco nocontlalia y noyolia y nanima canel ytlachihualtzi
ytlamaquixtiltzi. yeica yn oc no qualcā ca nicā nictecpana ȳ notestamēto y
sa tlatzaca y ni³⁷ ayac huel quixitiniz y notlanequiliz nosielis = ettᵃ =

v ynic cētlamātli niquitohua ytla oninomiquili ca icxitlatzinco nitocoz y
notlasotatzin san Juᵒ bauhᵗᵃ onca nitocos yn ixPantzinco noestra cēñora
del trancito no niquitohua momacatzinos totlasotatzin Pᶜ prior = 10 tᵒs yc
nechmanilihui [*sic*] catores — 6 tᵒs = ic motlanehuiz candela 2 tᵒs yc motlanehuiz tonba = 2 tᵒs yc tlatziliniz porificacion — mᵒ reyez mᵒ santiago
mᵒ dios piltzintli mᵒ — la concepcion mᵒ sentetl misa cantada de Requie
ypāpa mochihuaz nanimātzin ninocnoytohua ytechcopa notelpotzin dḡō
de la cruz —

v ynic 2 tlamātli niquitohua yn itechcopa sata maᵃ madalena yhua yn
[oc?] cequintitzintzin ypilotzintzihua dios ca niquinnomaquilitiuh
tepitzin tetlaltzintli mani caltitla tecomolco ypan icac ygus yetacatl cen-
taca[tl?] peras quahuitl oncā quiztias popochtzintli xochitzintli cande-
latzin in iquac ytlasoilhuitzin — quimotequipanilhuiz dḡō de la cruz + —

v ynic 3 tlamātli niquitohua yn itechcopa notelpotzi dḡō de la cruz + ca
nicnomaquilitiuh tepitzin tetlaltzintli mani teopacaltepotzco ypa ycac
amacapolquahuitl tlamelahua ypan otli moquaxochnamiqui tlacomolco
diegotzin yhua caltzintli tonatiuh ycalaquiāpa itzticac 2 m[e]tlatl

v ynic 4uh tlamātli niquitohua yn itechcopa noxhuiuhtzi pasquala maᵃ
ca nicmacatiuh tetlaltzintli ypa mani mēbrillo quahuitl motonehua amilcopahuic yc nechilnamiquiz canel noxhuiuh[tzi]

[v] *v* ynic macuillamātli niquitohua yn tehuehuec mani notetlaltzin
canel nocihuacha ca nicnomaquilitiuh y noxhuiuhtzin y pasquala maᵃ ca
concahuizque yn itatzin dḡō de la cruz quimoxelhuizque

v yni 6 tlamātli niquitohua in itechcopa nocalnemac yhua ytlalo yn opa
tehuehuec monamacaz nomisa yc mochihuaz — ca oticoncahuiyayā
ynatzin ytoca balˢᵃʳ manoel

v ca ye ixquich ynic ninomaquixtia yn ixpātzinco dios ca niquimixquetza
noalbaceashua yni nopa motlatoltisque ypapa ypalehuiloca nanimātzin =
ynic cetlacatl pablo juceph — y grauiel juguares — y Ju° agustin — sihu-
atzintzinti juᵃ maᵃ — y dg͞a gerᵐᵃ y jucepa maᵃ — nehuatl onicneltili yn itla-
tol cocoxcatzintli = en 29 de dicienbre de 1661 aᵒs

Juceph jacinto es = [R]

❧

Jesus, Mary, and Joseph

In the name of God the Father, God the Child, and God the Holy
Spirit; only one very true God, deity, Lord, everywhere in the universe. I,
Agustina Juana, whose tlaxilacalli is in Tlilac, say that I believe all that our
mother, the Holy Catholic Church of Rome, believes. The sentence of
God, sickness, has been issued upon me. My earthly body is very sick, but
my spirit is sound. When my Lord God wants me, I place my spirit and
soul entirely in his hands, since he made and redeemed them. While it is
still a good time, I here set in order my last testament. No one, whoever it
may be, can derogate my wish, my will. Etc.

First, I declare that, when I have died, I am to be buried at the feet of
my precious father San Juan Bautista. I am to be buried there before
Nuestra Señora del [Tránsito]. I also declare that our precious father, the
padre prior, is to be given ten reales; six reales, with which the singers
[will] come to take me; two reales, with which candles are to be rented;
two reales, with which the catafalque is to be rented; half a real, with
which [bells] will ring at Purificación; half a real at Reyes; half a real at
Santiago; half a real at the Child Jesus; and half a real at La Concepción. I
beg of my child, Diego de la Cruz, that one high requiem mass be held
on behalf of my soul.

Second, I declare concerning Santa María Magdalena and some other
saints,[38] that I am giving them a small piece of [rocky?] land next to the
house at Tecomolco, on which three fig and one pear tree stand; from
there will come the incense, flowers, and candles with which Diego de la
Cruz is to serve them on their precious feast days.

Third, I declare concerning my child Diego de la Cruz that I am giving him a small piece of [rocky?] land at the back of the church, on which
cherry tree[s] stand. It goes straight along the road bordering
Tlacomolco. And [I am giving] Diego the house facing west [and] two
metates.

Fourth, I declare concerning my grandchild, Pascuala María, that I am
giving her a [piece] of [rocky?] land, on which there are quince trees,

called Amilcopahuic [literally: towards the irrigated field], with which she is to remember me, since she is my grandchild.

Fifth, I declare that I am giving my [rocky?] land at Tehuehuec, since it is my home as a woman, to my grandchild, Pascuala María. She and her father, Diego de la Cruz, are to share it; they are to divide it among themselves.

Sixth, I declare concerning my inherited house and its land at Tehuehuec, that they are to be sold; with [the proceeds] a mass is to be held for me. The mother of [the one] named Baltasar Manuel and I used to share it.

This is all with which I redeem myself before God. I name as my executors, so that they will speak on my behalf for the aid of my soul, first, Pablo Josef; Gabriel Juárez; and Juan Agustín; the women, Juana María; Dominga Gerónima; and Josefa María. I verified the words of the sick person on the 29th of December in the year 1661.

Josef Jacinto, notary.

Notes

I would like to thank Eric Hinderaker, Susan Kellogg, Matthew Restall, and two anonymous readers for the press for their comments on an earlier version of this article.

1. For brief reviews of the field of Nahua studies, see Klor de Alva 1992 and Lockhart 1991a: 159–82. Much of this work treats limited geographic areas and time frames. What it lacks in breadth it makes up for in the greater attention to the local scene and the actual behavior of individuals drawn from all levels of post-conquest Nahua society. The publication of James Lockhart's *Nahuas After the Conquest* (1992) marks a certain maturation of the field.

2. At times this creates the impression that Nahuas crafted their own worlds and preserved an indigenous culture separate from that of the Spaniards. For one example of this interpretation, see Kellogg 1995a: xi–xxii.

3. Lockhart (1992: 7–8) discusses this point in the context of the overall value of Nahuatl language documents. See Horn 1997a for a discussion of Nahua naming patterns.

4. The portion of the corpus that dates from the mid-sixteenth through the mid-seventeenth centuries forms the basis (along with Nahuatl land-sale documents) for an examination of Nahua sociopolitical organization and land tenure in Horn 1997b.

5. For the administrative history of Coyoacan, see Horn 1997b: 67–76.

6. For a detailed discussion of Spanish landholding in sixteenth- and early-seventeenth-century Coyoacan, see Horn 1997b: 166–200.

7. For ties between Spaniards and Nahuas concerning land, see the many examples in Horn 1997b: 166–200 and appendix tables A.28–31; for labor, see 1997: 210–13.

8. For a detailed discussion of the Guzmán family, see Horn 1997b: 45–55.

9. Don Juan de Guzmán, who spoke some Spanish, enjoyed close relations with Spanish authorities. In the 1540s, he aided the Spaniards in the suppression of the Mixtón rebellion in western Mexico and on occasion hunted with the viceroy. As the viceroy stated, he "was always treated like a Spaniard" (Gibson 1964: 158). See Horn 1997b: 49.

10. Coyoacan as a whole is exceptionally well documented probably because of its location so near to Mexico City and its special jurisdictional status as part of Cortés's marquesado. Also see comments in Lockhart 1991a: 195.

11. CDC II: 16–25, 26–27. I rely almost entirely on testaments written in Nahuatl. When a testament is written in Spanish, I indicate so in the text.

12. For Spanish Coyoacan, see Horn 1997b: 213–16.

13. For ties between local Nahua elites and provincial Spaniards in early-seventeenth-century Xochimilco, see Lockhart 1991a: 5–87; for late-seventeenth-century Xochimilco, see Cline 1991: 267, 274; for late-sixteenth-century Culhuacan, see Cline 1986: 122.

14. AN, 497 Juan Pérez de Rivera, 352: 77r–77v (20 Feb. 1584). A similar wage obtained in the case of Juan Bautista of Coyoacan, who agreed in 1583 to work for a Mexico City carter for one year in exchange for food and four pesos for each month of service (AN, 497 Juan Pérez de Rivera, 3352: 378r–378v [23 Sept. 1583]). Advance wages put employers at some risk and carters might demand bondsmen (*fiadores*) as part of a labor agreement; Juan Bautista, just mentioned, presented two fellow Nahuas from Coyoacan to guarantee his contract. Carters sometimes pressed charges against employees for failure to carry out a contract. One 1607 case involved the considerable amount of 122 pesos, which the employer claimed he had paid to another Mexico City carter on behalf of the employee (AN, 374 Andrés Moreno, 2468: 227r–28v [8 Feb. 1607]).

15. The claims that Gómez was involved in lands from don Juan de Guzmán's estate may have had some validity. Testimony provided during a 1604 water dispute associates Gómez, along with Yépez, with the property Xoxocotlan, originally part of the tlatoani's landholdings. Testimony also indicates that in 1604 Gómez had been deceased about thirty years. See BL 84/116m: 191r, 204r, 210v–11r, and 212v–13r.

16. See Horn 1997b: 77–78.

17. For a detailed discussion of the Téllez landholdings, see Horn 1997b: 180–89.

18. As Nahuatl kinship terminology does not distinguish between siblings and cousins (Lockhart 1992: 75), doña Juana de Guzmán may have been don Juan's cousin.

19. Cline (1991: 274) argues in regard to late-seventeenth-century Xochimilco that "the mingling . . . of Indian elites and marginal Spaniards is evidence of the process of Hispanization but also the erosion of status of the native nobility."

20. For money lending and trade by Nahuas in late-sixteenth-century Culhuacan, see Cline 1986: 90–97; for other regions throughout the colonial period, see Lockhart 1992: 184–98.

21. Berdan 1982: 35–44; 1986: 281–90; Hassig 1985: 67–84, 110–26, 131–44. For descriptions of producer-sellers, see Sahagún 1950–82, 10:63–94.

22. For a discussion of postconquest markets, see Hassig 1985: 228–41; Gibson 1964: 353–58, 395; Lockhart 1992: 185–93.

23. Gibson 1964: 54–55. The order concerns Indians of Tlalmanalco who were selling wood in Mexico City.

24. BL 84/116m: 67r (1573, apples, apricots, peaches, quince); AGN Bienes Nacionales 1453, 12: 181v (1612, cherry, quince), 182r (1611, avocado), 182r (1619, fig), 183v (early seventeenth century, orchard), 184r (1608, orchard), 185v (1587, cherry), 193v (1610, orchard), 195r (1590, orchard); AN, unlabeled *legajo*: 290r (1632, orchard); Lockhart 1992: 463 (1621, zapote, quince,); BC: 54–57 (1588, orchard), 64–69 (1622, avocado, zapote, fig, peach, pear). For discussion of the Spanish loanword *huerta* (often appearing in the form *alahuerta*), see Lockhart 1992: 69, 303.

25. For cultivation of European fruit trees in late-sixteenth-century Culhuacan, see Cline 1986: 139.

26. For tribute, see AGN Bienes Nacionales 1453, 12: 183v–84r, and the Nahuatl letter concerning the apricots and pears demanded as "palace duty" that is reproduced in Karttunen 1982: 416.

27. AGN Bienes Nacionales 1453, 12: 184r (1610), 191r (1610), 194v (1597); AGN Tierras 1512, 7 (1607); BC: 64–69 (1622). For maguey cultivation in Culhuacan, see Cline 1986: 138–39; for the Valley of Mexico, see Gibson 1964: 317–19.

28. A Nahua resident of Coyoacan brought *miel de cañas* from Las Amilpas and sold it out of his house and in the markets of neighboring towns. See AGN Indios 10, 191–92: 104r–104v (1630).

29. AGN Indios 4, 145: 46v (1589); 795: 218r (1590); 6, 1ª, 52: 12 (1592); 1094: 300r (1595); 1166: 321v–22r (1596); 10, 191–92: 104r–104v (1630); 13, 103: 87r–87v. The licenses mention both *miel blanca* and *miel negra*.

30. AGN Indios 6, 2ª, 225: 50. See AGN Indios 6, 2ª, 226: 50 for another example of a female trader from Tacubaya.

31. See also Lockhart 1992: 184, 195. For a transcription and translation of the testament, see Karttunen and Lockhart 1976: 98–100.

32. For postconquest traders, see Gibson 1964: 358–60; Hassig 1985: 223, 240–41, 244–45; Berdan 1986: 292–97; Cline 1986: 93–97; and Lockhart 1991a: 234–35; 1992: 192–97. Hassig (1985: 240–41) and Gibson (1964: 358–59) argue that indigenous trading expanded after the epidemics of the 1540s.

33. AGN Indios 4, 344: 113v; 345: 113v. Licenses to engage in trade, granted to individual Indians from at least 1575, were intended to protect Indian traders from Spanish provincial officials who claimed exclusive rights to trade in their respective jurisdictions. By 1590 Indians were selling Spanish goods in quantity despite prohibitions against it; in 1597 Indians were permitted to trade in all goods (except arms and Spanish silks) (Hassig 1985: 237–38, 239, 241, 244–45; Gibson 1964: 359). For alcabala liability, see Gibson 1964: 205.

34. The testament is transcribed and translated in BC: 58–63. See also Lockhart 1991a: 184–85, 194–95. For Fuentes, see Horn 1997b: 78–79, 224.

35. See the following citations to testaments, all dating after the mid-seventeenth century. AGN Civil 1064, 1: 14r–14v (1734, apple, walnut); AGN Civil 1143, 6: 4r–4v (1674, maguey); AGN Civil 1168, 8: 5r–6v (1737, fig,

zapote); AGN Civil 1201, 9: 7r–9v (1748, orchard); AGN Civil 1213, 8: 2r–3r (1722, figs, quince); AGN Civil 1213, 10: 17r–18v (1737, maguey); AGN Civil 1230, 9: 1r–1v; AGN Hospital de Jesús 113, 21: 1r–1v (1659, maguey, quince, walnut); AGN Hospital de Jesús 210, 8 (1673, quince, zapote), 12 (1657, maguey, pear, zapote), 13 (1679, figs, maguey, zapote), 15 (1661, cherry, fig, pear, quince), 16 (1597, avocado, orchard, quince, zapote), 17 (1625, maguey), 54 (1676, avocado, orchard), 66 (1676, quince), 67 (1689, orchard).

36. Lockhart 1992: 197. For late-colonial traders, see Haskett 1991: 166–68. Also, see note 13 for a parallel example of Nahua elites associated with tailors in late-seventeenth-century Xochimilco.

37. "ma" written here, apparently as an afterthought.

38. Literally "children of God," apparently meaning "saints" in this context, although the form *-pillohuan* mainly means "nobles."

CHAPTER 4

Testaments and Títulos:
Conflict and Coincidence of Cacique
and Community Interests in Central Mexico

STEPHANIE WOOD

On the eve of the Spanish invasion of Mexico, don Bartolomé Miguel, an indigenous noble whom "God threw down to earth," nearly single-handedly transformed a place of brush, thorny trees, and weed clumps into an idyllic agricultural community eventually known as San Bartolomé Capuluac, in the central highland valley of Toluca.[1] At least, this is how the alleged founding father and his younger son tell the story in first-person, Nahuatl-language narratives that contain their brief, undated, and somewhat unorthodox testaments (see the wills at the end of this chapter).[2] These interwoven manuscripts have come to represent the community's most ancient recorded history and serve as a symbol of its territorial integrity.

Although they fall into the genre of "primordial titles," or *títulos*,[3] this group of manuscripts really fuses the two documentary traditions of municipal history (titles) with the founding family's final wishes (testaments). Don Bartolomé Miguel refers to the central account in Capuluac's títulos as "my true title" [Noneltiliztitonlo] telling how he had "deserved (or obtained) land" [onitlalmaceuh] for his town. In his testament, embedded in the longer historical narrative, he bequeaths this title to the younger of his two sons. Later copies of these manuscripts came into the custody of Spanish colonial officials in the mid-eighteenth century when heirs of this family and another prominent indigenous family were fighting over lands that had once pertained to the community

85

but were being treated at that late date as private property.[4] The origin and use over time of these primordial titles with their embedded, founding family's wills serve as a window into the evolving relationship between the indigenous elite and the community it supposedly served, as they all came under the domain of a new imperial power. The fusion of testaments and titles highlights a growing tension between conflicting and shared individual and group interests as power and resources such as landholdings became increasingly contested over the colonial period.

The Títulos Genre: Community History

Before exploring this Toluca Valley case in detail for insight into these issues, and before seeing how titles and testaments could become fused, it is important to review what is known of the less familiar genre of local history that we call "títulos." The label "titles" provides a clue to the significance they hold for landownership vested in the community, although few observers would equate them precisely with legal deeds.[5] A recounting of a boundary survey from the mid-sixteenth century or later is often a prominent feature in these titles, also attesting to their worth for establishing territoriality. But the land-tenure theme is only one of several topics that title authors held to be essential for the collective memory. They enthusiastically recount pre-Hispanic migrations and early settlements, the gathering of people to form more compact communities, visits of the first Christian clergy, the construction of Catholic churches, the selection of patron saints, the formation of the semiautonomous indigenous town councils that would serve the communities as well as the viceroy and Spanish king, and, occasionally, the honored presence of passing dignitaries. Sometimes they speak of tribute arrangements, or of conflict with neighboring towns or Spanish estate owners coming to live nearby, or of rivalry between political factions within the pueblos. In short, they are fascinating narratives with hints about precontact life and sometimes detailed descriptions of rearrangements at the local level set in motion by the Spanish intrusion and occupation of Mesoamerica.

In a context where indigenous voices have been neglected in favor of official, European-slanted versions of events over a period of centuries, source materials such as primordial titles, like testaments, facilitate a welcome change. They even differ from the official Nahua accounts written by well-trained historians, for they seem to have been put to paper, amended, and recopied over time by less educated writers who would insert less formulaic, more candid narratives of local events. An employee of the colonial courts once remarked that the style of one set of titles, actually written in Spanish, recalled the style of indigenous testaments, apparently because of their sometimes weak command of Spanish grammar and legal formulas (AGN Tierras 2936, 7: 125r). S. L. Cline (1986: 6) suggests that "the degree of inadvertent error in some of the introductory sections [of testaments] tells us that the notaries were napping while writing them." European models and periodic colonial impulses did have some effect on the evolution of the primordial titles genre, but the genre also seems to have pre-Hispanic antecedents, and it clearly presents original interpretations of indigenous realities. Some of the earliest content of títulos, most likely derived from oral tradition, can assume a mythical quality, stretching the life span and activities of figures such as don Bartolomé Miguel or his son don Miguel Bartolomé into the range of the superhuman. They are also intriguing for their collective perspective or, as James Lockhart describes it, "corporation-centered view" (1991b: 41),[6] appearing in a milieu that became and even today continues to grow increasingly privatized and individualized as a result of late-twentieth-century reversals to land reform (see, for example, Collier 1994).

The Town Founder: Divided Interests

Primordial titles' origins were inherently connected with the actions and later glory-seeking of individuals, opening the door to the insertion or attachment of their testaments. Títulos' speeches about the importance of protecting and preserving the community, its territory, and the memory of its origins are laced with the chest beating by one or more alleged community leaders.[7] Because of the prominent role of the proverbial town founders, and their personal stake in protecting and preserving the community and its land base for the sake of their own heirs as well as the town's children in general, it should not surprise us that their testamentary wishes might flow into the narrative. Both wills and titles often contain an emphasis on landownership, and both could be passed down through the generations as documentary "proof" of that alleged tenure.[8] Whether by design or through serendipity, when these two forms became fused, a tension could arise between accumulation of property at the individual level and the servicing of community political needs. The Capuluac manuscripts are especially revealing of this dynamic relationship between the two genres, as we shall see.[9]

Furthermore, from don Bartolomé's perspective (or that of his descendants), the longer narrative of municipal history complemented his brief will by allowing for more autobiographical (or biographical) material than the typical testamentary form allowed. The Capuluac documents, with their typical oratory or declamatory style, are riddled with the first-person pronoun "*nehuatl*" (Nahuatl for "I"). Don Bartolomé Miguel's name appears twenty-seven times in fewer than ten pages of text that either he directed a scribe to write or he inspired in a later descendant, who put oral tradition to paper.[10] The narrative is punctuated with remarks such as, "I came to settle first on the land," "I was the very first person who came to settle," "I became deserving of getting the land for the first time," "how very true it is that I won the land," and so on.

Despite don Bartolomé's self-aggrandizement, his account reflects some unselfish concern for the welfare of his subjects, "nomaçehualhuan" [my commoners]. To a great extent the land he "won," as he put it, was for the community. On this land he claims to have helped clear the brush and construct houses for other indigenous settlers, acts that may have had an important ritual significance. Nahua tradition held dear the obligations of the "good ruler" (*cualli tlatoani*) toward his subjects: "The ruler [is] a protector; one who carries [his subjects] in his arms, who unites them, who brings them together. He rules, takes responsibilities, assumes burdens. He carries [his subjects] in his cape; he bears them in his arms. He governs; he is obeyed. [To him] as shelter, as refuge, there is recourse; He serves as proxy, as substitute" (Sahagún 1950–82, 10:15). Don Bartolomé strove to fulfill the ideal of the good tlatoani both before and after the Europeans arrived—or so later writers described him, in terms that agreed with this still-surviving model of exemplary rulership.

Don Bartolomé was a Nahuatl speaker and therefore a representative of the privileged minority who had held power in the region since the Mexica conquest of the Toluca Valley in the 1470s. He strove to include the largest local ethnic group, the Matlatzincas, in the new community he was building. Although only one of these people could speak his language, he claims with satisfaction how "Really patiently, in a friendly fashion, they understood me."[11] Don Bartolomé recalls how he fed these people when he himself was at risk of going hungry. Later, when *nanahualtin* (translated into the Spanish as *nahuales*, here meaning evil spirits?) threatened the community, don Bartolomé prayed to God and the "saints" (even though this seems to have occurred in pre-Hispanic times) and built more houses, this time to include Otomí couples, and the nahuales did not return. He speaks proudly about the people's construction of the temple with its "stone saint" (because "we could not yet believe" in Christianity) that drew Otomí and Matlatzinca pilgrims from far around.

While the narrative provides no inkling of *macehualtín* (commoners') opinions on the European invasion of Mesoamerica, it shows don Bartolomé making the necessary adjustments without complaint. But, of course, he benefited personally through his service as intermediary. He proudly recalls how the *tlatoque* (plural for tlatoani) don Hernando Cortés, leader of the conquering Spanish expedition, and don Antonio de Mendoza, the first viceroy to Mexico, granted him the lofty title of *tlatoani juez* in 1534. Using such terminology, he presents himself as a peer of Cortés and Mendoza. Unfortunately, the historical facts do not precisely jibe with this account. Viceroy Mendoza actually came to Mexico in 1535, and it is highly unlikely that he and Cortés visited Capuluac. But perhaps representatives of these important Spanish leaders could have conducted some kind of ceremony in the 1530s honoring don Bartolomé (or his equivalent, if poor memory was placing don Bartolomé farther back in time in the town's history than it should have, as will be discussed below).[12] And, indeed, the first postconquest cacique would have become tlatoani juez or have received some variation on this title, such as *juez gobernador*, municipal governor (Gibson 1964: 167). As the narrative continues, don Bartolomé received the title "tlatoani juez" only after twelve witnesses verified under oath and by taking the cross that he was truly the town founder. Perhaps streamlined by memory, the proceedings were simple: witnesses were each asked in turn if this was don Bartolomé Miguel's land, with the simple question, "Don Bartolomé Miguel?," and each responded with an identical "Why, yes." While his brief testamentary statement lacks witnesses, perhaps he felt the memory of these unnamed people standing up for him at the ceremony of his appointment as municipal chief would be sufficient testimony of the position of power and access to land he enjoyed—his principal legacy.

Royal recognition usually came readily for cooperative, eligible caciques who would facilitate transition to Spanish rule at the local level. As tlatoani juez, the narrative explains, don Bartolomé Miguel would pay tributes to "God" and the "ruler in Spain." But he seemed especially delighted that he would have a grant of local rulership, control over a certain amount of land, and the right to have the people of the "entire region" pay him tributes—possibly perquisites he had been enjoying even before Spanish officials rubber-stamped them. Of course, he would soon have to pass a good portion of those tributes on to the higher colonial authorities, but this was not his concern for the moment (or even in retrospect).

Establishing and Documenting the Lineage

At an unspecified date, but seemingly early in the third quarter of the sixteenth century, don Bartolomé Miguel decided it was time to transfer the title of "tlatoani" to his elder son, don Miguel Bartolomé (the inverse of the father's name, with the two men thereby sharing the name of the town's patron, St. Bartholomew).[13] Here we see him taking advantage of both the testamentary and title forms to establish a noble lineage that would carry on after his death. According to the narrative, don Bartolomé's son, don Miguel, became deserving of the rulership when he and a Spanish priest, who "came to convert us for the first time," together "broke up the idols." Don Bartolomé also sent don Miguel to bring people from the "entire region" to build the "large church" that would house three saints' images and serve the three ethnic groups, with St. Bartholomew in the center for the Mexica,[14] St. Mary on one side for the Matlatzinca, and St. Nicholas on the other side for the Otomí.[15] Finally, don Bartolomé instructed his elder son and new tlatoani, don Miguel, to distribute land to the citizens of the town (*macehualtin*).

While don Bartolomé (or an heir) was making a concerted effort to document the lineage, possibly exaggerating family claims through the títulos and testaments, other historical sources uphold the veracity of such activities on the son's part. In 1590 the third Marqués del Valle, grandson of the conqueror Cortés, assembled documents about the indigenous communities in the Valley of Toluca, part of his special domain. He found records mentioning how, after the death of the famous conqueror and first marqués in 1547, the second marqués, don Martín Cortés, had commissioned a don Miguel Bartolomé to distribute lands in Capuluac among the barrios of the three main ethnic groups.[16] The precise date of the land distribution is unclear, but it could have taken place in the late 1550s or early 1560s, which helps clarify the timing of events in the primordial titles, with their two undated testaments. In 1557 an official grant designated an allotment the size of an *estancia para ganado mayor* (cattle estate, ideally 6.76 square miles) for the purpose of reshaping and regularizing the community (AGN Mercedes 84: 57v).[17] In 1558 authorities sent an indigenous *juez* (commissioned judge, arbitrator) from Culhuacan to Capuluac to supervise the redistribution of parcels, including the identification of uncultivated lands and their allotment to the landless (AGN Mercedes 84: 57v and 150). If don Bartolomé Miguel had a hand in helping the community win and distribute this very important grant, such action would have been more than sufficient impetus for instigating the written record that evolved into the testaments and títulos, if indeed his father had not already initiated the paper trail.[18]

The move to regularize indigenous settlement and redistribute lands was a colonywide effort and came in the wake of the terrible epidemic of 1546–47. An anonymous communication to the king in the 1550s, researched by historian Margarita Menegus Bornemann (1991: 177–78), clarified that a major motive was to increase the amount of land under cultivation and thereby ensure tributes. Since the principal tribute payers were the macehuales, they needed access to agricultural parcels, and many individuals did not have this. At the same time, the local leaders, here called *mandoncillos*, had more land than they needed and were renting it out to "españoles o mestizos [u] otras gentes." They were also taking advantage of their access to the "service" or labor from the macehuales to develop parcels for their own benefit rather than for the satisfaction of the community's tribute requirements to the colonial authorities (177). This anonymous author actually pointed to the recent implementation of this practice in the Marquesado del Valle, including the Toluca Valley, with apparent success (178).

Concern for Community Needs

One might argue that it was not simply greed that drove the Spanish colonial land redistribution programs in the mid-sixteenth century. While the government officers at various levels would have their tax income, access to valuable resources would, theoretically, become more evenly available to all, despite differences of socioeconomic status. In the order to the indigenous judge from Tula who oversaw redistribution in the pueblo of Metepec, not far from Capuluac, we find a note of concern for the "macehuales que no tienen muchas [tierras]" [tribute payers, or commoners, who do not have much land] (cited in Menegus Bornemann 1991: 178).

Did these programs result in some degree of social leveling? In Toluca itself, writes Menegus Bornemann "the judge Pablo Gonzales had orders to restrict the ownership of the lords and distribute parcels to the macehuales who lacked agricultural fields . . . [and] the process of redistribution of the land was carried out to the detriment of the properties of the indigenous elite, who saw themselves dispossessed by order of the colonial authorities" (1991: 182, my translation). And, indeed, some caciques complained vociferously (181–82). However, we need to remember that the indigenous elite was at least partially complicit in this process. The judges—such as the ones from Culhuacan and Tula mentioned above—appointed to oversee these programs came from the native nobility (see also Gibson 1964: 268; Wood 1984: 384). Also, local leaders were on hand to provide information or even help direct census taking and parcel allotment, if these municipal narratives and testaments can be taken at face value. Were office holders conscious of an obligation to serve first the needs of the group? Menegus Bornemann suggests there may have existed some greater degree of social cohesion between the "natural" lords and the macehuales in the mid-sixteenth century. In the Puebla region, possibly owing to the beneficent influence of the friars, the indigenous elite of Huejotzinco gave some of their properties to the landless in 1554. While this seems altruistic, the leaders expected the laborers to support them with the proceeds from one of the (probably larger) fields (Menegus Bornemann 1991: 152–53).

This fascinating mid-century interplay between individual and corporate interests arises in the Capuluac manuscripts. Despite the figurative and symbolic passing of the torch to the elder son, in the fusion of titles and testaments we still find don Bartolomé really making most of the decisions about what land (called *tlalli* and, more specifically, *tlatocatlalli*, or ruler's office land) would go to whom. He designated a waterfront parcel (or "at the place called Atenco") for a bilingual indigenous salt vendor, Antonio de Mendoza (named for the first viceroy), whom they hired to deliver the town's tributes to Mexico City.[19] Don Bartolomé also clarified which areas would be cultivated by the Matlatzinca and which by the Otomí;[20] his intention appears to have been for macehuales to have usufruct rights rather than outright ownership: "Even though I am giving it to them, they are just to take hold of it and till it." He stipulated how, after his son don Miguel distributed the land, "because he is the tlatoani," the son could then work what was left for his own family: "However little might remain, he is to sow it." Such language seems to place tlatocatlalli within the broader conception of community holdings, and the tlatoani himself would not appear to have had an especially large share.[21] This was true also of the allotment for the town founder's other son, who "is still a child," living with his mother "of advanced age": "In the same way my youngest, don Agustín Miguel, will distribute the land that I gave him." The sons may have received large tracts, but they had the corresponding responsibility to distribute it in usufruct parcels to the macehuales so that the latter could support themselves and produce a surplus with which to pay tributes.

The older tlatoani and his chosen successor, don Miguel, were supposed allies in the mid-century colonial rearrangements in Capuluac, unless activities actually carried out by earlier leaders were mistakenly attributed to them as a result of poor memory. The titles associate them both with assisting the Catholic clergy in its efforts to change the mace-huales' religious beliefs and practices. Did the clergy also convince them that the redistribution of land was in the best interests of all? We do not ·have the answer to this question. Perhaps surprisingly, the first-person voice of don Miguel, don Bartolomé's older son, never enters the municipal narrative, his will is not attached, and the existing testamentary portions leave us wondering why don Miguel did not inherit the primordial titles. It was the younger, minor son, don Agustín, who received his father's bequest of the "true title about how I, don Bartolomé Miguel, won the land." Perhaps the younger son's youthfulness would ensure the greatest possible longevity for the manuscripts. Perhaps it also represented the father's effort to equalize things between his sons. Knowing this unexpected gift would cause some friction between the sons, don Bartolomé counseled in his will: "Miguel, you are not to hate your younger brother. You two are to love each other in the name of God."

Building and Defending the Cacicazgo

Whatever the relation between the two brothers, the manuscripts increasingly seem to have spoken for the family more than the community. Don Agustín, their new ·guardian, added to them two more narratives and his own testament. He employed these documents to continue to build the *cacicazgo* (the cacique's hereditary estate, originally intended to be limited to the descendants of a community's original tlatoani) while simultaneously defending it from some ardent rivals. One of his greatest concerns in these new additions is the continuing status of the land designated for the salt vendor hired to deliver tributes, Antonio de Mendoza. The latter had decided to settle permanently in the town, making the alleged founding family nervous. Mendoza's principal home was on the edge of Mexico City, even though the community of Capuluac provided him with a house, an orchard, and "a little land where you will sow." Don Agustín perceived his growing permanence in the town as threatening. Perhaps Mendoza was becoming prosperous and politically ambitious; his ability to speak Spanish might have given him better access to Spanish colonial authorities, too. One suspects he was the first member of a rival family to capture the town governorship away from the traditional elite. This was a typical theme of pueblo histories and is especially notable in the added narratives of these Capuluac records. The addition of the younger son's testament is an attempt to shore up the supposed founding family's historical role, strengthen its claim to power, and fortify its privileged access to lands.

Subsequent worries on don Agustín's mind included the alienation of the property at "Chimali texcaltenco," supposedly bequeathed by his father but which, his statement laments, the elders (*huehuetque*) pawned to pay for a side altar in the church. (This property may have later formed part of the hacienda called Texcaltenco in the Capuluac jurisdiction.)²²
The town elders also purchased vestments with the proceeds from land sold or pawned in another location. Probably throwing land tenure into further confusion, the town underwent *congregación* in 1604, during which a colonial administrator oversaw the second wave of regularization of settlement, establishment of wards, allotment of families, remeasurement of lands, and the marking of boundaries with the planting of new trees.²³ To make matters worse, another epidemic struck—not unusual in the wake of congregación, which brought people, and whatever germs they were carrying, into closer proximity. Eventually, havoc caused by the epidemic might have required that usufruct plots be reassigned once more. At any rate, don Agustín complains in his narrative, "When the dying had passed in 1634, my brother began to steal my land from me. He gave it to his child, Juan Buenaventura." He reiterates the charge in his testament (ignoring the date this time).

By linking his brother to events in 1634, don Agustín tests his credibility with potential readers. Could this brother, who possibly died in the early seventeenth century, be the same don Miguel Bartolomé who took the title "tlatoani," aided in the earliest evangelization of the town, and helped redistribute plots in the mid-sixteenth century? Only if their father had really been responsible for most of the early-sixteenth-century activities, and then don Miguel came into prominence later in that century, might it just be possible that don Miguel died when his brother claims. There is some independent evidence, as noted above, that don Miguel was active in community affairs in the late 1550s or early 1560s.²⁴ We also find that a don Miguel de San Bartolomé was municipal governor in 1583.²⁵ On two occasions in that year he won a ruling that "his macehuales" had to obey him and perform various kinds of labor for him (AGN Indios 2, 750). Court records from the 1590s also pronounce that a don Miguel de San Bartolomé of Capuluac could enjoy the benefit of a *repartimiento* (contingent) of laborers, as long as he paid a fee for the privilege and paid the workers their wages (document cited in Quezada 1972: 140). If our don Miguel were, say, born in the 1540s, a young man fulfilling his first official functions in the 1550s and 1560s, in his forties and fifties when he was governor, and labor lord in the 1580s and 1590s, then he would have been in his nineties in 1634—representing a lengthy life span that is just barely conceivable.

Whatever the exact dates of don Miguel's activity, it was apparently sometime in the early seventeenth century that the son of the salt vendor Mendoza, who was called Juan Jiménez, obtained land from don Miguel. On two other occasions, according to the Capuluac narratives, this rival, Juan Jiménez, challenged property claimed by don Agustín. Some of this disputed land may have been contained in what later descendants asserted to be a grant given Jiménez by don Luis de Velasco Altamirano (AGN Tierras 2860, 1: 1v).[26] Possibly not really an outsider or social upstart, Jiménez got away with using the title *indio principal*, which could have been a notch lower on the social scale than tlatoani, or it may have been an approximate equivalent. The term was in transition in this period (Lockhart 1992: 133). Jiménez also captured the position of town governor and served in that capacity in the years 1590, 1591, 1592, and sometime (or still) during the period 1609–20, according to various court records.[27] This would make him a possible contemporary and serious rival of don Miguel Bartolomé. The fused titles and testaments try to cast doubt on Jiménez's hereditary rights by saying that he was a child born out of wedlock to Antonio de Mendoza. So-called illegitimacy of birth was a frequent charge rivals and unhappy subjects flung at politicians.

Another appendage to the narrative of don Bartolomé carries forward the continuing saga of the decline in power of the alleged town-founding family and the solidifying position of the rival family. Here, the son of (don) Juan Jiménez, (don) Andrés de los Reyes, became tlatoani. (In the resentful títulos neither man enjoys the noble title "don" before his name, but in separate litigation records this does appear, as is fitting of the high office they held and appropriate for mid-colonial-period usage.) Don Agustín describes (don) Andrés de los Reyes as a man who "is not of our lineage," who "is from someplace else," who "has a different kind of blood," and who "is an outsider," making every effort to discredit him. Possibly in the tradition of his grandfather, Antonio Mendoza, and clearly in that of his father, (don) Juan Jiménez, (don) Andrés de los Reyes "really made the town go to ruin." Don Agustín does not come out directly and say these men were *mestizos* (of mixed Spanish and indigenous heritage), but the references to a knowledge of Spanish and a "different blood" are suggestive of this typical accusation.[28] It was sometimes difficult for municipal governors to hold on to their offices if it could be proved that they were not fully indigenous (see Haskett 1991: 156–57).[29]

Don Agustín adds further charges about abuses and forced labor to which (don) Andrés de los Reyes subjected the townspeople until two justices from Mexico City came to arrest (don) Andrés and take him away on a pack saddle. He allegedly bribed them to leave him alone, claiming to be ill, and they returned to the viceregal palace to say he had been found dead when they arrived in the pueblo. His illness apparently did consume him at some point, and a certain palatial pronouncement, made more likely in the pueblo than in Mexico City, if at all, declared that no one else of that lineage (i.e., Mendoza-Jiménez-de los Reyes) could henceforth become tlatoani in Capuluac.[30] This charge was the last one don Agustín leveled at his adversaries before composing his testament.

Did that put an end to the competing lineage? Absolutely not. Whether the work of Cupid or a conscious strategy, sometime in about the fourth known generation the rival families became intertwined by marriage, shoring up the status and prestige of both. Another Nahuatl testament, this time dating from 1715 and pertaining to a don Tomás de los Reyes, "cacique y principal," claims both don Juan Jiménez and don Miguel Bartolomé as great-grandfathers (AGN Tierras 2860, 1: 1r–5r)! Furthermore, don Tomás went forth and became fruitful, leaving the community six children who all claimed to be caciques, used the title "don" or "doña," and were not reluctant to sport the surname de los Reyes, now in its third generation of use.

These and other descendants, certainly not in short supply, became very vocal in the mid-eighteenth century, vying for rights to use or dispose of properties of their *patrimonio* that once pertained to the "caci-cazgo of don Juan Jiménez" in Capuluac. Because many of them were descended from both sides of what were once rival lines, considerable confusion surrounded their claims, and cousins kept aligning and realigning, jockeying for position. The contested properties were of considerable size, in the multiple *caballería* (measure of land, each one about 105 acres) range, tended to be in the vicinity of the much desired *ciénaga*, bore toponyms that dated from the primordial titles and embedded testaments, and were sought after by neighboring hacienda owners, such as a don Josef de Montesinos, a Spaniard from Lerma (AGN Tierras 2860, 1, 2: 2v). A record from 1748 states that a number of caciques were trying to sell six caballerías to the hacienda owner. They had already sold off other properties, but the judge disallowed this sale, sympathizing with protests raised in the pueblo.[31] A few years later, in the 1750s, two different cacique factions, both claiming descent from don Juan Jiménez, disputed three caballerías that were a part of his supposed cacicazgo. The three caballerías were at "[Tzon]tecomatepeque, Quactepeque, and Coyotliapa" (AGN Tierras 1859, 2). Years before, don Agustín had mentioned in his narrative and testament a "Tzo[n]tecomatepetl" and "Coyotlyapan," among many other locations, when describing his own land and property (*notlal* and *nohuaxca*) that was threatened by Jiménez. Additional records indicate that Jiménez sold one caballería next to a ciénaga called "Çontecomatepec Coyotleapa" for four hundred pesos ca. 1609–20. He asserted that it pertained to his "patrimonio," seemingly a synonym for cacicazgo.[32] "Tlatocatlalli" also came to be translated as "patrimonio" on at least one occasion in the Cuernavaca region (Haskett 1991: 173), and Charles Gibson (1964: 260) recalls that judges decided that some disputed tlatocatlalli in Teotihuacan in the sixteenth century were a part of a cacicazgo.

Colonial Mexican cacicazgos originated as indigenous rulerships but increasingly came to represent a form of entailed estate that resembled the Spanish *mayorazgo* (Taylor 1972: 44; Chance 1994: 48). Cacicazgos seem to have had roots in the concept of tlatocatlalli and the custom of tlatoque families enjoying the proceeds from probably large and fertile tracts carved out from the corporate territory, but then, over time, as the laborers succumbed to the periodic, devastating epidemics, its holders or heirs began to treat it as something resembling private property and pertaining only to their family (Gibson 1964: 266).

A Mixtec manuscript and map studied by William Taylor sounds somewhat like this manuscript group from Capuluac in its content and reveals a similar emphasis on a founding-father figure whom Taylor calls the "first cacique." This man was cordial with the earliest Spaniards in the Oaxaca expedition and accepted Christianity. In return they affirmed his rulership and gave him dominion over three barrios with their lands. He was quick to pronounce how his children would inherit these rights: "I give my lands to my children so that they and their descendants may keep and inhabit them forever." Lest anyone jump to the conclusion that these were private properties, however, he stipulated a fine of three hundred pesos for any individual among his descendants who might try to take absolute hold over these lands, which really belonged to the whole pueblo. Taylor concludes that "the cacicazgo lands and the town" were "an integral unit" (1972: 40–41). One can imagine that this was particularly true of their first incarnation, but perhaps less so as time wore on.

Of course, it is not clear that Mixtec and Nahua practices coincided. But, in a similar gesture, don Agustín concludes his testament (and the primordial titles) with the statement that his son was to inherit the "true title . . . for the aid of the town" [ypanlehuilocan AlTepetl]. Nevertheless, by this date, sometime after 1634, one gets the impression that don Agustín was only giving lip service to the community interest. He continued to complain about the alienation of various properties his father had designated for him, including one he called "my land portion" or "land grant" [notlalnemac].[33] He says nothing here about its distribution into usufruct parcels for the macehuales. Of course, his concerns about the rival family could have a dual dimension, the way he paints them as threats to his own family's continued access to power and wealth but also as inadequate rulers who were "ruining the town." But the tone was far different from one generation to the next in these interwoven primordial titles and testaments. Whereas don Bartolomé did not want to see his sons take much land for themselves, this one heir, at least, became very concerned about his own access to and control over his inherited property. He also claimed don Miguel took one of don Agustín's parcels and gave it to his son, don Agustín's nephew. If this is true, neither of the brothers of the second generation was as selfless as their father had intended, and their subsequent behavior was precisely what their father had worried about.

Perhaps such was the desired or natural result of the encouragement the Spanish kings gave the cacicazgo. For example, the monarch had stated in 1557 that the colonial audiencias, or high courts, must listen to the "descendants of the first lords, with utmost dispatch if they seek justice in successfully holding and inheriting their cacicazgos" (cited in Taylor 1972: 39). It was certainly the caciques' own aim. These nobles regularly petitioned for official recognition and land grants, and they often met with a success that helped secure, unwittingly, the position of their eighteenth-century descendants in subsequent litigation. A considerable number of disputes pitted these nobles against their communities, which provides further substantiation of a growing conflict of interest (see, for example, Taylor 1972: 53 on Oaxaca, Münch 1980 on Oaxaca, Gibson 1964: 266 on central Mexico, and Münch 1976 on Teotihuacan). While the mid-sixteenth-century redistribution programs may have struck a blow against the native elite, in the second half of the colonial period the tlatoque recuperated and social inequality increased.[34] If we are to believe the testaments and títulos of Capuluac, don Juan Jiménez was one such second- or third-generation cacique. He may have come from outsider stock, but he climbed to the pinnacle of local indigenous politics and supposedly won a grant of land in the vicinity of the founding family's prized territorial possessions. Although

Jiménez's son, (don) Andrés, brought temporary scandal upon the family, numerous heirs were still anxious to use the family name as a means to prestige and subsidiary land rights.

In many towns and many elite indigenous families, primordial titles might have served a dual role as both community and cacicazgo papers. Testaments more clearly sustained the family estate, but títulos could, too. For example, the Mapa de Cuauhtlantzinco, from the Puebla region, praises the deeds of four caciques, one of whom exhorts, "honor my descendants and do not oppress them in distributing and working my lands since they ought to live as my sons and to work my lands, united to my pueblo" (see the transcription and English translation in Starr 1898: 19). The Metepec titles of the Toluca Valley state their purpose as wanting to make it known "who were the founders and caciques of the ancient pueblo of Metepec," especially one cacique named don Ignacio Carrillo, originally from Tlatelolco (see the transcription and Spanish translation in *Códice de Métepec* 1992: 26; English translation mine). Many primordial titles from the Cuernavaca region feature the activities of a don Toribio Sandoval de San Martín Cortés, municipal governor from the late 1560s through 1591, who, according to Robert Haskett, became an exemplar of corporate integrity but who was supposedly unconcerned with "the welfare of Cuernavaca's common indigenous citizens." On at least one occasion he settled a dispute by upholding private property rights to the detriment of community claims (Haskett 1992: 15–16).

Authenticity of the Testaments

Because of the strong interests and motivations behind the activities of caciques, their documentary production can sometimes attract questions about authenticity. With cause one might doubt whether the first of the two testamentary statements in the Capuluac titles, the undated will of don Bartolomé Miguel (see the wills at the end of this chapter), could stand on its own. If he truly had a hand in the early composition of these manuscripts, he probably would not have drawn a clear division between his testamentary statement and the remaining components of the títulos. The different units were integrated and supported one another. Don Bartolomé opens the titles with "Jesos, Ma. y Josep" and praises God in a way that is very reminiscent of the testamentary portion (AGN Tierras 2860, 1, 2: 69r, 70v). But if we try to examine just the will, alone, we find that it is relatively brief, especially for a tlatoani, and lacks elements one expects to find in more standard Nahuatl testaments.

Don Bartolomé's will has two principal themes. The first one encompasses his concerns regarding the church under construction for the town's patron saint, Bartholomew. Here we see the connection with the pictorial in the corpus, featuring as it does a church with what appears to be scaffolding and people possibly raising stones or roof tiles. The illustration also probably shows don Bartolomé as the central, dark figure holding the staff of authority, possibly at about the time he wrote his testament (AGN Tierras 2860, 1, 2: 74r). Because the church is incomplete upon his death, don Bartolomé must be interred at (the chapel of?) Santa María, but, as he explains in his testament, he hopes his coffin will eventually end up at the new church. To stipulate burial wishes was common, although it would probably have been rare and unlikely that his coffin would be moved. Don Bartolomé also designates properties for the support of the saints' images on the three main altars of the new church, another request that falls in line with testamentary custom.[35]

The second matter preying on his mind is his concern, already explored, that his younger son inherit the primordial titles, but without having this bequest cause animosity between his two offspring. For a powerful figure, don Bartolomé's will has surprisingly few details. We do not learn the name of his spouse. No witnesses appear for him. There is practically no formulaic matter about beliefs in God and the Holy Trinity, no begging of forgiveness for sins, no specific references to masses, no mention of specific monies to cover such masses, and no dispersal of specific properties, other than the house, to his wife and sons.[36]

The other testament (see the wills at the end of this chapter), that of the younger son, don Agustín, contains a longer, more convincing introduction full of praise and humility ("I am a very big sinner"), followed by the standard elements of so many pesos for an alb, so many for masses, and so many for his wife to bring up the children. He singles out a son, Pedro, who should inherit the "tlalnemactli" [granted land, or share of land] that don Agustín's older brother alienated, part of it being at the base of oft-mentioned Tzontecomatepetl (Skull Hill). Three men bearing the title "don" witness the document. With that, don Agustín concludes his testament and the titles, not to mention his own interlude on earth. If the wear of time, flagging memory, and occasional recopying simplified don Bartolomé's testament until only its essential thrust survived intact, don Agustín's last wishes were probably composed in concert with one of the more recent renditions of the community's history, allowing for the preservation of a few more details than his father's will contains.

In the highly charged environment of central Mexican land struggles and the Spanish colonial authorities' insistence on documentation, it is understandable that indigenous people would sometimes resort to the ad hoc composition of unofficial manuscripts to support their often legitimate genealogical or territorial claims. Both titles and wills can lend themselves to modification and contrivance.[37] Poor memory can also detract from the veracity of their contents. Recopying will result in inadvertent omissions and, sometimes, alterations by disgruntled heirs. On the other hand, these manuscripts can also represent the frank and earnest visions of reality of the people they represent. Since literate amateurs could put quill or paintbrush to paper (or cloth, as with *lienzos,* and even deerskins), we should not be startled to find deviant variations on the more polished work of educated indigenous notaries and historians. Nor should we automatically question their authenticity. One can imagine how there were times, such as in the midst of an epidemic, when individuals could not obtain the assistance of a Spanish priest—or even an experienced indigenous aide to an ecclesiastic—to help record a final will. Similarly, local histories from the smaller, outlying towns could have been written by people without much schooling and only irregular contact with Spanish authorities. Under such circumstances, fraud was not necessarily such authors' intention.

Conclusion

With the rare but logical feature of embedded testaments, the títulos of Capuluac shed a particularly bright light on their potentially tension-filled multiple purpose of sustaining the community while advancing the power and wealth of one or more of its noble lineages. The combination of the two genres, of testaments and títulos, can provide insights into the indigenous people's conception, adaptation, and utilization of each one that we might not otherwise fully appreciate. The titles, though primarily providing foundation to the community's antiquity, territoriality, and ostensibly its communality, increasingly generate a narrative aimed at advancing the interests of one particular family and deflating those of another. The wills, though clearly representing elite individuals and attaching to specific lands a private significance that would live on indefinitely, also had the ironic potential to shore up the pueblo's corporate interest in the land. In pre-Hispanic tradition, tlatocatlalli was supposed to be safe from sale or hereditary transfer. Such may explain the ruling in 1748 against the alienation of Capuluac's one-time community properties. Through proximity and interweaving, the two genres of testament and title become fused and facilitate each other's objectives.

The testamentary form played a significant role in the complex evolution of individual and community rights in early Mexican history. It reveals social differentiation and power relations within the indigenous community, still sometimes mistaken in the modern popular consciousness for a homogenous, communitarian utopia. In the primordial titles of San Bartolomé Capuluac, the presence of the two wills, pertaining to the town founder and his younger son, underlines the centrality of such figures in the history of what was probably in many ways a typical rural, indigenous community of the central Mexican highlands in the sixteenth and seventeenth centuries. It recalls the special status that Spanish colonial authorities gave to the cooperative indigenous elite and the communities in which they ruled. The wills remind us of the heated competition that the elevation and privileging of individuals (and families) led to, as members of rival families fought over local authority and the perquisites it afforded. This may not necessarily have been a phenomenon that originated in the colonial situation, but one that might well have been exacerbated by it. Testaments and titles show us how the colonial cacique as a social type might emerge, taking advantage of his valued status in the indigenous world while emulating Spanish-style accumulation of private property. These documents provide clues to the complex and evolving nature of tlatocatlalli in its possible journey from community lands distributed and governed by indigenous leaders to vast tracts that descendants felt authorized to use or sell in later years to facilitate hacienda formation and expansion. In short, the testaments provide a window onto issues of conflicting jurisdictions over resource control and distribution that begged for clarification but, alas, would continue to plague Mexico into modern times.

Last Will and Testament of Don Bartolomé Miguel, n.d.
(Attached to the títulos of San Bartolomé Capuluac,
Valley of Toluca)[38]

Jesus Ma y Joseph

Ycan inn inTocantzin Dos [*sic*] Tentantzin: yhua Dios Tepiltzin: Ynhua Dios espiriTo Sancto: Nican nictlalia: Noteztanmento: Ma n nicnoyecTenehuili: Y tto Dios Yhua yehuatzin: Notlaçotantzin: Sancto San Bartholomen: Yhua yiehuatzin: Santan maria: Yhua yehuatzin: Sancto San Nicolas: can ye onnechmolnanmiquilitzino: y noDios: can ye yman ye

ocan otlamico: canhuitl: Ytla onechmotlaçotili: yn Dios: Ma çan ipapan
tzinco: Y tto Dios: Anquimochihuilizque: Y tle nechtequipanchotiuh: yn
iTeocaltzin: Notlaçotatzin: Sancto San Bartholomen: Yn quename
onpeuh: yuhqui tlamiz: ma ixquich Amotlapaltzin: xicmochihuilican:
SanTa maria: SanTo San Nicolas: yn yeixtitzitzin: Mocanlaquizque: Ytla
omocencauh: can huell opan nichuechiuhtiuh: Yn tlali çoquitl: Y manel
axcan: ye nechmotlaçotilia: Yn Dios: opan SanTa maria: Ycan ce Jaxa:
Anechmotoquilizque canyac Teonpantlacatl: canyac Teonpixqui: can huel
huecan huitz: Ypapan nitlanahuatia: Yn icuac mocanlaquizque: Sanctos:
Ytla omocecauh: yn Teoncaltzin: Sancto San Bartholomen: SanTa maria:
Sancto San Nicolas Yhua nehuatl: oc cepa anechmoquixtilizque: onpan
yaz y notlalo noçoquiyo: ma huel ypapantzinco: Yn Dios: ye noyolo
panchiuhtiuh: Yhua nichuechiuhtiuh: yn tlali teopan: Sancto San
Bartholomen: Ytlaltzin yez: Atiçaco Santa mariatzi: Ytlaltzi yez: y san luiz:
Yhua sa nicolas: Ytlaltzin yez Ynic nechmopanlehuilizque: ye aquicacque:
Amochtintzitzin: Amo aquin tle nichuiquilia: Amo tle nechtequipan-
chohua: Agostin Miguel: oc piltontli: Nicanhuilitiuh: Noneltiliztitonlo:
Ynic onitlalmaceuh: Nehuatl: Don Bartholome miguel: Yhuan nochan:
niccanhuilia: Ayc aqui quiquixtiliz: yn n inantzin: y omochicanhualti: Auh
canmixpan nitlananhuatitiuh: miguel: Amo tictlayelitaz: y moteycauh:
Amotlaçotlazque: ycantzinco: Y Dios Nitlacuilohua: Nehuatl: ADres
Lopiz —

❧

Jesus, Mary, and Joseph

In the name of God the Father, and God the Son, and God the Holy
Spirit, here I set down my testament. Let me praise our lord God and my
dear father, the saint St. Bartholomew, and Saint Mary, and the saint St.
Nicholas. When my God has remembered me [with death], when [I am
in?] his hands[?], when time has run out, if God loved me, let [it be] just
for our lord God [that] you build that which is worrying me, which is the
temple of my dear father, the saint St. Bartholomew. How it began, so it
will end. Make every effort. Make sure [the images of] St. Mary, the saint
St. Nicholas, [and St. Bartholomew], all three go inside when [the
church] is ready. For really there I am dedicating the earth, the mud [i.e.,
my body]. If God loves me today already [with death], you are to bury
me in a coffin there at Santa María. For there is no church person, for
there is no priest [here], for he comes from really far. For this reason I
order that when the saints [i.e., their images] are ready, they will be
placed inside the church of St. Bartholomew, St. Mary, the saint St.
Nicholas. And [regarding] me, again you will make me leave [the church

at Santa María]; my earthly body will go there [at the new church]. Let it really [be] for God. Already my heart is satisfied. And I am making an offering of land to the temple. The land of the saint St. Bartholomew will be at Atiçaco. The land of St. Mary will be at San Luis. And the land of St. Nicholas will be used to help me. All of you already heard it. I owe nothing to anyone. Nothing is worrying me. Agustín Miguel is still a child. I leave to him my true title about how I deserved land, I, don Bartolomé Miguel. And I leave my home to him. No one is to evict [him and] his mother, who is of advanced age. For, before you, I am ordering: "Miguel, you are not to hate your younger brother. You are to love each other through [in the name of] God." I write. I, Andrés López. —

Testament of Don Agustín Miguel, n.d.
(Attached to the títulos of San Bartolomé Capuluac, Valley of Toluca)[39]

Jesos — ma. Y Joseph

Ycan yTocantzin Dios tentantzin: Dios Tepiltzin: Dios espirito Sancto: nican nictlalia: y noteztanmeTo: nehuatl notoca: Don Agostin miguel: nicnoyectenehuilia: Yn tto Dios: Yn onpa moyetztican: yn ilhuicac: Yhua Nican tlaltipac: nechmopielitica: can y otinechmotitlanilililitzinno: mocolotzin motzintzincantzin: Ma nicpancanceli: mochi can noyolo: ca Niquinnotlatlauhtilia: Yn Dios: can ycenmactzinco: nictlalia: nichuenmana: noyolia: nanima: Ma quimopacançelilitzinno: yn nitlatlacohuanni: can huel miec ynic onimitznoyolitlacalhuitzinno: yn nihueycetzotlatlanconhuani: ynic nechmolnamiquilitzinnozque: Ynic nechmotlaçotiliz: cannel niquixtlahuaz: Yn imiquilitzin: Y Dios can ye yma: can ye oncan oaçi Y notlapoal: Ynic nicnomaquilitiuh: cuetan: Y Dios: y notlalnacanyo can ycxitlatzinco Notlaçotatzin: Sancto San Bartholomen: Ninotocaz: Auh yn huetzintli: huel moxtlahuaz: ye anquimomachiltitincanTe: yn ocan AnmetzticanTe: ca ye yuhqui omotlali tlatolli: yn tehuatin: Yntla noço huel quitlanizque: motemacaz: ce peso: çann ixquich: Ynhuan nitlanahuctia [*sic*]: oncan ca yn ipatiuhtzin: Y tto Dios: onpohuali peso: çepohuali peso: nichuechihuan Teopan yc mocohuaz: Alba auh yn oc cepohuali peso: Macuili nomisa yes: Auh yn caxtolli peso: Yca quihuapahuaz: nopilhuan: Monicatzin: Noçihuatzin ca çann ome otechchimocanhuilili: Y Dios: ocan ca quezqui çitli quicuatiyezque: Nitlanahuatia: cali ca yaxcan: Pedro: yn notlalnemac: onnechmaquiltia: Notlaçotantzin: çan onechcuili noermano: Don miguel Bartholomen: quimaccac ypiltzin: Ma quita tle cueta quimomaquiliz: Y Dios: yn moztla huiptla: ytzintla

tzotecomatepetl: çanno tepitzin [added above: tlalli): tla quimonemiltiliz:
Y Dios ca yehuatl conanaz: yhua nicccanhuilia: noTatzin: onnechmocan-
huililitia: neltiliztitollo: Ytla nemiz Pedro: Ayc aqui [qui]quixtinliz: huel
quipiez: Ypanlehuilocan: AlTepetl Amo tle yn Nictehuiquilia: can ye
amixpatzico Nitlananhuantia == Don Juan == Don Locaz == Don Ynasio
== Amotech ninocancauhtiuh == Nitlacuilohua nehuatl: miguel peris —
Ma iuh mochihua —

❧

In the name of God the Father, God the Son, [and] God the Holy Spirit.
Here I set down my testament. My name is don Agustín Miguel. I praise
our lord God, who is there in heaven and here on earth. He is guarding
me. Let me happily receive for my heart all that you [God] sent to me,
your cross, your thistle. For I implore God. In his hands I place my
spirit, my soul. Let him receive it happily. I am a sinner, for very much I
have offended you [God]. I am a very big sinner. How will they [God
and the saints?] remember me [with sickness]? How will he [God] show
me attention [with death]? Since I will repay God's death. For already it
is time. For already my account has arrived, how I go to give the account
to God of my earthly flesh. For I am to be buried at the foot of my precious father, the saint, St. Bartholomew. The offering really will be paid.
Already you [plural] are handling the matter, you who are there. For
already in this way the statement was settled on. You all [were there].
Only if they really demand it, will a peso be issued, and that is all. And I
order there is [i.e., I have] an amount of money pertaining to our lord,
God, forty pesos. I make an offering of twenty pesos to the church; with
it an alb is to be bought. And [regarding] the other twenty pesos, five
will be for my masses, and with fifteen pesos, my wife will bring up my
children, Monica [and Pedro], [73r.] for God left us only two [children].
There are a few dried ears of corn. They are to eat them. I order that the
house is the property of Pedro. My brother, don Miguel Bartolomé, just
took from me my granted land [or my land portion] which my dear
father gave to me. He [my brother] gave it to his child. Let him see the
accounting that he will give to God in the future. At the base of
Tzontecomatepetl [Skull Hill] there is also a little piece of land. If God
shall let him live, he [Pedro] is to take it. And I leave to him the true title
that my father left to me, if Pedro lives. Never is anyone to take it from
him. He can have it for the aid of the town. I do not owe anything to
anybody. For already before you all, Don Juan, Don Lucas, [and] Don
Ignacio, I am ordering [this]. I leave you. I write. I, Miguel Pérez.
Amen.

Notes

1. The name of the town today is Capulhuac de Mirafuentes, according to Gerhard (1993: 273). It had a population of 1,653 in 1568 and 2,406 in 1595, as compared to Toluca's 16,550 and 6,220 for the same years (see Menegus Bornemann 1991: 208, citing Borah and Cook). The demographic decline experienced in Toluca was more the norm. Capuluac's civil jurisdiction, and therefore population size, possibly underwent some adjustments in the second half of the sixteenth century. Gerhard tells of changes in religious jurisdiction in this area in 1569 and 1573. The town was a *cabecera* in the colonial period and, of course, Nahuatl speakers called it an *altepetl*. (For a discussion of the meaning of *altepetl* see Lockhart 1992: 14–58, and for *cabecera* see Gibson 1964: 33–57.) In the 1770s there were 489 indigenous families in Capuluac, all Nahuatl speakers, and 108 families of other races or ethnicities, according to the local ecclesiastic's report to the Spanish king, a document also known as a *relación geográfica* (BNM, 2449: 84r–87v; on microfilm at the Library of Congress).

2. It is difficult to compare these two testaments with similar records. I have collected copies of nearly 200 testaments from the Valley of Toluca and studied more than 170 of these in some detail (see Wood 1991b and 1994). There remain in the local archives a great many more testaments. The bulk date from the eighteenth century, however, and surviving sixteenth- (and even seventeenth-) century wills are rare. There were proportionally fewer testaments recorded in the valley in the sixteenth century and during epidemics in subsequent centuries, when people were dying rapidly and in vast numbers in the more than one hundred towns that dotted the landscape. Many of the smaller towns had only infrequent visits from parish priests in the earliest colonial decades.

3. Lockhart, more than anyone, advanced the study of títulos with his important piece from 1982 (republished in 1991). Other studies include Wood 1991b; Restall 1991, 1997b: 276–92; Haskett 1992; Terraciano and Sousa 1992; Gruzinski 1993; and Wood 1997a, 1997b.

4. See AGN Tierras 2860, 1, 2: 59r–80v. This includes the Spanish translation (59r–66r) of the Nahuatl primordial title (67r–70v); the undated will of don Bartolomé Miguel (70v–71r) in the same hand; an added statement (71r–72v) by don Agustín Miguel, also in the same hand; the undated will of don Agustín Miguel (72v–73r), also in the same hand; a color painting (74r); and another partial copy of the primordial title, wills, and added statement, in Nahuatl but in another hand and with many discrepancies (74v–80v). Spelling in the latter version includes the increased use of the "s" in place of "z," indicating that this one was made after the one above. It omits material found on folio 67 of the older version. See the appendix for don Bartolomé's and don Agustín's testaments, excerpted from the transcription and translation I have in my personal files.

5. At times communities presented them to colonial courts as evidence of legal tenure, and occasionally the courts legalized them and allowed them to serve as legitimate titles. For example, the Ajusco town founding document won an official stamp of approval in 1710 (AGN Tierras 2676, 4). Similarly, authorities accepted what Haskett calls the "Díaz Titles," which a cacique presented in 1732 to support his land claims. They also reinforced, in 1707, community tenure in a

battle with sugar mills, basing this on a translated portion of Cuernavaca's "Municipal Codex" (Haskett 1992: 9–10). Finally, magistrates repeatedly legalized a "Techialoyan Codex" from Tepezoyuca in the late seventeenth and early eighteenth century (AGN Tierras 1873, 2).

6. Gruzinski (1993: 116) also emphasizes how títulos became "an instrument of protection and, beyond the shadow of a doubt, the basis of a communal identity."

7. I say alleged because questions raised in disputes between rival factions can call into doubt whether one or another "leader" was actually the legitimate or hereditary one or an upstart or outsider.

8. Studies of central Mexican testaments that incorporate discussion on land issues include, among others, Anderson, Berdan, and Lockhart 1976; Kellogg 1980, 1986; Cline 1981, 1986; and Wood 1991a, 1994. Cline (1986: 9) says, "Land tenure is perhaps the largest single matter which the wills illuminate." Studies of títulos have already been cited.

9. The títulos of San Nicolás Coatepec de las Bateas, a smaller settlement that pertained to the colonial parish of Capuluac, contains a near-testamentary ending, with the town founder speaking of his coming death and his need to leave his sons his final statement (*notlatol*). See the manuscript's transcription and translation in Máynez, Blancas, and Morales 1995: 318–19.

10. The founding father of Coatepec gives his name at least nineteen times in that town's historical narrative (see the Máynez, Blancas, and Morales transcription and Spanish translation, 1995: 269–319).

11. By the time of the relación geográfica of the 1770s, describing the parish of Capuluac, Nahuatl was the only language spoken by the indigenous residents. See BNM 2449: 84r (copy on microfilm at the Library of Congress).

12. Some "annals" (*anales*) held by the town as late as the 1770s claimed that the earliest inhabitants of Capuluac took up residence twenty-two years before the first land grant, dated April 5, 1557. (See the relación geográfica of 1777 in BNM 2449: 84r; copy on microfilm in the Library of Congress.) This would pinpoint town founding at about 1535, roughly consistent with these records. One wonders if the annals are really the títulos under study here or perhaps another Nahuatl-language historical record which could shed light on our titles and testaments.

13. Toluca Valley testaments reveal a fondness among indigenous families for naming children after favorite saints (Wood 1991a: 278–80). Many, particularly the founding families, favored the town's patron. According to fray Diego Durán (1971: 38), a patron saint was often chosen by its coincidence with the "birth sign of the chief of the town." As in the Capuluac manuscripts, in those of neighboring Coatepec the names of the founding father, his son, and the patron saint follow a similar pattern: (don) Nicolás Miguel, (don) Miguel Nicolás, and San Nicolás (see the transcription and translation in Máynez, Blancas, and Morales 1995: 272–73, 288–89). Incidentally, this record, in concert with the first section of the Capuluac narrative, consistently omits the title of "don" when referring to the founding father, which seems more in line with early usage. Later in the sixteenth century the use of "don" became more diffused. On the other hand, it may be evidence that these families actually had a lower status than they alleged. Their use of two given names is not impressive, but perhaps the "Miguel" component had a local significance, since we find it in the names of both the Capuluac and Coatepec founding families.

14. In the Nahuatl the word used is "*mexican*," with a standardly intrusive "n" at the end. With terms like "Aztec," "Mexica," and "Nahua" in scholarly use today, sometimes interchangeably and sometimes to mean very specific, finite groups, it seems worth clarifying the original term employed in these kinds of situations.

15. The phenomenon of having separate altars for different ethnicities may have recurred across the valley. Records from the church in nearby San Mateo Atenco in 1721 mention a separate altar for the Matlatzinca. See MNAH-AH, Fondo Franciscano 51: 7.

16. AGN Hospital de Jesús 277, 2: 248–49. Some of this is also quoted in Hernández Rodríguez 1954: 88. One wonders what sources the third marqués had access to when he was recalling the cacique of Capuluac. Was he using some early version of the primordial titles and testaments or more official records pertaining to the marquesado? There is also some confusion as to which man the marqués's records point to. In at least one place his name is given as "don Miguel Bartolomé," but, in another place, as "don brme. Miguel de San bartholome *cacique de* capuluhaque [another rendition of Capuluac]." Thus, was it the elder tlatoani or his first son who participated in the mid-century reorganization? If the father had helped found the town, allegedly in the 1530s, perhaps it was the son who had taken the reins by the 1550s. Because the names were so similar and they both shared the town's patron saint's name, it is no wonder that observers (then and now) could become confused.

17. Capuluac's relación geográfica (regional report to the Spanish king) of the 1770s provides a date of 5 April 1557 for this community land grant. See BNM 2449: 84r; copy on microfilm at the Library of Congress.

18. The primordial titles of neighboring San Nicolás Coatepec include two references to don Bartolomé Miguel participating in a boundary survey in that community in the year 1550 (see the transcription and translation in Máynez, Blancas, and Morales 1995: 292–93, 316–19). While such dates are sometimes questionable, this one could make sense. Alternately, since two *pinturas* (pictorial records) from the Toluca area and associated with the second marqués's census and land distribution order were made in 1563, some of the proceedings in Capuluac may also have occurred in that year. (See AGN Hospital de Jesús 338, 29 and 413, 3.) In 1567 Crown officials seized the marquesado from don Martín Cortés and did not return it to him until 1574, after which time he may have continued to pursue pueblo rearrangements (see Barrett 1970: 13), but I suspect the Capuluac and Coatepec events took place prior to 1567.

19. Salt was an important commodity. The salt trade was, according to Rosaura Hernández Rodríguez (1966: 219), a vital thread connecting the Valley of Toluca with the Valley of Mexico in pre-Hispanic times. In combination with chili peppers, salt was also so basic that it was the Nahua metaphor for food. See Ruiz de Alarcón 1984: 67. The travel that went with the salt trade possibly helped the vendor, Antonio de Mendoza, to pick up some Spanish. The reason given for his being hired was that he was bilingual and no one in this indigenous community spoke Spanish.

20. This ethnic component in the proceedings echoes in the records of the marquesado which recall how the cacique of Capuluac designated wards for the "naciones matalzingos Otomies y mexicanos" and gave names to the wards. See AGN Hospital de Jesús 277, 2: 248–49.

21. The record, unfortunately, is somewhat ambiguous about the actual extent of land that don Miguel would manage for himself. His portion (which he may have had to distribute among the macehuales) sounds quite extensive in one passage: "straight from San Sebastian up to the ocote woods, and all the marsh up to the basin. Another place it begins at Chimali Texcaltenco. All of it meets in this direction at San Luis where, for the first time, I came to settle; just I alone." As further examples of tlatocatlalli come to light we may gain more insights into its evolving meaning. Haskett (1991: 173) notes, in discussing the 1579 testament of a prominent indigenous family of Cuernavaca, "Prehispanic tlatocatlalli are generally believed to have been lands attached to the office of tlatoani but not private property. But in don Juan's will, the parcel was being treated as private property, suggesting that members of the elite had been able to claim exclusive ownership of such plots at the expense of their communities in the fluid years following the conquest." In an example provided by Cline (1986: 142) from Culhuacan in 1580, we find a Miguel Cerón, non-tlatoani, bequeathing tlatocatlalli, dividing it, ordering part of it to be sold, and generally treating it "as his private property." See also León-Portilla's (1992: 140–42) helpful summary of the state of knowledge—albeit frustratingly limited—on tlatocatlalli.

22. AGN Mercedes 59, 129 (Composición of the titles of the Hacienda de Texcaltenco, 250 pesos; June 28, 1675).

23. The sole volume (*tomo único*) of the Ramo de Congregaciones in the AGN upholds the timing of this congregación in Capuluac. But the detail in the municipal narrative is especially rich and valuable.

24. As already noted, his father, don Bartolomé, was still active as one of several elders who participated in the boundary survey of the neighboring community of Coatepec, if we can trust the dates of the títulos of that town, which close with a testament-like statement dated 1550 (Máynez, Blancas, and Morales 1995: 292–93, 316–19). By the end of that decade or the beginning of the next, it is conceivable that don Miguel would have been handling such affairs.

25. It was standard usage that the "de San" in the name don Miguel de San Bartolomé might or might not appear. The father, similarly, could be either don Bartolomé de San Miguel or don Bartolomé Miguel.

26. Seemingly, this is the same grant that established the town's official territory in 1557, discussed above. The rival family had also come to think of it as the seed to their cacicazgo.

27. He was gobernador and "indio principal de Capulhuac" in a document from 1590 (see AGN Indios 4, 282: 95r). In 1591 and 1592 he appears as "juez gobernador" (AGN Indios 6, 1ª, 116: 27v, and 6, 413: 108v). For the latter period, see AGN Mercedes 35: 52v. Don Juan Jiménez is here called "indio principal y gobernador."

28. Antonio de Mendoza's bilinguality and his Mexico City origin certainly make it feasible that he could have been a mestizo. There were also Spaniards in the vicinity in the early 1540s. Colonial officials granted an allotment of land between Ocoyoacac (then Ocoyacac) and Capuluac and near the ciénaga, or marsh, to two Spaniards from Mexico City in 1542 (AGN Mercedes 1, 6: 4v.). This may have been fairly close to the waterfront property of Antonio de Mendoza, although the brief summary of the grant provides no details. The famous utopian don Vasco de

Quiroga also bought a river island that had once pertained to Capuluac "sometime before 1536," according to Gerhard (1993: 271–72).

29. Of course, there are numerous examples wherein the law that required that caciques be fully indigenous was disobeyed. See Mörner 1966.

30. The narrative tells, additionally, that two townspeople had died at the hands of (don) Andrés de los Reyes, who customarily took people to "sell" in Mexico "as though they were horses." He prodded them with sticks and whipped them. Further research may illuminate this scandal. The Ramo de Indios in the national archives contains material on periodic battles by the macehuales of Capuluac to get out of a hated draft of laborers to Tacubaya. At some time before 1589 the courts had set a limit of forty-one Indians to be sent. The community was trying to get it lowered further in that year (see AGN Indios 4, 53: 16). Again, in 1591, the laborers fought an at least partially successful repartimiento battle in the courts against an Esteban Ferrofino (AGN Indios 5, 761: 271v). As for the ruling against the rival family, it was probably short-lived if it was not invented by don Agustín or his heirs, because the de los Reyes clan was very prominent in the eighteenth century. The grandson of don Andrés, for instance, a don Tomás de los Reyes, called himself "cacique y principal" of Capuluac in his will of 1715 (see AGN Tierras 2860, 1: 1r).

31. One of these men had the name Salvador de los Reyes, who was described in later records to have been a grandson of don Juan Jiménez. See AGN Tierras 702, 7: 2r and 1859, 2.

32. The sale of this caballería next to the ciénaga was to a Juan de Quirós (AGN Mercedes 5: 52v). To give some idea of the considerable sum four hundred pesos was, we might note that the annual salary of the municipal governor of Toluca in 1580 was two hundred pesos and the second-ranking town officers, alcaldes, earned a mere twenty-four pesos a year! Also, a tlatoani of a small town who claimed to be poverty-stricken, sought and obtained only ten pesos for his maintenance out of the tribute coffers one year (Menegus Bornemann 1991: 152, 214).

33. Cline (1986: 151–52, 232 n. 59) discusses "tlalnemactli" (here, in the absolutive form) in Culhuacan and cites other references to it, both colonial and modern. Horn (1989: 270–72) clarifies colonial meanings of "tlalnemactli" for the Coyoacan area.

34. Chance (1994: 47) summarizes these findings of recent research.

35. The singling out of multiple saints does strike me as a pattern that was more common in the middle of the colonial era, when what might be called the "cult" of the saints was in full swing (Wood 1991a: 289). But, since this is a reference to saints in the community church, and not on a home altar, it could be early. Cline (1986: 144) provides an example of a Culhuacan woman bequeathing land for the support of Santa María Magdalena, the patron of the testatrix's ward's church in the sixteenth century.

36. In format and content, this testament compares weakly to the (possibly) contemporaneous testaments of Culhuacan (Cline and León-Portilla 1984; and see Cline 1981, 1986). Kellogg (1995a: 133 and nn. 10, 11) outlines some of the principal features of Nahua testaments.

37. Kellogg (1995a: 51) discusses sixteenth-century lawyers' recognition of problems in testaments, such as the failure to meet procedural requirements and

outright fraud, which could include "false testimony and forged wills." Regarding potential problems with títulos, see Wood 1997b.

38. AGN Tierras 2860, 1, 2: 70v–71r; original punctuation and orthography preserved.

39. AGN Tierras 2860, 1, 2: 72v–73r; original punctuation and orthography preserved.

PART 2

Southern Mesoamerica

Map 3   Southern Mesoamerica

CHAPTER 5

Native Expressions of Piety in Mixtec Testaments

KEVIN TERRACIANO

The colonial native-language last will and testament seems to have continued a preconquest function rooted in the oral tradition. A passage from the *Florentine Codex* records a preconquest Mixtec tradition that approximated a function of the colonial testament. Nahua nobles wrote in the mid-sixteenth century:

> Ca quil in iehoantin mixteca: yn oc ipan intlateutoquiliz, in iquac ie ceme miquiznequi: quinotza in tlapouhqui in nonotzqui, ixpan muchi quitoa, muchi ixpan quitlalia, in tlein oax, in tlein oquichiuh in itlapilchioal, in inequal, in inequavitec: in at ichtec, in at itla quitecuili, muchi quitoa: atle quitlatia, atle quinaia. Auh in tlapouhqui, in manoço ticitl: quinaoatia in cocuxqui in tetlaxtlaviliz, in quitecuepiliz in teaxca in tetlatqui.

> ❧

> [It is said of the Mixtecs, that in the time of their idolatry, when one was about to die, s/he summoned the diviner, the advised one. Before him/her one told all, before him/her one placed all which one had done, all which one had performed—one's faults, one's good to others, one's harming of others. Perhaps one had stolen, perhaps one had taken something from someone. One told all, concealed nothing, hid nothing. And the diviner or the healer commanded the sick one to make restitution to people, to return property and belongings to people.][1]

The Mixtec tradition allowed a sick person to settle his earthly debts and concerns in the presence of a priest or priestess and other witnesses.

Though the Nahua writers from central Mexico who contributed to the *Florentine Codex* singled out the Mixtecs of Oaxaca for this tradition, their reference is part of a larger discussion of confession and penitence involving ancient deities and diviners throughout highland Mexico. Indeed, it is likely that many Mesoamerican groups performed similar rituals of reckoning upon death.

Like the native tradition, the colonial last will and testament entitled a sick person to settle accounts on earth and to make a final pronouncement of faith on his or her deathbed. Sometimes these statements in Mixtec wills went beyond the cursory remarks typical of many testaments, fulfilling a native oral tradition while conforming to the required Christian format. Though the model for the statement of faith in testaments was Christian, the resulting pious discourse reflected a native form of popular Christianity. It is difficult to know how Mixtecs may have interpreted Christian symbols in the absence of sources that speak directly to these issues. Natives did not have the opportunity to write down their impressions of Christianity. The statement of faith in the religious preamble of early-colonial testaments is one of the few sources for native expressions of piety in a Christian context.[2] Unlike the religious instructional materials produced by friars and their multilingual native aides (such as catechisms, speeches, and confessional manuals), the language of the testament was not selected or edited by friars. Native-language testaments reveal the daily vocabulary that testators and notaries used for Christian concepts such as the saints, the Virgin Mary, Purgatory, and Heaven and allowed them to articulate the thoughts that they considered most important at the time of their death. Thus the preamble presents what Christian natives said rather than what they were ideally supposed to say. Of course, these statements do not reveal the full complexity of the individual's faith, and since testators articulated pious expressions within a Christian context, they say nothing of conscious beliefs unrelated to Christianity.

This chapter consists of two main parts. The first section describes the format and function of the Mixtec-language testament and outlines the evolution of this genre in the region of the Mixteca from the sixteenth to the nineteenth centuries. The second and main section of this chapter examines the religious preamble of Mixtec-language testaments for expressions of piety and popular conceptions of Christianity among Mixtecs in the colonial period. Proceeding from the premise that the colonial testament drew upon a native precedent, the purpose of this analysis is to suggest how native beliefs influenced popular Christianity in Oaxaca. In examining native-Christian expressions, I hope to avoid making rigid distinctions between preconquest beliefs and introduced concepts. Rather, I want to focus on how indigenous ideology shaped the perception and understanding of European and Christian concepts, and how native expressions of piety in colonial testaments reflected a sacred, cultural dialogue. The limited dialogue initiated by ecclesiastics in the sixteenth century relied upon convergent European and native cultural constructions. If the two cultures offered an expansive arena for dialogue based on what was identifiable and familiar to the other, they also possessed different constructions of culture, gender, and society that influenced their imagination of sacred relations. Native articulations of Christian doctrine reflected these convergent and divergent ideologies, much as popular Christianity in early modern Spain represented local versions of Catholicism.

Though some Mixtecs in this period made their testaments in Spanish, the present study focuses mainly on native-language testaments for purposes of philological analysis. My interpretation of cultural expression and meaning is rooted in a reading of the native language. Spanish-language testaments are used to supplement observations drawn from the native-language record.

Speaking of language, it is important to clarify our use of ethnic terms. In the course of studying native-language sources from the region of the Mixteca, I came to realize that the authors of these documents never called themselves "Mixtecs." Rather, they expressed a conscious ethnic identity embodied by their own term, *Ñudzahui*, meaning "the rain place." In native-language archival documentation and church manuscripts, the term "ñudzahui" has been attested many dozens of times in reference to the language, the region, the people as a group, individuals, and cultural artifacts such as grinding stones, native fig-bark paper, and clothes. Spaniards and friars adopted the Nahuatl-derived "Mixtec" that is still used today; I will use the name by which they called themselves for the remainder of this chapter.[3]

Ñudzahui-Language Alphabetic Writing

After the Spanish conquest, ecclesiastics worked extensively with nobles, teaching them to write Roman script in their own languages and training scribes for the record-keeping responsibilities of Spanish-style government, a key element of Spanish colonial rule. In the western region of Oaxaca known as the Mixteca, the Dominicans developed a network of apprentices and educated informants or consultants who passed on written records and methods to successors decades before the appearance of the first church-sponsored texts written in the native language.[4] These early efforts by ecclesiastics and native nobles established a fairly consistent Ñudzahui orthography in spite of extensive dialectal and tonal variation. By the second and third generations after the Spaniards arrived, Ñudzahui-language alphabetic writing had been established in the *cabeceras* (head towns within a given jurisdiction) of the Mixteca. By 1600, native-language writing was practiced in dozens of Ñudzahui communities of the Mixteca Alta and Baja. The peak period of Ñudzahui-language writing in terms of quantity and quality was 1670–1720, when the practice of writing spread beyond larger population centers such as Yanhuitlan and Teposcolula to a number of smaller subject communities (*sujetos*), many of which had won independence from cabeceras during this time. By this later period, the native population had begun to recover slowly from the devastating epidemics that had reduced the population to a small fraction of its preconquest total.[5]

Extant Ñudzahui-language sources for which a date and provenance are certain date from the 1560s to the first decade of the nineteenth century, nearly until the end of the colonial period. In my research, I have located more than twenty types of archival sources written entirely in the Ñudzahui language, including testaments and inventories (of nobles and commoners, men and women); personal letters; criminal records (letters, testimony, confessions); land transactions (titles, transfers, sales, and rentals); sales of houses and businesses; personal business accounts and inventories; community fiscal accounts; election results; tribute records; baptismal registers; petitions to Spanish authorities; official decrees; ecclesiastical records; forged land titles; and entire civil proceedings. The documents range in length from one side of a page to as many as seventy pages. The collection is evenly spread across time—no five-year period is undocumented within a period of almost 250 years. More than sixty Ñudzahui *ñuu* (pueblos or towns) are represented, from Cuilapa in the Valley of Oaxaca to Tonalá in the Mixteca Baja, from Coixtlahuaca in the northern Alta to Chalcatongo in the south. The majority of these settlements are concentrated in the Mixteca Alta, in the colonial jurisdiction (*alcaldía mayor*) of Teposcolula and Yanhuitlan. In all, I have located approximately four hundred Ñudzahui-language documents.[6]

The last will and testament was the first genre of alphabetic writing to be practiced within the indigenous community. Most of the writing was done by trained notaries selected from the nobility, though some documents were written outside of notarial auspices.[7] Like most indigenous texts, testaments differed visually from their Spanish counterparts. These native documents often were written on slightly smaller paper that did not bear the official stamp and seal of Spanish legal documents. The preservation of native-language records was not systematic. Testaments exist in collections kept by the local church and in municipal archives; many in my present collection were used as evidence in civil proceedings. Many more testaments were kept in private collections and were filed in notarial archives only as a result of a legal dispute. Wills are the most common of all native-language sources in Mesoamerica from the colonial period. Testaments comprise approximately half of all extant Ñudzahui-language documents, or nearly two hundred of some four hundred documents in my collection. Testaments are valuable historical sources for the study of numerous topics and concerns, such as material culture, social and household arrangements, kinship, and sociopolitical organization.

Preconquest Precedents

The convergence of the European genre of written testaments with an indigenous equivalent explains its early success and proliferation. The testament incorporated a rich native oral tradition and a primary function of earlier pictorial writing. One notable function of preconquest-style Ñudzahui codices (painted and folded deerskin manuscripts) and colonial *lienzos* (painted cloths) involved keeping a record of ruling genealogies, place names, and lands. The succession of rulers in many Ñudzahui pictorial writings ends about two or three generations after the conquest, around the time when the first Ñudzahui-language testaments began to appear, and when wills had become more valid claims to lands and succession than pictorials in the Spanish legal system. For example, the *Codex Selden* and the *Lienzo of Natividad* terminate the depiction of lineages around the 1560s and 1570s, when the first alphabetic native-language writings appeared in the area. In the sixteenth century, *caciques* (a Spanish term for native rulers) produced both pictorial records and testaments to document their patrimonial claims before Spanish officials, but many native nobles came to rely increasingly on the latter for these purposes.[8] The importance of dynastic lineages and the occasion for inheritance disputes made testaments indispensable, just as pictorial writings were instrumental in the preconquest and early postconquest periods.

By the late sixteenth century, Spanish officials preferred alphabetic writings over pictorial manuscripts as legitimate legal documents. In a dispute between two Ñudzahui communities in 1569, one Spanish lawyer argued that the paintings introduced as evidence in the trial did not portray the truth but simply a community's "private and particular wish, based on fiction and fantasy." The paintings had no basis in fact, he argued, because "the Indians simply painted what they wanted to portray." Besides, he opined, the ancient system of writing was "a tradition from heathen times, when Indians lied to each other and were easily deceived by the devil" (AGN Tierras 24, 6: 13v). Such prejudices against using pictorial images as legal instruments hastened the eventual decline of pictorial writing and necessitated the learning of alphabetic writing.

Thus, in the indigenous world, the testament imparted a lasting legal record of property entitlement and confirmed one's kinship ties. By the second or third generation after the conquest, many rulers and nobles traced their dynastic ties to relatives inside and outside their communities and settled all types of accounts with them. The legal importance of the testament led many testators to explicitly admonish all those who were present, in typical native rhetoric, from attempting to obstruct, deny, or meddle with any declaration.[9]

If the introduced testamentary genre fulfilled a function of preconquest-style pictorial writing, adapted to suit Spanish demands, native testators took the form and reshaped it to meet their own needs. The testament consisted of a speech to a surrounding circle of close relatives and friends and was more of a statement before an assembly of witnesses than the typical private European testament.[10] In most colonial indigenous testaments, the assembled persons played an important role in the proceedings; many men and women, and often the entire *cabildo* (the Spanish-style municipal council staffed by native nobles), attended the event.[11] Not every testament drew a crowd, but since many town officials normally attended the ceremony as witnesses, the testator would often speak before a familiar audience. The testament of a high noble occasioned a large gathering. For example, sixty men witnessed the testament of don Pedro Osorio, the governor and cacique of Teposcolula in 1566. Women were also present, but they did not sign their names to the document because they were not members of the cabildo (AGN Tierras 24, 6: 4v).

Natives guarded testaments as valuable papers demonstrating kinship ties and claims to property; they also documented the transfer of papers and paintings that solidified those claims. Several lords referred to chests and desks in their houses or palaces (*aniñe*), where they kept documents pertaining to their patrimonies. Don Juan Agustín, a cacique in the Mixteca Baja, kept "all of his titles and testaments in his palace" [niy cuto titulos si testamentos yonehy hua aniy]; CAGN Tierras 245, 2: 77–79, document of 1642). The testament of don Jorge de la Cruz Alvarado from Guaxuapa, written in 1678, mentions a "chest of papers" [satno tutu] and a "chest of land documents" [satno ñuhu tutu] containing "the land documents and testaments of my grandparents" [ñuhu tutu testamendo si siy sitnayu] as well as "all the papers concerning the lands and the lienzos of borders" [dihi cutu tutu saha ñuhu dayu dzoo dzaño] (AGN Tierras 245, 2: 85). Don Raymundo de Santiago y Guzmán, the cacique of Coculco in 1676, referred to the "testament and borders-painting" [testamendo dzaño pintura] that documented his "lands and poor dependents" [ñoho dayu ñadehi ñadahui] (AGN Tierras 571, 1: 75–77). Women also referred to important written records in their testaments. Doña Josepha de Salazar of Chilapa said in 1750 that she owned a "little chest with a lock containing all the testaments of her ancestors" [satno duchi yondey ndaha caá sihi ndihi taca testamento sanaha] (AJT Civil 10, 873: 9). Petrona de Osorio of Yolomecatl recorded in her testament of 1738 a "chest of land documents and other papers" [satnu ñuhu ndihi taca tutu] (AJT Civil 10, 866). Thus in addition to naming heirs for all types of possessions from houses and lands to dancing feathers and clothing, nobles used testaments to document and bequeath pictorial and alphabetic writings related to their properties and kinship relations. In their testaments, nobles often referred to other testaments, titles, and paintings in their possession that documented their hereditary rights.

By the eighteenth century, some Spanish officials questioned the validity of using testaments as legal instruments for documenting property possession. In a lengthy court battle between the native cabildo of Yanhuitlan and its caciques over possession of the royal palace, the Royal Audience judge expressed doubt as to whether testaments, submitted by the caciques to document continuous possession, represented valid legal instruments in lieu of official titles, even though earlier titles were based mainly on testaments (AGN Tierras 400, 1: 382). The judge ruled in 1759 against the caciques, despite their collection of testaments dating back to the mid-sixteenth century. The ruling reflected changing Spanish attitudes toward native writings and legal documents.

The Transformation of Native-Language Writing

Just as the testament was the first genre of alphabetic writing to be employed within the indigenous community, it was also the most enduring. In my current collection of nearly four hundred Ñudzahui-language sources, more than 90 percent of the documents from the middle of the eighteenth century forward are testaments, whereas testaments for the whole colonial period represent a little more than half of all documentation (55 percent). More than a third of all wills were women's (35 percent). After 1700, 78 percent of all Ñudzahui-language documents in this collection are testaments, and after 1750, 91 percent are testaments.

The practice of native-language writing persisted until the first decade of the nineteenth century but declined from about 1770. Bilingual Ñudzahui spoke and wrote Spanish as early as the late sixteenth century, a process that became more noticeable with each generation and culminated in the community's ability to execute its business without native-language records, a development encouraged and decreed by colonial authorities in the late eighteenth century.

By the late-colonial period, the testament was no longer associated directly with the corporate community. Whereas all sources generated by the native cabildo (criminal records, proceedings, community accounts, etc.) were being written in Spanish by the eighteenth century, many native notaries continued to write native-language testaments for individuals who knew no Spanish. The will became less of an official document, done more often in the cabildo's absence. Such documents bear the signatures of only one or two witnesses who were close to the testator; they are usually brief, poorly written documents (in terms of handwriting and grammatical conventions) (AJT Civil 18, 1564). For example, the testament of Nicolasa María, written in Chilapa in 1764, skips the religious preamble and simply lists her lands and goods before closing hastily. The case in which this document is enclosed contains two posterior testaments of relatives that, by 1776 and 1787, were written in Spanish. In most of these later documents the statements are terse and tend to focus on simply what was to go to whom, conforming more to the Spanish model of a legal document.

Spanish-language writing became more pragmatic and expedient as the colonial period came to a close. As a legal language, it needed no translation in court, and documents written in Spanish were more likely to be recognized as legitimate. At the same time, the Ñudzahui nobles who normally served as notaries were especially good candidates for bilingualism. Bilingual or *ladino* (outwardly acculturated) natives often prided themselves on knowing how to speak and write Spanish; they readily declined the assistance of translators to transact official business. Some Ñudzahui, such as María López of Santa Catarina Adequez, had testaments written in both languages (AJT Civil 18, 1516: 51). In 1784 her will was recorded in her native language and then written again in Castilian a few days later. Nonetheless, the Spanish in this testament reveals a Ñudzahui-speaking author, with such words as "mungeres" for *mujer*, "totnasa" for *tomasa*, "loniete" for *poniente*, "quanreta" and "quarreta" and "quanrenta" for *quarenta*.

Ñudzahui writing was gradually supplanted by Castilian in the cabeceras where writing first appeared, and where contact with Spanish culture and language was most pronounced. On the other hand, many testaments from the late-colonial period written in the Ñudzahui language come from remote, smaller communities where the cabildo remained actively involved in native-language writing. The testament of Casimiro de los Santos, written in Tonaltepec in 1807, exemplifies how some communities continued to produce native-language records even as places such as Yanhuitlan adopted Spanish as the official written language. This neat and lengthy document includes all the reverential vocabulary of the early period and is signed by the entire cabildo (AJT Civil 18, 1578). Though it is the latest extant sample of Ñudzahui-language writing, the testament's polished prose defies a dying tradition. Nonetheless, the tradition was not maintained in the nineteenth century.

The transition from native- to Spanish-language writing marked the end of an era but did not signify the demise of native communities. In many of the more centrally located areas of the Mixteca, writing in Spanish became more practical and widely recognized, much like alphabetic writing had become more pragmatic than pictorials two centuries earlier. Native individuals and communities adopted alphabetic writing to preserve their own traditions while adapting to the demands of Spanish authorities. The eventual use of Spanish reflects increasing contact with the dominant language and culture of Mexico, and represents profound changes among native peoples in late-colonial society.

Thus, throughout much of the colonial period, the writing of Ñudzahui-language testaments constituted a community event that drew upon an elaborate oral tradition and fulfilled a basic function of pictorial writing. Testaments served both secular and spiritual needs. The document featured an important religious component, allowing one to pray and pay tribute to Christian sacred figures, to provide for burial and masses, and to pledge money to various images, chapels, brotherhoods, and charities. The second part of this chapter focuses on the religious content of testaments.

Writing and Religious Discourse

Alphabetic writing was a powerful tool of religious conversion. The first extant Ñudzahui-language publication—the *doctrina* (catechism) of the

Achiutla region, published in 1567—was produced in the area where the majority of earliest extant testaments were written. The religious orders disallowed most public forms of native religion and usurped the traditional public function and privileges of the former priestly class, targeting local nobles as intermediaries for religious conversion and cultural indoctrination. Native-language alphabetic writing facilitated this process.

Testaments were the first Ñudzahui alphabetic documents produced outside of the direct auspices of the church, though friars were involved in this genre from the beginning. Friars promoted the writing of testaments, especially among the nobility, in which the first order of business was to commend one's soul to God and then to entrust one's body and part of one's earthly riches to the church. The earliest extant Ñudzahui-language testament—written in 1571 for doña María López, the *cacica* (*yya dzehe toniñe* in Ñudzahui) of Yucucuihi (called Tlazultepec by Spaniards, based on the Nahuatl name)—comes from the same dialect area where the first doctrina was produced. She referred to five Dominican friars by name, including the author of the only colonial Ñudzahui grammar, fray Antonio de los Reyes, requesting him to say several masses on her behalf. Doña María personally associated with the "precious fathers" [zutu manindi], as she referred to them, who played such a prominent role in the development of native-language alphabetic writing in the area. Among the many books in doña María's possession, she bequeathed a "doctrina book" [tutu dotrina]—very likely a copy of the religious text published four years earlier.[12] Appropriately, doña María's testament is accompanied by a preconquest-style genealogy, testifying to the continuing tradition of pictorial writing that was complemented by, then shared space with, and ultimately was supplanted by alphabetic writing.[13]

Another early testament from the dialect area of Achiutla reveals a coexistence of certain native and Christian concepts. In 1573, don Felipe de Saavedra, the *yya toniñe* (Ñudzahui term for hereditary male ruler) of Tlaxiaco, may have written his own will before a noble audience. The testament bears no signature other than his own and those of the literate witnesses who were present; in the apparent absence of a notary, don Felipe indicated in the closing paragraph that he wrote the document. The neat document was written in a reverential vocabulary befitting don Felipe's high rank. For example, don Felipe referred to the Christian year in which the lord Jesus was born on earth as the number of years since "the face of the lord appeared" [yotuhuinana hitooya], using a common metaphor for birth in the honorific register typically spoken among

Ñudzahui nobles.[14] He also referred to the current year with the native calendrical equivalent, 2-deer [coo quaa], revealing the continued importance of the ancient calendar some fifty years after the conquest. The three-page document contains ninety lines of tiny, neat writing with an extensive religious preamble and a long list of place names associated with his individual patrimony and rulership. Among his numerous possessions are five books [hoho tutu libronde], a "writing box" [hatnu escrivania], and a pair of eyeglasses [antojos]. Don Felipe was clearly well versed in reading and writing by the time of his death in 1573 (AJT Civil 7, 654).[15]

The Religious Preamble

The last will and testament was a sacred act. The Spanish-Christian model testament began with an invocation of the Holy Trinity and the identification of the testator. The religious preamble followed, consisting of a supplication, a meditation on death and the final judgment, and a profession of faith. The profession of faith usually included a statement of belief in the church and affirmed basic tenets of the Christian faith. The statement of faith was immediately followed by the encommendation of the soul and body. After the preamble and encommendation, the testament moved on to concrete matters concerning one's burial and masses, pious bequests, the division of one's estate, and the naming of one's executors and witnesses to the will.[16]

The religious preamble of testaments has attracted the attention of only a few scholars. For Europe, Michel Vovelle uses religious invocations in testaments as sources for changing religious beliefs in eighteenth-century Provence, and Carlos Eire discusses the religious preamble as a source for popular conceptions of Christianity in sixteenth-century Madrid (Vovelle 1978; Eire 1995). For Mesoamerica, S. L. Cline considered expressions of Christian piety among Nahuas from early-colonial Culhuacan (Cline 1986).[17] Though it is true that much of the preamble in native wills is formulaic and unremarkable, mimicking the invocations of Spanish testaments, several Ñudzahui-language testaments dedicated many lines to the statement. Sometimes these religious reflections were eloquent speeches packed with reverential vocabulary and expressions, continuing for entire paragraphs. The honorific language resembles that of the early-colonial doctrinas. When a testament was later translated into Spanish, entire sentences or paragraphs of the religious preamble were sometimes condensed or omitted because the translator did not consider them essential to the legal proceedings.

Considering the diversity of doctrinal points one could espouse in the preamble raises an important question: who was responsible for the written words in this passage—the testator or the notary? Given the oral nature of this discourse, I suspect that the notary recorded the testator's speech in the form of a transcript. No doubt the notary was still an important actor in this process. The notary was the local expert who presumably led testators through the stages of the document, supplying words or standard phrases and editing passages according to the appropriate conventions of the day. As Cline noted for testaments from Culhuacan, even though testators could influence the wording of the religious preamble, the majority of invocations did not appear to be verbatim statements (Cline 1986: 19). In the case of lengthy statements, however, it is doubtful whether the notary would have written so much on his own. A comparison of religious preambles in three different testaments done by the same notary in Teposcolula demonstrates differences in the length and substance of these passages, suggesting that the testators themselves were responsible for the discrepancies.[18] Furthermore, even if the notary did augment or edit the testator's speech, the writing still represents an indigenous perspective since all notaries were members of the native cabildo. In this sense, invocations may be viewed as potential sources for native statements about the Christian faith.

In the beginning of the document, most testators immediately expressed their belief in the Holy Trinity. They referred to the Father, the Son, and the Holy Spirit [dzutu dios, dzaya dios, espíritu santo dios], using the loanword "dios" for each one, but then qualified this usage by acknowledging three persons and only one true God.[19] I have seen more than one testament that confused this part. One notary clearly referred to three persons and three gods, whereupon he (or someone) scratched out the second "three" (written *uni*) and inserted "one" (*ee*). The preferred term for God in the religious preamble of the testament was *stoho Dios*, meaning "high lord God." God was also referred to as *ñuhu*, an ancient term for "deity," and by the name for "male ruler" (*yya toniñe*). Jesus was also called by this latter title or simply *yya* (lord). A straightforward loanword was adopted for the Holy Spirit.

After referring to the Trinity, wills usually identified the testator's sociopolitical affiliations. Writers used the Ñudzahui terms *yuhuitayu* (complex community, also abbreviated as *tayu*), *ñuu* (community), and *siqui* (subentity of a community). The latter category had two regional variants, called *siña* (in the Yanhuitlan area) and *dzini* (in the Mixteca Baja). The three entities were usually translated into Spanish as "ciudad," "pueblo," and "barrio," respectively. Every sociopolitical entity had a specific Ñudzahui name, associated with a toponym or lineage. For example, in 1672 a lord of Teposcolula (called "Yucundaa" in Ñudzahui), don Gerónimo García y Guzmán, was introduced as "don Gerónimo García y Guzmán, from the siqui Yaasahi of this yuhuitayu San Pedro and San Pablo Yucundaa" [don geronimo garcia siqui yaaçahi yaha yuhuitayu san pedro san pablo yucundaa] (AJT Civil 4, 417; see the will at the end of this chapter). Testaments from Yanhuitlan normally listed these affiliations on the top margin of the first page.

The preamble then proceeds to a declaration of belief in basic Christian principles, especially the Ten Commandments and Articles of Faith; at this point requests are made for the intercession of the Virgin Mary and other saints on behalf of the soul and one's entry into Heaven.[20] In reference to statements of faith in Spanish wills from sixteenth-century Madrid, Eire observed that this was the least likely part of the will to find individual expression because of pressures to conform to Christian doctrine: "There could be a great variation in the number of doctrinal points that were affirmed by each individual, but as far as the actual doctrines were concerned, the last thing anyone would have wanted to do was to express creativity" (1995: 79). The length of these parts varied greatly in Spanish wills, ranging from perfunctory statements to lengthy affirmations. In many Ñudzahui testaments, this declaration was subject to spontaneity. The declaration of faith represented the doctrina's teachings and language in action; it recorded how ordinary people understood and referred to the most fundamental Christian concepts, and showed which concepts they chose to address in their final hour. Though the words in this part of the document were based on the ideals and models of native-language church writings and teachings, and these models were often reduced to formulaic statements, I have found that Ñudzahui testators and/or native notaries elaborated upon those ideals in various meaningful ways. In this sense, testaments not only demonstrate the resulting language of native-Christian discourse but also reveal how natives actually used or elaborated upon this language when thinking about Christian concepts. Since the full range of sacred concepts articulated in statements of faith is too broad to consider here, I will focus on two related and frequently mentioned Christian ideas: the Kingdom of Heaven and the Virgin Mary.

Mary in the Ñudzahui Kingdom of Heaven ✸ In the affirmation of faith, some testaments reveal interesting native interpretations of Christian concepts and metaphors. Testators often spoke of their own ascent and succession to the "yuhuitayu andehui gloria," the Christian "Kingdom of Heaven," employing Ñudzahui vocabulary for the largest political entity (yuhuitayu) and the sky (andehui), modified by a Spanish loanword (gloria) in reference to its everlasting glory. Sometimes the Ñudzahui term "toniñe" (rulership) also was employed in association with the above phrase; "toniñe" was used in reference to the titles of male and female rulers ("yya toniñe" and "yya dzehe toniñe," respectively). Of the many Ñudzahui-language tropes adopted for Christian concepts in the sixteenth century, the "Kingdom of Heaven" stands out because of its symbolic associations. The term appears in the earliest native-language records in the area, including the *Doctrina en lengua misteca* (1567) and the first extant Ñudzahui-language last wills and testaments.

Before and after the Spanish conquest, Ñudzahui used the term "yuhuitayu" in reference to a community represented by a male and female ruler, symbolically depicted in the preconquest-style codices and lienzos as a man and a woman seated together, facing one another, on a reed mat. The term is a metaphorical doublet: *yuhui* is "reed mat" and *tayu* is "pair" or "seat," depending on tonal pronunciation. "Tayu" is a tone pun or homonymic device for both the seat of rulership and the married, ruling couple.[21] In this social and political arrangement, male and female lords ruled jointly, each representing the lineage and patrimony of a separate community, called a "ñuu." In this sense, the Ñudzahui "kingdom" placed as much emphasis on the female as the male ruler. The glyph represented a given place and its seat of rulership, a complex political institution that the Spaniards recognized only as "kingdoms," focusing on the male ruler of the ruling couple. The term "andehui" (sky) was applied by Dominican friars and converted Ñudzahui to the Christian concept of "Heaven," much like the Spanish *cielo*. The yuhuitayu andehui exemplifies the early-colonial dialogue between friars and native aides to reach reasonably equivalent terminologies in order to avoid the borrowing of loanwords that conveyed little meaning to native speakers. In this dialogue, even some native-language terms were charged with ambiguities or associations unrelated to the Christian concept.[22]

The popular imagination created a sacred realm in the image of the secular world. Christian ideology portrayed God as the King of Heaven, superior to all kings on earth; His domain was the ultimate kingdom. All others in His celestial court were subordinate figures and potential intercessors between God the Father and His children on earth. Popular conceptions of God cast the Creator in patriarchal terms, as an almighty father with no equal. Medieval Christianity viewed the Virgin Mary as a prominent queen or empress in the Kingdom of Heaven, but she was still a mortal who became a saint because of her motherly virtue. She was not a goddess, and she was not God's equal. In sixteenth-century wills from Madrid, Eire (1995: 69–71) points out that Mary was the most popular intercessor between God and testator, and that she was asked to act in her role as mother of Jesus.

The native concept of a sacred yuhuitayu included a woman as much as a man, a female creator as much as a male creator. Ñudzahui origin legends recorded in preconquest codices and articulated in the sixteenth-century oral tradition spoke of a sacred male and female creator couple who constituted the first yuhuitayu.[23] Just as popular conceptions of the Kingdom of Heaven in early modern Spain were based on a projection of the earthly sociopolitical order, modeled on the European court, the Ñudzahui yuhuitayu andehui represented a sacred version of male and female rulers on earth (Eire 1995: 68–72). Thus, from the Ñudzahui-Christian perspective, Mary should have figured prominently in the yuhuitayu andehui.

In fact, statements of faith often associated Mary directly with the yuhuitayu andehui. In a testament from Chalcatongo, for example, don Diego de Velasco offered his soul to the high lords (*hitoho*) God and Mary, and to all the saints and angels that accompanied them in the kingdom of heaven (AGN Tierras 637, 1: 74–79). The passage reads: "I offer my soul to our high lord God and our high lady Saint Mary, and to all the saints and angels who are with them in the rulership in the sky of glory" [yonaçocondi animandi noo nana hitohoyo ndios hiy noo nana hitooziyyo sata maria hiy noo nana ndiy taca sato hiy ageles hihi yohi taca daa yuhuitayu toniñe adihui gloria]. In this example, the writer referred to Mary and God in the same manner, using an honorific parallel construction "nana hitoho" [in the presence of the high lord]. The term "stoho" or "hitoho" (orthographic variations based on dialect) always connoted a sacred ruler. It was sometimes applied to human lords and thus blurred distinctions between current rulers, sacred ancestors, and deities. The reference to Heaven was translated later into Spanish as *corte del cielo* (celestial court) instead of using the more commonly written *reino* (kingdom).

Many Ñudzahui testators and their native notaries referred to Mary as a "female ruler" [yya dzehe toniñe]. I have found dozens of such examples. For example, in his testament of 1718, Salvador de Zelis of Teposcolula referred to Mary as "yya dzehe toniñe Santa Maria del Rosario," employing the operative title for female ("dzehe") ruler, just as

Jesus and God both were called "yya toniñe" (male ruler) in the course of the same document (AJT Civil 7, 689: 16). Likewise, doña Lazara de Guzmán, a cacica of San Juan Teposcolula in 1691, referred to Mary as "yia dzehe toniñe santa maria" and "stoho dzehendo toniñe santa maria"; in the same document, she referred to God with the same superlative titles—"stoho" and "yia toniñe" (AJT Civil 4, 417). Thus some Ñudzahui believers emphasized her sacred, ruling qualities, as if she were a female deity.

Other Ñudzahui called Mary a goddess. In an elaborate testament from Teposcolula, written in 1717, Domingo de Zelis referred to Mary as "ñuhu Santa Maria," using the same word for "deity" (ñuhu) usually applied to God. Again, the term "ñuhu" was the preconquest word for a deity. In 1726, Petronilla Calderona called Mary "ñuhu yya dzehe toniñe Santa Maria," combining the words for "god" and "female ruler" (AJT Civil 8, 726: 1). The latest extant Ñudzahui language testament, written in 1807 on behalf of Casimero de los Santos of Tonaltepec, refers to the "yuhuichayu toniñe andehue gloria" (Kingdom of Heaven, written in Yanhuitlan area dialect) and calls Mary "mani ndios Maria Santissima del Rosario" [the precious God Holiest Mary of the Rosary], employing Ñudzahui and Spanish superlatives for this deity (AJT Civil 18, 1578). By this later period, the writer used the Spanish "dios" instead of the Ñudzahui equivalent "ñuhu." Spanish translations of testaments ignored or simplified most of these terms.

Many Ñudzahui also recognized Mary as a sacred mother, though few emphasized her virginity. Petronilla Calderona referred to God as "dzutu maniya" [precious father] and Mary as "dzehe maniya" [precious mother] (AJT Civil 8, 726: 1). Domingo de Zelis called her the "precious mother of the true God's son" [yya dzehe santa maria mani dzaya ndisa ñuhunDios] (AJT Civil 7, 689: 14). Domingo also described her as "the mother of all of us and all the saints there in the Kingdom of Heaven" [yya dzehe sindehe tacando sihi ndehe taca santos ysi siyo yuqua yuhuitayu toniñe andehui gloria]. Mary was often paired with God in the "yuhuitayu in the sky," followed by all the angels and saints. In general, angels and saints usually bore no titles such as "yya" (or the female "yya dzehe"), "yya toniñe" (or the female "yya dzehe toniñe"), "stoho," "ñuhu," and certainly not "Dios." Occasionally, saints were assigned the title of "yya," but most Ñudzahui simply referred to them with the Spanish *santo/a*.

Not all Ñudzahui referred to Mary in terms of a ruling female deity; many used the more conservative title of "yya dzehe" (noble woman), much like the term *cihuapilli* in Nahuatl. The Nahuas of central Mexico may have found a similar attraction in the Virgin of Guadalupe, considering her as much a goddess as the mortal mother of Jesus, regardless of whether or not they associated her specifically with Tonantzin, a preconquest female deity.[24] In this sense, it is not important to correlate a specific image of the Virgin with a particular preconquest deity in order to understand how Mary appealed to native piety. Tonantzin and Guadalupe had no effect upon Ñudzahui interpretations of Mary, though the Guadalupe cult had become increasingly popular among Ñudzahui Christians by the eighteenth century.

Natives interpreted introductions in familiar terms and interpreted Mary in native ways that resembled aspects of popular Spanish Christianity. Spaniards adored Mary, and the religious orders actively promoted Marian devotion in the Americas. Just as Mary was an ideal successor to pre-Christian female deities in Europe, she appealed to the imagination of Ñudzahui Christians.[25] However, Spaniards in the sixteenth and seventeenth centuries were more inclined to emphasize her virgin qualities, and her role as the suffering bearer of the sacred child, than her position as a ruling goddess, equal in status to God. She was more of a mediatrix than a ruler, and certainly not a goddess. Statements of faith in Ñudzahui-language testaments suggest that many imagined her as a sacred ruler, a goddess in the yuhuitayu andehui. Indeed, Mary was a powerful native-Christian image who figured prominently in the minds of Ñudzahui testators.

Sacred Offerings ❧   The affirmation of faith in testaments was followed by the disposition of the body and soul, arrangement of masses, and offering of money to the church. With standard Christian phrases, most testators acknowledged the inevitable return of their bodies to the "earth" and "mud" (*ñuhu ndayu*) from whence they came. Many spoke of their time on earth in terms of *tniño*, a term referring to community labor service and other duties organized by the nobility and ruling lords—the yuhuitayu. In this sense, they had served on earth as they would in the yuhuitayu andehui. All testators hoped to make an expeditious passage through Purgatory, which was called *huahi caa purgatorio*, "the jail of purgatory" (literally, "iron house"), doubtless in reference to an undesirable holding place.

An important part of every will involved the offering of money to several holy images inside the church, to various *cofradías* (lay confraternities associated with the church), and to the priest. Though the act of giving money to images and organizations within the local church was encouraged and perhaps enforced by the friars, it is clear that Ñudzahui accepted Christian images as their own and paid great attention to their care and sustenance, as in European Christianity. The offerings could be extensive, for there were many images to bestow gifts upon before one's death. Some testators gave as much as a hundred pesos to more than a dozen images and cofradías. Nobles and commoners customarily offered coins to these images, even if they had to sell things to acquire the money; even the poorest people gave a few *tomines*, coins of low value, to the saints and the Virgin Mary. In the Yanhuitlan area, it was not uncommon for witnesses to join in the offering by pledging pesos for masses on behalf of the testator. Witnesses entered into the proceedings, and the notary recorded their statements in the first-person narrative form. For example, in Juan Domingo's testament, written in Topiltepec in 1668, the notary included the line "And I María Hernández request a high mass" (AJT Civil 8, 705). This spontaneous affirmation of faith and sign of solidarity with a sick one recalls the participatory, public nature of native testaments. However, it is unclear whether people pledged money out of sheer beneficence, or if individuals were obligated to meet a quota of pledges and thus relied upon their family and friends when they could not fulfill those payments. It is unclear whether the money was actually paid in these cases.

Many Ñudzahui arranged to give money to multiple images of Mary in their churches, and many others possessed various Marian images in their houses and palaces. Don Gerónimo García y Guzmán left money to three different images of the Virgin in his church of Teposcolula: "yya dzehe solidad" [the Lady of Soledad]; "yya dzehe Rosario Español" [the Spanish Lady of Rosario]; and "yya dzehe chisi coru" [the Lady beneath the choir] (AJT Civil 4, 417; see the will at the end of this chapter). Don Gabriel de Guzmán, yya toniñe of Yanhuitlan, bequeathed four different images of the Virgin Mary in 1591 (AGN Tierras 985, 2: 14v–23). Salvador de Zelis possessed a large lienzo of the Virgin of Guadalupe in 1718 (AJT Civil 7, 689: 16). In 1621, Catalina García of Yanhuitlan had various images of the Virgin when she made her testament, including a tobacco pouch bearing the image of the Virgin of Chachuapa (AJT Civil 2, 188). Some testators bequeathed land to an image of the Virgin. In 1749, Rosa Hernández gave some of her land in Chilapila to the Virgin of Guadalupe; don Lorenso Vasquez followed her example just a few months later (AJT Civil 20, 1684). In describing the borders of these lands, they referred to Mary as an owner not unlike their neighbors.

The same García y Guzmán who left money to different images of the Virgin also bequeathed pesos to a "Ñudzahui Christ" inside the church (AJT Civil 4, 417). Don Gerónimo left money to a "Santo Christo tay ñudzahui" [Holy Christ Ñudzahui person] and to a "Santo Christo español" [Holy Spanish Christ].²⁶ The ethnic distinction is not mentioned in a brief translation of the document accompanying the case (see the will at the end of this chapter). Did the Ñudzahui Christ represent a native version of the deity, or did the image simply belong to a native cofradía in Teposcolula? Perhaps the Spanish images were actually made in Europe and the Ñudzahui figure was crafted by local artisans. This possibility would accord with many references in the documentary record to indigenous objects such as cultural artifacts, flora and fauna, and clothing as Ñudzahui items. Such references were made to distinguish local products from those attributed to other parts of New Spain, Spanish America, Europe, Asia, and Africa. However, the reference to "Ñudzahui person" (tay Ñudzahui) seems to allude to the physical qualities of the image. There were at least five different images of Christ in the church of Teposcolula at this time. A few years later, García y Guzmán's wife gave money to multiple images of Christ, but referred to only the "santo christo español" (AJT Civil 4, 419).

Such references to ethnic images are rare in testaments. Whatever the case, it is clear that Ñudzahui considered the images in the church to be their own, and that they used testaments to sustain the images by feeding their offertory boxes (*satnu*) with coins. On the saint's feast day, part of the money was used to feed the community, or at least those members who belonged to the cofradía responsible for maintaining the image. The tradition of giving to the saints in return for divine intercession was imbued with a spirit of native-Christian reciprocity and sacrifice, and also corresponded to European-Christian practice.

Conclusion

Religious knowledge and ritual were instruments of power and status. Native nobles invoked the Christian God, Mary, and the sacred saints through the religious discourse of testaments. In the early-colonial period, reciting holy words and phrases before one or more priests and a convocation of nobles confirmed one's status vis-à-vis the new religious elite—the *dzutu* (fathers), as priests customarily were called, who lived beside the *huahi ñuhu* (sacred house, or house of the deity, in reference to the church). Like Europeans, nobles requested to be buried inside the temple, before the main altar. Some lords bequeathed land to the church to help sustain its activities. Since the written Ñudzahui language did not overtly mark plurals, "huahi ñuhu" could also be interpreted as "house of the deities," considering the many versions of Christ, Mary, and all the saints inside the church. Significantly, no loanword was ever employed in Ñudzahui for the actual church structure, suggesting an identification of the new sacred house with the preconquest temple. The identification of the church with a preconquest structure is appropriate since the church usually was built on the same site as the earlier structure, with the same materials, and by the same group of people through the same mechanisms of community labor. To some degree, ecclesiastics promoted Christianity by encouraging certain associations of the new faith with certain ancient traditions.

Whether by choice or coercion, local rulers associated with the new priesthood and embraced the new faith. Though many lords and nobles may have adhered to remnants of ancient beliefs, Christianity became the dominant state religion just two to three generations after the conquest. Just as the priestly, noble elite wrote codices in preconquest times, the new religious elite taught nobles a new form of writing that would supplement and later supplant the ancient writing tradition. The Christian doctrinal texts were the new sources of sacred knowledge; all other texts that spoke of sacred truths were to be burned. The codices served a similar function in associating elites with certain deity figures, sacred ancestors, cosmic and natural forces—an association dependent upon ritual sacrifice and other divine practices. Now Ñudzahui were instructed by Christians to embrace the doctrine of the one, true God who sent His Son for the ultimate human sacrifice and resurrection. Many Ñudzahui took the new faith and made it their own.

Statements of faith in native-language testaments impart a complex range of beliefs illustrating the convergence of native and Christian ideologies, despite nuances of difference. Of course, these statements are incomplete and only reflect a fleeting impression of one's faith. An individual's belief cannot be assessed through the limited format of a will. But such statements, taken as a whole, divulge certain patterns of belief and mentalities about life and the afterlife. Wills reveal the mundane language used by natives to express themselves in those sacred and somber moments. The Ñudzahui-Christian dialogue created long-lasting native-language phrases and metaphors to convey certain Christian concepts; these approximated their original meanings but left much to the native imagination.

Over a period of nearly three centuries, the spontaneous religious components of testaments appear to fade in relation to their legal content. In most places the native testament conformed increasingly to the Spanish model, until it was written entirely in Spanish. However, even the last testament in my collection, written in 1807, features an extensive religious preamble that pays tribute to the "yuhuitayu toniñe andehui gloria" (AJT Civil 18, 1578). Native-language testaments reveal how some Ñudzahui spoke about and imagined fundamental Christian beliefs, and how their words and images were influenced by indigenous cultural constructions. Future research on popular Christianity in native communities, informed by the use of new and original sources, will no doubt contribute to the study of popular religion and culture in early Mexico.

Last Will and Testament of Don Gerónimo García y Guzmán,
Teposcolula, 1672
(AJT Civil 4, 417)

saha sa nani ni dzutu ndios ndehe dzaya ndios ndehe dzaya ndios ndehe espiritu santo ndios ndehe nuni persona dza ee ni ndisa ñuhu ndios ndehe huaha ndehe cuhuiya yosinindisa nduhu Don gr[mo] garcia siqui yaa cahi yehe ndahuindi sihi yonahihuahandi nee cutu mandamiento articulos de la fen sa usi sahu simaa stohondo ndisa ñuhu ndios ndehe huaha ndehe cuhui dzahua nacuhui saha sananiya Jesus—dzahua huitna naconaha ndehe taca yya toho yondu ndehe cotondaa tutu testamentondi yaha yoquidzahuahandi

huitna hua dzehui saha cuhuindi ndahua dzehui saha cacundi yondiyoynindi sadza yochihinda tuca ynindi ta quadzuhua siqui codzo cahui yuquiti quahi Justiçia si maa stohondo ndios yotnahanino yequicoñondi dzoco yyo ca si ynindi yocachindaa yocachicuitindi ndehe ndudzu ñuhu ynindi condaa tutu yaha ndudzundi yaha nacuhui cutu nacuhuindaa nee chihi taa qhhu huacuhui yoonacane huacuhui yoodzatuhu huacuhui yoodzatihui dzahua tnaha yotasitnunindi huitna sa cuhui sianimandi sihi yequicoñondi tucu

dzahua huitna dzinañuhu dzina huii yonadzocondi animandi nuu nana stohondo ndios yonatniñondi nduhua ndayaya cuhui uhui sichi yonachihitnahandi yequicoñondi ñuhu ndayu sa nisiyonahi nuu nisiyonahi yecandi neecutu nisiyo nisicandi ñuu ñayehui yosicatahuindi huahi ñuhu cano condusi yequicoñondi yodzocondi usi pesos dzahua quehui nasaa 9 quehui nisiyohuaha yiquicoñondi yosicatahuindi vigillia ee missa cano ndatu tahui animandi yodzocondi 2 pesos dzahua quehui saa uhui dzico quehui nisiyohuaha yequicoñondi yosicatahuindi bigillia sihi uni dzutu cachi missa ndatu tahui animandi yodzocondi 4 pesos

[f.2] dzahua sa yonadzocondi nana stohondo ndios tucu nana sacramento yodzocondi uhui rr.— nana san p.º, san pablo yodzocondi ee rr.— nana yya dzehe solidad yodzocondi me.º— nana S.ᵗᵒ Dgo soriano yodzocondi me.º— nana S.ᵗᵒ Cristo Español yodzocondi me.º— nana yya dzehe Rosario Español yodzocondi me.º— nana Jesus nasareno yodzocondi me.º— nana sa Reymondo yodzocondi me.º—nana sa xacindo yodzocondi me.º— nana s.n miguel yodzocondi me.º— nana s.ᵗᵒ dgo yodzocondi me.º— nana s.ᵗᵒ Christo tay ñodzahui yodzocondi me.º— nana santiego yodzocondi me.º— nana yya dzehe chi[s]i coru yodzocondi me.º— sianima yodzocondi me.º— ndehe dzahua sa yonadzocondi nana stohondo ndios ta nicuhuindiya sani naquacaya animandi

dzahua huitna saha sa si ñuu ñayehui sa nisinindahui ñaha stohondo ndios nicuhuitahuindi sihi ñaha dzehendi Donña lasara de gusman saha maa ñaha dzehendi conducundaha stohondo Rey sindi sihi ndaha maaya yonachihindi ytu huahindi ndehe taca ñuhu ytu chiyo sihi huahi nama ᵑᵘ ani ᵑᵃ ñendi ta cotnee ya saha ysi siyo dzayandi sihiya cooya huahi dzahua tnaha yyo ya huitna yca saha yoqhtasindi toho nisano p.º de andrada si alcaldes loreso gonsales nduhui to cuhui albaçeandi yuhu nuu animandi qhhu saha to dzanumini no quiye

to coo huaha yequicoñondi sihi cuhui sihi toñaha dzehendi coto to tniño ñuu ñayehui sindi tucu nda dzahuata nicuhuindiya may stohondo ndios niquitnaha ninosasihi maa ñaha dzehendi quehui dzahua cana chihi tnuni yni niyasihi nduhui albaçeandi tanda ytu chiyo huahi dzuchi dzuchi cana nihi ee ee dzayandi dzahua ni yotasitnunindi nuu taca Justiçia yondito nuu ndehe taca yya toho yyo yaha testigo çebastian de palma andres de tapia gr.ᵐᵒ Baup.ᵗᵃ

sa ndaa cuiti yuhu ndudzu may yya yocuhui nitaa nduhu Ess.ⁿᵒ nombrado huitna biernes sa ñeni caa uni oras 6 de mayo 1672 a.ˢ yaha yuhuitayu san p.º san pablo yucundaa.

Ess.ⁿᵒ Domingo de Belasco

❧

In the name of God the Father, and God the Son, and God the Son [*sic*], and God the Holy Spirit, three distinct persons, one true and good God in whom I, don Geronimo García from the siqui [named] Yaa cahi, have believed. I am a poor man and I guard all the commandments and articles of the faith, the ten [commandments] of our true lord God, so that good will be done in the name of the lord Jesus.

Today it will be known to all the nobles who are present and to all who will see this testament of mine, which now I make. Whether I die or I am saved, I truly desire only that I obtain complete satisfaction in my heart, despite this sickness that is the justice of our lord God. My body is sick but I am sound of heart. I speak with certainty, I speak clearly and with God's will I put down my words on this paper. This will be done, all will be recorded and written. Nobody is to obstruct it, nobody is to deny it, nobody is to change it.

Thus I now arrange things for my soul and also for my body. Now first and foremost, I offer my soul before our lord God, whom I have served as a slave. Secondly, I give my body to the earth, the mud. All that I have possessed, living in this world, I have borrowed. I ask that my body be buried in the great church. I offer ten pesos. Then, when nine days have passed, and my body has been cared for, I beg that a high vigil mass be said on behalf of my soul. I offer two pesos. Then when forty days have passed, and my body has been cared for, I ask for a vigil and that a mass of three priests be said for the benefit of my soul. I offer four pesos. Then, I offer to our lord God and also to the sacraments two reales; before San Pedro [and] San Pablo I offer one real; before the Noble Lady of Soledad I offer half a real; before Santo Diego Soriano I offer a half a real; before Santo Cristo español [the Spanish Christ] I offer half a real; before the Noble Lady Rosario español [Spanish Rosario] I offer half a real; before Jesus of Nazareth I offer half a real; before San Raimundo I offer half a real; before San Jacinto I offer half a real; before San Miguel I offer half a real; before Santo Domingo I offer half a real; before Santo Cristo tay Ñudzahui [the Ñudzahui Christ] I offer half a real; before San Diego I offer half a real; before the noble lady below the choir I offer half a real; to the souls I offer half a real. This I offer before our lord God. If I am worthy, may you collect my soul.

Now that I have served my time on earth I leave matters to my wife doña Lázara de Guzmán, because my said wife will look after the tribute to our lord King. I leave in her hands my house plots and all the patrimonial lands and the house of my palace, where my children live together in the complex. Thus, now I will appoint the elder lord Pedro de Andrada and the alcalde Lorenzo Gonzales to be my executors. So that my soul will be taken, take care of things quickly. Take care of my body. Keep my wife company and see also to my worldly obligations when I die.

May our lord God guard my wife until her final day, and may she consult with the executors who will divide the patrimonial house plots between each little one. Each child will have some of it. Thus, I order before all of the officials who are now in attendance, and all the lord nobles who are witnesses to this: Sebastian de Palma, Andrés de Tapía, Gerónimo Bautista.

True and certain are the words and speech of the lord which I have written, the named notary. Today Friday, three hours in the afternoon, the sixth of May, in the year 1672, here in the yuhuitayu of San Pedro and San Pablo Yucundaa (Teposcolula).

Domingo de Velasco, Notary

Notes

A version of this essay was presented at the Annual Meeting of the American Society for Ethnohistory in Tempe, Arizona, on Nov. 13, 1994. The title was "Dead-Giveaways: Preconquest Vestiges in Colonial Mixtec Testaments." I would like to thank S. L. Cline, Susan Kellogg, Matthew Restall, and Lisa Sousa for insightful commentary on an earlier version of this work.

1. Sahagún (1950–82, 7:34). The transcription and translation is mine. I translate pronouns referring to the "diviner" as "him/her" because the language is not gender specific. I contend that Mixtec diviners may have included women, in light of evidence for women rulers and priestesses in this society. For a discussion of women in Mixtec politics and religion, see Terraciano 1994.

2. Inquisition records deal more with preconquest vestiges than native interpretations of Christianity. Studies of the Passion Play genre have revealed the many ways in which Nahuas took a Christian model and shaped it according to native perceptions (see Lockhart 1992: 402–10; Burkhart 1996). But there are no such sources for the Mixtecs.

3. In the Nahuatl language, *mixtlan* means "place of the clouds" and *mixteca* is the plural of *mixtecatl*—"people of the cloud place." The concept and term *Ñudzahui* also existed in preconquest times and the name survives among native-language speakers in many parts of the Mixteca today.

4. For a discussion of the development of alphabetic writing in the Mixteca, see Terraciano 1994.

5. At the time of the Spanish conquest, the Mixteca constituted one of the most populous culture areas contiguous to that of the Nahua, located just south of central Mexico (some two hundred to three hundred kilometers from Mexico City) and just northwest of the Valley of Oaxaca and the Zapoteca. Population estimates for the densely settled Mixteca Alta (one of three subregions that comprise the Mixteca) at the time of the Spanish conquest place the total number of inhabitants at approximately 700,000. This figure was reduced to about 57,000 by 1590, reaching its nadir toward the middle of the seventeenth century and leveling off at about 30,000 by 1670. After the mid-seventeenth century the population began a slow and nearly constant climb until the present day, never reaching the preconquest estimate. All population figures for the Mixteca Alta are taken from Cook and Borah 1968.

6. These documents constitute a major part of the primary sources examined in my forthcoming book, titled *Mixtec Writing and Culture in Colonial Oaxaca*.

7. For example, see the murder note written by Pedro Caravantes in 1684 and the personal letter written by don Diego de Guzmán in 1572, translated in Terraciano 1994 (appendix B).

8. The case containing the Genealogy of Tlazultepec, for example, is accompanied by a Ñudzahui-language testament (AGN Tierras 59, 2).

9. The common expression is "hua cuhui yoo nacane, hua cuhui yoo dzatuhu, hua cuhui yoo dzatihui." The admonition is also common in Nahuatl and Maya wills.

10. For a discussion of testament writing among the Nahuas, see Cline and León-Portilla 1984; Cline 1986; and Lockhart 1992.

11. See Molina 1984 [1569]: 58v–60; and Lockhart 1992: 471.

12. The *Doctrina en lengua misteca* by fray Benito Hernández was published in 1567 and again in 1568. The first version was written in the dialect of the Achiutla area, which was similar in its orthography to that of Tlazultepec, where doña María gave her testament.

13. This pictorial portion is known as the Tlazultepec Genealogy, discussed in Spores 1964 and Smith 1973.

14. This is the type of metaphorical, honorific register that grammarian fray Antonio de los Reyes associated with the Ñudzahui nobility. In his *Arte en lengua mixteca*, published in 1593, Reyes included a chapter (25) titled "De los nombres y verbos reverenciales de que usan los naturales con los grandes señores o haziendo relacion dellos." In this chapter, he listed the above verb under "nacer el señor" (Reyes 1976: 79).

15. Incidentally, two other versions of this testament appear in a land dispute in 1749 between Santiago Nduaxico and San Juan Numi, both dated 1573. They were presented as evidence on behalf of Nduaxico, who claimed don Felipe de Saavedra had died and had made his will there. The first is a fairly accurate copy of the original, but it is incomplete and its orthography and handwriting betray a date later than 1573, suggesting that it may have been copied much later. The second is obviously fraudulent. The religious formula is about a line long and then all of the lands are promptly enumerated and handed over to Nduaxico. Moreover, the document is unsigned (AGN Tierras 3030, 8).

16. See Eire 1995: 36 for a summary of the standard format of sixteenth-century Spanish testaments, and Lockhart 1992: 468–74 and Cline's chapter in this volume for a model testament in Nahuatl, published by fray Alonso de Molina in 1569.

17. See also Lockhart 1992 on Nahua testaments; Restall (1997b: 155–57) compares the opening religious formulas in Nahua, Yucatec Maya, and European wills.

18. For example, three wills written by the notary Domingo de Velasco in the 1670s and 1680s have been preserved; each shows significant variation in its preamble from the others, despite the use of similar religious language (AJT Civil 4, 417; AJT Civil 4, 488; and AJT Civil 6, 575). Two testaments written by Juan Domingo in 1691 and 1712 reveal the same behavior (AJT Civil 4, 417 and AJT Civil 7, 682). Two other examples (Juan Diego in 1727 and 1731, and Nicolas de la Cruz in 1724 and 1726) seem to confirm this pattern. Restall (1997b: 152–58) found that formulas in Maya wills reflected community, rather than individual, variations. This is also true for Ñudzahui testaments, though individual variation did occur within communities, as well.

19. In his discussion of fray Alonso de Molina's model testament, contained in the 1569 edition of his *Confesionario mayor*, Lockhart (1992: 469) noted that Molina did not include "Dios" in reference to every member of the trinity, but that Nahuas invariably used the term in mundane documentation. In Ñudzahui, the three items were often connected by the term *ndehe*, meaning "and." But similar to the function of *ihuan* in Nahuatl, it was not necessary.

20. In his examination of Molina's model Nahuatl testament of 1569, Lockhart (1992: 470) observed that this component of the preamble, also typical in most Nahuatl wills, was missing from the model; also see Cline's chapter in this volume.

21. For a discussion of social and political relations, and joint male and female rulership in the Mixteca, see Terraciano 1994.

22. Burkhart (1989, 1996) makes similar observations for the interpretation of certain moral concepts among the Nahuas.

23. The creator couple is depicted in the codices. See the *Codex Vindobonensis,* for example, studied by Anders, Jansen, and Reyes G. (1992). See also the sixteenth-century oral legend from Cuilapa, a Ñudzahui community in the Valley of Oaxaca (García 1981).

24. For a discussion of possible associations of the Virgin of Guadalupe with Tonantzin, see Poole 1995; Taylor 1987; and Lockhart 1992.

25. For a discussion of popular devotion to the Virgin Mary in sixteenth-century Spain, see Christian 1981: 21.

26. The Ñudzahui word "tay" is the personal agentive pronoun, meaning "person" or "one who."

CHAPTER 6

Interculturation and the Indigenous Testament in Colonial Yucatan

MATTHEW RESTALL

Introduction: Mixed-Up Differences

"A persistent myth," one anthropologist has written (Fabian 1983: 149), "shared by imperialists and many (Western) critics of imperialism alike has been that of a single decisive conquista, occupation, or establishment of colonial power." Fabian goes on to indict anthropological practice as an imperialist exercise in perpetuating a West-Other relationship. If there is any validity to this sweeping judgment, historians of colonial Mexico must also fall under the gavel; long and overly (but not surprisingly) influenced by the colonists themselves, those who wrote about New Spain worked from an assumption of indigenous irrelevance or utter submission or appropriate isolation—or any combination of the above—often insisting on colonialism's "single decisive" imposition with such eagerness as to make one suspect wishful thinking in the tradition of that consummate colonial Mexican commentator, don Carlos de Sigüenza y Góngora.[1]

In the decades since Charles Gibson's pioneering studies of central Mexico (1952, 1964), most historians of colonial Latin America have ceased believing in Fabian's "persistent myth" while nonetheless continuing to perpetuate a binary-oriented perspective on culture history. With the security offered by the totalist vision of the conquest undone by the new social history, by subaltern studies, and by the New Philology, ethnohistorians, like anthropologists, have been tempted by the romanticism of indigenous resistance and cultural persistence, in absolute form an equally pernicious pendulum-swing solution.

In between lies the heart of the matter, that fascinating grey zone of interethnic interaction, that "gradual spectrum of mixed-up differences" (to steal from a different context a phrase of Geertz's [1988: 148]). In between, too, lies much of the recent work on colonial Mexico and Peru (see the introduction to this volume); the analysis therein tends to navigate a more or less safe passage past the rocks of cultural extinction on one side and conscious cultural resistance on the other. Without at all wishing to take issue with or to distance myself from this scholarship, I would like to suggest, by using the example of Yucatan, that the dangers of these interpretive rocks are perhaps not always adequately recognized.

Certainly it is clear that the colonial period saw a steady diminution of the initial barriers between the indigenous and invasive peoples and their cultures. But it is also clear that the subdominant majority were not passive instruments of cultural change, but rather responsive (albeit not altogether conscious) agents in "a dynamic process of adaptation" (Lockhart 1992: 443). Lockhart's comment that the Nahuas were "self-centered realists and corporate survivors" (1994: 219) certainly applies to the Mayas, probably to all colonial Mesoamericans, and perhaps to Andeans, too; this implies that the processes of cultural intercourse and alteration were multiple and varied, but not necessarily under the aegis of cultural defense or resistance.

Susan Kellogg has argued in this volume and elsewhere (1995a) that Nahuatl-language wills dictated by men and women in Tenochtitlan/ Mexico City reveal the gradual but significant impact of Spanish legal concepts upon Mexica culture; economic, demographic, and cultural forces of change were fortified as a result of Mexica engagement with the colonial legal system, a process that was also evident at the same time in the nearby Nahua community of Culhuacan (Cline 1986). Leslie Offutt has examined several dozen Nahuatl wills from the early seventeenth to late eighteenth centuries from San Estebán de la Nueva Tlaxcala, a community of Nahua colonists in Coahuila; she argues that such documents illustrate "increasing exposure to, and integration into, the hispanic world" on the part of Nahua individuals (1992: 412).

In her study of Culhuacan, Sarah Cline's presentation of her sources showed that cultural continuities from preconquest times and the influx of Spanish elements were in some sense parallel and compatible phenomena; Kellogg has emphasized that culture change must be placed in the context of power relations, for only then can we understand how Nahua strategies of protection and resistance became culturally counterproductive; Offutt viewed her testamentary sources in the temporal and spatial context of culture change offered by evidence from the center, with the pace of change slightly slower in San Estebán than in central Mexico—as revealed by the delayed acquisition of Spanish-language elements by Nahuatl speakers.[2]

Such evidence from Nahuatl-language wills would suggest that indigenous testaments from the colonial Mexican province of Yucatan might also reveal a delayed and slow, but nevertheless steady, process of acculturation, with the language used in such wills revealing a growing grammatical and lexical Spanish influence, and lists of material items betraying a gradual integration of Maya and Hispanic worlds. Indeed, such a pattern can be clearly demonstrated (Restall 1997b: chap. 14 and 22). On the other hand, this approach also comes dangerously close to romanticizing the subject culture as an agent of persistence and resistance. Part of the problem is terminological; the term "acculturation" implies that individuals or groups are primarily engaged in acquiring another culture, reacting to its imperatives rather than acting according to their own traditions and needs. Fernando Ortiz pointed this out half a century ago, but his proposed alternative term, "transculturation" (1947: 97–103), arguably places too much emphasis on deculturation, on "the loss or uprooting of a previous culture."

The notion of culture loss is problematic because it too easily becomes something to be lamented, sometimes only by implication, sometimes as though all colonial-era culture change were a direct result of conquest-era violence, destruction, and repression. Colonial circumstances made unequal partners in cultural intercourse, but the subordinate partner was by no means passive; colonialism was by definition victimizing, but indigenous peoples were far more than mere victims. Their activism, their "riposte" to the "challenge" of colonial realities, did not necessarily amount to conscious resistance but certainly might be characterized as "counter-hegemonic formulations."[3]

The evaluation of indigenous cultures in terms of their ability to persist or their "success" at self-defense tends to be based upon two misconceived assumptions. The first assumption is that culture can have integrity or purity; thus acculturation taints, compromises, and diminishes the subject culture. Yet culture exists to be used; the value of cultural forms lies in their utility, and the resourcefulness of a culture lies in its ability to make creative use of cultural forms, regardless of their origin, and give them symbolic meaning. As a result, cultures are perpetually in transition, confounding any attempt to pinpoint a moment of cultural purity. The only circumstance under which this assumption becomes valid is that of a conscious effort to manipulate concepts of cultural integrity for political purposes—which brings us to the second assumption, that subject peoples strove to defend their culture from dilution and reduction.

Perhaps this fact can be demonstrated with respect to some of Spanish America's indigenous peoples, but it is difficult to make the argument stick for colonial Yucatan, particularly for the long period between the end of the conquest and the decades preceding the Caste War.[4] If the political will to strategize cultural protection existed, there would be evidence of a strong sense of ethnic consciousness; instead, there are overwhelming signs of a society divided by multiple identities of class, *chibal* (the patronym-group of extended families), and *cah* (the self-governing municipal community). Indeed, if the Mayas were committed to cultural defense in a purist sense, they would hardly have been so willing to adopt new cultural forms.[5]

What is important here is the nature of the process whereby the Mayas adopted new cultural forms—and the symbolic meaning given to those forms. The process was more than the simple acquisition of a new culture through acculturation, more too than the transition from two separate cultures to a new hybrid culture, as implied by transculturation. New cultural forms were seldom taken wholesale with their original meanings intact, but were adopted in fragments or as part of complexes consisting of fragments from both cultures whose usages and meanings depended on the beholder.[6] The process was, in the words of Sidney Mintz, writing on the Caribbean (1974: 25), "neither a seamless synthesis nor a potpourri," but it did contain both of these elements. Perhaps a neologism may be permitted to capture the multiple aspects of this interaction between cultures: "interculturation." This term does not restrict culture change to a single direction or a single end result, nor does it overemphasize culture loss or acquisition, expressing instead the colonial-era process of cultural intercourse.

To demonstrate the applicability of "interculturation" to Yucatan, this chapter draws upon the surviving body of more than five hundred Yucatec Maya-language wills, emphasizing the three corpora from Cacalchen, Ixil, and Tekanto, but also referring to other individual testaments (see table 6.1). To make the potentially contradictory patterns of culture change accessible, I have chosen a somewhat perverse, but I hope persuasive, methodology. First, I will examine three documents that might represent the early, middle, and late stages of a spectrum of culture change, one with relatively tidy spatial and temporal parameters. These documents are the Maya-language testaments of Ursula Ake, who died in Cacalchen in 1649, and Juan Cutz, whose children inherited his property in Motul in 1762, and the will of Enrique Chan of Seyba Playa, who dictated his dying wishes in Spanish in 1818. Having presented these wills as more or less indicative of such a spectrum, I then hope to show how Maya testaments, and corresponding patterns of culture change in colonial Yucatan, paradoxically also reflect more complex interculturative processes—and in turn help to articulate the nature of culture change and contribute toward a theory of interculturation.

Three Testamentary Tales

We might imagine that it was a hot and sticky evening in northwest Yucatan when in late June, 1649, Ursula Ake realized that she was facing death. Perhaps she sent her son, Marcos Itza, to notify one of the members of the *cabildo* (municipal council) that it was time for Ursula to dictate her will; perhaps Marcos went to the house of Francisco Uicab, a respected citizen of Cacalchen to whom Ursula had entrusted the task of executor. Certainly it could not have been long before Ursula's three children and a small group of relatives and friends were joined at her bedside by one of the two alcaldes of the cah, Joseph Couoh; one of the regidors, Felipe Kuk; and the community notary, Antonio Chi.

Ursula probably asked the notary to begin the will for her; having written them out many times before, Antonio knew the customary opening phrases better than anyone.[7] He began to write: "Tu kaba dios uchuc tumen tusinil . . ." [In the name of Dios, who has power over everything] (or, as our formula would have it, "In the name of God Almighty") (LC: 16). As always on these occasions, Antonio went on to cite the Virgin Mary, to name the testator's parents, and to record her request that candles be lit and that the local friar, Juan Lorenzo, say a mass for her, the customary fees for which were two *tostones*,[8] two measures of maize, and four chickens.

Ursula then told Antonio how she wished to settle her estate. Like that of many colonial-era Maya women, Ursula's involvement in the local economy went beyond vegetable gardening, animal husbandry, and weaving so as to feed and clothe her family and pay her taxes. She does not appear to have been a veritable banker like Ana Xul (who died in Cacalchen in 1678; LC: 33) or a virtual domestic clothing factory like Pasquala Matu (of eighteenth-century Ixil; TI: 29), but she probably borrowed and lent money, and bought and sold yarn and lengths of cloth; on her deathbed she gave 120 measures of yarn to a Lucia Pech and settled a debt of one *real* with an Ana Euan, neither woman her apparent relative. Ursula also owed three different small sums of money to three men; to pay them off, she sold her horse. In addition, Ursula kept three score

Table 6.1

Extant Colonial-Era Testaments in Yucatec Maya

Cah of Origin	Date	Type/Number	Source
Cacalchen	1646–78	corpus/34	LC in TULAL
Ixil	1765–68	corpus/65	TI in CCA [Restall 1995b and 1997b]
Tekanto	1724–1835	corpus/approx.400	DT in ANEY
Bokoba	1775–84	individuals/2	ANEY
Chicxulub	1759	individual/1	ANEY
Cuncunul	1699	individual/1	TE [Roys 1939]
Dzan	1700	individual/1	TT in TULAL
Dzan	1764	individual/1	AGEY Tierras
Ebtun	1785–1813	individuals/9	TE [Roys 1939]
Homun	1763	individual/1	AGN Tierras
Izamal	1795	individual/1	AGEY Tierras
Izamal district	1706–1831	individuals/9	ANEY Protocolos
Ixil	1738–69	individuals/3	ANEY [Restall 1995b]
Kanxoc	1814	individual/1	MT in TULAL
Mani	1629	individual/1	TT in TULAL
Mani	1760	individual/1	DTi in TULAL
Motul	1762	individual/1	ANEY [the present article]
Pustunich	1726	individual/1	TS in TULAL
Sicpach	1680–1709	individuals/3	Titles of Chichí in CCA
Sicpach	1820–32	individuals/2	ANEY
Tehaas	1805	individual/1	ANEY
Tekanto	1661–79	individuals/3	DT in ANEY
Tekax	1689	individual/1	ANEY
Ticul	1736	individual/1	TS in TULAL
Tiho	1741–89	individuals/5	ANEY

Note: Citations in brackets under "Source" indicate where wills have been published. Most of these sources are discussed in Restall 1997b, while the Tekanto collection is analyzed in Thompson 1978. Full citations of archival sources are in the bibliography, save for the following manuscripts in TULAL: DTi (Documentos de Ticul); MT (Montes de Tsek etc.); TS (Tierras de Sabacche); and TT (Tierras de Tabi) hives of bees, divided among her son and two daughters; the latter also inherited her piglets (including those of her pregnant pig), two chairs, and one set of female clothing (a Maya dress and petticoat).[9]

Judging from thirty wills covering a decade of Cacalchen's history (1646–56), Ursula Ake was neither the richest nor the poorest of that small community's inhabitants. In terms of the type of items she owned, as well as their number, Ursula might be taken as a typical *cahnal* (Maya citizen) of mid-century Cacalchen. Rather than compare her property in detail to that of her contemporaries, however, let us compare it to that of Juan Cutz, who lived in the following century and died in Motul in 1762 (ANEY 1796: 205; see the will at the end of this chapter). The cah of Motul was larger than nearby Cacalchen and more important—both to the Maya, for whom it had been a regional economic center since the days when it was also the capital of the preconquest province of the Pech, and to the Spanish colonial and ecclesiastical authorities, for whom it was a regional administrative head town, or *cabecera*. By this time there was also a growing number of Spaniards and mestizos living in Motul.[10] While both *cahob* (plural of "cah") were geographically equidistant from the colonial capital, we might expect 1760s Motul to be culturally closer to Mérida than 1640s Cacalchen.

The will of Juan Cutz would appear to support that supposition. For example, Juan leaves four house-plots to his children; neither Ursula nor her contemporaries mentioned house-plots at all. Always referred to in Maya documents with the Spanish term *solar*, the house-plot à la Juan Cutz was a colonial innovation; preconquest-style clusters of houses whose gardens had traditionally been marked off with stone mounds were gradually reorganized in the colonial period into a grid system of plots demarcated by stone walls (Restall 1997b: chap. 3 and 8). Larger, more important cahob were given this facelift more quickly.

A comparison between these two wills also suggests that there was an architectural dimension to the contrasting looks of Ursula's Cacalchen and Juan's Motul. Juan leaves to his son a house-door and frame ("u hol na y[etel] u marcoil"). As the Nahuas did,[11] the Mayas left these items in lieu of houses themselves partly because doors, frames, and beams were understood to represent houses, and partly because such items were prized as the manufactured product of a carpenter's skills (as opposed to common or garden house ingredients such as palm leaves for roofs and wattle and daub for walls). House-doors and frames are standard items in eighteenth-century Maya wills; in the roughly forty extant seventeenth-century wills (mostly LC; see table 6.1) there are no mentions of house-doors and just one mention of an unspecified frame. Not only did the Cacalchen of 1649 and the Motul of 1762 look different, reflecting stages of architectural Hispanization, but their inhabitants conceived of their residential environment differently; like Juan Cutz, Ursula Ake lived on a house-plot in a house with a doorway, but she viewed differently their value and the appropriateness of their inclusion in her will.[12]

Another item left by Juan Cutz to his son that does not appear in the will of Ursula Ake is a silver spoon (*cuchara takin*). One of Ursula's contemporaries (LC: 9) mentions a spoon, but it probably falls into the same category as other food-related objects bequeathed in Cacalchen, such as the plate (*frado* or *plato*) and the gourd (*luch*). Juan's spoon, on the other hand, not only seems to hold greater economic value but also indicates that eighteenth-century Mayas may have adopted something of the cultural value ascribed to silver spoons by Spaniards; common items in Spanish wills, such spoons were symbols of prosperity (however modest) and, as the English adage suggests, western European symbols of inherited wealth.

Accompanying the changes in municipal layout were also changes in the form and outward structure of colonial administrative status and local political office. A cah became, from the Spanish perspective, a *pueblo*, an official part of the *república de indios*, complete with a cabildo or municipal council of elected officers holding Spanish titles (Restall 1997b: chap. 3, 5, and 6). But while a community's classification may have been unambiguous from the viewpoint of colonial government, Maya-language records such as testaments reveal that the transition was sometimes (perhaps usually) gradual. Cacalchen had pueblo status by the 1640s, and cabildo officers are named as present during the dictation of all extant wills, but the cabildo's form is uneven in several ways. This can best be explained by examining Juan Cutz's will, which contains an example of the complete and full-fledged ritual presentation on paper of the Maya cabildo. The document ends (again, see the will at the end of this chapter) with a brief statement that the cabildo officers were present, followed by a paragraph of ratification and validation in which confirmation is made of, first, Juan Cutz's identity and the truth of his statement, and second, the location, date, and the names and office titles of the cabildo members present.[13] Ursula's will (like other Cacalchen wills) features no such statements, listing cabildo officers as present in a sentence in the middle of the will (between religious formula and the settling of the estate) and ending simply with a record of the date. Furthermore, Cacalchen wills of Ursula Ake's time tend to mention one alcalde and one regidor, the identities of which differ between wills, and there is no mention of the *batab* (cah governor) in the 1646–52 testaments. The mature-period norm, as reflected in Juan Cutz's will, was always to not only mention but prominently feature the batab, and to list all alcaldes and regidors (the numbers of which varied between cahob—eighteenth-century Motul had three of each—but not from year to year or document to document [Restall 1997b: chap. 6]).

If these two wills seem to illustrate a gradual process of Hispanization affected by location and time, can we detect a progression of the process by extending this partially anecdotal method to a later cah more heavily populated by Spaniards (and Hispanized *castas* [Africans and mixed-race people])? The testament of Enrique Chan (CCA X-1818, 007) suggests we can. The document was dictated in the final years of the colonial period in the community of Seyba Playa, a cah down near the Bay of Campeche, far from Cacalchen and Motul and the most thickly populated Maya regions of the colony, a town whose inhabitants were mostly not *cahnalob* (plural of "cahnal," Maya citizen) as such, but *vecinos*—Spanish residents—whose identity was rooted in the pueblo, not the cah.[14] Seemingly caught between these two worlds, or in a world that appears to us Janus-faced, was Enrique Chan. The cover page to his will describes him as a vecino; the text itself categorizes him as "yndio, natural de este pueblo." The latter was presumably more accurate, but the ambiguity remains and is reflected in the form and content of the document.

On the one hand, Enrique was a cahnal, a Maya citizen of Seyba Playa, the son of Maya parents—Pasqual Chan of the same cah and Maria Couoh of the nearby cabecera, Seyba. He was married to a Maya woman, Maria Petrona Mut; together they had four children. He was illiterate, as were all Mayas save for the elite notarial and gubernatorial (batab) class; the cah notary, Josef Chel, signed his name for him. Also present were two other members of the cah cabildo, the alcaldes Dionisio Puch and Justino Tun. Enrique did not live near the center of town, where Spaniards tended to reside, but on the outskirts, on the road to Xkeulil, a neighboring cah less than a third the size of Seyba Playa and demographically almost twice as indigenous.[15] His household property included modest items common in mid- and late-colonial Maya homes, such as a washing bowl, a bench, and some clothes chests.

On the other hand, the testament is not in Maya, like our previous two sample wills, but in Spanish, written not by the cah notary, despite his presence, but by the local *juez español* (a local Spanish official of modest rank). Accordingly, the form and phrasing of the testament is

Spanish: Maya formulations are replaced by Spanish legalese, and instead of the customarily brief religious opening of indigenous wills (eleven lines in Ursula Ake's will, none at all in Juan Cutz's) there are almost three pages of religious formula and provisions from Enrique Chan. In addition to three official cah representatives were three Spanish witnesses, in effect representing the pueblo; at the foot of the document, in lieu of cabildo ratification and signatures, are the self-signed names of these Spaniards. Furthermore, although Enrique's children are Mayas, they carry not only their father's patronym (Chan), as is overwhelmingly the colonial-era Maya naming pattern, but also their mother's, in the Spanish style (Chan y Mut).

Symbolizing the existence in Enrique's will—and in his life—of these two cultural systems were his two houses. One was Spanish-style, a "solid" house (that is, of limestone: "de cal y canto") with a timber roof; the other is Maya-style, roofed with palm leaves and walled with wattle and daub ("de cololche y embarro"; the Maya term "cololche" means "something made from sticks [palisade, fence, wall]"). From Enrique's description of these structures it is clear that he recognized how different they were, and the use of a Maya term to describe the nature of one of the houses is significant; through this metonymy Enrique is saying that he has one *casa* and one *na*, each representing two different ways of doing things. Yet just as important was the fact that the two structures sat side by side on the same plot of land, both contained stores of maize, and both served the daily needs of family members who surely would not have been conscious of separate cultural systems as they walked from one building to the other. Symbolically adding this theme of integration to that of cultural duality was the existence of the kitchen, a wattle-and-daub addition attached to the back of the stone house ("una cosina de cololche y embarro").

The image of two things distinct yet integrated within a single framework is pertinent not only to material objects but also to personnel. We have seen that the six witnesses to Enrique Chan's testament were three Mayas and three Spaniards, representing cahnal and vecino communities; yet all lived in Seyba Playa, and all appeared to witness the same ritual and be included in the same document. Likewise, of the two landowners whose property bordered on plots of Enrique's, one was a vecino (Lucas Bera, the "capitan de pardos"[16]), the other a Maya nobleman (don Ermenejildo Balam). Five men owed Enrique sums of money, four of them Mayas and the fifth a non-Maya (José Grasales); all five were to settle accounts through the agency of one of the debtors, Juan Mian.[17]

Enrique's testament thus reflects the fact that people of Spanish, African, and Maya descent all lived in Seyba Playa, in some senses separated into indigenous and Hispanic worlds, but to some extent tied to each other politically, economically, and culturally.

On Enrique Chan's house-plot the culture-change spectrum ends, at least for our purposes. We pass from the unspecified Maya structure of Ursula Ake to Juan Cutz's Maya house with valuable wood-worked door and frame to Enrique's pair of houses—one traditional, let us say, the other modern. The Maya cabildo goes from ill defined to deeply rooted to marginalized. There is an apparent shift in the culture of meaning, in the values assigned to objects and words. We move from an overwhelmingly Maya environment to one that seems permeated by "the modern" on every level; the moment when Maya culture seems to flourish, in Juan Cutz's day—strengthened by its adaptation to colonial innovations since Ursula Ake's times—seems also to be pregnant with a profound Hispanization.

Yet we have also seen signs of a pattern featuring less of a simple shift between cultures and more of a cultural cohabitation and intercourse. Clearly the model of a spectrum of culture change requires the modification suggested by the image of the Chan y Mut family continually and (we might conjecture) un-self-consciously passing between their two houses.

Toward a Conclusion: Cultural Intercourse

More than a century passed between Ursula Ake's and Juan Cutz's deaths; Juan lived in a community several times larger than Ursula's; in the former's home cah, about one in three residents were Hispanic. Given these facts, perhaps what is surprising is not that the wills of 1649 and 1762 reflect culture change, but that they are so similar—in language, in the material items they contain, in the social world onto which they let a little light. The major lexical impact upon Maya has taken place before Ursula Ake's lifetime; her will contains a representative sample of Spanish nouns borrowed by Mayas in response to the colonial introduction of coins, horses, Spanish-style furniture, the Spanish calendar and religion, and new titles of political office. Juan Cutz's will reflects the same process, almost to the same degree. Juan uses more loanwords, but he has more property and dictates a longer statement. Even if we accept that Juan's will reflects the gradual increase in loanwords evidenced by the wider corpus of Maya-language material, the fact remains that there has been no change in the *nature* of the impact of Spanish upon Maya; in particular, there are no signs of grammatical influence.[18]

Furthermore, the material worlds of Ursula, Juan, and Enrique are notably similar. Comparing their three wills, we find that all three lived in a municipality whose material environment was—from an urban Spanish perspective—rural; that is, revolving around the use and husbandry of animals (Ursula's colt, pigs, and bees; Juan's mare, cow, and calf; Enrique's mules) and the gender-specific economic staples of farming and weaving (Ursula's yarn; Juan's maize fields; Enrique's corn and rice fields and his stash of dried maize). All three participated in the cash economy, all three discussing loans or debts, installment payments, or coin bequests. The household property of all three was modest but reflecting the early-colonial introduction of Spanish-style furniture (Ursula's bed and chairs; Enrique's bench; and the chests mentioned by all three testators).

This comparison can be given an empirically stronger foundation by placing it in the context of four corpora of testaments, contrasting the Cacalchen wills of 1646–79 with the later collections from Ixil (1765–68), Ebtun (1785–1813), and Tekanto (1725–1835) (LC; TI; TE; DT).[19] While a detailed such comparison would have to take into account a variety of factors (such as the incidence and number of samples within each corpus, as well as other factors discussed here), the general sense given is parallel to the impression lent by the philological comparison of the previous paragraph. The nature or typology of material life remained little changed: plots of house and farming land; trees and vegetables; horses, cattle, pigs, and chickens; small pieces of wooden furniture; machetes and a variety of tools for farming, horse keeping, apiculture, and so on; petty valuables, such as plates, spoons, and small amounts of cash; unchanging gender-specific styles of clothing, and measures of cloth and yarn. There is, however, an increase in the variety and quantity of items within these categories. In the later wills there are more species of trees, and donkeys and mules make an appearance, as do such tools as well pulleys and branding irons, and items of value such as saint images. (Conversely, turkeys disappear from the record, perhaps because they were no longer considered worthy of mention; even pigs and chickens are given scant passing attention in late-colonial wills.)

In demonstrating the material similarities between wills over time, I have already hinted at alternative factors that explain differences, factors that indicate culture differences not related to Hispanization. One of these is gender: female roles in the domestic and local economies are inevitably and strongly reflected in testaments. Another is the existence of variations between cahob, variations that were often independent of temporal developments. Such variations were manifested in a myriad of ways and amounted to integral cah subcultures of ways of doing and viewing things. Substantial elaboration is offered elsewhere (Restall 1997b); let it suffice to say here that some of these variations were determined by locale (for example, Ebtun, its lands less fertile than those to the west, specialized in apiculture from preconquest to modern times; from shortly after the conquest, Dzaptun became caught up in the economy of transport along the nearby Campeche highway), others by traditions of probable precolonial origins (numbers, combinations, and compositions of political offices made colonial cabildos highly varied from cah to cah; while the dictionaries tell us that *col* meant "field" and *kax* "forest," some cahob used kax to mean any nonresidential plot—cultivated, cultivable, or not). Other variations resulted simply from the fact that human organizations, when given some autonomy and when enjoying the close affinity and loyalty of their members, as was the case with the cah, tend to develop customized patterns of behavior. The logical extension of this point is the theme of what I have termed "cahcentrism" (Restall 1997b); the ubiquity of the cah in the Maya-language documentary record reflects the centrality and vitality of the Maya community in the colonial period. From this perspective, contrasts between source materials such as wills can not only be subsumed within the dominant pattern of cahcentrism but can also contribute to its supportive evidence. The three wills selected above could thus be interpreted as reflecting the cah's ability to adapt to colonial innovations in the early period; its continued integrity and maturity as late as the 1760s; and its survival on the very eve of independence in a community where Mayas were a minority.

We can de-emphasize or recontextualize the differences between the Maya-language wills, but there is yet another way to view these contrasts. For example, the length of Juan Cutz's will, about twice as long as the testaments of Ursula Ake and her neighbors, might be taken as another indicator of cultural change. Spanish wills tended to be far longer than indigenous ones, but of course Spaniards tended to be wealthier. My point, rather, is not that length indicated Hispanization, but that what makes Cutz's will longer is the detail he chooses to include, detail that earlier Maya wills tend to exclude. While there are certainly examples of Spanish testaments that feature lengthy personal asides or accounts,[20] wills by Spaniards more commonly featured item-by-item lists of property. Instead, the personalization of wills—including the use of reported speech, laudatory or deprecatory remarks about relatives, and the shifting of pronominal perspective as relatives or cabildo officers add comments—seems to be an indigenous phenomenon, a cultural form that was subject to change independent of any Spanish influence. Such features are visible in the Nahuatl wills from sixteenth-century Culhuacan (Cline and León-Portilla 1984) and in Ixil's eighteenth-century testaments (Restall 1995b) (giving the impression that they developed earlier in central Mexico, although this may be a distortion created by the uneven survival of testament corpora).

In other words, Maya culture change and Hispanization are not necessarily synonymous simply because during the period under study the Mayas were increasingly exposed to Spaniards and their culture. Late-colonial testators such as Juan Cutz, along with the notary and cabildo in his home cah of Motul, may have felt more comfortable with the ritual of the will—in the sense that its format and validity were perceived as deeply rooted and secure—making its written record an appropriate place to clarify a matter such as the digging of a well and the purchase of the land around it. Certainly, the written testament was a Spanish innovation, but it was culturally familiar to Cutz and his contemporaries as something Maya.

Indeed, while in an analysis of testaments and other texts we can detect and label some cultural elements as deriving from Maya or Spanish "systems of representation" (as William Hanks [1986: 739] has put it), often such elements cannot be so easily categorized. This is because, to use Hanks's terms, they can be "fused within the larger whole," a process of "hybridization" that produces an "ambivalence in discourse." The process of cultural fusion, however, does not result in a hybrid culture that we can then place under the microscope. The process remains incomplete; it is its own end, in essence a continuous and infinite dynamic interplay or intercourse between cultural forms that is not necessarily progressive and certainly not teleological. There remains a duality to the process, but the two cultures are in constant communication; the "ambivalence in discourse," or what has been referred to earlier as an ambiguity of cultural identity, lies in the fact that in this cultural dialogue it is not always apparent who is doing the talking.

In fact, Maya-language notarial documents are conversations on a variety of levels. In one sense, these written records are dialogocentric within cah culture; that is, they center on conversations between ritual participants acting as both individuals and corporate representatives. In the case of testaments, the conversants are testator and heir (representing generational interest groups and/or the extended families or patronym groups called *chibalob*), testator and notary (representing the cah citizenry and the cabildo, the cah ruling body), and various other pairs of interested parties ranging from the batab to a family creditor.

In another sense, the very nature and format of indigenous notarial documents represents a dialogue between cultures, of which testaments are a fine example. A clerically imposed genre satisfying colonial legal and ecclesiastical requirements, wills were also Maya rituals, probably based on some form of preconquest oral tradition, that helped to maintain community ties of family, property, social hierarchy, political office, and corporate identity. The dual purpose of the document was reflected in the terms used by the Maya to describe it: "yn takyahthan [t]in testamento" [my final statement, (in, of) my testament]. The terms are like Enrique Chan's two houses: one is Maya, the other Spanish, but the two sit side by side to constitute a single phrase and identify a single document; their purpose is both singular and dual. Bilingual couplets were omnipresent in colonial cah life—take the names of our testators, for example, or the full name of any cah (such as San Juan Baptista Motul)—and drew upon a tradition of semantic couplets that seems to have preconquest Mesoamerican roots (Edmonson and Bricker 1985; Hanks 1986; Restall 1997b: chap. 18; Lockhart 1992: chap. 9). Monolingual semantic couplets in colonial Maya texts are common, reflecting cultural continuity; their bilingual counterparts are indicative of the intercultureative yet inclusive process of Maya adaptation to colonial realities.

Not just the form but also the content of indigenous wills contain fragments of cultural conversations, detectable within both corpora of wills and individual documents. For example, taking material possessions as indicative of cultural alignments, not surprisingly we find that some individuals in Ixil in the 1760s were more Hispanized than others (TI). Some Ixil cahnalob lived only in homes and wore only clothes that were wholly colonial Maya (in the sense that such objects, mostly precolonial-rooted, would not have been possessed by a contemporaneous Spaniard); the same applied to most of their tools and kitchen implements. In the same cah, at the same time, were individuals whose material world approximated that of a poor Hispanic. Yet rather than representing contrasting groups within the community, such individuals were contributors to a cultural intercourse that existed not only on a community level but also within the confines of individual house-plots.

Pedro Mis, for example (TI: 30), owned some objects not included in the estates of any other Ixil cahnal dying during the same period (sixty-five wills span November 1765 to January 1768). Two of these were Spanish-style items: a writing desk ("papirera," i.e., *papelera*) and a door lock and key ("yabe," i.e., *llave*) to go with one of his two houses (only one other Ixil testator mentions a house, per se, the rest refer to house-doors and frames; I believe the distinction is that the former are stone houses and the latter represent wattle-and-daub structures). Both items are culturally symbolic: literacy was reserved for Spaniards and elite Mayas holding certain offices (Pedro Mis was probably a former notary in Ixil), and houses have been a leitmotiv of this discussion of interculturation. Yet Pedro was also the unique possessor (the afore-mentioned caveats still applying) of items whose cultural associations were Maya: an orchard of sapote trees, a "nuc" (a seat of some kind), and a "dzopatancochbol" (a blunt-ended digging stick). Comparing Pedro's entire estate to those of his contemporaries, the picture becomes clearer. His property is not just more varied, it is more exten-sive (only one other testator has as many plots of farmland [four] as Pedro). Pedro was not simply more oriented toward the Hispanic world, he was wealthier. Given the realities of colonial socioeconomic structures, it is not surprising that exceptional wealth might mean the possession of items unusual in a cah.

In her analysis of indigenous testaments from a community in Coahuila, Leslie Offutt concluded that her Nahua subjects "straddled both the Indian and the Hispanic worlds" (1992: 424). I have argued here that the existence of Hispanic elements in an indigenous testament and in indigenous lives did not necessarily signify acculturation toward the Hispanic world, that the straddling process was not always a one-way progression into Hispanization, that it was more comfortable than the image of straddling suggests, and that it was as reciprocal, natural, and potentially ambiguous as a conversation. Drawn as we are to the West-Other relationship cited at the start of the chapter, and valid as it can be as a tool of analysis, the binary paradigm of conflicting absolutes needs to be modified by an understanding of indigenous perspectives. While Mayas surely perceived themselves as subject to systems of hierar-chy and accordingly granted cachet to Spanish-style forms and objects, they also did not always view the world in binary terms; or, if they did, the terms were not ours or those of the Spaniards (what is to us Hispanic could have been to them Maya or, more likely, simply local, pertaining to the cah). The nature of the interculturative process was in many ways determined by each Maya individual's subconscious percep-tion of it, by each individual's contribution to the cultural intercourse of mixed-up differences.

Last Will and Testament of Juan Cutz, Motul, 1762
(ANEY 1796–97: 205)

ten cen Juan cutz Ah cahalnal en Uay tu mektan cahil ca yumilan Ah bolon pixan San Ju.º Baptista Uay ti cah motul lae cin mentic yn hahal than lae tohil in uol Utial in dzaic hecex solar yan ten ti in palilobe y hecex kax u lumil colob yan tene = Bay xan yax chun lae cin dzaic[21] lay hunac solar yn cah lic lae ti in mehen Andres cutz heix lay solar lae [yan][22] u chenil ten tin holah u cenil = oxlahunpis peso catac hunpel toston tin [bot]ah u men cenil heix tun lay u cotil u pach lae tomas Aguilar cote yoklal u yoltic cahtal cachii Bay bic tun utial yn yum Pablo cutztze ma tin chaah ti ti lay tomas Aguilar lae tin botah hecex u tohol lay cot tu betahe uaxacpel peso tin betahix u hanalil xan u chic u betabal canpel peso u cuentail u tohol lay cot y u hanalil lae lahcapis peso lay tumenel cin patic ti lay in mehen lae y tulacal hecex xanob pakanie y tulacal he.. ..[c]heob yanie maix mac u chac u thanan cal yoklal uamax tu hok uba than yoklal [t]u kinile ca u tucin cakal peso ti lay in mehen lae ca u hokes ubae bay bic coh yanil lay solar ten lae lay tumenel cin mentic lay in hahal than lae tac tanil yn yum Batab y in yum Justisias li[c i]n kubic lay solar ti lay in mehen lae ychil u tohol in uol = Bay xan cin dzaic ti lay in mehen lae hunpok yeua in mandzil na yxim col y hunpok baca y u yal in man yoklal hopel toxtones y hunpel u hol na y u marcoil in man yoklal hunpel peso u ci y hunpel caja in matan ti i[n] na y hunpel cuchara takin in matan ix ti in na xan lay cin dzaic ti lay in mehen Andres cutz lae mix mac bin than nac yoklal

Bay xan cin dzaic ti in mehen Joseph cutz hunac solar minan u cotil bin cah lae u palilob tu kinili heix lay solar lae in matan ti in Na heix lay solar lae te yan tu lakin cah bel cibalame u yohelob =

Bay xan cin dzaic ti in uixmehen luisa cutz y Josepha cutz hunac solar yan tu lakin cah bel cibalam canupop yoklal bin u ...b tu kinil hecabin yol cah tolobie catanili u pache

Bay xan cin dzaic ti in uixmehen Antt.ª cutz y Rosa cutz hunac solar canupop yoklal heix lay solar lae yan u chenil ti li tu hol cah bel cibalam heix lay solarob lae mix ca u conol mix ca u siob bin cah lae yalobi tac tu kilacabilob tu kinil =

[f.205v] Bay xan cin patic tu kab yn mehenob Joseph cutz y Andres cutz canac u lumil col h[eix] hunacie hokal u kanil lay yan tu lakin cah tu xaman bom yan chenil ychil potbil .. heix u lak hunace tu kin u estansia cah hokal u kanil u yohelob = heix u lak hunace te yan tu chikin yaxleula u kal u kax D.ⁿ francº Ake u yohelob hokal u kanil y u lak hokal u kanil u lumil ... man kax in Na ti lorenso Kuh escriba[no] te yan xaman

chenkelem u yohelob ..n hun bak lay kax tu pakkil lae cin patic tu kab in
mehen Joseph cutz y Andres cutz bin u mul col yetel u bal tu kinil bay bic
tun tu tohil in uol cin mentic lay in hahal than lae bay test[amen]toe cin
pecoltic u than ca yumil ti Dios he tux cin manel tin mol patan bic tusan
in bel tumen ca yum encomenderroe lay hahal than cin mantic .. tu tanil
yn yn [*sic*] Batab y yn yum Justisias y Regidoresob y escribano lay u
ha[hal] [hele] en 13 de Agosto de 1762 años

ten Juan cutz =

toon con Batab y Justisias Regidores escribano Uay ti cah motul tanil
tu dzah u h[a]hil u than lay Juan cutz lae licil u mentic lay u hahal than lae
cu pecoltic u.. yal tumen ca yumil ti Dios tux ci tan tumenel ychil u mol
patan lay [tu]mentah lay u hahal u tanil lay u hahil lic ca dzaic ca firma
yalan [ca]bal hele en 13 de Agosto de 1762 años

Nicolas balam	Dⁿ Matheo Koh [*rubric*]	Julian Tzek
Ber.ⁿᵒ pech	Batab	Seuastian chan
Santiago Koh	Pasqual Pech theᶜ	Matheo Ake
Alcaldesob	Ambrosio kuh	Regidoresob
	escribano=	

❧

I who am Juan Cutz, I am a citizen here in the cah governed by our lord
the blessed San Juan Baptista, here in the cah of Motul, where I make my
true statement and affirm that I give this house-plot of mine to my children and this forest of milpa lands that is mine.[23] Therefore first I give this
one house-plot where I reside to my son, Andrés Cutz. This house-plot
has a well of mine. I made the well hole; thirteen pesos and one tostón I
paid for the well construction. Here too is the stony ground around it. It
was Tomás Aguilar's stony ground, because he used to live there when it
was the property of my father, Pablo Cutz. I didn't take it from this Tomás
Aguilar; I paid him bit by bit. The price of this stony ground came to eight
pesos; a resale payment of four pesos was also made by me. The cost, the
price of the resale of this stony ground was therefore twelve pesos. Thus I
leave it to my son here with all these planted palm trees[24] and all its other
trees. Nobody shall have much to say about it. Whoever does come out
with words about it, at that time let them come out with forty pesos for
my son here. This is how expensive this house-plot of mine is because I
made it what it is. This is my true statement, before m'lord the Batab and
m'lord the Magistrates. I now deliver this house-plot to my son here, as is
my wish. Likewise I give to my son here one mare bought with my
mother's corn field; and one cow with its calf which I bought for five
tostones; and one house-door with its frame which I bought for one peso

of henequen; and one chest, inherited from my mother; and one silver spoon, also inherited from my mother, which I also give to this son of mine, Andrés Cutz. Nobody shall say anything about it.

Likewise I give to my son, Josef Cutz, one house-plot without stony ground. His children shall live there in time. This particular house-plot I inherited from my mother; it is to the east of the cah on the road to Cibalam, as is known.[25]

Likewise I give to my daughters, Luisa Cutz and Josefa Cutz, one house-plot that is to the east of the cah on the road to Cibalam. It shall go to both of them at the time when they are ready to spin thread there; then they will take possession.

Likewise I give to my daughters, Antonia Cutz and Rosa Cutz, one house-plot for both of them. This house-plot has a well; it is near the cah's entrance, on the road to Cibalam. These house-plots we are neither to sell nor to give away; they dictated this impediment in the time of our ancestors.

Likewise I leave in the hands of my sons, Josef Cutz and Andrés Cutz, four milpa fields. Here is one of them, of one hundred mecates, to the east of the cah and to the north of Bom. There is a well dug in it. Here is another one of them at the corner of the cah estancia; it is known to be one hundred mecates. Here is another one which is to the west of Yaxleula and the twenty-mecate forest-plot of don Francisco Ake—it is known to be one hundred mecates—and the other one-hundred-mecate field, a forest-plot my mother bought from the notary Lorenso Kuh, which is to the north of Chenkelem. The cultivated area of this forest-plot is known to be four hundred mecates.[26] I leave the whole field with its contents in the hands of my sons Josef Cutz and Andrés Cutz. Thus my wish at this time is just. I make this my true statement, as a testament, that I swear by the word of our lord Dios whereby I passed my tribute collection, according to my appointed office, on to our lord the encomendero. This true statement I make before my batab and my lords the magistrates and regidors and notary. This is the truth. Today on the 13th of August of the year 1762.

I, Juan Cutz.

We who are the batab and magistrates, regidors, and notary here in the cah of Motul, to whom Juan Cutz gave his true statement. He now makes his true statement; he hereby swears by the sayings of our lord Dios regarding where he stands in his tribute collection. He made his true statement. This is the truth. We now give our signatures below. Today on the 13th of August of the year 1762.

Don Mateo Koh: Batab.

Pasqual Pech: Lieutenant.

Ambrosio Kuh: Notary.

Nicolas Balam; Bernardino Pech; Santiago Koh: Alcaldes.

Julian Tzek; Sebastian Chan; Mateo Ake: Regidors.

Notes

I am grateful to Sarah Cline, Susan Kellogg, James Lockhart, and William Hanks for comments made on earlier versions of this chapter.

1. Among the best-known examples of this old school are, from the late nineteenth century, W. H. Prescott and H. H. Bancroft, and from the early twentieth, Robert Ricard. For some succinct historiography on this topic, see Lockhart 1992: 2–3. As Lockhart observes (1994: 220), a particular version of this view still survives (and is certainly dominant outside the community of academic specialists) with respect to the conquest of central Mexico.

2. The frame of reference for culture change in the philological ethnohistory of Mexico tends to be the "stage" theory first proposed in Karttunen and Lockhart (1976, cited by Offutt 1992) and further articulated in Lockhart 1992, especially chapter 7.

3. Comaroff and Comaroff (1992: 236) describe colonial relations as a process of "challenge and riposte"; also quoted by Burkhart (1996: 5), who suggests that "counter–hegemonic formulations" may be found as "muted messages" in postconquest native-language texts.

4. If specificity was required, the conquest's terminal date could be taken as 1570 and the Caste War as originating in 1800, following the titles of two persuasive studies by Clendinnen (1987) and Rugeley (1996); also see Restall 1998.

5. These assertions are explored below to some extent, but also see Restall 1997b.

6. It is essentially this aspect of the process of cultural interaction that has been characterized by Mintz (1974: 25; context of the Afro-Caribbean) as "culture disguise" and by Lockhart (1992: 445; context of the colonial-era Nahuas) as "double mistaken identity."

7. Over the preceding two years, Antonio Chi had written a dozen wills (that are extant) (LC).

8. There was also a fee of two *tomines* (*tumin*) "for Jerusalem," effectively a supplemental priest's fee. A tomín was the same as a real (although Mayas and Nahuas used the term generally to refer to cash or coin); four reales made a tostón, and two tostones made a peso. Sung masses cost an extra tostón. (On mass fees paid by Mayas, see Restall 1997b: chap. 12; in the context of all taxes paid by colonial Mayas, see Farriss 1984: 41.)

9. For further discussion of Maya women in colonial Yucatan see Restall 1995a and 1997b: chap. 10, as well as Hunt and Restall 1997.

10. There are available estimated populations of these cahob in 1700 and 1716, respectively: Cacalchen, 860 and 956; Motul, 1,169 and 1,274. It is probable that

Motul in 1762 was three or four times the size of Cacalchen in 1649. By the 1780s Motul was 48 percent non-Maya. See Patch 1993: app. A, B.

11. Lockhart 1992: 69, citing the Tulancingo Collection in the UCLA Research Library, a corpus also discussed, with sample documents presented, in Lockhart 1991a: chap. 6; Cline and Léon-Portilla 1984; and Cline 1986: 101–2.

12. This perception of Ursula Ake's was presumably shared by those who witnessed and possibly prompted her dictation. On Maya houses and households, see Restall 1997b: chap. 8.

13. The signing of documents by Maya cabildo officers was a typical incomplete imitation of the form of the Spanish model: a document might state (as does Juan Cutz's will) that "ca dzaic ca firma yalan" [we give our signatures (or, we sign) below], but the notary actually wrote the names, with only the batab (governor of the cah) sometimes signing his own name (as was the case with Juan's will). (Nahua, Mixtec, and Cakchiquel practices were similar; see Anderson, Berdan, and Lockhart 1976; Terraciano 1994; Hill 1989; and Restall 1997a; also see the wills included at the end of each chapter of this volume.) Of course, whether the signators actually signed (as Spaniards did) or not (as illiterate Mayas did not and could not) made no difference to the legal validity of the document. Because a document was in Maya, it was expected and acceptable for its form to be an "imperfect" imitation of a Spanish genre; in effect, by late-colonial times, if not sooner, Maya notaries employed their own legal forms (as well as some that were not accepted as legal) (Restall 1994, 1997a, 1997b: chap. 18–21).

14. Seyba Playa had a population of about four thousand in 1794 and five years earlier was about 55 percent vecino (Patch 1993: 173, 259). We can assume that both these figures would have risen a little by 1818. "Vecino" usually refers to Spaniards, but sometimes, in Yucatan at least, it included castas, making "non-Maya" or "Hispanic" more accurate glosses.

15. Based on the population estimates offered by Patch (1993: 259), which include Xkeulil at 24 percent vecino relative to Seyba Playa's 55 percent (1789).

16. There was a militia company of eighty-five armed pardos installed in Seyba Playa in the late eighteenth century; the term "pardo" was used in Yucatan to mean mulatto, and sometimes applied to all people of African descent. On Africans in Yucatan see Patch 1993: 94–96, 232–36; García Bernal 1972: 17–19; and various brief entries in Hunt 1974; I am currently working on an article and book chapter on the African and pardo experience in colonial Yucatan, drawing upon archival material in AGEY, AGI Escribanía and AGI México, AGN, and ANEY.

17. These business ties were related to the two ways in which Enrique Chan appears to have made a living: as a muleteer (he owned five mules with corresponding riding gear and bags) and as a farmer (he had plots devoted to maize and to rice).

18. For discussions of colonial-era Maya language changes see Karttunen 1985 and Restall 1997b: chap. 22. William Hanks is also at work on a study of the impact of Franciscan evangelization upon the Maya language. With respect to the Nahuatl-Maya comparison, the fact of minimal language change during the period of the three selected wills (1649–1818) does not imply Maya incompatibility with the "stage theory" analysis of Nahuatl (Karttunen and Lockhart 1976; Lockhart 1992: chap. 7), as Maya appears to have passed very rapidly (within a

decade or two of the conquest) through a "stage one" equivalent while not entering anything like a "stage three" until the mid-nineteenth century at the earliest.

19. Such a comparison can be found in itemized and table form in Restall 1997b: app. E.

20. One well-known example which comes to mind is Diego Mendez's tale in his 1536 will of Columbus's fourth transatlantic voyage (included in the Penguin edition of *The Four Voyages*). More mundane examples can be found scattered through the volumes of ANEY (covering Yucatan from the 1690s on).

21. Shortly after the Spanish conquest a letter resembling a backwards "c" was invented for the colonial Maya alphabet (see Restall 1997b: chap. 18, 22); it is represented here by its modern equivalent, "dz" [ts'].

22. Worm damage to the document has necessitated a number of spaces in the transcription; where possible these are filled with syllables or words suggested by context and thus placed in brackets.

23. This testament, while representative of colonial Yucatec Maya wills in many ways, is unusual in not including an opening religious formula. However, the formula used by Yucatec notaries was similar to that used by other colonial Mesoamerican notaries (see other wills in this volume; also Restall 1994, 1995b, 1997a, 1997b: chap. 12).

24. This is the xan, or *abal mexicana*, whose leaves were used by the Maya as roofing material (I thank Eugene Anderson [pers. comm. Nov. 1997] for identifying the botanical Latin name of this tree; I misidentified it in Restall 1997b: 204).

25. Literally, "they know it" ("they" being the community in general, represented by the cabildo witnesses, and specifically the Cutz heirs).

26. The measurement here is one *bak*; the *kan* and *kal* are also used in this will (one bak equals 20 kal equals 400 kan; a kan is equivalent to a mecate) (see Restall 1997b: chap. 15).

CHAPTER 7

Land, Family, and Community in Highland Guatemala: Seventeenth-Century Cakchiquel Maya Testaments

ROBERT M. HILL II

This chapter is concerned with one specific use of writing among the seventeenth-century Cakchiquel: the preparation of testaments or wills.[1] Like other colonial Mesoamerican peoples, the Cakchiquel Maya of highland Guatemala were heirs to a preconquest tradition of writing, complete with its own formal document types. The writing system introduced by the Spaniards in the sixteenth century, while differing in form and materials, was readily understood by the Cakchiquels, who soon put it to use both in preserving aspects of their preconquest culture and responding to the demands and possibilities of the new colonial regime (see Hill 1989, 1991, 1992).

As a document type, Cakchiquel wills do not appear to be of preconquest origin in the region. At least, there is no clear evidence at present of an equivalent class of preconquest wills from either the descriptions of the Spanish chroniclers or from other documents of the Cakchiquel themselves. Accordingly, we should view the Cakchiquel *testamento* as essentially a colonial-period innovation, and address ourselves to its characteristics and the reason(s) for its creation.

At a basic level, wills—be they Cakchiquel or European—are produced for the same purpose: to ensure that the transmission of the testator's property proceeds according to his/her wishes. From the limited corpus of extant Cakchiquel wills, it is clear that land, as in any agricultural society, was the crucial form of property. Naturally, according to their wealth and position, testators could also transmit other kinds of property to beneficiaries. But land was clearly central.

Characteristics of the Corpus

The entire corpus of surviving early-colonial Maya wills from Guatemala is small (see table 7.1), and this may be due (aside from the physical deterioration of documents in an earthquake-prone, tropical climate) to the seeming tendency of families to keep such documents in their own possession rather than in municipal, church, or notarial archives. Indeed, the documents in this corpus were preserved only by virtue of the fact that they were presented as evidence before Spanish authorities and thus entered into the formal record of legal proceedings.

Only five indigenous Guatemalan wills date from the sixteenth century, and only two of these are Cakchiquel. Both were written in 1596: one for Diego Can (town unknown), the other by Diego López Ch'uti Pacal (contained in the Annals of the Cakchiquels; see Recinos 1950: 202–4). Like the other wills from this period, the Can and López testaments are short, simple statements, unlike the often more elaborate, formal documents of the seventeenth century.

There are eleven extant texts of wills for the seventeenth century and references to the provisions of two more, representing seven Cakchiquel-speaking towns. Of these, three pertain to the Pirir family of San Juan Sacatepéquez (Hill 1989). Three are from Patzicía. There are two wills (one fraudulent, see below) from Chimaltenango and one will each from Sololá, Santiago Sacatepéquez, and Comalapa. The provisions of Tecpán resident Francisca Yeol's will (ca. 1635) are known only in part from legal proceedings in 1689 (Hill 1992: 60). Some of the provisions of Patzicía resident Andrés Pérez Cuat's will (pre-1689) are also known from their mention in court records. Apart from the 1708 Thomás Jocón will (directly connected with the Pirir family) there are currently only two other known Cakchiquel wills from the eighteenth century, and these are from a married couple (Restall 1997a). The significance and implications of this chronological distribution will be considered later in this chapter.

Structure

The wills were all deathbed statements, and the physical condition of the testator at the time may well have been significant in terms of the length of the document and complexity of the formulas employed. Even in the small

Table 7.1:

Inventory of Early-Colonial Indigenous Guatemalan Testaments

Year	Testator (Language & Provenance of Will)	Reference
1569	Catalina Nijay (Nahuatl)	AGCA A1 5930, 51849 (in Carmack 1978: 371–72)
1569	Gerónimo Mendoza (Tzutuhil)	AGCA A1 5942, 51997 (in Carmack 1978: 372–74)
1583	Magdalena Hernández (Kekchí)	(in Burkitt 1905)
1596	Diego Can (Cakchiquel, town unknown)	AGCA A1.43, 6071, 54705
1596	Diego López Ch'uti Pacal	Annals of the Cakchiquels: 10
1608	Gaspar Uuch (Cakchiquel, Chimaltenango)	AGCA A1.20, 6074, 54894
1608	Baltasar López/Hernández /Uuch (Cakchiquel, Chimaltenengo [fraud])	AGCA A1.20, 6074, 54893; A1.43, 4836, 41598
1627	Miguel Sanon (Cakchiquel, Patzicía)	AGCA A1.45.1, 5322, 44813 (in Hill 1991: 298)
ca. 1635	Francisca Yeol (Lolmay) (references only, Tecpán)	AGCA A1, 6063, 53970 (Hill 1992: 60)
1642–48	Miguel Pérez Pirir (Cakchiquel, San Juan Sac.)	AGCA A3.15, 2787, 40301 (in Hill 1989)
1651	Juan Pérez Tzamol (Spanish trans., Patzicía)	AGCA A1, 5954, 52144
1662	Miguel Juan Queh (Cakchiquel, Santiago Sac.)	AGCA A1, 5945, 52040 (In Hill 1989)
1669	Domingo Pérez Pirir (Spanish trans., San Juan Sac.)	AGCA A3.15, 2787, 40301 (in Hill 1989)
1680	Juan Pérez [Tzamol] (the younger) (Spanish trans., Patzicía)	AGCA A1, 5954, 52144
pre–1689	Juan Hernández Oxlah (Cakchiquel, Comalapa)	AGCA A1, 5960, 52246
1689	Andrés Pérez Cuat (references only, Patzicía)	AGCA A1, 5954, 52144
1708	Thomás Jocón (Cakchiquel, San Juan Sac.)	Municipal Archives, San Juan Sac. (In Hill 1989)

corpus of Cakchiquel wills at our disposal there is great variation in the texts. The shortest wills take up barely half a page (see the will at the end of this chapter and table 7.2), while the Miguel Pérez Pirir will and codicils run verso and recto in tiny print for eight pages. Apart from the most common formulas, such as the invocation of the Holy Trinity, there is considerable variation in the phrasing employed. Even among wills of approximately the same length and complexity there is still variation in terms of the precise topics addressed and their sequence. This makes it difficult to determine if all the wills might have been based on a single model such as Molina's 1565 sample testament (Molina 1984b; also see Cline's chapter in this volume). It is true that most of the longer wills at least touch upon most of the topics in the Molina sample. However, they do not do so consistently nor in the same order as in Molina. It seems likely, then, that similarities between the seventeenth-century Cakchiquel wills and Molina's sixteenth-century model may simply be due to the fact that, as wills in both the Spanish legal and Catholic religious traditions, there was simply not much possible variation in structure, phrasing, and content.

The wills begin uniformly with an invocation of the Holy Trinity, the Holy Family, and/or other saints. The first expressed concern of testators was always the care of their souls through the performance of memorial masses, and at least some money was set aside for this purpose. Wealthy individuals also made sizeable donations of land, money, and other goods to their town church and to individual *cofradías* (religious sodalities dedicated to the veneration of a saint). In the case of Miguel Pérez Pirir, these gifts (called *hornamentos*) totaled 3,360 pesos (Hill 1989: 5). Apparently, he was not unique. Thomas Gage writes that in his time (the 1630s) a Cakchiquel man of Chimaltenango left 5,000 "ducats" (pesos) to the church of that town, and a Cakchiquel man of Santiago Sacatepéquez reportedly left 6,000 pesos to his town's church (1958: 172, 210). However, the section on gifts to the church could occur at different places in different wills, again arguing against strict adherence to a model.

Similar to Molina's model, most testators indicated that they were ill and dying, but they generally did not profess their mental competence. Nor did they generally indicate their place of residence. As one would expect, the enumeration of goods and their assignment to heirs took up the bulk of all of these documents. Debts due to and owed by the testator were also noted. The Cakchiquel did not appoint executors (*albacea*, in Spanish) as was common in wills from other areas. The phrase in Molina's model rescinding any previous will is never present. Witnesses always

Table 7.2

Summary of Bequests in the Last Will and Testament of
Gaspar Uuch, Chimaltenango, 1608

Heir	Bequest
Cilia	grindstone for corn
Ana	grindstone for cacao
Both daughters	1 milpa
	1 hatchet
	1 scissors
	4 turkey hens
	4 "maa castelan" [some kind of thread?]
Diego Anís	1 mule
	land in ravine
	3 tostones
Melchior	house and lot #1
	house and lot #2
	3 tostones
"Sons"	25 nets of corn
	4 small hoes

Note: See the end of this chapter for the complete text of this
will (source: AGCA A1.20, 6074, 54894).

included at least some of the town's justices and might also include the
heads of the testator's *parcialidad* (corporate social unit) as well.

Testamentary Patterns

From the limited corpus of wills at our disposal, it is clear that bequests of
land were testators' main concern and that males were the primary beneficiaries. However, women—as aristocrats, or at least as members of
wealthy families—could inherit land and (in the case of Francisca Yeol)
even swap tracts with their brothers. Still, most land was given to male
heirs, usually as either a group of brothers or as pairs of brothers in a family corporation arrangement (Hill 1989, see below). An elder brother
might inherit and act as a guardian for his younger brothers until they
reached adulthood. Alternatively, in family corporations possessing large,

widely distributed holdings, older and younger brothers might be paired as beneficiaries in order to provide as much security of possession as uncertain individual survival would allow. If no male beneficiaries had reached adulthood, they might be taken in by a paternal uncle (and henceforth referred to as his "sons") or even a maternal uncle, with land being turned over to them as they matured.

Lands could be strictly for cultivation or include grazing, timber, and even hunting tracts. Depending on the wealth of the testator, other property could include houses, money, debts due the testator at the time of his or her death, livestock (especially oxen, mules, and horses), blacksmithing forges, tools, feathered dance costumes, and other clothing, furniture, metates and manos, and saints' images (along with the attendant obligation to celebrate the saint's day, called a *guachibal* [Hill 1986]).

Fraud and Its Consequences

Of course, among the implications of writing in general are both the possible falsification of the information contained in documents and the creation of fraudulent documents. From the fragmentary corpus at our disposal, we cannot tell how often either of these might have occurred. Nevertheless, in the small corpus of Cakchiquel wills there is one case of fraud. This case was thoroughly investigated and the perpetrators severely punished, thus providing us insights into the difficulties and dangers associated with fraudulent wills. Based on this one case, it seems there were safeguards adequate to discourage widespread fraud or at least to detect such attempts as might occasionally be made.[2]

Don Baltasar Uuch of Chimaltenango died suddenly on January 12, 1608, during an episode of epidemic disease (perhaps typhus or plague) then rampant across the Guatemala highlands. A widower and childless, he left a considerable estate with no obvious heir (see table 7.3; compare to table 7.2). Diego Anís, an orphan boy of Chimaltenango who worked as a muleteer for don Baltasar, saw his opportunity. While many of the details of this case remain obscure (as is natural with criminal conspiracy), it seems that Diego already had a relationship with the prior of the Dominican order in Guatemala, fray Rafael de Luján.[3] Upon don Baltasar's sudden demise the two sent for the town scribe, Diego López. Somehow, López was cajoled or intimidated by the prior to draw up a will, the contents of which were dictated by Anís, with himself as the sole beneficiary.[4] López even forged the signatures of the town's alcaldes. Don Baltasar's closest relative, his brother Gaspar, died shortly afterward on

February 19. With this document and no immediate competition, Anís was able to gain possession of don Baltasar's property. By 1610 this orphan muleteer had become *fiscal* of the town's church (presumably in return for donating a considerable portion of the estate to Luján and the Dominicans), a position that exempted him from tribute and labor obligations. But the conspirators had not counted on other, more distant relatives laying claim to the estate. These included don Baltasar's sister and her husband (both of whom lived in the neighboring town of Sumpango) and his father-in-law.

In 1610, claims and counterclaims (and perhaps the 1609 ordinance mentioned in note 4) finally led to an official investigation by Spanish authorities. One reason for the length of the case was that no one seemed capable of believing that an official town scribe could have written a fraudulent will. However, under interrogation by Spanish officials, the two Maya conspirators finally admitted their crime and were severely punished. Anís had to pay half the costs of the investigation, totaling some twenty-two pesos, and return all goods from don Baltasar's estate plus any profits he had derived from them, and he was banished from Chimaltenango for two years. Diego López was sentenced to one hundred lashes, was forbidden from practicing again as a scribe, and was required to pay his half of the costs. The severity of his sentence clearly indicates that, as a literate public official, he was held largely responsible for the fraud. Certainly, it could not have occurred without his complicity. With such punishments awaiting potential conspirators, fraudulent wills were almost certainly rarities. Presumably because of his position, fray Rafael was neither charged nor interrogated, and there is no record of his having been reprimanded.

The Development of Testaments

Why did testaments apparently develop among the Cakchiquel over the course of the seventeenth century? Assuming that this is not simply a question of sampling error, I think that the answer may lie in the changes in principles of land tenure and family organization. As I have discussed at length elsewhere (Hill 1992: 48–64), the seventeenth century was a period during which some traditional, preconquest landholding practices continued while Spanish principles were increasingly imposed and adopted in creative ways by the Cakchiquel. The result was considerable dynamism in land transactions and surprising latitude in the legal bases of its possession.

Table 7.3

Probate Inventory, Estate of Baltasar Uuch, 1610

Houses

Las casas de adobes cubiertas de paja con un corredor y dos aposentos a los lados. Y una cocina y otras dos casas pequeñas, cubiertas todas de paja, y la casa principal con tapanco.

Land

"tierra labrada junto al agua"

20 mecates en el llano[a]

20 mecates junto a las casas del pueblo

8 mecates en los Aguacates

7 mecates junto al pueblo

6 mecates en Pantzaramac

6 mecates cerca al pueblo

4 mecates

Goods and Livestock

4 sillas de madera con sus barandillas

4 sillas de sentar

4 banquillos

2 tapescos [beds made of saplings lashed together]

2 cajas chicas

4 azadones

2 hachas

4 piedras de moler [in other contexts, 3 metates and manos, 2 for corn and 1 for cacao]

1 casa llena de maíz

6 cargas de sal

1 carga de cacao pataste

20 mulas aparejadas

20 cabezas ganado prieto, chicas y grandes [swine]

6 gallinas

60 tostones

dance costume inventory

---

[a]It is unclear just what the *mecate* as a unit of measure refers to here. The Cakchiquel texts use the term *chicam*, based on *k'am*, usually translated as "cuerda." However, the cuerda is not a fixed unit either. Thus it is not possible to gauge the extent of the plots listed in the inventory.

Source: See note 2.

To summarize briefly, it appears that preconquest highland Maya land-holding took two main forms. Commoners in this aristocratic society appear to have enjoyed only usufruct to lands corporately controlled by their respective *chinamit*. The chinamit (later called *calpul* or *parcialidad* by the Spaniards) was the basic social unit of the late-preconquest Maya highlands. The word itself is a borrowing from the Nahuatl *chinamitl*, a term used in some parts of central Mexico as a synonym for *calpulli* (a subdivision of an *altepetl* or Nahua municipality). Indeed, the highland Maya chinamit seems to be very similar to the Mexican calpulli. It appears to have been a corporate, territorially based type of social unit. Among the highland Maya, possession of chinamit land by individual members seems to have depended very much on its use, and it may have been possible to inherit rights to the use of specific tracts (Hill 1984; Hill and Monaghan 1987). In contrast, for members of the highland Maya aristocracy, landownership by individuals or families seems to have been the pattern.

From the Spaniards' point of view, all of this changed with the conquest, by virtue of which all land technically became part of the Spanish monarch's royal patrimony and was so indicated by use of the term *tierras realengas* (royal lands). However, Crown policy was to permit indigenous peoples to continue in their use (though not ownership) of lands they had previously enjoyed. The door was also open for indigenous individuals and groups to own land via the process of *composición*, whereby land was purchased from the Crown. In highland Guatemala, this seems to have been mainly an eighteenth-century phenomenon (see below).

The Cakchiquel viewed things rather differently. First of all, they had suffered catastrophic population losses through the sixteenth century, and populations remained low through much of the seventeenth century. These losses must have resulted in the decline or disappearance of many chinamit groups and the subsequent melding together of the survivors of some groups. The Spanish policy of *congregación* (forced resettlement in towns) undoubtedly contributed to this process of amalgamation. Population loss meant that unoccupied land was relatively abundant and that individuals potentially could bring into production any tract not currently used with little fear of dispossession. Thus, prior to the eighteenth century, most Cakchiquel seem not to have seen any reason to purchase their own lands from the intrusive colonial regime. Instead, land rights could be protected more easily and economically through any of a number of written instruments that generally were accepted as valid evidence of prior possession by the *audiencia* (the governing council of colonial Guatemala) in any dispute over land.

Still, as families grew larger or smaller over time, as they grew wealthier or more impoverished, there was a constant need to redistribute land at a microlevel. Land sales appear to have been an important means for achieving such redistributions. While we do not know the exact status of land before the conquest, it was clearly commoditized very soon afterwards (for an Andean parallel, see the chapter by Ramírez in this volume), a process no doubt abetted by the introduction of true, general-purpose money in the form of Spanish coin. Yet such "sales" were technically illegal since all lands were realengas. How could buyers assure themselves that their purchases would not be forfeited at some later date? *Cédulas de compra* (bills of sale), written in indigenous languages, were part of the answer. Among the Cakchiquel these documents formed part of a formal "ownership" transfer ceremony, overseen by the justices of the town. In order to pass land on to the next generation, testaments were used. Again, it must be pointed out that these documents did not confer legal ownership from the Spanish perspective. Their chief benefit was as *títulos*—the generic term employed by the Cakchiquel and other highland Maya people for documents that could be presented in court as evidence of prior possession of land.[5]

In this way, a wealthy individual might specify in his or her testament which lands were to go to each beneficiary and present them with a cédula as proof of the transfer and "ownership" as of a specific date. Beneficiaries would then have two títulos to present if their possession of the land was ever challenged: the cédula and the testament. If, as a result of a successful defense of land in court, an individual was granted a *despacho de ámparo* (similar to a restraining order, which prevented the summary expropriation of landholdings) then his or her descendants then would have yet a third título. This pattern was, in fact, followed by Domingo Pérez Pirir in his 1669 testament (Hill 1989: 56, 58, 60, 61, 64). This document, his father's will, and the ámparo he had obtained in 1650 were all used by his descendants in their successful 1707 defense of the land against encroachment from other residents of the growing town of San Juan Sacatepéquez (97–98). Diego Xpantzay made similar, successful use of his mother's testamento in defending land in 1689 (Hill 1992: 60–61).

While protecting landholdings was a general concern, wills seem to have been especially important in perpetuating a form of organization that I have referred to elsewhere as "family corporations." These appear to have been a highland Maya response to the special conditions of the seventeenth century. Family corporations may be characterized briefly as attempts to engage in diversified, commercial agricultural production and distribution, relying almost exclusively on family members' labor. Our best-documented example, the Pirir family of San Juan Sacatepéquez, numbered over thirty members in the 1640s (Hill 1989). Such labor practices were necessary due to the drastic population losses of the sixteenth century and continued low populations (as well as periodic epidemic outbreaks) through most of the seventeenth century. This resulted in such a temporarily favorable population/land ratio that even lands lost to Spanish colonists did not evidently cause much hardship. However, the relative abundance of land meant that most Cakchiquel could work for themselves rather than for someone else. The ability to work for oneself, combined with Spanish demands on indigenous labor through *repartimiento* (a program of forced labor on Spanish farms and other enterprises), made wage laborers almost unobtainable.

In the few well-documented examples, the activities of such corporations included growing Spanish crops such as wheat and sugar cane as well as the more traditional tending of beehives (presumably now for honey as well as for candle wax). Livestock was raised, including cattle, oxen, horses, donkeys, and even mules. All these forms of livestock, except for cattle, were used as draft and/or pack animals in both the production and transport of agricultural products. As noted in the proceedings concerning the Baltasar Uuch will (see table 7.3), mules in particular were employed in trading activities that might extend from the Cakchiquel region all the way to El Salvador.

The very diversity of their activities meant that family members, while a group in the socioeconomic sense, could not necessarily be a residential group. For example, Pirir family landholdings were scattered among too many different altitudes and too widely across the rugged municipal territory of San Juan Sacatepéquez for them to have commuted daily from a single home, no matter how centrally located. Instead, the different adult male members lived on or near the lands they worked, along with their sons, grandsons, and perhaps nephews (see below).

With fully partible inheritance, this form of organization would have fragmented quickly and completely, with each heir in each generation being left with a consecutively smaller land base with fewer potential uses. Special inheritance practices, validated by wills, were a means to avoid such fragmentation as well as to ensure continued family possession and use of its lands, despite the uncertainty of individual survival. One practice was to name a specific heir as effective head of the corporation, and this need not have been the eldest brother. Don Miguel Pérez Pirir named son Domingo as head rather than eldest brother Gerónimo, evidently because Domingo had living children while Gerónimo did not. Domingo could thus ensure continuity of both the family and its holdings. Another practice—and one that Domingo himself used—was to leave specific tracts to pairs of brothers. This served at least two purposes. First, control of the land remained in the family if one brother or the other suddenly died. Second, if this did happen, the surviving children were provided for. The surviving brother would automatically adopt them (in seventeenth-century Cakchiquel kinship, a male classed his children terminologically with those of his brothers) and they retained their full rights to the combined landholdings. Even if the second brother died, there hopefully would be some male descendant old enough to run things. Such was evidently the case for both Juan de la Cruz Pirir and Domingo Ramos Jocón in the early eighteenth century.

Eighteenth-Century Developments

As noted above, at present we know of only two Cakchiquel wills from the later eighteenth century. Had the writing of wills ceased? Were the two we have exceptional? The answer to both questions is probably no, though the functions of wills and testamentary procedures apparently did undergo some significant changes.

The two wills in question were produced for Manuel Jiménez and Juana K'otuc, a husband and wife living in Sololá, in 1758 and 1762, respectively.[6] The husband's will is a document of two and a half pages written in a large hand. The wife's will is only three-quarters of a page. Both documents are concerned primarily with burial and masses (the husband having endowed a cofradía with the impressive sum of five hundred pesos on the condition that they perform a mass for his soul each year). They were preserved only because of their inclusion in the *protocolos* (file of documents that were written or reviewed in an official capacity) of a visiting Spanish *alcalde mayor* (administrative official). In this instance, the wills were presented by the town's justices, requesting that the alcalde mayor approve the terms of the wife's will. He ordered the documents to be translated by an "Indio ladino" (a native who spoke Spanish in addition to his own language; who seems not to have noticed that there were two wills, not one). Both originals and the translation were duly included in the alcalde mayor's protocolos.

The alcalde mayor noted that the documents were written "en lengua en el estilo que acostumbran los yndios [*sic*; the language {and} the style to which the Indians are accustomed]." This phrasing strongly suggests that wills were still commonly produced in the later eighteenth century. Because the wills are presented by the town's justices instead of family members or a beneficiary, it suggests that they were kept in official rather than private hands, according with later eighteenth-century Quiché practice.

The Gates collection in Tulane University's Latin American Library contains photostats of some fifty Quiché wills, all dating to the later eighteenth century (Edmonson 1964: 288–89). These eighteenth-century Quiché wills were evidently kept together as a book or file by the town authorities. In turn, these authorities conducted a formal reading of the will at the house of the deceased, in the presence of the beneficiaries. In contrast to the most elaborate seventeenth-century Cakchiquel wills, these eighteenth-century wills are much shorter, simpler statements—all that was needed to dispose of the generally scant possessions of a largely pauperized, peasantized population. Unfortunately, at this point, we do not know from which town the Quiché wills come, though they are probably from the Quezaltenango area.

Why did wills and testamentary practices change during the eighteenth century? At this point, the answer seems to be a combination of a worsening population/land ratio, a resulting pauperization of the Cakchiquel, and the emergence of towns as basic landowning units via the purchase of their *ejidos* (common lands) through composición. As a process, composición for individual Maya people was both time-consuming and ruinously expensive. First, Spanish legal counsel had to be retained in the capital (present-day Antigua Guatemala) in order to create an initial petition and see it through the maze of officialdom. Once this was received, the audiencia would commission an official to conduct an on-site inspection of the land in question (called a *vista de ojos*). Typically, an interpreter was also appointed to ensure that the Cakchiquel could communicate effectively with the Spanish official. Both of these individuals had to be paid for their time (including travel to and from the town in which the inspection occurred), as well as fed and housed while conducting the inspection. The official had also to notify neighboring individuals or towns of the inspection and give them the opportunity to object based on any claims they might have. Both the petitioner's and any other claimant's títulos then had to be exhibited. In the case of disagreements between two or more claimants, both sets of documents had to be remitted to the audiencia for evaluation of their relative merits. Due to the elaborate appeals process under colonial Spanish law, disputes could (and did) run actively for years and even decades.

The next step in the process was a survey, for which a two- or three-man Spanish crew was commissioned. These individuals also had to be paid, fed, and housed. Depending on the size of the tract, a day to a week or even more might be needed. With the boundaries established and area determined, the next task was to place some value on it. This was usually based on local opinions concerning its quality and potential uses, with good, level agricultural land being most valuable. Such land was scarce in the generally rugged Cakchiquel country, and land typically was valued between one to three pesos per *caballería* (approximately 111 acres). While land was thus relatively cheap, officials' salaries could total anywhere from about forty to several hundred pesos, astronomically expensive for all but the wealthiest Cakchiquel, who were becoming rare by the eighteenth century.

By that time, highland Maya populations generally were on the increase (Hill 1992: 27–30). While the actual numerical increases were small, they occurred against an inflexible land base from which losses to Spaniards and to cattle raising had already occurred. One result was increased pressure on landholding, reflected in more frequent and acrimonious disputes both within and between towns. Yet individuals increasingly were unable to afford the costs of litigation. The apparent solution to the problem was that the community as a whole would undertake to secure its holdings. By pooling its financial resources, an entire town might be able to afford the composición process and receive an unassailable royal title—the only true *título*—for its lands. In fact, this trend was well under way throughout the Maya highlands by the mid-eighteenth century (Hill 1992: 156). With town ownership of land and increasing populations, the tracts used by family corporations were broken up and the individual "ownership" common in the seventeenth century passed away. As it did, and as people became poorer, the need for elaborate testaments and other documents also waned. The testamentary tradition continued because individuals still possessed some property and still needed to make the ritual arrangements for their passing. However, given the generally low survival of documents in the region's town archives, we may never know how long this tradition endured.

Last Will and Testament of Gaspar Uuch, Chimaltenango, 1608
(AGCA A1.20, 6074, 54894)

chupam ru lo3olah bi Dios tatatz Dios caholatz Dios espiritu santo Santa trinitat. Yn yaua gaspar uch tahin ynaj chupam ru justicya Dios ti uaho ca tin ban nu testamento Rumal uequi ru lo3oh Dios lo chuva3 mani uetam

Ruquin timu3 nu tiohil chupam utziriçam uleu Rumal yn xpianos
3ahina3 Ru ya Dios pa nu vi — Ruquin ti uaho ti ban nu missa nu
responxas xuae u ochoch xa nim hay mani puerta chuchi. xahucam xolar
coh ui ti richinah can nu cha3 ronohel. xaqui ru lo3oh chirichin osi tte.
nu cha3 melchior. xaui huvi chi xolar coh tzan hay. xaui richin can nu
cha3 melchior. xaui hun macho. xaui ti richinah can nu cha3. Dio. Anis.
xauae chenbal uleu hun etabal chenbal uleu quichin nu mial çiliya ruquin
ana. tiqui chinah xaui tiqui chinah ri osi tte. tan qui ru lo3obeh nu cha3.
xaui 25 yalhal xaui quichin nu cahol xaui cahi qui te ac xaui quichin nu
mial. xaui cahi maa castelan xaui quichin nu mial xaui hun ca quebal tzo.
ti richinah nu mial çiliya xaui hun ca quebal uqui ya. xaui ti ri chinah nu
mial ana. xaui cahi chuti3 açatom xaui quichin nu cahol. xaui hun ycah
xaui hun taxeres xaui quichin nu mial. xauae çivan pa chu pap.xaui Dio. ti
cohe can chuvi e nu cha3. xaui coh chic hala che chuvi bah xaue que cohe
can nu cha3 chuvi. xcauae hun nima xera xaui ticais xa 3a mixa ti ban
chirichin. Rumal oh.8. chuvi xere ri hun chic ri caz. xaui ca tu ya Justiçiya
chuvi ru 3a cayi tte. Ru banom. xalis cham. ti ya ca chirichin. xere ca ri
halo nu tzih xtin yacan. xcauae xhot xel richin nu mixa uahxa3i tte. coh
richin nu mixa xaui hun tte. richin santa mariya xere ca halaui chiri mis
chayaua chiquiva chinamital. chu vach ah tzalam thomas mich xaui chu
vach ah tzalam gaspar mich xaui chu vach dio. ulom chu pam 19 3ih iq
hefrero 1608 anos

❧

In the blessed name of God the Father, God the Son, God the Holy Spirit,
[the] Holy Trinity. I, the infirm Gaspar Uuch, enter into the justice of
God. I want to make my testament because I believe in the grace of God;
tomorrow I know not if they will bury my body in consecrated ground.
Because I am a Christian the water of God has descended on my head; for
me they will celebrate my masses, my responses. Just this house, this big
house, without a front door. There is a measure of land. All his possession,
my younger brother/cousin. Just this gift of three tostones for him, my
younger brother/cousin, Melchior. Just another house lot at the head of
the town. Just for my younger brother/cousin, Melchior. Just one mule.
Just his possession, my younger brother/cousin, Diego Anís. Also one garden plot, one measure of garden, for my daughters Cilia, along with Ana,
to possess. Just to possess three tostones I give his gift to my younger
brother/cousin. Just twenty-five net-loads of corn, just for my sons. Just
four turkey hens, just for my daughters. Just four skeins of Spanish
thread[?], just for my daughters. Her possession, my daughter, Cilia. Just
one grindstone for cacao. Just her possession, my daughter, Ana. Just four

small hoes, just for my sons. Just one hatchet, just one pair of scissors, just for my daughters. Just one ravine at Chupap, just to remain with Diego and my younger brother/cousin. Just a small digging stick[?], just to remain with my younger brother/cousin. Just one big field. Just two masses are to be made with it. Because I gave eight tostones for just this one debt. Just two tostones into the hands of the Justices. It is done. . . . Give it to him. Just this, then, my word, will I leave behind. Just here for my masses, eight tostones for my masses. Just one tostón for Santa María. And whatever is left is to be given to the chinamital. In the presence of Tomás Mich, Ah Tzalam. In the presence of Gaspar Mich, Ah Tzalam. In the presence of Diego Ulom. On the 19th day of the month of February, the year 1608.

Notes

1. The research upon which this paper is based was made possible in part by a Summer Research Grant from Tulane University.

2. Information on the Uuch estate and fraudulent will is contained in a series of documents from the AGCA. These include A1.43 4902, 41917; A1.43 4836, 41598; A1.43 6074, 54893; A1.43 4838, 41611.

3. Luján had been nominated by Archbishop Gómes de Córdoba as his coadjutor in 1596, but the Crown declined to appoint him. He was elected prior of the Dominicans in Guatemala in 1601. He died during an epidemic in 1631 (Ximénez 1929–31, 2: 205–7).

4. Such direct interference in testamentary affairs was not at all unusual and was limited neither to the Dominican order nor to Guatemala. Indeed, the practice was so widespread and troublesome that the Crown issued an ordinance in 1609 in an attempted crackdown:

> Porque ordinariamente mueren los indios sin testamento, y cuando disponen de sus haciendas en memorias simples y sin solemnidad, y conviene ocurrir a los daños que proceden de introducirse los doctrineros y otras personas, recogiendo sus bienes y alajas, y disponiendo que se gasten en limosnas y sufragios. Y para que no se queden ex-heredados los hijos, padres o hermanos, y los demas que conforme a derecho deben suceder, rogamos y encargamos a los arzobispos y bispos y provinciales de religiones, que con efecto remedien los escesos que en estos casos intervinieren, haciendo las diligencias que son obligados. Y mandamos a nuestros vireyes, audiencias y gobernadores, que cerca de lo susodicho hagan guardar y guarden lo dispuesto por derecho y leyes de estos reinos de Castilla, y libren las provisiones y mandamientos necesarios. (Recopilación 1973 [1681], libro 1, título 13, ley 9)

This edict had little long-term effect and the ordinance was reissued in 1631. Still, as late as 1662, a considerable portion of Miguel Juan Queh's estate was turned over by his mother to the local friar, presumably at his instigation (Hill 1989: 12).

5. The use of the term "título" to refer to a land title is not to be confused with the use of the same term to refer to the closely related—but not identical— genre of the primordial title (see the chapter by Wood in this volume for a discussion of testaments and primordial titles in central Mexico; also see Restall 1997a).

6. I am grateful to Matthew Restall for bringing this document to my attention, for graciously making a copy of it available to me, and for allowing me to make reference to it in this paper. The wills appear in AGCA AI.20, 4551, 38560. The fact that they were included in the official document registry of a Spanish official suggests that the examination of such collections might produce additional examples.

PART 3

The Andes

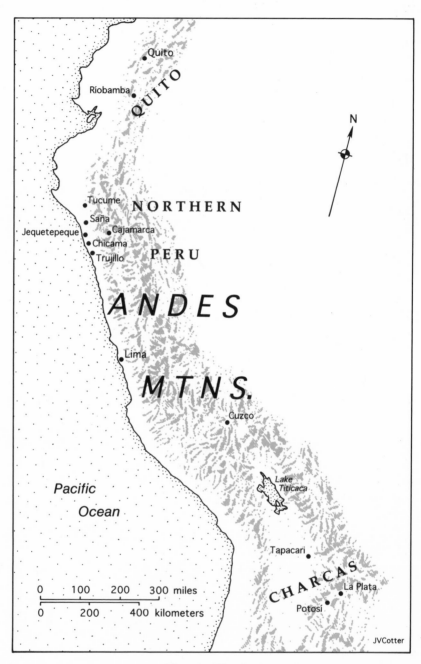

Map 4   The Andes

CHAPTER 8

A Battle of Wills:
Inventing Chiefly Legitimacy
in the Colonial North Andes

KAREN VIEIRA POWERS

Surrounded by five snow-covered volcanoes, the spectacle of Riobamba's landscape can be matched only by the political dramas that its indigenous peoples have created and performed for centuries. From ca. 1450 to the present, the region has been subject to successive invasions and colonization schemes, first by the Inca, then by the Spaniards, and more recently by Ecuadorian national agrarian capitalists. The demographic and political upheavals that ensued defy cultural survival, yet Riobamba's ethnic groups are among the largest and most cohesive in contemporary Ecuador. Known among members of the dominant culture as *vivos* (sharp, cunning), the region's native peoples have met these challenges by developing their individual and collective imaginations as well as their political and theatrical skills. It is to these strategies, created and refined on the stage of a tumultuous history, that this chapter will be devoted.

When the Spaniards arrived in Riobamba in 1534, they encountered a highly atomized political scenario. With the Spanish conquest of the Inca, the area's indigenous inhabitants were first polarized into aboriginal Puruhuayes and Inca *mitmaq* (colonists), and then further fragmented on both sides into constellations of small, independent groups. According to most scholars of the northern Andes, this political decentralization was characteristic of pre-Incaic Ecuador and resurged after the Incaic veneer was lifted.[1] The political infighting, both between and inside these small units, that must have been suppressed by Cuzco, resurfaced as Inca-appointed and -demoted leaders, both mitmaq and puruha, all vied for position in the new political configurations of yet another invasive force—the Spaniards. This left the local indigenous leadership disunited and its legitimacy in serious question throughout the early-colonial period.

The Spaniards, already familiar with larger, more politically centralized ethnic groups in the southern Andes, attempted to apply what they thought they knew of that model in the northern Andes. Their centralizing administrative reorganization, especially of the Riobamba region, was therefore akin to forcing square pegs into round holes and unleashed centuries-long hostilities both within and between indigenous communities and between the Indian republic and the Spanish regime. For this reason, the corregimiento of Riobamba, in the audiencia of Quito, is especially interesting for studying the institution of the colonial *cacicazgo* (indigenous rulership) and attendant issues of chiefly legitimacy. Perhaps nowhere in the viceroyalty of Peru was there as much need for "invention" in order to fit local realities to colonial imperatives. And perhaps nowhere in Riobamba was there a chiefly lineage more adept at "inventing" themselves than the Duchiselas of the town of Yaruquíes.

An examination of the Duchiselas' rise to local and regional power is especially timely since they have recently become the "darlings" of Ecuadorian nationalist histories—belated *indigenista* and/or integrationist attempts to construct a national identity in the present through the "imagined community" of a glorified indigenous past (Anderson 1991). The Duchisela lineage plays a crucial role in this modern construction, where it is placed at the pinnacle of a chiefly hierarchy composing a "Kingdom of Quito" that is both pre-Hispanic and pre-Incaic—that is, pre-Peruvian to "patriotic" Ecuadorians currently embroiled in the border war with their neighbors to the south (Costales 1992; Velasco 1979; Carrera Andrade 1963). What I seek here is not the truth or the lie, but rather how the historical actors, the Duchiselas in this case, were "made."[2] The main sources for this drama derive from a late-eighteenth-century suit over the cacicazgo of Yaruquíes in which seven testaments of members of the Duchisela lineage are presented as evidence.[3] The wills range from that of don Juan Duchisela (the elder) in 1605 to that of his grandson, don Manuel, in 1769, providing a century and a half of clues about the imagination and shrewd political maneuvers that went into the "making" of the Duchisela cacicazgo and the "inventing" of the family's legitimacy. This chapter is divided into two parts: the first is composed of three vignettes extracted from the Duchisela wills that narrate, in theatrical form, the lived experiences of the Duchisela family under colonial rule;

the second part is a more serious, academic analysis focusing on the strategies used by the Duchisela lineage to "invent" internal legitimacy—that is, to justify their position to their local subjects as opposed to the Spanish regime.[4]

"A Battle of Wills": A Family Drama in Three Acts

Act I: Wooing Legitimacy: A Colonial Love(?) Story

It is the year 1605 and the community of Yaruquíes has now passed through decades of unrelenting epidemic disease (Alchon 1991: 37). At the age of thirty-five, don Juan Duchisela has just lost his third wife and is himself ill enough to write a last will and testament.[5] As the cacique dictates his will to don Juan Paguay, the Indian scribe, a colorful life story unfolds that is in vivid contrast to the pervasive misery that must have enveloped the town during prolonged periods of sickness. It is a story filled with philandering, strategic liaisons, internecine conflicts, and extortion. Among the main characters are a mestiza lover, a prodigal son, a favored son, and six illegitimate children.

As a young man, don Juan has a son with his lover, doña Barbola Cabatio, whom he marries three years after the boy's birth, thereby legitimating him. This son, don Gaspar Duchisela, would so bitterly disappoint his father that don Juan would later dispossess him not only of the cacicazgo but of any share in the family's considerable assets. Disenchantment with his original family begins early on, for the whole time that he is married to doña Barbola, don Juan carries on an illicit affair with doña Isabel Carrillo. The union of this powerful Indian cacique and wealthy mestiza lover produces six illegitimate children and an awesome family fortune.[6] Upon doña Barbola's death, don Juan marries doña Isabel but refuses to legitimate her children, probably because they are mestizos and will not legally have rights to the cacicazgo.[7]

From what we know of doña Isabel Carrillo, she is a veritable worldbeater. Not only has she inherited properties from a presumably Spanish father, but according to don Juan's will, she has amassed considerable wealth in money and land from her own hard work and industry ("de su propio trabajo e industria"). She finances don Gaspar Duchisela's (don Juan's first son) stint as alcalde mayor in the city of Quito, where he is said to have racked up two thousand pesos of debt. She is also especially adept at buying up lands in ecological zones that yield highly sought after products. As we shall see shortly, the efforts of this shrewd mestiza businesswoman will play a pivotal role in the survival of the Duchisela cacicazgo and in the invention and maintenance of the family's chiefly legitimacy. It is enough to make one wonder about the texture of their love affair and subsequent marriage. Was she in love with him? Why else would a wealthy mestiza have an affair and six illegitimate children with an Indian, even if he was a cacique? Considering Spanish America's race-based social hierarchy, women like doña Isabel usually aspired to marry, and to marry "whiter," or at least "wealthier." Was he in love with her? This is a more difficult question to answer, especially in view of his attempts to maneuver her assets into his will.

By 1605, doña Isabel has died and don Juan has already married and buried his third wife. With doña Barbola Curiguarmi, don Juan has three children—don Antonio, don Joseph, and doña Faustina—this time all of them legitimate. His decision to step over his first-born son, don Gaspar Duchisela, and name the twelve-year-old don Antonio as his successor in the cacicazgo is not only a stunning rebuke to don Gaspar and his sons but is so unfathomable that his descendants would describe it as a family mystery for generations to come.[8] To add fuel to the fire, he names his illegitimate mestizo son, don Juan Carrillo, to administer the cacicazgo until don Antonio comes of age. He then proceeds to distribute the majority of his assets to his three legitimate children with doña Barbola Curiguarmi, his last wife. In the 1605 will, many of these assets, especially lands, were doña Isabel's but appear as his own, and the two-thousand-peso debt his son owed her has been forgotten.

Unlike his unfortunate spouses, don Juan bounces back from his illness and lives a long life. In 1655, at the age of ninety, we find him making amendments to his will. Apparently, during the ensuing years he is either badgered by doña Isabel's children or has suffered from a guilty conscience about the incorporation of Carrillo resources into his cacicazgo. In this codicil, he makes arrangements to pay his illegitimate children for the two-thousand-peso loss—a change of heart that will later lead to bitter fraternal strife. He also admits that doña Isabel wrote a will naming all her properties, but he "suspects" that it has been lost. He then rearranges the distribution to compensate her six children for at least those lands that belonged to her before their marriage. This still leaves considerable properties in his and his heirs' names, which will be carried on as part of the Duchisela cacicazgo. And when, in 1685, don Antonio Duchisela, his heir, finally writes his last will and testament, he succeeds in incorporating into the cacicazgo even some of the lands that were designated by his father, don Juan, as part of the Carrillo estate—this by claiming doña

Figure 8.1 Duchisela Genealogy

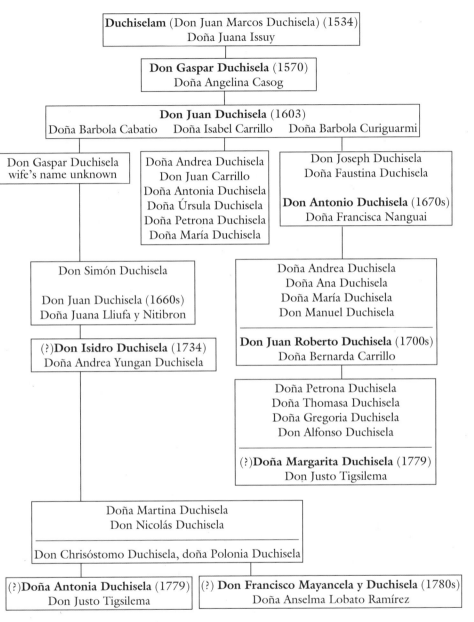

Note: Names that appear in boldface type are those of persons who were appointed as caciques of Yaruquíes; names that are preceded by a question mark are persons whose legitimacy was questioned in litigation. Names of issue do not always appear in birth order owing to design flow of family tree, and dates that appear alongside chiefly names represent the first mention as cacique of the town.

Isabel as his mother, when he is clearly the son of doña Barbola Curiguarmi, don Juan's third wife.[9] More than eighty years later, in 1769, doña Isabel's private lands still appear as part of the cacicazgo in the last will and testament of don Antonio's son, don Manuel Duchisela.[10] Evidently, a protracted love affair and subsequent marriage with a wealthy mestiza was quite a strategic liaison and translated into a political instrument of chiefly legitimacy across generations.

Act II: Sporting Legitimacy: The Story of the Prodigal Son

It is 1655 in the town of Yaruquíes, and don Juan Duchisela the elder, now on his deathbed, asks his lifelong friend, Sargento Juan de Guadalupe, to draw closer. He implores him to honor the friendship and love they have always shared by executing his will in a manner that will alleviate his conscience, and by fulfilling the special promise he made to him regarding this matter.[11] The Indian scribe, don Juan Paguay, dutifully records these words, and only these words. It is clearly a secret promise.

Although the centuries since this mysterious scene have left no trace of evidence that would help us to unlock the secret of don Juan's heart, the historian/playwright suspects that it was about don Gaspar. Both the old man's will and his codicil take on a distinctive tone whenever he refers to his firstborn son—an almost acerbic tone—a tone perhaps born of the contempt that a man of means and power might feel toward a son for whom he had wished great things, but who consistently failed him. Whatever the motive for his bitterness, it is evident that don Juan and his presumed successor had had a serious falling out.

There is something at once defensive and scolding about the way don Juan alludes to don Gaspar's less than exemplary history. He states repeatedly that he has already given don Gaspar his inheritance when he came of age, and that he owes him and his heirs nothing. Styling himself the generous though unappreciated father, he lists everything he ever gave his eldest son—two thousand pesos in silver, fancy clothes, fine furniture, houses, lands, and orchards—all of them described in the minutest detail. In the codicil, he enumerates all the debts that don Gaspar had incurred in Quito while he was the *alcalde de naturales* (administrator of indigenous people), a prestigious, but apparently costly, position. How had he spent two thousand pesos of doña Isabel's money on clothes, banquets, and other luxuries in a single year?[12] Disgusted and ashamed, he feels compelled to pay his son's debts from his own assets in order to relieve his conscience and to account to God. He then warns that there might still be some lands out there that don Gaspar is using, but they are not his; he stipulates emphatically that he did not give those lands to him as possessions, but only loaned them to him.[13] Indeed, don Gaspar Duchisela comes off as a spendthrift dandy; a talentless, irresponsible gad-about who has squandered part of the family fortune and whose wealthy mestiza stepmother naively paid the bill.

In the half century between his will and his codicil, don Juan Duchisela has had sufficient time for his resentments to accumulate toward a vengeful, draconian solution. He now names his and doña Isabel's illegitimate mestizo son, don Juan Carrillo, as one of the executors of his will, instructing him to take from his possessions the equivalent of the two thousand pesos that don Gaspar owed his mother.[14] In addition, he arranges to pay doña Isabel's children for some of their mother's properties, which turn out to be the very lands he had originally given to don Gaspar as his inheritance when he came of age. Between these two moves and the bequeathing of the cacicazgo to don Antonio, don Gaspar Duchisela becomes the family's *desheredado* (disinherited one). The prodigal son, however, would not be the one to bear the onerous burden of this vindictive maneuver; it would, instead, be shouldered by don Gaspar's issue, the truly "unfortunate" don Juan and don Simón.

In fact, the life and death of don Juan the elder would leave a grievous legacy for the whole Duchisela family. His descendants from three separate marriages would engage in bitter internecine rivalries over both the cacicazgo and its assets for nearly two hundred years. The retaliatory acts and shifting alliances of this protracted battle scene begin immediately after don Juan the elder's death, when the seventeenth-century protagonists— don Antonio Duchisela, don Juan Carrillo, and don Juan Duchisela (don Gaspar's son)—come into collision over the political and economic control of the cacicazgo. Although don Juan the elder has named don Juan Carrillo to administer the cacicazgo until don Antonio came of age, his tenure in the position does not last long (Costales and Costales 1992: 153). Apparently, the old man had not counted on the meddlesome nature of Spanish colonial officials, who had an unshakable belief in the concepts of legitimacy, primogeniture, and racial purity (Díaz Rementería 1977: 119, 132). Their sensibilities, no doubt, were offended by the specter of a mestizo bastard occupying the town's highest office. They instead appoint don Juan Duchisela, the first-born son of don Gaspar—an event that is sure to have caused don Juan the elder to roll over in his grave.

The second don Juan Duchisela manages to maintain political power until his pending death but remains without rights to the family's economic resources. In his will of 1670 he speaks bitterly of the manner in which his grandfather summarily disowned his father, don Gaspar, ultimately resulting in his and his brother's complete disinheritance. But he reserves his most acrimonious accusations for don Juan Carrillo, who he says went about collecting his mother's two thousand pesos with such a vengeance that there was now nothing left of the Duchisela fortune. He portrays don Juan Carrillo as a greedy viper who usurped his position as executor of his grandfather's will to force payment of the two thousand pesos and then some. In the process, he sold the family finery and silver at public auction, rented lands and ranches at will, and seized all manner of livestock and other prized possessions. He then distributed the proceeds among his five sisters, leaving the legitimate heirs completely "destroyed." Don Gaspar's son reiterates several times that the Carrillos have been more than well paid for his father's debt to their mother, and warns Juan and his family not to demand anything further of his heirs. Of course, this is a gross exaggeration, considering that his successors in the cacicazgo retain many of doña Isabel's lands for generations to come. His portrayal of don Juan Carrillo is undoubtedly the distorted perception of a man who, through no fault of his own, is made to live out the consequences of his father's reckless behavior and his grandfather's vindictiveness—and what better scapegoat than a "bastard half-breed." As for the cacicazgo, don Juan Duchisela, eldest son of don Gaspar, dies without issue and names the favored don Antonio as his successor in fulfillment of his grandfather's wishes.[15] And so, don Juan the elder's will, though temporarily thwarted, is carried out.

Act III: "Forging" Legitimacy: The Imposter Caciques

As the *visitador*, don Juan Josep de Villalengua travels along the flank of Chimborazo, the most dazzling of Riobamba's snow-covered volcanoes, he cannot imagine what political intrigues await him in Yaruquíes. The year is 1779 and he has been charged with conducting a royal inspection and census of the audiencia of Quito's Indian subjects (Alchon 1991: 120); it is also the year that doña Antonia Duchisela, the town's *cacica* (female ruler), has died without heirs. In the Riobamba region, as elsewhere in the audiencia, the untimely death of a ruler is always an occasion for the usual protagonists to dredge up bitter injustices of the past in multiple and protracted bids for power. Typically, descendants of the direct line, lateral lines, and female lines—as well as bastards and imposters—all vie for control of the cacicazgo, often supported by regional factions that cut across race and class. Litigation goes on interminably while the legal maneuvers, unorthodox practices, and downright deceptions used to wrest the prize are too numerous and varied to be recorded here.[16] Yaruquíes is no exception, and a more experienced visitador would have braced himself for the inevitable.

Immediately upon the inception of the royal *visita* (inspection), one contender, don Francisco Xavier Mayancela y Duchisela, steps boldly forward to request possession of the cacicazgo of Yaruquíes.[17] He claims he should rule by right of inheritance because he is a descendant of the direct line; he is, after all, the legitimate grandson of don Isidro Duchisela, who, in turn, claims to be the son of don Juan Duchisela, grandson of don Juan Duchisela the elder, and great-grandson of don Gaspar Duchisela, trunk of the chiefly line. The *visitador* (royal inspector) Villalengua, following established procedures, then publishes the request with a warning that don Francisco will be granted the cacicazgo provided that no one with more right claims it.

At this juncture, the usual cast of characters predictably appears on stage. Doña Margarita Duchisela, followed by an entourage of supporters, comes to object. Indignant, she charges that don Francisco Mayancela y Duchisela is an imposter who has usurped the Duchisela surname. Her allegation focuses on the legitimacy of don Francisco's grandfather, don Isidro Duchisela, who she says was not the legitimate son of don Juan Duchisela, but a bastard to whom don Juan's wife, doña Juana Lliufa y Nitibron, gave birth after her husband's death. According to doña Margarita, don Isidro had not one drop of Duchisela blood. Others paint a more lurid scenario: that not only was he illegitimate, but also he was the progeny of an illicit love affair that the widow, doña Juana Lliufa, had with her husband's brother, don Simón.

What then ensues is a veritable "battle of wills," as Doña Margarita, claiming to be the legitimate daughter of don Juan Roberto Duchisela, brings suit against don Francisco Mayancela for the cacicazgo of Yaruquíes. There is no end to surprises as the contenders and their respective factions present several of their ancestors' last wills and testaments to prove or disprove the legitimacy of the late don Isidro. From this bizarre parade of dead Duchiselas, the ingenuous don Francisco calls forth his grandfather to give witness to his legitimacy. There, in his will of 1758, don Isidro stated repeatedly (perhaps too repeatedly) that he was, indeed, the legitimate son of don Juan Duchisela and doña Juana Lliufa y Nitibron, as well as the grandson and great-grandson of the original caciques of the town.[18] Considering the almost sacrosanct nature of last wills and testaments, one would think that the presentation of such a legal instrument would be sufficient to truncate the proceedings. In a stunning reversal, however, doña Margarita presents two more wills, those of don Juan Duchisela (1670) and doña Juana Lliufa y Nitibron (1682), in which both declared that there had been no issue from their marriage.[19] Furthermore, doña Juana stated explicitly that after her widowhood, God had seen fit to give her a son, don Isidro Lliufa y Nitibron. Doña Margarita's lawyer interjects here that not even don Isidro's mother had had the nerve to confuse his name with that of the Duchiselas, as he had so brashly done in his own will.

This unexpected turn of events leaves both don Francisco Mayancela and his lawyer abashed and prompts the latter to desist upon examination of the latest evidence. Doña Margarita now presses to receive costs and damages. To counter this, don Francisco's lawyer, still believing in the veracity of the opposition's evidence, charges that if his client had known about these wills and thus his real genealogy, he would never have pursued the case. Giving the story yet another twist, he accuses don Justo Tigsilema of hiding these wills from don Francisco and encouraging him to claim the cacicazgo. It turns out that don Justo is the widower of doña Antonia, the cacica who has just died; he has consequently been administering the cacicazgo for years and is apparently seeking a way to maintain influence. According to don Francisco's lawyer, however, he suddenly switches sides in the suit because he has conjured up a better way to ensure control—he simply marries doña Margarita, the plaintiff—a maneuver that would once again place him in direct administration of the cacicazgo should she win the case. It was at this point that he supposedly whipped out the two wills proving don Isidro's illegitimacy. Don Justo Tigsilema, of course, vehemently denies this and claims that he never had the wills in his possession to begin with and that he and doña Margarita had to round them up and even had to pay off a pawnbroker in Riobamba for one of them.[20]

In the interim, however, don Francisco's lawyer comes up with a couple of new angles and requests that the case be reopened. First, he presents another will as evidence, that of don Juan Roberto Duchisela of 1734.[21] Don Juan Roberto, a member of the direct line, was the *cacique principal* (paramount lord) and *gobernador* (Spanish-appointed ruler) of the town by right of inheritance from his father, don Antonio Duchisela. Don Antonio was the son of don Juan Duchisela the elder, but according to don Juan Roberto there was an irregularity in his father's succession. For some "unknown" reason, don Juan Duchisela the elder had passed over his first-born son, don Gaspar Duchisela, to grant the cacicazgo to don Antonio, a younger son from his third marriage. In a stunning deathbed reversal, don Juan Roberto stated that because of the laws of primogeniture and mayorazgo, the cacicazgo really belonged to the heirs of don Gaspar, the formerly disinherited branch of the family. He thus named don Isidro Duchisela, whom he described as don Gaspar's legitimate son, as his successor.

Second, don Francisco Mayancela's lawyer also claims that after more careful examination of the wills of don Juan Duchisela and doña Juana Lliufa y Nitibron, it is evident to him that they are forgeries and that the charges of his client's illegitimacy are completely false. He maintains that the handwriting of the two wills is not that of the seventeenth century but that of the contemporary period. He also compares them to earlier documents written by the same scribe and signed by some of the same witnesses and points out that the writing and signatures are different. Evidently, don Isidro's bastard status has been trumped up by doña Margarita and her new consort through the creation of falsified legal instruments.

The plot now thickens as doña Margarita and don Justo respond by adding yet another intrigue to the scenario. They insist that don Juan Roberto made a big mistake in assuming don Isidro to be his legitimate cousin, as evidenced by the wills of don Juan Duchisela and doña Juana Lliufa. But even worse, he had allowed the parish priest to dupe him into believing this was so and to coerce him into inserting a completely erroneous, last-minute "confession" in his will. The priest, Dr. don Joseph de la Vega, they allege, had some interesting reasons of his own for this maneuver. It seems that he had arranged a marriage between don Isidro and his favorite "maid" (probably his lover or his daughter) and then engineered the couple's takeover of the cacicazgo at the expense of the town's legitimate caciques. Don Isidro, supposedly a bastard who usurped the Duchisela name and possessed not a drop of Duchisela blood, did indeed become the cacique and even succeeded in passing the cacicazgo on to his granddaughter, the recently deceased doña Antonia.

As for the variations in handwriting and inconsistent signatures of the wills, the court examines the evidence carefully and moves that while the boldness of the letters varies, the characters all exhibit more or less the same formation, and so the wills cannot be proven to be forgeries. In the end, the Spanish administration, its decision resting on the damning evidence of illegitimacy contained in the two wills, names doña Margarita to the cacicazgo. And the "bastard" line of don Isidro supposedly passes into oblivion, but not really. Because "déjà vu" is the leitmotiv of north Andean succession stories, the audience will get to revisit this drama.

A few years later, doña Margarita Duchisela, cacica of Yaruquíes, dies without heirs. Once again the usual cast of characters appears on stage, don Francisco Mayancela y Duchisela among them. Now, don Alfonso Duchisela, legitimate grandson of don Juan Roberto Duchisela, assumes doña Margarita's former role and reenacts the challenge to don Francisco's legitimacy. This time the Spanish courts rule in favor of don Francisco Mayansela, the usurper of the previous case, leaving the audience to wonder whether "legitimacy" isn't just a battle of wills.

Inventing Chiefly Legitimacy: The "Making" of the Duchisela Cacicazgo

Upon deeper analysis of the Duchisela wills and some historical contextualization, the human-interest story that bubbles easily to the surface can be fleshed out to construct a wider window on the meaning of the "cacicazgo" as a colonial institution. For embedded within the thick description of these seven legal instruments are many important clues as to how caciques were made and their legitimacy constituted over time, at least in the town of Yaruquíes. Efforts to globalize these local conclusions will be made through comparisons with studies of other cacicazgos both in the audiencia of Quito and in the Andean region as a whole.[22]

The Stage is Set

At the time of Spanish colonization, the north Andean highlands were characterized by a multiplicity of small political units, each headed by an autonomous lord. In the interests of more efficient administration, the colonial regime carried out a program of centralization in which a number of independent groups were often aggregated into a cacicazgo, with one of several leaders of equivalent rank promoted to the position of cacique principal. This policy led to protracted conflicts over chiefly legitimacy as demoted lords and their descendants carried on bitter, intergenerational struggles to regain power (Powers 1995: 134–41). The tenure of the ruling lineage, then, would depend on its ability to legitimate itself, both externally and internally; that is, to the Spanish regime and to the local community.

True to the policy described above, the Duchisela cacicazgo was a Spanish creation. From the materials that surface in the various lawsuits over legitimacy and in the Pérez and Costales studies, the story surrounding the family's rise to power can be reconstructed as follows. Before the Spanish arrival, the area around Yaruquíes was inhabited by the ayllus of Cacha, Quera, Suclla, Yaruquíes, Sidlag, Siviquíes, and others, each of which had its own autonomous cacique. During the century prior to the European invasion, the leadership of these groups varied according to the vicissitudes occasioned by serial Inca campaigns emanating from Cuzco. Both Tupac Yupanqui and Huayna Capac rewarded the Puruhuayes, who had allied with them during these battles, by appointing them caciques of their respective groups. According to Juan de Velasco, a prolific Ecuadorian historian of the eighteenth century, the Duchiselas alternately resisted and supported the Inca invaders, initially losing power and then recuperating it.

In a careful study of both Velasco's work and existing Spanish documentation, however, Aquiles Pérez concludes that the Duchiselas were never a ruling lineage before the arrival of the Europeans. When the Spaniards came on the scene in 1534, the family sided with Sebastián de Benalcázar, the expedition's Spanish leader, and was apparently awarded a *señorío* (lordship, dominion) (Pérez 1969: 343–83). By 1545, Viceroy Blasco Nuñez Vela described Duchiselam (the first leader's pre-Christian name) as lord of the whole province of Puruguay, allegedly confirming a previous appointment made by Francisco Pizarro (Pérez 1969: 349–50). Apparently, the Duchiselas had succeeded in vindicating themselves not only by consolidating the leadership of their own ayllu, Cacha, but in gaining power over other ayllus that had not previously been under their control.[23] During the *reducciones* (town relocations) of the 1570s, when six (and possibly up to fourteen) of the area's ayllus were relocated in Yaruquíes, Spanish officials appointed the first don Gaspar Duchisela as cacique principal of the town (Costales and Costales 1992: 151).[24] His heirs were then legitimated in that position, at least juridically, by successive visitas and by their own last wills and testaments. Nevertheless, as in other cacicazgos of the Riobamba region, the rancor of Yaruquíes's demoted leaders would be played out across generations, both in and out of the courts (Powers 1995: chap. 5). And like other newly created caciques principales, the Duchiselas would have to expend considerable energy justifying their position to the community—that is, inventing and reinforcing legitimacy.

The Duchiselas Create a Family Fortune

The Duchisela family used a number of strategies to achieve and maintain politico-economic control of the cacicazgo of Yaruquíes. As in other studies of Andean cacicazgos, the accumulation and consolidation of chiefly wealth and community resources played a pivotal role.[25] We will therefore start by reconstructing, through exegesis of their last wills and testaments, the ways in which the Duchiselas managed to build a sizeable family fortune while maintaining the good will of most of their subjects. Of the strategies for land accretion, clearly don Juan Duchisela the elder's marriage to doña Isabel Carrillo was the most lucrative. A detailed examination of his will and codicil of 1605 and 1655 is instructive. Of the forty-two properties recorded in this document, twenty-four belonged to don Juan's cacicazgo before his union with the wealthy heiress, while eighteen either belonged to doña Isabel or were purchased with her money during their marriage. When sizes are totaled, don Juan's holdings amounted to 33.2 *caballerías* of land—or between 374.4 and 531.2 hectares.[26] Doña Isabel was responsible for bringing an additional 28.25 caballerías to the cacicazgo—or between 315.8 and 452 hectares.[27] This means that by marrying doña Isabel, don Juan almost doubled the amount of land to which he had access. Together they controlled 61.45 caballerías, which totals between 693.15 and 983.2 hectares. This number does not include properties for which sizes were not recorded in the will, nor smaller properties measured in *brazas* (measurement of about five and a half feet), some of which were quite important, either for their high yields or because they produced specialty crops such as fruit and barley. In the audiencia of Quito, where cultivable land was at a premium, the couple's combined assets represented a spectacular fortune, even in comparison to Spanish holdings.[28]

After doña Isabel's death, don Juan the elder explored a few different avenues for moving his wife's handsome assets permanently into the cacicazgo. In his will of 1605 he listed six properties that he had already given to his eldest son, don Gaspar, when he came of age; five of the six were among doña Isabel's largest lands.[29] Presumably, these would be passed on as part of the Duchisela domain. Apparently outwitted by his and doña Isabel's illegitimate children, he amended his will in 1655 to pay her heirs for nine of the properties she had brought to the marriage, and he bequeathed to them a tenth property, eight caballerías of land in Chimborazo; the other eight lands associated with doña Isabel he recorded as his own, describing some of them as "paid for with doña Isabel's money but belonging to him," and distributing them among three of his legitimate children.[30]

His conscience getting the best of him, don Juan also confessed in his codicil about the 2,000-peso debt his eldest son owed to the late doña Isabel. He instructed his executors to use some of his assets to pay her six children for both the lands and the debt—a combined value of 4,640 pesos.[31] We know from the 1670 will of don Juan Duchisela (don Gaspar's son) that the Carrillo children were indeed paid for don Gaspar's debt, but it is unclear as to whether they ever received payment for their mother's lands.[32] Some of these properties, along with those retained by don Juan for his own estate, however, continued to appear in the Duchisela wills up to 1769 and perhaps beyond—showing a substantial incorporation of Carrillo lands into the cacicazgo.

Beyond the accumulation of land, don Juan's "strategic liaison" with doña Isabel Carrillo also aided the Duchisela family in formulating a sophisticated economic plan. First, the will of 1605 attests to a deliberate land-buying strategy rather than random acquisitions. The properties that don Juan and doña Isabel bought in the early seventeenth century were scattered throughout multiple ecological zones and included fruit orchards, sheep ranches, sugarcane fields, and high-yield cereal lands. They were purchased from Spaniards, mestizos, and Indians within a short period of time, giving the impression of a methodical scheme, and more often than not with doña Isabel's money.[33] This buying spree was apparently an attempt to put together a varied set of resources, perhaps an effort to recuperate traditional vertical control of the economy after the dislocations of the late-sixteenth-century reducciones.[34] As we shall see, however, this was not all it was.

In addition to the expenditures on land, don Juan also used doña Isabel's considerable assets to purchase various pieces of equipment necessary to set up an *obraje* (textile workshop), iron pieces to establish a mill, a breeding stallion and riding gear, and five mules with harnesses.[35] Most of these items are what would be needed to spin, weave, dye, and transport cloth. Obviously, don Juan used his second wife's money to diversify his investments and enable him to participate in the colonial textile economy. In short, he and doña Isabel employed a strategy that combined the best of both the Andean and Spanish economic systems: the reestablishment of vertical control for the maintenance of the Andean ideal of self-sufficiency, and the establishment of infrastructure necessary for participation in the new Spanish market economy.

Considering doña Isabel's mestiza background, this strategy represents a glaring example of resource transfer from Spanish to Indian hands—a type of "reverse" appropriation that puts into question the traditional historiography of linear and unidirectional land divestment. Rooted in binary analyses of conqueror and conquered, previous colonial land studies have had a tendency to totalize the phenomenon of Spanish expropriation of Indian lands.[36] At least in the town of Yarquíes, land tenure seems to have had a more variegated history.

Much of the incorporation of doña Isabel's lands took place during the tenure of don Antonio Duchisela, don Juan the elder's heir. Despite the loss of five of the cacicazgo's original properties, don Antonio kept pace with, and even superseded, his father in lands, mostly owing to the incorporation of precisely five of doña Isabel's properties.[37] In his will of 1684, he merely recorded these as if they were a part of the original cacicazgo. Evidently, however, problems must have surfaced regarding them because he wrote a new will in 1685 in which he repeatedly claimed that doña Isabel was his mother, leading the reader to believe that her lands were his maternal inheritance.[38] As mentioned previously, he was the son of don Juan the elder's third wife, doña Barbola Curiguarmi.

Most of the original Duchisela lands he still held remained constant in size, at least those that are calculable, and these, in combination with the 11 caballerías of land he "inherited" from doña Isabel, brought his assets to 35.25 caballerías, as compared with his father's original 33.2 caballerías.[39] So, without doña Isabel's lands, don Antonio's chiefly domain would have shrunk to 24.25 caballerías, a loss of 27 percent, from that of his father before his marriage to doña Isabel Carrillo.

A century and a half later, don Manuel Duchisela, don Antonio's grandson, still maintained holdings of 29.5 caballerías, most of which were the lands recorded in don Juan Duchisela the elder's last will and testament of 1605.[40] Although many of the family's traditional lands, such as Pachanlica, Llagpizan, and Amala, no longer appeared in don Manuel's will of 1769, he still managed to keep pace with his grandfather's holdings by retaining the incorporation of 7 caballerías of doña Isabel's lands and inheriting 5.25 caballerías from other sources. Don Manuel's total was down only 3.7 caballerías from that of don Juan the elder's before his lucrative marriage. Once again, without doña Isabel's lands and his other inheritances, don Manuel's assets would have been reduced to the remaining Duchisela lands, or 17.5 caballerías. In other words, only half of don Juan the elder's original lands were still intact after 164 years. Nevertheless, through the incorporation of new lands and the retention of some of doña Isabel's contributions, the cacicazgo's holdings were more than respectable for the period. At a time when many surrounding cacicazgos, not only in Riobamba but throughout the audiencia, had long since collapsed, the Duchisela family was able to stay the course.[41]

The Duchiselas Create a Political Machine

The accumulation and maintenance of wealth also translated into political capital for the Duchiselas. Although these lands and other assets appear in their last wills and testaments as seemingly private holdings that are passed down from one generation of heirs to another, there is a curious mix of European and Andean concepts embedded in the language used to describe them.⁴² The testators' use of verbs such as *tengo* (I have), *poseyo* (I possess), *compré* (I bought), *vendí* (I sold), *empeñé* (I pawned), and *mando a mis herederos* (I bequeath to my heirs) all attest to an understanding, however culturally modified, of the Western idea of individual proprietorship.⁴³ Also woven into these Spanish-style legal instruments, however, are substantial vestiges of the Andean principles of collective ownership, reciprocity, and redistribution. Regarding lands, especially large tracts, the phrase "mando a mis herederos" often appears linked to the phrase "partibles con mis deudos" (to be shared with my kin/subjects).⁴⁴ Since there is rarely any mention of community lands in these wills, it is my opinion that what we see here is a hybrid form of communal land masquerading as individual private property, or at least being described in the language of European land tenure.⁴⁵

The continued value placed on reciprocity and redistribution is evident not only in the dominant place of the community in the chiefly lands recorded in the wills, but also in the extraordinary lengths to which the Duchiselas went to take care of their subjects. If we examine don Antonio's will of 1685, which is the most explicit of all seven with regard to "shared lands," we discover that twenty-eight of the thirty-five caballerías he listed—the overwhelming majority—were shared with the community. This might not seem unusual if they were lands inherited from the original caciques of the town (lands assigned to the community during the reducciones of the 1570s), but more than half (fifteen caballerías) were deliberately purchased in the early seventeenth century by don Juan. Apparently, his and doña Isabel's land-buying scheme was a strategy not just for familial aggrandizement but also for community survival. Once again, we see the meshing of two economic systems—those of European and Andean land tenure—to achieve the greatest possible benefit.

This hybrid tenure arrangement has many advantages. The most obvious, and one that has been discussed in other studies, is that privatization could have been a chiefly strategy to protect subsistence lands from confiscation by the Spanish regime.⁴⁶ Unlike communal property, private property simply was not subject to the wholesale public auctions of "surplus" land that took place throughout the seventeenth century. As the Crown's financial crisis intensified, several campaigns of confiscation and regularization occurred throughout the north Andean countryside, especially in the 1640s and 1690s, leaving many indigenous communities almost completely divested (Powers 1995: 131). During these agrarian onslaughts, lands held under European, as opposed to Andean, precepts—that is, private lands purchased with money and titled as such—were usually respected. This could be one reason why the Duchiselas were so careful to record in their wills which lands had been purchased, from whom, and for how much money.

A less obvious reason for purchasing private land that would be communally shared was the political control that such an arrangement bestowed upon the Duchiselas.[47] Because privately held lands were shared with the community but not legally owned by the community, the Duchiselas, now supported in their possession of the land by an externally imposed Spanish judicial system, could exercise considerably more power over their constituency than under the pre-Hispanic contract between rulers and ruled. In other words, the overlay of European individual property ownership onto an Andean communal land/labor structure altered the principles of reciprocity and redistribution in ways that would favor the cacique's position vis-à-vis the community.

Probably the most important development of the trend toward privatization, however, was that the Duchisela family was able to turn both the Spanish land-tenure and judicial systems to one supreme advantage. Its culturally modified use of Western private property rights, bolstered by Spanish legal instruments such as titles and last wills and testaments, gave the family a kind of power within the community that had an immutable quality, especially with regard to the intrusions of the Spanish regime. Because the lands were privately held by a designated heir or heirs and bequeathed from one generation to another, the chiefly lineage was able to monopolize economic (and hence political) power, no matter whom the Spanish regime appointed to be cacique and gobernador of the town.[48] Even when the colonial administration selected an alternate leader, such as don Isidro Lliufa y Nitibron or don Francisco Mayancela, thus splitting the community's politico-economic leadership, the Duchiselas' control of lands endowed them with a permanence of power that was difficult to rival. Because the use of Spanish inheritance practices ensured that the economic resources of the cacicazgo would remain with the chiefly lineage, the community's subsistence was left in the hands of the Duchiselas, giving them an internal legitimacy with which the Spanish bureaucracy could not tinker.[49] What we have here is an ingenious manipulation of Western concepts and legal tools against a Western colonial regime.

Although the family's control of the community's resources gave them de facto power no matter who was at the official helm, most of the time they also managed to exercise raw political control over the town. By manipulating political appointments in the ayllus under their rule and arranging strategic marriages with both the leading families of the town's ayllus and with chiefly families of other towns, the Duchiselas were able to compose a vast network of alliances that served to secure both their continued leadership of Yaruquíes and their central position in regional politics.

Analysis of both the last wills and testaments and lawsuits over the family's legitimacy reveals that the Duchiselas succeeded, through corrupt practices, in orchestrating the town's political organization from early on. In his codicil of 1655, don Juan Duchisela the elder intruded directly on the leadership of the Cacha ayllu, strongly recommending that its hereditary leader not be permitted to exercise office. In a scathing attack on the competence of don Fabián Puncho, he stated that although legitimate heir to the *principalazgo* (rulership of an ayllu), don Fabian was an unruly, runaway Indian ("un indio cimarrón y fugitivo") who had no talent or ability whatsoever to assume the responsibilities of the position. He insisted that the arrangement made by the visitador, don Antonio de Arteaga, in 1654 should remain in place; that is, that don Juan Tenelema and don Lorenzo Duchisela—no doubt his partisans—should continue to administer the ayllu of Cacha.[50] In addition, he claimed that although don Esteban Lobato was not the "legitimate" leader of the Quera ayllu, he had been administering it for many years and should continue to do so unless the courts decided otherwise. The Lobatos, a powerful mestizo family, were related to the Duchiselas through marriage.[51]

Nearly a century later, we find don Juan Roberto Duchisela, don Juan's grandson, being accused of the same kind of nepotism insinuated above. In a suit of 1754, don Juan Chagpalbay, contender for control of the Cacha ayllu, claimed that a few generations earlier, don Juan Roberto had forcibly ("con mano poderosa") removed his father, don Basilio Chagpalbay, from office and had awarded the position to don Alfonso Daqui—the descendants of whom had continued to administer the ayllu. Chagpalbay explained that don Alfonso was don Juan Roberto's brother-in-law, being as he was married to doña María Duchisela, don Juan Roberto's sister, and that the demotion was part of a move to consolidate all the town's power inside the Duchisela family (ANQ Cacicazgos 32, 52, 1754: 2v, 105v). Whether this is true remains to be seen, but what is clear is that there was indeed a perception abroad in the town that the Duchiselas were unfairly monopolizing power. This can be ascertained from a related suit in which several of the principales of Yaruquíes attempted to have the embattled don Juan Roberto removed from the office of gobernador (ANQ Cacicazgos 34, 59, 1773: 40).

A related strategy for the consolidation of power, the marriage alliance, was one that the Duchiselas used masterfully, perhaps better than any other chiefly lineage of the audiencia. Although the formation of political conglomerates through marriage is commonly described for the Andean cacicazgos of the eighteenth century, the Duchiselas seized upon this strategy almost at the inception of Spanish rule.[52] Nearly every member of the chiefly line married outside his or her ayllu—with alliances being formed in a concentric circle whose circumference radiated out over time to cover an increasingly larger political surface. Inter-ayllu marriages between the Duchiselas and other elites of Yaruquíes eventually ended in the genealogical convergence of all the town's ayllus.[53] As the seventeenth century wore on, members of the chiefly line increasingly married into the chiefly lines of other towns in the region of Riobamba, and as the eighteenth century approached, the strategy was extended to form alliances with cacicazgos in distant areas of the audiencia. Throughout the entire colonial period, this formation was punctuated by interracial marriages with important Spanish/mestizo families of Riobamba—a strategy that was sure not only to accrue new resources to the Duchisela cacicazgo, but also to add clout to the family's already pivotal position within the regional power structure.

Examples of the Duchisela penchant for marriage alliances are abundant in both their last wills and testaments and in secondary sources on the lineage. Of don Juan the elder's three marriages, two were strategically exogamous. The origins of his first wife remain unknown, but his second, doña Isabel Carrillo, was most certainly from a local Spanish/mestizo family of means. And his third wife, doña Barbola Curiguarmi, judging by the partial anthroponym "Curi," was most likely from a chiefly lineage of nearby Macaxí or Licán (Costales and Costales 1992: 125–26). In addition, don Juan's daughter, doña Petrona, married into the ruling family of Licto, and two of his grandsons were Llangarimas, an important lineage of Calpi.[54] As the analysis proceeds chronologically into the seventeenth century, marriage patterns begin to cut across a wider swath of the Riobamba region. Don Antonio Duchisela, don Juan's heir, married doña Francisca Nanguai, whose parents were caciques of Licto and Punín, thereby linking three of the area's major cacicazgos.[55] The second don Juan Duchisela, don Juan's grandson, contracted marriage with doña Juana Lliufa y Nitibron, who was cacica of the Niti ayllu, also in the town of Calpi.[56]

In the eighteenth century, the network continued to both deepen and expand as don Antonio's son, don Juan Roberto Duchisela, backtracked to connect once again with the famous Carrillo family by successively marrying two of doña Isabel's female descendants.[57] His son, don Manuel, then married doña Antonia Lopes of San Andrés, another important native town in the region, and after her death he took yet another Carrillo, doña María, as his second wife. His son-in-law, don Ventura Tumay Guaraca, was also the cacique principal and gobernador of the town of Licán.[58] By the time doña Margarita Duchisela of Yaruquíes married don Justo Tigsilema of Calpi in the late eighteenth century, the marriage-alliance strategy had resulted in extensive consanguineal integration of the cacicazgos of Calpi, Licto, Punín, Licán, San Andrés, and Yaruquíes, with forays into those of Guano and Asancoto.[59]

As the eighteenth century progressed, the Duchiselas extended their marital tentacles to the cacicazgos of other regions such as Ambato and Latacunga, and even to the far reaches of the audiencia in Carchi.[60] Other scholars have posited that these extra-regional marriage alliances are evidence of a pan-audiencia chiefly hierarchy with the Duchiselas at the pinnacle—a type of colonial kingdom that reflected the Duchisela lineage's supremacy in a pre-Hispanic "Kingdom of Quito."[61] The existence, however, of concurrent colonial documentation pointing to constant local conflict over Duchisela legitimacy leads me to more measured conclusions.[62] The colonial marriage alliances, when carried out regionally, were an important strategy for overcoming this conflict through the creation of kinship bonds and for the consolidation of local and regional power—a strategy that was undoubtedly a kingpin in the "invention" of internal legitimacy. The extension of this strategy to other areas of the audiencia in the eighteenth century may have widened the Duchiselas' political influence and resource base, but considering the indigenous elites' disparate responses to the eighteenth-century rebellions, it is unlikely that the family dominated an organized chiefly hierarchy during the colonial period.[63]

Conclusion

In the audiencia of Quito, the cacicazgo was, for the most part, a colonial invention, and, as such, its holders were left with the awesome responsibility of "inventing" their legitimacy. In their scramble to integrate themselves into the new hegemonic formations of the Spanish colonial regime, the Duchiselas used a number of imaginative strategies to "make" their cacicazgo and to legitimate their leadership both locally and regionally. Most of their efforts were based simultaneously on coercion and consensus, leading to odd strategic juxtapositions such as interracial love affairs with extortion; primogeniture/*mayorazgo* (entailed estate) with disheritance of a prodigal first son; private landownership with communal land use; and brute political force with integrative marriage alliances. Many of these seemingly improbable juxtapositions were the result of combining the best of Andean and Spanish institutions and led to highly effective hybrid forms, especially in the areas of land tenure, resource management, economic success, and political hegemony.

The making of the Duchisela cacicazgo and the invention of the family's legitimacy were ongoing processes that were continually contested, not only by outsiders, but also by members of the lateral, female, and bastard lines of the lineage. In the highly fragmented and contentious political arena that was Riobamba, the outcomes of these power grabs were often the literal and figurative result of a "battle of wills." It is the author's hope that through the exegesis of seven indigenous testaments, the interior meaning of this "battle of wills" is brought to light, both at the experiential level of the historical actors and at the analytical level of the historian.

Last Will and Testament of Don Juan Duchisela, Cacique Principal and Native Lord of the Town of Yaruquíes, 1605
(ANQ Cacicazgos 38, 75, 1788: 8–21; ANQ Cacicazgos 32, 52, 1754: 43v–69v)[64]

. . . sepan los que vieren este mi testamento y última voluntad como yo don Juan Duchisela casique prinsipal y señor natural de este mi pueblo de la Limpia Concepción de Yaruquíes, hijo lexítimo de don Gaspar Duchisela y de doña Angelina Casug y nieto así mismo lexítimo de don Juan Duchisela y de doña Juana señores naturales de este dicho pueblo, estando enfermo pero en mi juicio natural . . . ordeno y dispongo el dicho testamento en la forma y manera siguiente . . .

Yttem declaro que fui casado según orden de la Santa Madre Yglesia con Doña Barbola Cabatio en quien tube por mi hijo lexítimo a don Gaspar Duchisela al qual lexitimé por matrimonio tres años despues de nasido y en teniendo hedad sufisiente para tomar estado le dí y entregué toda la herensia que de mi parte le pertenesía y por parte de su madre no tubo ninguna herensia, a él ni a sus herederos les debo cosa alguna.

Yttem declaro que por muerte de la dicha doña Barbola casé segunda bes con doña Ysabel Carrillo en la qual no tube hijo alguno lexítimo y a los que tube en la susodicha durante el primer matrimonio que son a doña Andrea Duchisela, don Juan Duchisela, doña Úrsula Duchisela, doña Petrona Duchisela, y doña María Duchisela. Les he dado para tomar estado lo que buenamente he podido, sin quedar a deberle cosa alguna de justisia, ni de grasia.

Yttem declaro que por muerte de la dicha doña Ysabel Carrillo casé tersera bes segun orden de Nuestra Santa Madre Yglesia con doña Barbola Curiguarmi ia difunta en la qual tube a don Antonio Duchisela de hedad de dose años y a don Joseph de dies años y a doña Faustina Duchisela de nuebe. . . .

Declaro por mi subsesor lexítimo sin perjuisio de mejor derecho en el casicasgo y señorío natural de este dicho pueblo a mi hijo don Antonio Duchisela por que le pertenese de derecho, y en el entretanto que tenga hedad bastante para servir el dicho señorío, quiero, y es mi voluntad que tenga, posea, y administre, mi hijo don Juan Carrillo Duchisela.

Yttem declaro que el aillo de Cacha pertenese y toca de derecho a don Favián Poncho hermano lexítimo de don Gabriel Poncho que por ser suyo de derecho le administró mientras vivió pero por ser el dicho don Favián yndio simarrón y fujitivo que nunca ha querido asistir en el pueblo, y prinsipalmente por ser yncapas y de ningun talento, para la administrasión del dicho aillo jusgo conbenir al servisio de ambas Magestades, Divina, y Humana que administre y gobierne la dicha Parsialidad de Cacha don Juan Thenelema que al presente la está administrando a medias con don Lorenzo Duchisela. . . .

Yttem declaro que dí y entregué a don Gaspar Duchisela mi hijo lexítimo durante su vida, y en la ocasión que tomó estado cantidad de más de dos mil pesos en preseas de plata, vestidos, cama, y aderesos de espadas y otros vienes muebles, y raises, como son, una quadra entera en la trasa deste pueblo, y en ella una casa grande enmaderada con madera gruesa con puertas y ventanas y mucha clabasón de hierros, y otro quarto de casa de dies brasas de largo poco más, o menos, y una huerta de arboles frutales, como son membrillos, durasnos, y mansanas, peras, tunas y algunas drides, y granadillas, todo lo qual con otro quarto demás de ocho brasas de largo, y muchas alajas y aderentes de casa, como son sillas, bufetes, otra chacra en Baiusi tiene sinco o seis quadras poco más, o menos que compró la doña Ysavel Carrillo con veinte y sinco pesos, linde con las tierras de Fransisco Sisalema barrero y con otras tierras de yndios de Penipe.

Otras tierras o chacra llamada Casintu que es de quatro quadras poco más, o menos, linde con tierras Santiago Ynsillungu, por un lado con tierras de Gonsalo Vijai.

Otra chacra llamada Chibunga que coje el río hasta el mojón de Juan Urcun que le costó sien pesos de una mujer de Puni llamada doña Luisa de tal que es de seis o siete quadras poco más o menos, linde con tierras del dicho Juan Urcun.

Más otra chacra en Ventus abajo de Chibunga, coje desde el río hasta donde tenía yo una casa y está amojonada con unos cabuyos, tiene quatro quadras, linde con tierras de don Fransisco Bedon, que esta en posesion don Juan Carrillo Duchisela.

Otra chacra en términos del pueblo de Ylapo que son de una caballería, linde con las tierras de los indios de Ylapo.

Otras tierras llamada Chipsa que es junto al río grande abajo de la puente de Pungala, que es de quatro quadras, un pabellón balor de treinta pesos, más dies y siete tornos con sus seguiñuelas de hierro, dos pares de cardas=más unos hierros de armar molino=más una silla brida con unos estribos de hierro y guarniciones=más ûn sillón con sus guarniciones==todo lo qual declaro por verdad notoria.

Es hecho en este pueblo de Yaruquíes en ocho de marso de mil y sei-scientos y sinco años siendo testigos don Juan Thenelema alcalde ordinario de este dicho pueblo, y Fransisco Rodrigues maestro del obraje, Diego Ortis de Taguada vesino de este pueblo, don Fransisco Ramos, don Miguel Garsia Lema, Balthasar Paguai, don Phelipe Yungan=Arruego: Fransisco Rodrigues=ante mí: don Juan Paguay, escrivano nombrado de este pueblo.

↬

. . . let all who look upon my last will and testament know that I, don Juan Duchisela, cacique principal and native lord of the town of the Immaculate Conception of Yaruquíes, legitimate son of don Gaspar Duchisela and doña Angelina Casug, and legitimate grandson of don Juan Duchisela and doña Juana, native lords of this town, being ill but of sound mind arrange my last will and testament in the following manner. . . .

. . . I declare that I was married according to the precepts of the Holy Mother Church to doña Barbola Cabatio with whom I had a legitimate son, don Gaspar Duchisela, and whom I legitimated through marriage three years after his birth. And when he came of age I gave and delivered to him all the inheritance that belonged to him. . . . I owe him and his heirs nothing by law or otherwise.

. . . I declare that upon the death of doña Barbola I married for a sec-ond time with doña Ysabel Carrillo with whom I had no legitimate chil-dren, and to those children I had with her during my first marriage—doña Andrea Duchisela, don Juan Carrillo Duchisela, doña Damiana Duchisela, doña Antonia Duchisela, doña Ursula Duchisela, doña Petrona Duchisela, and doña Maria Duchisela—I have given what I could and owe them nothing.

. . . I declare that upon the death of doña Ysabel Carrillo I married for a third time with doña Barbola Curiguarmi who is deceased, and with whom I had don Antonio Duchisela, twelve years old, don Joseph, ten years old, and doña Faustina, nine years old.

. . . I declare my son don Antonio Duchisela as my legitimate successor to the chiefdom and lordship of this town because he is the rightful heir, and in the interim until he comes of age, it is my will that my son, don Juan Carrillo Duchisela hold, possess, and administer the chiefdom.

. . . I declare that the Cacha ayllu belongs by rightful inheritance to don Favián Poncho, the legitimate brother of don Gabriel Poncho, who administered the ayllu during his lifetime, but because don Favián is a runaway, fugitive Indian who has never wanted to reside in the town and who is incompetent and talentless, I judge that it is more fitting that don Juan Thenelema, who is at present administering the ayllu jointly with don Lorenzo Duchisela, should continue to do so.

. . . I declare that I gave and delivered to don Gaspar Duchisela, my legitimate son, during his life and on the occasion of his marriage: more than 2,000 pesos in silver ornaments, clothes, a bed, trappings and swords, and other furniture and properties such as an entire block in this town, with a large house constructed of thick wood with doors and windows and many sets of iron nails and a room in another house approximately 360 square feet, a fruit orchard with quince trees, apple trees, peach trees, pear trees, fig trees, . . . and granadillas, along with another room of approximately 288 square feet, and many household ornaments and other finery, such as chairs, buffets, a farm in Baiusi of approximately five or six hectares, which doña Ysabel Carrillo bought for twenty-five pesos and which borders on one side with the lands of Francisco Sisalema the potter, and on the other with the lands of the Indians of Penipe.

Another farm of approximately four hectares called Casintu which borders on one side with the lands of Santiago Ynsillungu and on the other with the lands of Gonsalo Vijai.

Another farm of approximately six or seven hectares called Chibunga which follows the river up to Juan Urcun's boundary marker. It was bought from doña Luisa, a woman from Puni, for one hundred pesos. It is approximately six or seven hectares and borders on the lands of Juan Urcun.

Plus another farm in Ventus below Chibunga which follows the river to a place were I used to have a house, and it is marked with agave plants. It is four hectares and borders on the lands of don Francisco Bedon. It is in don Juan Carrillo Duchisela's possession.

Another farm in the district of the town Ylapo which is sixteen hectares and borders on the lands of the Indians of Ylapo.

Four hectares of land called Chipsa which are next to the large river below the Pungala bridge, a canopy worth thirty pesos, sixteen spinning wheels . . . , two pair of cards (machines for carding wool)=plus iron pieces for building a mill=plus a saddle and bridle with iron stirrups and a harness=plus a side saddle with harness=all of which I declare to be true and publicly known.

Made in the town of Yaruquíes on March 8, 1605, witnessed by don Juan Thenelema, magistrate of the town, Francisco Rodrígues, administrator of the textile mill, Diego Ortis de Taguada, citizen of the town, don Francisco Ramos, don Miguel Garsia Lema, Balthasar Paguai, don Phelipe Yungan=I now fold it: Francisco Rodrígues=before me: don Juan Paguay, official scribe of the town.

Notes

1. See, among others, Moreno Yánez 1983; Salomon 1986; Oberem 1993; and Burgos Guevara 1975.

2. The methodological orientation of this work is derived from suggestions put forth by Jean and John Comaroff (1992).

3. ANQ Cacicazgos 38, 75, 1788. The wills and their dates are those of don Juan Duchisela the elder (1605 and 1655), don Juan Duchisela (1670), doña Juana Lliufa y Nitibron (1682), don Antonio Duchisela (1685), don Juan Roberto Duchisela (1734), don Isidro Duchisela (1758), and don Manuel Duchisela (1769). North Andean lawsuits over cacicazgos and landownership often include either original indigenous testaments or copies of them. Eighteenth-century litigation is especially rich for its inclusion of sixteenth-, seventeenth-, and eighteenth-century indigenous testaments. Frequently, original sixteenth- and seventeenth-century testaments are found inserted into eighteenth-century documentation, rather than copies, owing to continual paper shortages in the audiencia of Quito. In the Archivo Nacional de Quito, indigenous testaments are also found in the Cacicazgos, Indígenas, and Notariales sections.

4. For treatment of the ways in which caciques established external legitimacy—that is, with the Spanish regime—see Powers 1991.

5. All subsequent data for Act 1 are culled from two eighteenth-century copies of the following document unless otherwise specified: "Testamento de don Juan Duchisela, 1605 y su codicilio, 1655," presented as evidence in ANQ Cacicazgos 38, 75, 1788: 8–21; and ANQ Cacicazgos 32, 52, 1754: 43v–69v. The combined study of both copies was necessary for a complete paleographic transcription and to determine authenticity.

6. Both Pérez (1969) and Costales and Costales (1992) have studied the Duchisela family and have pondered over whether doña Isabel Carrillo was a

mestiza or simply adopted a Spanish surname. While she is never actually described in the documentation as a mestiza, there is strong evidence that she was not an indigenous woman. Her name never appears with the suffix *india* or *natural*, nor is she ever associated with an ayllu. Her seemingly independent wealth and the fact that don Juan was not interested in legitimating her children are also indicators of non-Indian status. Lastly, the empirical data suggest that interracial marriages were quite common among the indigenous elite in colonial Riobamba as well as in other parts of the audiencia of Quito. Also, I am using fictional license when I describe doña Barbola as don Juan's lover whom he marries three years later, and when I describe doña Isabel as don Juan's mestiza mistress. Since both premarital sex and elite male polygyny were the norm in the pre-Hispanic Andes, they may have continued residually into the early-colonial period.

7. According to a law of 1576, a mestizo son could not inherit a cacicazgo. In the eighteenth century, as mestizaje proceeded unabated, mestizo caciques began to appear with regularity, in spite of the law (ANQ Cacicazgos 26, 24, 1768: 179). See also Díaz Rementería 1977: 132.

8. For example, when don Juan's grandson, don Juan Roberto Duchisela, describes this succession in his own will of 1734, he uses the words "for some unknown reason" ("Testamento de don Juan Roberto Duchisela, 1734," presented as evidence in ANQ Cacicazgos 38, 75, 1788: 53).

9. "Testamento de don Antonio Duchisela, 1685," presented as evidence in ANQ Cacicazgos 38, 75, 1788: 131v–39v; and in ANQ Cacicazgos 32, 52, 1754: 37–43. Once again, both copies were examined together.

10. "Testamento de don Manuel Duchisela, 1769," presented as evidence in ANQ Cacicazgos 38, 75, 1788: 127–30.

11. "Codicilio del testamento de don Juan Duchisela, 1655," presented as evidence in ANQ Cacicazgos 38, 75, 1788: 20v.

12. Ibid.: 16v–18v.

13. Ibid.: 18–19v.

14. Ibid.: 15, 18v.

15. "Testamento de don Juan Duchisela, 1670," presented as evidence in ANQ Cacicazgos 38, 75, 1788: 60–61v.

16. For a more elaborate treatment of this theme, see Powers 1995: chap. 5.

17. All subsequent data for Act 3 are culled from the eighteenth-century suit between don Francisco Mayancela and doña Margarita Duchisela unless otherwise qualified (ANQ Cacicazgos 8, 75, 1788).

18. "Testamento de don Isidro Duchisela, 1758," presented as evidence in ANQ Cacicazgos 8, 75, 1788: 5–6v.

19. "Testamento de don Juan Duchisela, 1670" and "Testamento de doña Juana Lliufa y Nitibron, 1682," presented as evidence in ANQ Cacicazgos 8, 75, 1788: 60–61v and 37–38.

20. Testaments were valuable documents in the colonial Andes that were sometimes used as collateral for loans during critical periods.

21. "Testamento de don Juan Roberto Duchisela, 1734," presented as evidence in ANQ Cacicazgos 8, 75, 1788: 41–54.

22. The methodology used here is based on deep analysis of a discrete body of documentation fleshed out by published primary and secondary sources. This

method owes much to the Subaltern Studies Group and especially to Guha (1987: 135–65).

23. This is also the story told by don Juan Chagpalbay in his suit against the Duchiselas in 1754 (ANQ Cacicazgos 32, 52, 1754: 99–103).

24. This don Gaspar was don Juan Duchisela the elder's father, not his wayward son.

25. See Choque Canqui 1993; Oberem 1993; Pease 1992; Powers 1991; Ramón 1987; and Salomon 1975.

26. According to Christiana Borchart de Moreno's calculations (1989: 150), 16 cuadras were equivalent to a caballería, and one caballería equaled between 11.28 and 16 hectares. The reason for the range is because the cuadra was measured by the size of the town square, including its streets, and in the audiencia of Quito the extension of the "plaza mayor" often varied.

27. Lands belonging to don Juan Duchisela before his marriage to doña Isabel are Elen (no size given), Pugtus (6 cuadras), Sillpata (2 caballerías), Guacona (5 cabs.), Aguagllanchi (3 cabs.), Pachanlica (5 cabs.), Gataso (4 cabs.), Pollongo (6 cabs.), Guazazu (4 cuadras), Llagpizan (1.5 cabs.), Sinin Caguan (0.5 cuadra), Chibunga Pudcasacucho (200 brazas by 30), Pul (no size given), Tap Tap Caguan (2.5 cuadras), Marcaguan (2.5 cuadras), Callicacha (0.5 cuadra), Jutun (1.5 cuadras), Silmit (300 brazas by 200), Changañag (2 cuadras), Chapancucho (4 cuadras), Yuntas (300 brazas by 200), Ventus (4 cuadras), Pifan (16 cuadras), Amala (4 cabs.). Lands that either belonged to doña Isabel Carrillo or were purchased with her money are Guazaite (3 cabs.), Puela (1 cab.), Bayusi (6 cuadras), Casinto (4 cuadras), Chibunga (7 cuadras), Ylapo (1 cab.), Cago (2 cuadras), Cuntus (8 cuadras), Chimsa (4 cuadras), Pisiquis (6 cabs.), Chaso (12 cuadras), Sillsi (300 brazas by 200), Sucusquid (2 cuadras), Chimbopata (no size given), lands in Chimborazo (8 cabs.), Cajabamba (1 cuadra), Angañag (4 cabs.), Gualayqui (2 cabs.), Tunsi (6 cuadras).

28. In the 1690s, a period of more extensive land monopolization, don Antonio de Ron conducted a visita of the audiencia's lands and found the largest lands in Quito to be about 100 caballerías each. According to Borchart de Moreno, landholdings as large as these were less common at the beginning of the seventeenth century (1989: 164–65).

29. "Testamento de don Juan Duchisela, 1605 y 1655," presented as evidence in ANQ Cacicazgos 38, 75, 1788: 16v–17.

30. Ibid.: 17v–20.

31. Ibid.: 17v–18v. His pledge to pay a debt of 4,640 pesos, an enormous amount of money at the time, is an important indicator of the size of the family fortune in the mid-seventeenth century.

32. "Testamento de don Juan Duchisela, 1670," presented as evidence in ANQ Cacicazgos 38, 75, 1788: 60–61v.

33. According to both the wills of don Juan the elder (1605 and 1655) and don Antonio (1685), lands such as Pisiquis (sheep ranching), Cuntus (fruit orchards), Sillsi (high-yield maize), and Guazaite (potatoes and barley), among others, were all bought with doña Isabel's money during her marriage to don Juan. That they were bought quickly can be deduced from a review of don Juan's marriage history. Since he was already married to his third wife by the time he was

twenty-three years old, this does not leave time for a long marriage to doña Isabel, his second wife (ANQ Cacicazgos 8, 75 and 32, 52).

34. More than half the lands that appear in don Juan's will of 1605 were purchased as opposed to inherited—that is, at least 31 caballerías of 61.45 are explicitly described as purchased during don Juan's lifetime, and most of them during his marriage to doña Isabel. Many of the lands listed as belonging to doña Isabel (as opposed to purchased with her money) were probably also purchased but were not described as such.

35. "Testamento de don Juan Duchisela, 1605," presented as evidence in ANQ Cacicazgos 2, 52, 1754: 48.

36. Examples are Chevalier 1963; Keith 1976; Ramírez 1986; Spalding 1984; and Larson 1988. Certainly, there are studies that underscore the retention of indigenous lands, such as McLeod 1973 and Taylor 1972, but none, yet published, that suggest a reverse appropriation. Susan Ramírez, however, has also found cases of reverse appropriation in her current research.

37. The lands that were evidently lost are Gataso (4 cabs.), Sinin Caguan (0.5 cuadra), Amala (4 cabs.), Yuntas (300 brazas), and Ventus (4 cuadras). They total 8.5 caballerías or between 95.8 and 136 hectares. Those he retained of doña Isabel's lands are Pisiquis (4 cabs. [6 cabs. in don Juan's will]); Gualayquis (3 cabs. [2 cabs. in don Juan's will]; Guazaite (3 cabs.); Chibunga (7 cuadras); Sillsi (300 brazas by 200); and Cuntus (8 cuadras). They total almost 11 caballerías.

38. "Testamento de don Antonio Duchisela, 1684," presented as evidence in ANQ Cacicazgos 32, 52, 1754: 37–43; "Testamento de don Antonio Duchisela, 1685," presented as evidence in ANQ Cacicazgos 38, 75, 1788: 131v–39v.

39. Ibid.

40. "Testamento de don Manuel Duchisela, 1769," presented as evidence in ANQ Cacicazgos 38, 75, 1788: 127–30.

41. The period from about the mid-seventeenth century through the eighteenth century was one of the wholesale confiscation of chiefly assets for the payment of tribute arrears (see Powers 1995: chap. 5).

42. According to Díaz Rementería's juridical study (1977: 162), cacicazgos in the Viceroyalty of Peru began to incorporate the patrimonial rights of the Spanish mayorazgo as well as its rights of succession in the sixteenth century. As we shall see, however, this colonial variant of the cacicazgo-mayorazgo was highly Andeanized.

43. Most of the Duchisela wills were prepared by Indian scribes, making it unlikely that this language was the simple infusion of Spanish official ideology into the legal document of an indigenous person. On the other hand, Ramírez (1986: 428–37) has uncovered evidence that there was a pre-Hispanic, north Andean concept of chiefly property—though not in the Western sense of private ownership—that was shot through with reciprocal and redistributive obligations. Land was also bequeathed and inherited in terms of distributive jurisdiction, not private ownership (Ramírez 1996b: 49–53).

44. The term *deudos* is technically translated as kin, but in the North Andes where ayllus were based on descent from a common ancestor and inter-ayllu marriages had, by the seventeenth century, created consanguineal relations among most ayllus, the word "deudos" often takes on the connotation of "subjects" in

colonial caciques' testaments. In the case of Yaruquíes, the Duchiselas made a
concerted effort to form exogamous relationships with all the principales of the
town's ayllus. These principales were the Duchiselas' "deudos" with whom they
"shared" chiefly lands. The principales were then responsible for "sharing" those
lands with their "deudos" (the ayllu members). This redistributive mechanism,
however, did not necessarily apply to *forasteros* (outsiders); the latter made private
arrangements with caciques and principales. This often led to intracommunity
conflicts, since distribution to forasteros usually translated into less land for the
original ayllu members.

45. Pease (1992: 166) also suggests that seemingly private resources appear to
have a communal feel in the seventeenth-century will of don Gabriel Fernández
Guarachi, wealthy cacique of Alto Peru.

46. There is a debate among Andeanists as to whether caciques privatized
community lands and purchased individual private properties for self-aggrandizement or community survival (see Choque Canqui 1993: 39–41, 95–107; Larson
1988: 152–70); Pease 1992: 166–68; Rivera Cusicanqui 1978; Spalding 1984:
228–30; and Stern 1982: 162–64).

47. Not only do they describe these lands as being shared among family members of the direct line, but also with lateral, natural, and illegitimate members of
the Duchisela line, as well as with key leaders of other ayllus; in other words, the
Duchisela heirs maintain redistributive control over everyone's lands, elites and
commoners alike.

48. Spanish law guaranteed the retention of the chiefly lineage's property,
lands, privileges, and services, even in the case of the hereditary cacique's removal
from office (Díaz Rementería 1977: 123).

49. The roots of this pattern come not only from Spanish inheritance practices,
but also from North Andean precedents. According to Ramírez (1996b: 50–51),
lands in northern Peru were transmitted through a chiefly line from one generation to another during pre-Hispanic times. Caciques did not, however, own the
land in the Western sense; they had jurisdiction over their subjects and the land
and other resources that the latter occupied and improved. They also had rights to
the labor of subjects on lands used to support them while they were in office.

50. "Testamento de don Juan Duchisela, 1605 and 1655," ANQ Cacicazgos
38, 75, 1788: 49.

51. According to Costales and Costales (1992: 168), the leaders of the Quera
ayllu were descended from a Spaniard, Mateo Lobato, who resided in Riobamba
from 1540 to 1576; they later married into the Duchisela family.

52. For eighteenth-century marriage alliances see, for example, Spalding 1984:
236–37 and Choque Canqui 1993: 106.

53. With the marriage of don Francisco Xavier Mayancela Carrillo and doña
Anselma Lobato Ramírez in the late eighteenth century, we find the consanguineal
and administrative integration of all of Yaruquíes' ayllus (Costales and Costales
1992: 170).

54. "Testamento de don Juan Duchisela, 1605," ANQ Cacicazgos 8, 75,
1788: 8–21.

55. "Testamento de don Antonio Duchisela, 1685," ANQ Cacicazgos 8, 75,
1788: 33v; Costales and Costales 1992: 154–55.

56. "Testamento de don Juan Duchisela, 1670," ANQ Cacicazgos 8, 75, 1788: 60–61.

57. "Testamento de don Juan Roberto Duchisela, 1734," ANQ Cacicazgos 8, 75, 1788: 41–54.

58. "Testamento de don Manuel Duchisela, 1769," ANQ Cacicazgos 8, 75, 1788: 127–30.

59. Ibid.: n.f.; Costales and Costales 1992: 166.

60. Members of the Duchisela family eventually married into many extraregional cacicazgos, some of which are Quisapincha, Angamarca, Isinlibi, Sigchos, Guantahalo, and Pilalo in the central sierra and Tulcan and Pasto in the north (Costales and Costales 1992: 170–72).

61. Juan de Velasco, the eighteenth-century historian, was the originator of the idea of a pre-Hispanic "Kingdom of Quito" in which the Duchiselas predominated (Velasco 1979). He was challenged in 1969 by Aquiles Pérez, who claimed that there was no evidence for Duchisela preeminence anywhere outside Yaruquíes (1969: 343). More recently, Costales and Costales have supported Velasco by positing these colonial marriage alliances as being rooted in pre-Hispanic political organization (1992: 172–73).

62. Three examples of the extensive litigation over Duchisela legitimacy in the cacicazgo of Yaruquíes are ANQ Cacicazgos 32, 52; 34, 59; and 38, 75.

63. For treatment of the caciques' responses to the late-eighteenth-century indigenous rebellions, see Moreno Yánez 1985: 389–96.

64. This paleographic transcription of don Juan Duchisela's last will and testament of 1605 was derived primarily from the eighteenth-century copy appearing as evidence in ANQ Cacicazgos 38, 75, 1788: 8–21. When parts of the copy were indecipherable, another eighteenth-century copy was consulted which appeared as evidence in ANQ Cacicazgos 32, 52, 1754: 43v–69v.

CHAPTER 9

Rich Man, Poor Man, Beggar Man, or Chief: Material Wealth as a Basis of Power in Sixteenth-Century Peru

SUSAN E. RAMÍREZ

The fateful meeting of Europeans and Native Americans in the late fifteenth and on into the sixteenth centuries began a process of adjustments in the ways of life of both groups. Speaking very broadly, two different cultures confronted one another and were forced to accommodate. The resulting cultural borrowing and acculturation left both of the original lifestyles altered in important ways. But, as in other colonial situations, the lifeways of the dominated tended to change more drastically than those of the dominators.[1]

This is certainly true for the native peoples of the Andes, who are the subject of this study. Their culture was assaulted from various angles as Spanish ways and concepts gradually modified or replaced native ones. Andeans were taught to understand and speak a foreign language and worship a single deity instead of several. Defense-minded native political authorities were replaced with persons willing to bow to the dictates of the Europeans (AGI Justicia 458: 927v). Communities were divided and entrusted to individual Spaniards. Andeans were forced to abandon their dispersed settlement patterns and to live in nucleated villages (*pueblos* or *reducciones*) for more efficient colonial tax collection and religious indoctrination. This physical reorganization, coupled with community division and demographic collapse, disrupted and, in some instances, destroyed patterns of resource use and exchange. Familial and neighborly reciprocity and communal redistribution, two underlying principles of social organization, were eroded as a monetarized economy became the norm in Spanish *villas* (small Spanish towns) and cities. Native peoples were also exposed to different measures of wealth and means of acquiring power.

Dreams of riches—starting with Columbus's own misguided plan to trade for pearls, silks, and spices in the Orient—proved powerful motivations for the invasion, exploration, and settlement of what became known as Spanish America. Some of the Europeans who crossed the Atlantic were rewarded for their risks with trade goods, booty, plunder, or ransom acquired from the native inhabitants they encountered. The first European men at Cajamarca in 1532, for example, immortalized by James Lockhart (1972), became wealthy once the gold and silver ransom of Atahualpa was melted down and divided into shares. For some, this newly acquired bullion and what it could buy became the basis for their status and power. Reports of their good fortune circulated widely and stimulated others to sail for Peru. Sixteenth-century chroniclers spread such stories of easy wealth throughout Europe.

Given the fact that the native Peruvians did not learn the language of the invaders immediately and did not write their own descriptions of the encounter until the late sixteenth and early seventeenth centuries, it is not surprising that one European gauge of position and power, namely material wealth, was prominent—the one that the Spaniards used in their comments on native customs and habits.[2] Lost and of little concern to most of the sixteenth-century European participants in the colonizing of the "New World" and Peru, in particular, was the significance and meaning to the native peoples of the gold and silver taken from them.

The Spanish who came to Peru at the time used bullion to buy the material trappings of nobility, to establish a *casa poblada* (literally, a "populated house," which refers to the Spanish ideal of being able to sustain in a befitting manner a large house, populated by one's family, servants, and retainers), to acquire political office, and to obtain titles, coats of arms, and other privileges in a quest for individual and familial aggrandizement. Pre-Hispanic and early colonial Andeans, in contrast, esteemed these metals primarily for their malleability and used them for collective ceremonial purposes. Gold and silver proved of special importance for adorning central personages such as the Inca (i.e., the son of the sun god) and native chiefs or *curacas* during rituals and celebrations. Ceremonial drinking cups, used to dispense the maize beer (*chicha*) so necessary in mobilizing labor and in reinforcing the loyalty of commoners (see below), were also sometimes made from these metals. Bullion, then, represented important paraphernalia of ritual dramas meant to honor the gods, and especially the ancestors, and to portray the collective principles of reciprocity and redistribution.

On the provincial level, people believed successful ritual propitiation of the ancestors by their lord brought fertility and prosperity. Acceptance by the spirits of a lord's periodic sacrifices, which were sometimes burned or otherwise destroyed, was manifested as an absence of natural disasters, droughts, and epidemics and interpreted as divine favor. Good times and healthy and well-fed subjects guaranteed the survival, reproduction, and growth of the community. Successful mediation between the departed and the living became equated in the people's minds with the divinely sanctioned legitimacy of a lord's authority and rulership.

It follows that the size of this community indexed a lord's rank vis-à-vis others. In the Andes, an individual's following was a measure of a person's power (Cobo 1956, 2:121). The more tribute labor a lord could mobilize, the more his people produced. The more surplus they generated, the more a lord could give away: to lift the standard of living of less fortunate members of the community—especially of the orphans and the old; to reward loyalty and outstanding service; to attract more loyal followers and their kinfolk into his circle from the ranks of other lords; and to burn to honor the gods. To traditional Andeans, then, power and wealth were not measured as much by a person's collection of material objects as by the number of persons who obeyed and respected him. Unlike the European system, in which gold and silver was converted into other tokens of wealth and power, the Andean redistributive system's emphasis on gift-giving allowed a native chief to accumulate good will that could be converted, when needed, into all kinds of support.

In this chapter, I will use a diachronic analysis of the last wills and testaments and papers related to the estates of three sixteenth-century native chiefs to indicate how they adapted to changing conditions to maintain their cultural values and personal power. I assume that what is recorded in these last testaments represents what the dying person most prized. These primary sources, although written in Spanish following models of European origin, enable outsiders to trace the progressive appropriation of the values, concepts, and definitions of an alien culture. These wills show, on the most apparent level, a shift from direct concern about the welfare and number of a lord's followers, reminiscent of the Andean ideal, to a growing preoccupation with the control of natural resources and the acquisition of nonhuman tangible assets, more related to the European norm. On another level, I would argue that this shift, while also self-interested, masked a continuing preoccupation with living up to traditional, pre-Columbian collective values. The change evidenced in these documents represents an expedient shift in strategies, made necessary by the colonial reality in which native peoples were forced to live. These lords, prohibited from claiming large numbers of dependents by the Spanish and forced to deal with multiple political pressures and economic demands, began to accumulate material wealth in order to give it, or at least part of it, away. The colonial state made lords responsible for tribute collection and obliged them to cover tribute shortfalls or be imprisoned or worse.[3] By accumulating capital and engaging in productive activities, they acquired the means to subsidize tribute deficits and arrears. These gifts or subsidies reinforced the loyalty of their supporters and maintained what was left of their communities. Thus the accumulation of material wealth was not a complete surrender to a foreign model. Instead, it allowed lords to satisfy and even impress their Spanish masters and representatives of the king while living up to the reciprocal obligations to gods and subjects. Such obligations forged bonds that were the traditional bases of the hegemony of the lords in their followers' eyes.

Northern Peru to 1565

Change did not occur overnight, nor did it occur evenly. At any given time, the gradient of change or acculturation was strongest near concentrated Spanish influence, at and near their hubs of settlement, and weakest in distant areas. Thus we would expect, and do indeed find, that Andeans living in the Valley of Moche, closest to the coastal Spanish city of Trujillo (founded in 1534), would be affected by Spanish culture more directly than those living in the highland region of Cajamarca, immediately inland and to the east of Trujillo, which remained a frontier of Spanish settlement into the seventeenth century. Likewise, those native peoples who had the most contact with the Europeans, usually the indigenous elite rather than the commoner, were the first to adopt selected Spanish ways.[4]

Before 1532, the vast majority of peoples of northern Peru lived scattered across the Andean landscape in small clusters of houses. Some farmers planted corn, potatoes, and other crops on land that was regarded as open to cultivation by anyone for as long as they used it. In the highlands were shepherds of camelid herds, and on the coast, fishermen. These commoners recognized the leadership of a hierarchy of lords, from their local lord to the *hatun curaca*, or paramount lord, who was both a political and religious leader. The hatun curaca facilitated communication with the ancestors, and his reputation hinged on how well he propitiated the spirits and gained their favor, and how well he managed his followers' labor on the available resources to provide for the subsistence and well-being of all (Ramírez 1996a, 1996b: chap. 2). On several occasions during the year, the curaca, carried on a litter or in a hammock and surrounded by a numerous retinue, made the rounds of his followers' homesteads.[5] Along his route, his attendants liberally dispensed chicha as a sign of his hospitality and largesse. In return, his subjects worked for him planting fields whose harvests supported him, his family, and the group's ritual obligations. On festive occasions his followers gathered at his administrative and ceremonial center, where the curaca would provide the food, beer, and pageantry. He also gave the needy whatever goods they might lack or did not produce themselves. Such redistribution proved the norm.

This life changed after 1532. In northern Peru, Spanish influence was felt from the start, for it was at the place called Cajamarca that Francisco Pizarro first encountered and captured the Inca Atahualpa on November 16, 1532. That Atahualpa quickly understood the Spanish desire for gold and silver is obvious from his offer of ransom. Once the bullion was melted down and divided, Pizarro continued to found Spanish settlements and began, in 1534, to give out groups of natives in trust to his men as *encomiendas*. The community that lived in the Jequetepeque (or Pacasmayo) Valley, for example, was divided into four encomiendas, undermining the integrity of the original polity. The native people headquartered in the Túcume Valley answered to two Spaniards. Three years later, citizens of Trujillo herded European cattle into the Valley of Saña. By 1540 the encomendero (holder of an encomienda) of Cajamarca demanded, besides labor to shepherd his cattle, that his charges work the silver mines of Chilete for him. Sugarcane was planted and a crushing mill was built in the Chicama Valley about the same time. The Franciscans built a monastery at Chiclayo about 1551. And another Spanish settlement, called Santiago de Miraflores, was founded in the Valley of Saña in 1563. Spaniards living in Trujillo asked Governor Lope García de Castro for land grants for farming in the Chicama Valley for the first time in 1565 (Ramírez 1995).

But these signposts of Spanish presence did not necessarily mean the immediate acceptance of foreign ways by the region's native peoples. The paramount lord of the Moche Valley, for example, although he used a Christian name, did not speak Spanish and had not converted to Christianity in 1558, when he was still practicing ancient rites including ancestor worship (Ramírez 1996b: chap. 5). Many commoners remained true to their original beliefs into the seventeenth century, refusing even to be baptized and change their names (Duviols 1986: 44). Before 1566–67, when Dr. Gregorio Gonzáles de Cuenca, the judge of the *Real Audiencia* (Supreme Court), visited the north, people remained in their homesteads scattered over the countryside. Native lords continued their polygynous lifestyles; tribute was still calculated mostly in labor; traditional dress remained in fashion; and men wore their hair long.[6] Individual ownership of land remained a poorly understood concept. Exchange was embedded in ritual, and money was not used in day-to-day interactions within a native community.

The visit of Dr. Cuenca and the naming of district administrators (the *corregidores*) in the mid-1560s, combined with Viceroy Francisco de Toledo's proactive administration and reorganization of 1569–81, introduced and accelerated change in the communities. Religious conversion intensified. The 1560s and 1570s saw two campaigns to resettle the native population in Spanish-style, nucleated villages, called "reducciones." A system of governance of these reducciones by *cabildo* (council) was introduced. Spanish administrators also reconceptualized the tribute and labor obligations to the encomendero and the state. It is in this context of transition that one should judge the three wills presented below.

Don Melchior Carorayco, 1565

My analysis begins in 1565 with a will that illustrates the measure of a powerful man and the essence of traditional Andean society from the emic point of view. Don Melchior was the scion of a long line of rulers. One of his forefathers, Concacax, ruled when the Incas under Pachacutec conquered the area, ca. 1460–70.[7] Concacax's son Chuptongo was taken to Cuzco as a boy by Túpac Inca Yupanqui, where he later served his son, the Inca Huayna Capac. Chuptongo accompanied Huayna Capac on his campaign in Quito and afterward returned to his native community, at the old site of Guzmango. One of his two legitimate sons died in November 1532 at Cajamarca in the ambush that Pizarro used to capture Atahualpa. The other, named Carhuarayco, submitted to Pizarro and was confirmed by him and accepted by his father's people as curaca. He eventually received baptism and a new Christian name, Felipe. Don Felipe Carhuarayco was the paramount lord of the people of Guzmango, in the province of Cajamarca, when Pizarro entrusted his person and subjects to Melchor Verdugo as an encomienda in 1535. Carhuarayco's son and heir, baptized with the same first name as the encomendero (though each spelled his name slightly differently), is the same person who is sick and testating in Trujillo in 1565.[8]

Don Melchior Carorayco, as a high lord of the peoples of Cajamarca, was personally responsible for the *guaranga* (unit of administration, theoretically equal to a thousand households) of Guzmango[9] and two more *parcialidades* (lineage or other groupings that are part of a larger community): Colquemarca (Espíritu Santo de Chuquimango) and Malcaden (later, San Lorenzo de Malcadan) (Rostworowski and Remy 1992: 94). As shown in table 9.1, about five thousand adult[10] males, under various lords, composed the broader polity of which don Melchior was a part. Counting their families, the population he was responsible for governing must have been about six thousand. Most of these mountain people subsisted by farming and herding camelids. Tribute duty included rotating temporary service at the silver mines of Chilete (Ramírez 1996b: 93; AGI Justicia 1063, 3, 1570: 10).

Don Melchior made the long trip down from the highlands to the coast and was visiting the nearest Spanish city, Trujillo, when he was stricken by sickness. He prudently dictated his last will and testament before the local Spanish notary, Juan de Mata, on June 20, 1565 (ART Mata, 8, June 20, 1565).[11] Coming as he did from a relatively remote area where very few Spaniards resided, his will (transcribed and translated at the end of this chapter) reflects most closely traditional organizational conceptions and Andean values. This is evident in the care he takes to list his retainers as part of his legacy. He claimed ten potters in the place or hamlet (*asiento*) of Cajamarca, a mayordomo or overseer from the parcialidad of Lord Santiago, a retainer from the parcialidad of don Francisco Anganapon, and a beekeeper who lived near a river. In the town of Chulaquys, his followers included a lesser lord (*mandonsillo*) with jurisdiction over seven natives. At the silver mines of Chilete, he listed twenty workers who served him. He claimed fifty-six Indians with no specific residence and at least twenty-four corn farmers and twenty-two pages in the town of Contumasá. Nine different subjects cared for his chili peppers and corn either in Cascas or near the town of Junba (Santa Ana de Cimba?) (Rostworowski and Remy 1992: 92). He claimed the towns of Gironbi and Guaento, whose inhabitants guarded his coca and chili peppers; another town called Cunchamalca whose inhabitants took care of corn; and another town called Churcan de Cayanbi. Finally, he mentions two towns that he was disputing with don Pedro.[12] In short, he named and claimed a minimum of 152 individual followers and six towns (including the two in dispute).

Table 9.1

Native Population of Cajamarca, 1536–1611

Year	Tribute Payers	Total Population
1536	8,000–10,000[a]	
1540	3,493[b]	
1566	5,169[c]	
1567	5,229	
1571	5,008	28,915
1572	4,263	23,691
1578	5,224	
1581	4,420	21,639
1611	4,000	

Sources: Del Busto 1959: 325; Rostworowski 1966: 90; AGI Justicia 458: 1479v; Hampe Martínez 1986–87: 79; Remy 1986: 40–47.

[a]This is an estimate by an early visitor named Verdejo (Del Busto 1959: 325).

[b]Readers should consider these figures minimums. Some natives escaped censusing into the seventeenth century.

[c]Governor Vaca de Castro gave the guarangas of Chondal, Bambamarca, and Pomamarca to another Spaniard in 1543. Dr. Cuenca reunited the seven guarangas in 1567 for administrative purposes. Since the caciques of Cajamarca claimed to be lords of all seven guarangas, I have included the figures above without separating out the populations of the three guarangas taken from Melchor Verdugo to give to another Spaniard (Hampe Martínez 1986–87: 67).

This preoccupation with his retainers shows how strong Andean tradition remained over thirty years after first contact in this highland region. In a society without markets, money, or merchants,[13] the wealthy and powerful man was the man with the most followers. A lord's status grew proportionately as the number of his followers increased, and vice versa. Felipe Guamán Poma de Ayala wrote that lords "will gain rank if the numbers [of their subjects] multiply according to the law of the dominion over Indians. And, if their numbers decline, they too lose [status]" (1980 [c. 1615]: 458 [456]). This concept of wealth (power and status) was the same one held in common empirewide in the Inca decimal division system. The hatun curaca or *huno apo*, lord of ten thousand households, ranked higher than a *guaranga curaca*, the lord of a thousand. The latter dominated the lord of a hundred Indians, (a *pachaca camachicoc*).[14] And he was superior to the overseers (*mandones* and *mandoncillos*) with responsibility for as few as five households (Guamán Poma de Ayala 1980 [ca. 1615]: 65 [65]). Don Melchior is a provincial reflection of this system. As a chief of a guaranga, he had jurisdiction over other lesser lords, who themselves ruled individual lineages.[15]

Don Melchior's concern for his subjects is also reflected in the clauses of his will where he leaves the poor some food and other items. He leaves a total of 15 *fanegas* (each approximately 1.5 bushels) of chili peppers, 5 fanegas of peanuts, 20 fanegas of corn, 10 fanegas of potatoes, 8 fanegas of yuca, 3 goats, and 1 *oveja* (a Castilian sheep or Andean camelid?) to the sick and needy in Cajamarca, Contumasá, Chilete, and Cascas. Such legacies reflect the redistributive rule of Andean society.

Don Melchior's will also lists inanimate items, all of them of Andean origin or manufacture. They include five houses in Cajamarca, Guzmango, or Chilete and fifteen planted pieces of land, noted as "chac[a]ras y tierras." Other objects worthy of mention are all ceremonial items: the hammock in which the Inca and presumably he himself was carried, a trumpet, and four large *cocos*, or ceremonial serving vessels, from which two persons could drink.

Don Diego Farquep, 1574

The second case concerns the will of don Diego Farquep, also known as don Diego Mocchumí, *principal* (lesser lord) of Túcume, who died between the tenth and the thirteenth of October 1574. He lived in the Valley of Túcume on the coast, north of Chiclayo and Trujillo, which according to a Spanish chronicler writing in the 1540s was large, scenic, and heavily forested (Cieza de León 1984: 205; Brüning 1922–23, 3: 4, 12). The Valley had been incorporated late into the growing Inca system by Huayna Capac (d. 1524–25), the last Inca emperor to govern a united empire (Cabello de Balboa 1951: 468).

Don Diego, like don Melchior, probably succeeded another lord of the same rank and last name, mentioned in the encomienda grant made by Pizarro on January 29, 1541.[16] Based on the population numbers of that date, he probably held the rank of a pachaca since his predecessor's followers numbered a hundred, or about 10 percent of the total number of adult male tribute payers (1,190) enumerated by the Spanish (ART Corregimiento, July 13, 1570; AGI Escribanía 502A: 54). Don Diego had held the position at least as early as 1566, when Dr. Cuenca visited the community (AGI Justicia 455, 1691; AGI Justicia 461, 1558 and 1572). In that year he appeared before Dr. Cuenca, petitioning him to allow his fishermen subjects to commute tribute corn to cash since they had given up farming (AGI Justicia 458: 1936v–37). To the day of his death, he never learned to sign his name, so others wrote down his last disposition for him (AGI Justicia 418, 1323).

Don Diego's goods are listed in table 9.2 in the order they appeared in his will. Among his possessions are many more items reflecting Spanish influence than don Melchior left, such as silverware and plate, furniture, and animals of European origin. Prominent, too, are Andean items such as ceremonial goods, including his silver, gold, and wooden (imported from Mexico) drinking vessels; nine silver crowns "with which they dance" [con que baylan], and six hundred strings of Andean beads (*chaquira*). He also lists nine "ovejas de la tierra" (camelids: llamas and alpacas), which were used continuously into the next century as offerings to the spirits as well as for their wool and as transport. More than two hundred pieces of textiles of various sizes, types, and uses are listed, most of which, given the descriptive terms used, were of Andean design and manufacture. Don Diego also mentions houses and one plot of maize next to his garden. In passing, he records or names some of his retainers, but not in such a deliberate way as don Melchior. "His Indians" included a potter, an unknown number of "widows," five subjects who kept seven thousand salted sardines in their care,[17] and seven lesser lords who had been charged with dyeing various numbers of skeins of wool (totaling 630).

A new element in this will is don Diego's inventory of receivables and debts. He owed a total of 24.5 *pesos corrientes* (or 9 *reales* each) to two individuals, but was owed 63.5 pesos plus two sets of clothes. This indicates that he used money, especially to settle scores for such things as wheat, flour, and women's clothes, with people outside his group of followers, including Francisco García, citizen of Payta, a port to the north of Túcume, and don Antonio, chief of Sinto, an indigenous community to the south. Redistribution and reciprocity remained the norm among his human dependents.

Don García Pilco Guamán, 1582

The third will is one dictated by the *gobernador* (governor, interim leader of a group of Indians) of Moro and town of Pisopon, don García Pilco Guamán, in the Jequetepeque Valley in 1582.[18] Moro was one of the four

Table 9.2

Possessions of Don Diego Farquep, 1574

–3 drinking cups, 2 of silver, 1 of gold

–1 gold cup

–1 silver pitcher

–1 silver salt–cellar [*salero*] with two spoons

–6 silver plates

–2 pregnant mares

–1 mare

–2 mules

–2 fillies

–1 he–mule or he–goat [*macho*]

–1 cup

–4 silver drinking vessels in the shape of gourds [*mates*]

–4 silver pairs of drinking vessels [*cocos*] to drink with

–2 gold cocos

–4 wooden cups from Mexico, made by Indian hands

–9 silver crowns, with which they dance

–9 camelids [*ovejas de la tierra*]

–2 sheep

–10 castrated pigs

–30 female pigs

–2 saddles

–8 chairs

–2 tables in his house

–50 tunics [*capuzes*]

–200 silver pesos in a chest with a key

–one empty chest

–houses that are next to the houses of his father in this town

–2 cloaks of woven cloth [*capotes*]

–1 chacara of corn near my garden

–67 *piernas* [literally "legs," an indigenous measure] of tunics being made by my "widows"

–1 tent or awning [*toldo*]

–100 pesos

–1 small piece of gold

–3 gold rings with their stones

–2 mattresses

–6 pieces of clothing

–600 strings of Andean beads

–7,000 sardines being held by his Indians

–6 corn husks and stalks [*chalas* con sus palos]ᵃ

–19 sets of women's clothes

–2 piernas of canvas or sail cloth [*lonas*]

–15 napkins

–630 skeins of wool to be tinted by 7 Indians

Note: Tables 9.2 and 9.3 were translated using (in part) the 1832 edition of the *Diccionario de la lengua Castellana.*

ᵃThis may be a copying error. The word might originally have been *chalana*, which refers to a lighter, square boat or scow—especially given the notation for sailcloth that follows. Don Diego was known to be a lord of fishermen.

encomienda grants created by Pizarro of the people of the Valley. According to Jorge Zevallos Quiñones (1989: 95), a noted local historian, Moro was small, with a population concentrated between the towns of Chepén and Guadalupe, south of Chiclayo and north of Trujillo. In 1583 the community numbered 189 tribute payers and 728 persons in total (Anonymous 1925 [1583] and AGI Lima 464), having been more than twice that size in 1567, when Dr. Cuenca assigned about 200 *mitimae* (Indian colonists uprooted from their community of origin by the state) families living in the highlands to serve Melchor Verdugo, the encomendero of Cajamarca (AGI Justicia 458: 1915v–16; Justicia 460: 457v).

As governor, the acting head of the community, don García assumed power during the minority of the legitimate curaca or when he was away, sick, or otherwise incapacitated. In other manuscripts he is listed as the "cacique" (an imported Caribbean word for "chief") or "cacique principal" (principal lord) of the people of Moro as early as 1565.[19] He may have become governor that year as a result of a dispute between two brothers: don Pedro Maxa Paico (who claimed to be cacique principal of Moro) and his younger brother don Diego Bilca (AGI Justicia 458: 1889v–90).[20]

According to a study by Guillermo Cock, don García was born between 1500 and 1520, making him at least sixty-two at the time he died. He had married doña Juana Chumpi and had a son named Juan, who was, by one account, only about eight months old and still breast feeding when his father passed away.[21] Don García regularly traveled south to the city of Trujillo to sell goats, and he once invested eleven hundred pesos that had been left to his people by their encomendero (Francisco Luis de Alcántara) and his wife (doña Ana Chacón). Yet, despite such interactions with the Spanish legal and financial systems, don García never learned to read or write, not being able to sign his will in 1582.[22]

A list of don García's belongings appears in table 9.3. Again, among those possessions are traditional goods, including textiles, clothing, and ceremonial paraphernalia. Indications of European influence are found in his list of tools and weapons; jewelry; cash; and European animals, including beef cattle, horses, sheep, and goats.[23] As did don Melchior and don Diego, he lists persons who have served him, including two herders of sheep (*obejeros*) and two other men. He names six others to whom he leaves two to fifteen pesos each, but it is not clear whether these sums represent past wages for service, debt repayment, or a legacy. In the records on the settlement of his estate, these six are named along with the shepherds and two others to receive their due. The corregidor and executor also paid several others amounts varying from one to five pesos, some for debts and some for past service. Included in the latter were a cook, three swineherds, and one tunic ("capuz") painter. Counting these individuals, his personal retainers might have numbered as many as fifteen.

The list of don García's debts in pesos implies an active involvement in the money economy, although some of his other obligations show the persistence of nonmonetary exchange. Unlike don Diego, though, he owed more than he was owed. His obligations totaled more than eighty-five pesos in cash, plus some textiles, a mare, and twenty fanegas of corn. He was owed fifty fanegas of wheat and a little more than nine pesos. In contrast to don Diego's will, his 1582 will indicates that he used cash to reward his workers (Gaspar Pir and Marcos Monfe, two shepherds) as well as to settle obligations with individuals who were not his direct subjects (e.g., Juan Portugués and Hernán García).

He makes little mention of lands and *chacaras* (planted fields), although he and his subjects were probably using land to grow chickpeas. He sold some to Juan Portugués, who still owed him nine pesos from the sale at the time of his death. In fact, the word "chacaras" occurs only once, in a clause that directs his executors to give twenty fanegas of corn to the principal named Pucalá to compensate him and his subjects for

Table 9.3

Possessions of Don García Pilco Guamán, 1582

–1 trunk with a lock and key, made in Spain

–long, loose breeches or trousers [*calças*] and a suede doublet or jacket [*jubón*]

–1 new jacket of hemp cloth

–1 worn buff doublet of jacket [*coleto*]

–3 pairs of boots

–8 (?) sets of clothes with their colored belts

–1 new set of painted clothes

–2 pieces of new hemp cloth, measuring 5.5 *varas* [a measure equal to 8.36 decimeters or 33 British inches]

–2 new sets of women's clothes

–5 sets of male clothes

–4 sets of male clothes

–2 blankets or mantels [*manta*], 1 new, 1 used

–1 trunk with a lock containing 4 new hand towels, 2 handkerchiefs, 3 varas of taffeta made into a shawl; 1 vara of taffeta in the form of a poncho, 2 shirts, 1 satin jacket

–3 wide breeches [*zaraguelles*]

–2 painted mattress covers

–3 new pairs of sandals

–2 pairs of shoes

–1 white cotton tunic

–1 pair scissors and 1 box of new knives

–3 pairs of gloves

–2 pillows

–1 cord [*cordon*] of black silk, another of silver, and one string [*çarta*] of earrings [*çarçillos*]

–5 pesos of gold and 1 more like an enameled gold pendant [?, *antojo*, which literally means "fancy" or "whim"]

–98 pesos in reales less 2 reales, all in the above trunk

–8 silver gourd–shaped vessels [*mates*] with which to drink

–3 pairs of silver cocos from which to drink

–1 silver cup and its stand [*con su pie*]

–24 pesos in 4 pieces of silver

−some feathers [headdresses?]

−1 silver pitcher

−2 black hats

−some tablecloths

−1 estancia at a place called Chule in this valley with 36 beef cattle

−1 field of corn [*sementera*] measuring 3 acequias[a]

−1 horse with the brand of Don Francisco

−1 mare with a filly

−1 mare

−1 bota for wine

−1 arcabuz

−2 chairs or saddles [*sillas*]

−1 bit or reins

−2 breast plates [or breast–leathers of a horse] [*pretales*] with bells

−2 pairs of spurs

−2 trumpets from Mexico

−1 pruning–knife [*podadera*]

−new reins

−1 chopping knife or cutlass [*machete*]

−1 bridle or bit for a mule [*freno*]

−7 crank or joint pins [*pernos*] for carts [*carretas*]

−2 pairs of new horse–shoes

−1 pair of iron fetters [*sueltas*]

−4 iron arches [*çinchos*] for cart wheels

−1 butteris [*pujabante*, an instrument for paring a horse's foot], a hammer, and tongs or pincers

−1 chisel [*escoplo*]

−3 cow bells [*cençeros*]

−2 candlesticks

−some stirrups

−some spurs

−4 plough–shares

−1 estancia for 860 sheep and goats in this valley at a place called Hiço

[a]An indigenous measure of land based on the amount of water running through irrigation ditches over a specified period of time.

damage to their fields caused by don García's oxen. He also mentions one *sementera* (cornfield) and two *estancias* (corrals or cattle stations): one for holding his beef cattle (*ganado mayor*) and another for holding his sheep and goats (*ganado menor*).

From Wealth in People to Wealth in Things

To understand the significance of these testaments, it is necessary, first, to consider the definitions of some key words and phrases. It would be wrong to interpret these expressions out of their historical contexts. For example, in don Melchior's will, "Indian" cannot be taken literally. It is a shorthand way of referring to native family units or households, which were the tributary unit. As the population data presented for Cajamarca in connection with don Melchior's will show, one must multiply the number of tribute-paying commoners by a numerical factor to approximate the total population. This factor changes over time as extended families became smaller or were perhaps listed as nuclear units for Spanish censuses.

Another word worthy of comment is "pueblo." In this geographical and temporal context, the word does not always refer to a native "town or village" as a nucleated settlement in the European sense. Before 1566–67, it is better translated as "people" united by kinship, clientelism, and/or loyalty to a lord. As noted earlier, the people of Cajamarca, Túcume, and Jequetepeque lived scattered and dispersed over the landscape. In 1567, for example, the population of the province of Cajamarca lived in forty-two villages (Remy 1986: 41).[24] Most people in northern Peru did not live in settled, Western-style towns laid out following a grid pattern until the systematic reducciones carried out under Dr. Cuenca in 1566–67 and again under Viceroy Francisco de Toledo in the 1570s. There is no telling how big some of the "pueblos," lineages, or ethnic groups don Melchior mentions were at the time he dictated his will. Only later were systematic, detailed censuses by individuals taken of the highland region (see Rostworowski and Remi 1992).

In don García's and don Diego's wills the phrase "pieza de ropa" also needs clarification. A "pieza de ropa" cannot be translated as a piece of clothing; rather, a better understanding is suit of indigenous clothes. A woman wore a long, broad sleeveless tunic or sarong (*anaco* or capuz) and a mantle, cape, or shawl (*lliquilla, manta,* or *chal*) (ART Mata, Feb. 22, 1564). A man wore a short tunic or shirt (*camiseta*) and mantle (manta or *capa*). Therefore, two separate pieces of clothing made up one suit of clothes for tribute purposes (AGI Justicia 461: 1261v).

Similarly, the term "cocos" must be discussed. These were drinking vessels of great ceremonial importance for distributing chicha on formal occasions. Juan de Betanzos, writing in the 1550s, reminds readers that the amount of chicha served on such occasions was another indication of a lord's hospitality or redistributive generosity; that is, his power (Betanzos 1987 [1551]: 68–69). Chicha was served usually in "paired vessels" that were carried with a lord when he visited his people. This was an important obligation of lords toward their subjects: "and this is the highest honor that they observe among themselves and if this is not done when they visit each other, the guest considers it a great affront" (Betanzos 1987 [1551]: 73). Dr. Cuenca prohibited curacas from having taverns where they served chicha to their followers in 1566 (AGI Patronato 189, 11, 1566; AGI Justicia 458: 1779). Protests were many and strongly worded. Don Juan de Mora, the cacique principal of Chicama (north of Trujillo), petitioned Cuenca for an exemption and the right to give chicha to his followers: "I say that the Indians who gather to go to work in the fields and on other necessary projects are given drink and if on such occasions providing drink to the Indians was prohibited, they would not gather to work on communal fields" (AGI Justicia 461: 1469v).

In other words, subjects would not work for the lord if he did not distribute chicha to them. Don Cristóbal Payco, a principal and "third person" of Jequetepeque, complained, too, saying that the prohibition was a "great inconvenience because the principal cause for the Indians to obey their chiefs and lesser lords is the custom that they observe of giving them drink" (AGI Justicia 461: 1470).

Another phrase, "chacaras y tierras," also deserves comment given Western conceptions regarding ownership of land. It is probable that don Melchior, speaking certainly in his native Quechua language, and don Diego and don García, probably expressing themselves in their native Mochica, used the term "chacara" or its equivalent alone. Chacara referred to a planted field, land that had been worked. It is no longer land in a natural state, covered by wild (unplanted) vegetation. Native Andeans considered unplanted land a medium, free in nature. It was theoretically available for use by anyone for as long as (s)he occupied and improved it. Once abandoned, it reverted to a natural state, once again becoming available to anyone for use (Ramírez 1996b: chap. 3).

Don Melchior, when using the word "chacaras," is undoubtedly referring to his rights to harvest the corn, chili peppers, and coca that were growing on such plots of land. He has rights to the harvest because his labor, or that of his followers, planted the seeds from which the plants grew. Following the principle that one controls what is processed (*cocido*, or cooked) or what is the result of one's labor, he claimed the harvest. He could not assert a right to the land as a personal possession (whether worked or not) because it originated unprocessed or wild (*crudo*, or raw). Once he abandoned the field and it reverted to its raw, unplanted state, it could be "cooked" or "processed" or planted by another.[25] The notary, being a Spaniard, undoubtedly added "lands" to the word for the benefit of Spanish readers. This faulty assumption—that the use of the land gave the occupier "ownership" rights (in the Western sense of control over the resource, whether worked or not)—clouded reality and led to misinterpretation of the historical record for years to come.

Proof of the validity of this interpretation comes from the records of the distribution, disbursement, and auction of the deceased's goods. The one plot of corn next to his garden that don Diego Farquep (Mocchumí) left, in 1574, passed to his heirs along with the six hundred strings of chaquira and the seven thousand salted sardines by order of a Spanish official (*alcalde mayor*) of the villa of Saña (ART Residencia, 313, Apr. 30, 1576). His *huerta* (garden or orchard) is not mentioned explicitly again, confirming that it was the harvest that he "owned" and could dispose of, not the land on which the plants grew.

More telling are the records of the auction of don García's goods. No lands or estancias were sold. One cornfield is described as three *acequias* (an indigenous measure of land based on the amount of water running through irrigation ditches over a specified period of time) of planted corn. The executor, Juan Rodríguez, is ordered to have it harvested, paying for the collection out of the resulting take: "Item: there remain three acequias of corn of the said don García so that the said Juan Rodríguez can have them harvested and from that which is harvested he can pay 20 fanegas that the said don García ordered given to the principal Pucala and to his Indians for damage that his oxen did as it appears in the clause of his will" (ART Corregimiento, 13, Aug. 11, 1582: 24).

These documents, in sum, provide us with one clue to the thinking of these Andean lords and the people they represent. The only possessions that could be claimed as one's own were items made or created or worked by one's labor, hence the importance of controlling human energy.[26]

Likewise, throughout the sixteenth century pastures grew wild and were common and open to all, as much from Castilian tradition as Andean. The estancias mentioned by don García in his will refer specifically to corrals. These corrals or cattle stations usually consisted of one or more holding pens made of brush, wood, adobe, or packed mud.

Occasionally, a one-room hut nearby provided shelter for the shepherd.[27] These complexes were not equivalent to ranches in the modern, territorially bounded sense. Those who constructed them did not legally own the land on which they were built before the mid-1590s. The estancias, per se, had no value. Typically, if mentioned at all, they were included in the sale of a herd, as an afterthought. In sales contracts of the time, a herd sold for so many reales (a division of a peso) or pesos per head (ART Mata, 1596 and 1598). The corrals and hut, if one existed, of these early estancias were not valued but transferred along with the herd. In this sense, estancias were not ranches, just cattle stations, or one or more corrals that were of so little consequence that they had no intrinsic value. It was only in the *visita de la tierra* (land title review) of 1594–95 that the first land grants were made to the owners of herds so as to give them legitimate title to the land on which they had built their pens. Thus, in none of these examples do the heirs or the Spanish executors of the estates sell the chacaras or estancias as real estate after the deceased's death. They sold or disposed of the crops and the animals, but land per se is not mentioned as an object that can be alienated.[28]

Given these etymological clarifications, this sequence of wills shows the uneven and gradual process of acculturation of these three lords and, by extension, the people of northern Peru. There is an apparent steady decline in the importance of people and retainers and a growing preoccupation with material possessions, increasingly of European origin or design, and with transactions in the expanding money economy. In 1565 don Melchior still claimed hundreds of retainers as his legacy. Don Diego refers to a potter, a group of widows, five Indians, and seven lords, each of whom probably had at least a parcialidad or lineage under his administration—still many fewer than don Melchior mentions.[29] Don García's list of retainers, in contrast, included no more than fifteen, even if we include those whose true status is in doubt.[30]

In the context of the times, this decrease in the number of retainers is not a surprising trend. Specific Spanish policy and programs gradually restricted the curaca's unpaid use of native labor. Traditionally, subjects of the lords did his bidding subject to known and recognized restrictions imposed informally by use and custom. Besides the individuals and towns he listed, recall the "chinas," or young women, whom don Melchior left to serve his wife. Dr. Cuenca, in readjusting tribute obligations, drastically cut these labor obligations (AGI Justicia 461: 1453v, for Moro; Justicia 458: 1851). Cuenca assigned curacas a few household servants, but these were vastly reduced in number from what they had once been

(AGI Justicia 458: 1413). This occurred at about the same time that the cities of Trujillo and Saña siphoned off labor, in a Spanish version of the indigenous *mita* (rotating draft-labor obligation), for municipal projects and for individual Spanish needs (ART Hojas Sueltas 1562). Fears of prosecution and punishment for cohabiting with several women probably prevented lords from declaring and enumerating "their widows" in later wills after the curaca don Juan of Collique was hanged for continuing his polygynous ways and having an open affair with a mistress in 1566.[31] In other words, even though lords continued to receive service, don Diego and don García might not have openly claimed as many retainers as had earlier lords such as don Melchior.

As the numbers of explicitly mentioned retainers dropped, the number and types of European goods increased. Recall that don Melchior owned only two items of European origin, the mares. These were highly prized possessions, having supplanted in some instances his *hamaqueros* (hammock bearers), who used to carry him about in his litter. The European goods owned by don Diego increased exponentially. Counted individually, don Diego Farquep had 90 items of European origin or form, including his animals, but not counting his cash and debts. He had 773 items of Andean origin, plus 630 skeins of wool. Don García's European possessions numbered 83 items and 860 head of European cattle, or 943 in total, not counting his cash or debts. Don García's Andean possessions numbered only 29, not counting the feathers.

The continued noting of sumptuous and ritual goods and regalia is important. All three lords had drinking cups with which to serve subjects chicha; some had ritual paraphernalia such as trumpets and crowns for the dancing and singing that accompanied their ceremonies and celebrations. These items attest to the persistence of ancestor worship and other devotions that, if recognized by the Spanish, were overlooked. Active participation in ceremonials propitiating their forbears was tied to the basis of legitimacy of the lords, as noted above. The lords orchestrated the ceremonies and sometimes officiated on these occasions (Duviols 1986: 32, 24, 44, 325), functions necessary to justify their position in the eyes of their followers (Martínez Cereceda 1988; Ramírez 1996a). Over time, religious persecution made such lords hide these activities, and yet we know from another corpus of documents that ceremonials of non-Christian origin continued into the seventeenth century.[32]

Another point to emphasize is that, as late as 1582, landownership was not claimed. Ideas that land was a medium continued. This was not changed completely by the reducción system, which sometimes removed scattered native peoples to a distant central location. In those instances, the Spanish assigned the resettled community specific lands to be held and used by those living in the new village.[33] These lands were bounded, but within these tracts, access was still governed by the same principles that traditionally held. Natives, both lord and commoner, could possess land as long as they worked it. They "owned," to use the Western concept of control, what they planted with their own labor. Land continued to be considered free in nature, belonging exclusively and permanently to no one, except to the community as an institution. Once abandoned, the land reverted to the wild or raw state and was open for use by others.[34]

Simultaneously, too, evidence of an active involvement in the monetarized economy grew. Don Melchior instructed his executors to pay for masses from his estate by selling his two mares. His two obligations totaled 40 pesos. The second chief, don Diego, owed 24.5 pesos corrientes to two people. His debtors owed him 63.5 pesos and two sets of clothes. Money had become a means of exchange with people outside his community. Don García, the third chief, was even more active, selling goats and investing large sums of capital in Trujillo. He died in debt, owing creditors more than he was owed. He used money to deal with people outside his community and also to pay and reward his own workers. Thus, between 1565 and 1582 monetary exchange began to supplant reciprocity and redistribution even within communal circles.

Evidence of nonmonetary exchange and explicit reference to the indigenous subsistence strategies in these three wills becomes more elusive over time. Don Melchior's testament refers to his people and the products that they grew: chili peppers, coca, peanuts, corn, potatoes, yuca, and cattle. His people included farmers, herders, potters, pages, and at least one beekeeper. Young women served his wife. They lived in dispersed settlements. His remarks also indicate competition for subjects and possessions (e.g., a house) between various lords (don Sancho, don Pedro, and don Diego). His ceremonial goods (e.g., the cocos) and the hammock and trumpet elicit scenes of a yesteryear when curacas were carried from hamlet to hamlet, to the sound of the trumpet, with retainers dispensing chicha at every stop. The possessions of don Diego and don García give us clues about their activities. Don Diego was involved in cattle raising, fishing, and cloth production.[35] Don García engaged in herding, too. For all three men, traditional subsistence needs, which in 1566–67 were, in part, codified and written into new tribute lists, continued to be provided through customary channels by their followers. Commoners carried the water, collected and delivered the wood for fuel, and cleared, plowed, planted, weeded, guarded, and harvested fields to support the lord's activities.[36] But these labors go unmentioned, suggesting that these wills were created more as a way to comply with Spanish dictates than for intracommunity purposes. This implies that for most of these years two systems were operative: one for extra-community affairs or relations, another for internal consumption.[37]

Rich Man, Poor Man, Beggar Man, or Chief

As late as 1565, natives and Europeans continued to see each other through their own respective cultural filters. At first glance to European eyes, don Melchior was poor—decidedly not powerless, but poor—the leader of even poorer subjects. He possessed few material possessions of note. At the time, Spaniards expressed puzzlement at the general lack of acquisitiveness of the natives in general. A few years later, don Diego, though a lower-ranking lord, proved richer in material possessions; and don García was wealthy, even by local Spanish standards, if we separate out the encomenderos. To Andeans, however, the opposite was true. Don Melchior was respected, even feared, as a lord of vast human resources. His retainers, who worked highlands and lowlands, embodied his wealth and power. Through them, he had access to products of many ecological niches with which to guarantee subsistence and a surplus which he could distribute to the disadvantaged and the needy. Don Diego and don García had apparently lost much of that type of human support. Both lords ruled over only one group that had been amputated from a broader pre-Hispanic polity by the Spanish distribution of encomiendas. Their access to widespread ecological niches had been curtailed because they managed few people, and these were concentrated, after the reducciones, in new towns and assigned only certain lands for their use. They were therefore considered of much lower status and power than their predecessors by their own people (Ramírez 1986). Wealth and its associated power were, and remain, relative concepts that, like beauty, reflect community standards and values.

Don Melchior represents here the conservative end of the acculturation scale because he valued people first. Without people, the natural resources—whether we refer to the silver mines of Chilete or the abundant lands all around him—were of little use. Without labor, resources would remain in a wild, unproductive state. Without followers, he would be reduced to the status of a commoner who dedicated his time and effort to familial subsistence and the whims and requirements of others.

By 1574, to some extent, and by 1582 to a greater extent, the European concept of wealth as a means for acquiring other tokens of power had begun to pierce the cultural divide. Don Diego and don García each showed a progressive incorporation of and assimilation to Western material culture and acceptance of European notions of "wealth" and, by extension, power. To don Melchior, to be wealthy and powerful meant having retainers who could produce a surplus that could be redistributed to provide for the needs of the living as well as those of the dead. Note how he left corn, peanuts, and other foodstuffs to destitute subjects in various locations. To don Diego and, especially, don García, wealth and status were increasingly measured in the size of their herds and the comfort in which they lived.

But don Diego and don García's wills, which seemingly point to the acceptance of acquisitiveness, make no mention of how they used these possessions while alive. Other colonial administrative documents show that native lords were made responsible for the collective tribute of their people. If some commoners did not appear for their turn of mita labor, if they failed to deliver the corn or wheat that was due, or if they fell short of cash for tribute, the lord was expected or, more accurately, obligated to make up the difference.[38] Thus, material possessions, a manifestation of power in a European culture, proved to be a creative means for Andeans to cover tribute shortfalls, thus garnering goodwill and maintaining the support of numbers of retainers, too. These goods, in part, were, like the earlier surpluses generated by the followers of don Melchior, meant to be given away in times of need. Such actions reinforced mutual obligations between subject and lord, bolstering the latter's future requests for labor and lending credence to his claims of legitimacy, thus helping to preserve a semblance of the traditional Andean community.

Last Will and Testament of Don Melchior Carorayco,
Cacique [Chief] of Cajamarca, 1565
(ART Mata, 8, June 20, 1565: 308–10)

T[e]stamy[en]to don M[elchio]r Carorayco [Caciqu]e de Caxamalca
[Leng]ua de myguelyndio

Enel nonbre de dios todo pod[e]roso y de la sienpre Virgen Santa Maria subendita madre yseñora n[uest]ra sepan quantos esta carta vieren comoyo don Melchior carorayco yndio caçiq[ue] y señor prençipal delas probinçias decaxamalca questan E[n]comendadas Enel com[enda]dor melchior Verdugo estante questoy al presente Enesta çibdad detrugillo destos rreynes yprobinçias del piru estando como estoy enfermo del cuerpo y sano dela voluntad yen mi Juizio y entendimyento natural tal qual dios n[uest]ro Señor fueserbido demelo dar y cre yendo como creo como cristianoenlasantisma trenydad padre y hijo yespiritusanto tresp[er]sonasy Vn solo dios berdadero y todolo quetiene e de la santa madreygleçia deRoma otorgoecono[z]co que hagoEordeno estemytestamy[en]to a onra e gloria dios n[uest]ro s[eñ]or edesubendita madre E porlengua demyguelyndioladino en la l[e]nguaespañola naturalde caxamalca enla forma emanera siguyente

—prim[er]amente digo q[ue] por quanto abnq[ue] estoy enfermo yo querrian [*sic*] a my tierra Enatural q[ue] si dios fuereser bido de q[ue] muera enesta çibdad que myCuerposea enterrado en la ygleçia del señor sanfran[cis]co desta çibdad y me aco[m]pañen la cruz Edosclerigos desta çibdad ysi muriere en mytierra mando q[ue] my Cuerposea enterrado en la ygleçia desan mateo q[ue]sta en elpueblo de C[o]nt[u]masa q[ue]s enlas d[ic]has probinçias de caxamal[ca] y sedepositemy Cuerpo enlaygleçia bieja p[ar]a q[ue] f[ec]halaygleçia nueba sepaseaella

—Yten mando quemediganenlad[ic]haygleçia desan mateo de C[o]nt[u]masa Cinco mysas cantadas con sus birgilias [vigilias] y ofrendas alparesçer de sus albaçeas y sepaguedesus b[ien]es lo acostunbrado

—Yten mando q[ue] me[roto] la[roto]n enlad[ic]haygleçia siete mysasresadas [roto]

[f.308v] —Yten declaro q[ue] soy casado segunhorden de lasanta madre ygleçia con doña madal[ena] cabislachos yndia myligitima mu[ger] qual duranteelmatrimonyo habido e [roto] pormyshijosligitimos a luys y ana [cecilia] y luysa myshijos ligitymos losquales [roto] portales

—Yten declaro q[ue] debo a don Seb [astian ?, roto] mando q[ue] selepague

—Yten declaro q[ue] debo alcon[enda]dor M[elch]or Verdugo my [encome]dero treynta p[es]os y medixo q[ue] abnq[ue] noselos d[roto] noseledaria nada demas deloqualledeb[roto] botija de bino q[ue] me dio quando tomelapos[roto] caxamalca mando q[ue] se lepaguen y descarguen

—Yten declaro q[ue] debo a Ju[a]n deaguylar diez p[es]os m[an]do q[ue]selos paguen de mysb[ien]es

—Yten mando q[ue]se dealospital de caxamalca p[ar]a lospobres del çinco hanegas deaxi y çinco hanegas de many ymas Vna obeja lo qual sededemys b[ien]es

—Yten mando q[ue]se de alos pobres del ospital y ygleçia de san Mateo q[ue]esen C[on]t[u]masa don deme mando enterrar diez hanegas de maiz yotros diez hanegas depapas y otros diez hanegas de agi

—Yten mando alosyndiospobres delasiento deChilete diez hanegas demaiz y ochohanegas de yuca

—Yten mando alos yndios pobres de cascas tres cabras

—Yten mando q[ue] den a la d[ic]ha doña madalena my muger quatro yndias chinas p[ar]a su serbiçio

—Yten declaro q[ue] tengo por myshijos abidos de otras mugeres dos hijos y vna hija q[ue]losconosçe myher]ma]no don X[rist]obal mando que acadaVno dellos selede vnapiesa de ropa de algodon

—Yten declaro q[ue] no debo ny soy a cargo otra cosa nynguna ymando q[ue] por nynguna cosa semoleste nyhaga daño a mymuger y hijosy her[ma]no

[f.309r] Declaro q[ue] tengo pormysbienes dos yeguas mando q[ue]se bendan p[ar]a pagar las mysas

Yten declaro q[ue]tengo los yndios ypueblos y tierras siguyentes q[ue]son myas

q[ue]don P[edr]o metienequatro cocos grandes depalo q[ue] por cada Vno podian beber dos yndios juntos mando q[ue]se cobren del

—Yten tengoen elasiento de caxamalca diez yndios olleros

—mastengoVn yndio mayordomo q[ue]se llama puerq[ue] q[ue]esdela parsialidad de Santiago emesirbe

—Otro yndio q[ue]sellama Culliq[ue] delaparcialidad de don Fran[cis]co angasnapon

—Ymasotro yndio q[ue]sellama ant[oni]o piq[ue] q[ue]esta en el rio y es apiero

—Yten declaro q[ue]tengo en el d[ic]ho asient[o] de caxamalca en dos partesypueblos casas de mymorada ymas Vna chacara e tierras y mas otra chacara q[ue] me quyto don Sancho quando murió mypadre todoloqual se cobre e ayan myshijosy her[ma]nos

—en otro pueblo q[ue]sedize san pablo de chulaquys Vn yndio man-donsillo q[ue]sellama anquiman con sieteyndios

—Yten tengoenelpueblo q[ue]sellama chunquys Vn solar q[ue]esp[ar]a my her[ma]no ymas tengo seys suertes detierras Echacaras

—mas mas [*sic*] Vna hamaca pitca enq[ue] andaban los yngas y Vna tronpeta decobre loqual metomo don p[edr]o y lo tiene e secobre del

—mas tengoen Chilete diezyseys yndios q[ue]sonp[ar]a myshijos y her[ma]nos

—declaro q[ue]tengo en chilete Vna casa grande q[ue]hera de mypadre la qual me tomola mytan [*sic*] don p[edr]o yla otra mytad don diego y mando q[ue]se cobre

[f.309v] —yten declaro q[ue]tengo [çin]queteseys yndios q[ue] P[edr]o delos Rios me diop[ar]a my serviçio [roto] mando q[ue]sirvana myshijos en chilete otros quatro yndios q[ue] [roto] d[ic]ho P[edr]o delosRios juezdeResidenç[ia, roto] amyshijos

—mas tengo enelpueblo de C[o]nt[u]masa [roto] y quatro yndios sembradores de maiz y [roto] y dos yndios q[ue] me sirben de pages

—mas tengo en el d[ic]hopueblo deC[o]ntum[asa, roto] otras dos-suertes detierras echacara que sellaman Vajucot q[ue]son myas

—mastengo en otro pueblo q[ue]sellama [roto] chaden çinco suertes de chacaras e tierras

—mas tengo en Cuzmango trescasas myas

—mas tengo en cascas seys yndios queme guardan agi q[ue]sellaman manya yotro Condul y otro tumao yotro Cusma y otro mychon yotro chico y otro quynyn y otro biejo q[ue]sellama quymyspe

—en el pueblo de junba tengo tresyndios q[ue] me guardan el maiz y axi q[ue]sellaman quiymo y masdos yndios q[ue]mequyto don p[edr]o q[ue]sellaman en ban y guayta

—mastengo dos pueblos q[ue] me quyto don p[edr]o quando murio my padrey andoenpleyto porellos

—mastengo vnpueblo q[ue]sellama gironvi que me guarda lacoca y el axi yotro pueblo q[ue]sellama gua ento q[ue]tambien meguarda coca y axi

—masotro pueblo Cunchamalca q[ue] me guarda maiz

—Otro pueblo q[ue]sellama churcan de cayanbi [roto]

todoslosqualesd[ic]hospueblosyndios ytierras son myos Ede mys herederos Eportallo declaro eposeo q[ue]loherede [roto] demy padr[e] [don fel]ipe carorayco caçiq[ue] y señor pr[inci]pal [roto] probinçias Cuyohijo mayor ynatural [roto]

[f.310r] Ep[ar]a CumplirEpagarestemy testamentos [*sic*] ylas mandas ylegatosyobraspiasen el contenydos dexo ynombro por mys albaçeas Etestamentarios a don sebastian [roto]ny nalingon my cuñado y a don X[rist]oval mosa [roto] [roto]ingon myher[ma]no yndiosprinçipales de Caxa[ma]lca alosquales y a cada Vno de ellos por si ynsolidun doypor cumplido tal qual deder[ech]o ental Caso serequyere p[ar]a q[ue] entren ytomen todos mys b[ien]es olosq[ue]les paresçiesen Elosbendanyrematen enpu[bli]ca almoneda e fuera della Edesubalor CumplaEpaguen este-mytestamy[en]to ytodo loenelcontenydo no enbargante q[ue]sea pasa-doel año delalbaçeasgo sin que nynguna persona nyjust[icia] sele entremetaenello porq[ue]esta es my voluntad

—yen el remanyente que quedan de todos mys b[ien]es der[ech]os y avçionese yndios tierras echacaras pueblos y casas y todolo demas q[ue] me perteneçe Eyo abia deaber egozar en qualq[ui]er manera quesea non-breycostituyo pormys Vnybersales herederos entodoello alosd[ic]hos luys

y ana y sesilia y luysa my[s]hijos ligitymos Edela d[ic]ha doña madalena
my muger p[ar]a quelos ayanE posean por ygualespartes tanto el vno
como el otro como mys ligitimos herederos y como mejordeder[ech]o
ayalugar

—Y en el entretanto quelosd[ic]hos mys hijos son de hedad nonbro
por su tutorE CuradordesuspersonasEbienes ald[ic]ho don X[rist]obal
my her[ma]no elquallas tenga E gobierne a ellos y sus b[ien]es como tal
su tutor E c[urador ?, roto]

[f.310v] Yporeste mytestamy[en]to y prostimera boluntadreboco yanulo
E do[y por, roto] nyngunos todos e qualesquier [roto] Cudiçilios escrituras
pu[bli]cas En [roto] Eotros qualesq[uie]r cosas que [roto] eldia deoy aya
f[ech]o Eotorg[roto] escrito o porpalabra qualq[roto] quenobalgan ny
hagan fee [roto] estemy testamy[en]to yprostimerabo[luntad] que agora
hagoEotorgoelqualquy[roto] yes my boluntad q[ue]balga pormy [roto,
tes] tamy[en]to Eprostimeraboluntad [roto] talmytestamy[en]to yescritu-
rapublica Epor aquellabia y forma que mejordeder[ech]o ayalugar en testi-
monyo de lo qualotorgoesta carta de testamento ante el es[criva]no
publicoE testigos ynsoescritos q[ue] f[ech]a Eotorgada enesta çibdad de
trugillo del piru en beynte dias delmes de junyo demyll E quy[ent]os
Esesentae çinco a[ñ]os t[estig]os que fueron presentes a lo que d[ic]ho es
Baltazar de çamora y P[edr]o deaguylar y Fran[cis]co perezdeloya y diego
de segouia Ebar[tolom]e Sanchez y myravel y el d[ic]ho otorgante alqual
yoel es[criva]no pu[bli]co ynsoescrito doyfee que conosco porq[ue]
nosupofirmar rogo a baltazar de çamora ya don X[rist]obal suher[ma]no lo
firmen porel los quales lofirmaron desus nonbres en este [illegible] y el
d[ic]ho myguel lengua juro por dios epor Santa m[ari]a segunder[ech]o
q[ue] a ynterpretado verdad Etodo lo quen el d[ic]ho don M[elchi]or
otorgante yno firmo porq[ue] no supo a su ruego por t[estig]os

Baltasar   don X[ris]p[o]val
de çamora

                                        J[ua]n demata
                                        Es[criva]no pu[bli]co

                          ❧

Will of don Melchior Carorayco Cacique [chief, or paramount lord]
        of Cajamarca Interpreter Michael Indian
In the name of omnipotent god and of the always Virgin Saint Mary his
blessed mother and our lady know whomever this letter sees that I don
Melchior Carorayco Indian chief and principal lord of the provinces of
Cajamarca that are entrusted to the Comendador Melchior Verdugo
being as I am at present in this city of Trujillo of these kingdoms and

provinces of Peru being as I am sick of body and healthy of will and with my natural judgment and understanding as God our Lord deemed fit to give me and believing as I do as a Christian in the blessed Trinity Father and Son and Holy Spirit three persons in one true and all-encompassing God and of the blessed mother church of Rome I dictate and recognize that I state and order this my will for the glory of God our Lord and of his blessed mother and through the interpretation of Michael bilingual Indian in the Spanish language, born in Cajamarca in the form and way that follows

—first I say that although I am sick I would have wished [*sic*] to my homeland and place where I was born that if God is served that I die in this city that my body should be buried in the church of the lord San Francisco of this city and the cross and two clergymen of this city should accompany me and if I die in my homeland I order that my body be buried in the church of San Mateo that is in the town of Contumasá that is in the said provinces of Cajamarca and my body should be deposited in the old church so that when the new church is built it can be moved to it

—Item I order that five masses be sung for me in the said church of San Mateo of Contumasá with their vigils and songs and offerings as my executors see fit and they should be paid for from my estate at the going rate

—Item I order that . . . in the said church seven masses resadas

[f.308v] —Item I declare that I am married according to the blessed mother church with doña Madalena Cabislachos Indian my legitimate wife [and] that during our marriage Luís, Ana, Cecilia, and Luisa were born as my legitimate children the same [I declare ?] as such

—Item I declare that I owe don Sebastián [?] . . . I order that he be paid

—Item I declare that I owe the Comendador Melchior Verdugo my encomendero thirty pesos and he told me that although I do not . . . he should not be given anything more than what I owe him . . . jug of wine that he gave me when I took the . . . Cajamarca I order that he should be paid and relieved

—Item I declare that I owe Juan de Aguilar ten pesos I order that he be paid from my goods

—Item I order that the hospital of Cajamarca be given for the poor in it five fanegas of chili peppers and five fanegas of peanuts and more one oveja [sheep or camelid?] to be taken from my estate

—Item I order that the poor of the hospital and church of San Mateo that are in Contumasá where I wish to be buried should be given ten

fanegas of corn and another ten fanegas of potatoes and another ten fanegas of chili peppers

—Item I order that the poor Indians of the place called Chilete be
given ten fanegas of corn and eight fanegas of yuca

—Item I order for the poor Indians of Cascas three goats

—Item I order that the said doña Madalena my wife be given four
young female Indians for her service

—Item I declare that I recognize as my children born to other women
two sons and one daughter who are known to my brother don Cristóbal I
order that to each of them be given one set of cotton clothes

—Item I declare that I do not owe or have any other responsibility and
I order that for no reason should my wife and children and brother be
bothered or molested [on such account]

[f.309r] I declare that I have as my goods two mares I order that they
be sold to pay for the masses

Item I declare that I have the Indians and towns and lands that follow
that are mine

that don Pedro has four wooden drinking vessels that are large enough
for two Indians to drink from together I order that they be recovered
from him

—Item I have in the place of Cajamarca ten Indian potters

—Furthermore I have one Indian overseer who is called Puerq[ue]
who is from the parcialidad of Santiago and he serves me

—Another Indian who is called Culliq[ue] of the parcialidad of don
Francisco Angasnapon

—And yet another Indian who is called Antonio Piq[ue] who resides
near the river and is a beekeeper

—Item I declare that I have in the said place of Cajamarca in two
places and towns houses where I live and more a planted plot and lands
and more another planted plot that don Sancho took from me when my
father died all of which my children and brothers should recover and have

—in another town that is called San Pablo of Chulaquys one Indian
overseer who is called Anquiman with seven Indians

—Item I have in the town that is called Chunquys a house site that is
for my brother and more I have six pieces of lands and planted fields

—more more [*sic*] one hammock *pitca* [?] in which were carried the
Incas and a copper trumpet which was taken by don Pedro and he has it
and [I order that] it be retrieved

—more I have in Chilete sixteen Indians who are for my children and
brothers

—I declare that I have in Chilete a large house that belonged to my father half of which was taken by don Pedro and the other half by don Diego and I order that it be retrieved

[f.309v] —Item I declare that I have fifty-six Indians that Pedro de los Rios gave me to serve me I order that they serve my children

In Chilete another four Indians that . . . said Pedro de los Rios Judge of the Residencia . . . to my children

—more I have in the town of Contumasá . . . and four Indian corn farmers and . . . and two Indians that serve me as pages

—more I have in the said town of Contumasá ... another two pieces of lands and planted fields that are named Vajucot that are mine

—more I have in another town that is called . . . Chaden five pieces of planted fields and lands

—more I have in Cuzmango three houses that are mine

—more I have in Cascas six [sic] Indians that guard my chili peppers who are called manya and another Condul and another Tumao and another Cusma and another Mychon and another Chico and another Quynyn and another old man who is called Quymyspe

—in the town of Junba I have three Indians who guard my corn and chili peppers who are called Quiymo and another two Indians who don Pedro took from me who are called Enban and Guayta

—more I have two towns that don Pedro took from me when my father died and I have a suit pending [ando en pleito] for them

—more I have a town that is called Gironvi that takes care of my coca and chili peppers and another town called Guento that also guards my coca and chili pepper

—more another town Cunchamalca that guards my corn

—another town that is called Churcan de Cayanbi . . .

all of which said towns and Indians and lands are mine and of my heirs and as such I declare and I possess it [and] that I inherited . . . from my father [don Fel]ipe Carorayco cacique and principal lord . . . provinces whose eldest and natural son . . . [f.310r] and to execute and pay this my wills [sic] and the orders and legacies and good works that in it are contained I leave and name as my executors and testamentaries don Sebastián . . . ny Nalingon my brother-in-law and don Cristóbal Mosa . . . ingon my brother principal Indians of Cajamarca to whom together and to each one individually I give whatever power in whatever case is required to enter and take all my goods or those they deem necessary and sell them in public auction or outside of it and from the results comply with and acquit this my will and all that is in it even though it is past the year of the executor without any person nor authority getting involved in it because this is my desire

—and in the remaining goods, rights and actions Indians and lands and planted fields towns and houses and all the rest that belongs to me and that I should have and enjoy in any way I name and constitute as my universal heirs in all of it the said Luís and Ana and Cecilia and Luisa my legitimate children and the said doña Madalena my wife so that they can have and possess it in equal parts one and all as my legitimate heirs and as best determined by right [*como mejor de derecho aya lugar*]

—And until my said children are of age I name as their tutor and guardian of their persons and goods the said don Cristóbal my brother who should keep them and govern them and their goods as said tutor and guardian

[f.310v] And by this my will and last volition I revoke and annul and declare . . . of no value all and every . . . codicils public instrument in . . . and other and every thing that . . . the day of today I may have made and executed . . . written or orally . . . that are not valid nor certify [*ny hagan fee*] . . . this my will and last volition that I now make and execute . . . and it is my desire that it stand for my testament and last will . . . such my testament and public instrument and this way and form that it be legally recognized as right [*mejor derecho aya lugar*] in testimony of such I execute this letter of testament before the public scribe and witnesses written dated and executed in this city of Trujillo of Peru on the twentieth day of the month of June of one thousand and five hundred and sixty and five years witnesses who were present to said testament Baltasar de Camora and Pedro de Aguilar and Francisco Pérez de Loya and Diego de Segovia and Bartolomé Sanchez y Miravel and the said testator who I the aforementioned public scribe certify that I know because he did not know how to sign he begged Baltazar de Camora and don Cristóbal his brother to sign for him [and] they signed their names in this [illegible] and the said Miguel interpreter swore by God and by the Blessed Maria by right that he has interpreted the truth and all that the said don Melchior [declared] and he did not sign because he did not know how at his petition as witnesses

Baltasar   don Cristóbal
de Camora

Juan de Mata
Public Notary

Notes

1. This is true for South America as well as other parts of the globe. See, for example, the discussion on Africa in Guyer 1995: 83–90 and Eno Belinga 1995: 91–120.

2. Both contemporary chroniclers and modern historians often used European concepts of power and wealth in describing the position and status of native lords. See, for example, Gutiérrez Flores 1964 [1574]: esp. 301–63; and Pease 1988: 92.

3. For example, when the lord of Bambamarca was asked for gold that he could not produce, his encomendero, the notoriously cruel Melchor Verdugo, sicced his dog on the curaca's son. The beast attacked, ripping the child apart before his father's eyes (del Busto D. 1959: 364–65).

4. See Frank Salomon's discussion of acculturation, miscegenation, ethnic redefinition, and the "ethnic continuum" (1988: 326). Also see Restall, chapter 6 of the present volume.

5. Cieza de León 1964: 219; Silva Santisteban 1982: 301.

6. Compare their long hair, for example, with Guamán Poma de Ayala's page-boy hair style, ca. 1615 (Guamán Poma de Ayala 1980 [ca. 1615]: 975 [961] and 1105 [1095]).

7. Urteaga 1919: 9; Silva Santisteban 1982: 308–10; Espinoza Soriano 1967: 13; Hampe Martínez 1986–87: 66.

8. Villanueva Urteaga 1975: 10–12; Silva Santisteban 1982: 312. See also Urteaga 1919: 16–25.

9. The spelling of toponyms and personal names varied a great deal in sixteenth-century documents. I have standardized these in the text.

10. Adult males, for tributary purposes, were usually defined as aged 18–50 (Hampe Martínez 1986–87: 68). In 1575, many natives still did not calculate their ages in years; therefore, the Spanish assigned them ages according to their appearance.

11. I believe that he survived this bout of sickness, because a lord with the same name (but spelled slightly differently [Caroaraico and Carua rayco]) was alive and well in the town of San Antonio of Cajamarca on Feb. 9, 1567, and in Guamachuco on June 14 of the same year during Dr. Cuenca's visit (AGI Lima 128, June 2, 1587; Justicia 458: 1480v *bis*).

12. It was probably not don Pedro Angasnapon, who according to Villanueva Urteaga (1975: 11) died in 1562.

13. Whether or not there were "merchants" (in the capitalistic sense) in the Andes is the topic of an ongoing debate. A growing body of scholarship suggests that there was exchange, but that this exchange was state administered. For a longer discussion, see Ramírez 1982, 1997; Rostworoski 1977; Salomon 1986; Sandweiss 1992; Craig 1997.

14. Santillán states that the Inca "gave responsibility of each 100 Indians to a curaca, who they called a lord of pachaca; and among each ten curacas of these they picked the ablest and most dominant (*más hombre*) to rule, and he was made curaca over the other nine, and he had charge of the nine curacas and their people, and he ordered them about and they obeyed him and were his subjects; . . . and to govern an entire valley where there lived many guarangas, they appointed

as lord over all one who they called Huño who was governor over all lords of pachaca and of guaranga and they obeyed him as a lord" (1927: 15–16).

15. The earliest written notice of the area also reflected this organizational principle. The first encomienda grant named Carnaarayco, as the paramount lord of Chuquimango, who ruled over Colquiensma, Tantaguata, Guaygui (lord of Mambamarca); Parintingo (lord of Pumamarca); Caranasas (lord of Chonda); Poenlli (lord of Ychinca); Espalco (lord of Cuysmango); and Otusco (Espinoza Soriano 1967: 4).

16. I qualify this statement with "probably" because earlier documents mention a lord "Mocchumí" but do not give him a first name. He was a lord of fishermen, whose followers lived in a place (*asiento*) called Payazuna. He was subject to a principal called Yllimo, who was himself a subject of the curaca of Túcume. Don Melchior could have been the same man if he died at a relatively old age for the time (e.g., at age sixty) and had been invested in his leadership position as a young man. Given the demographic decline and general crises of these years, I think that this is unlikely, but not impossible. See AGI Justicia 418: 369v; Escribanía 502A: 54.

17. These and other types of fish were probably preserved by burying them in the dry sand, as other fishermen did on the coast in the 1570s and still do today (Huertas Vallejos 1987 [1578]; Américo Herrera Calderón, pers. comm., 1994).

18. ART Corregimiento, 154, 208, Aug. 11, 1582. See also ART Corregimiento, July 3, 1578.

19. ART Múñoz Ternero, 1578: 131; Mata, Apr. 25, 1565; AGI Justicia 457: 887v; Justicia 458: 2041v, 2043; Justicia 461: 1453v.

20. Zevallos Quiñones (1989: 95) names son Alonso de Morales as "Cacique y Señor Principal del Valle de Moro" in 1576.

21. I do not believe that don Diego had fathered no other children. At his age and rank, he should have had dozens. He may have been reluctant to name them, given Dr. Cuenca's prohibition of multiple wives in 1566 and the fresh memory of the hanging of the paramount lord of Collique, who refused to live by Dr. Cuenca's dictates in this regard (Ramírez 1996b: chap. 2).

22. Cock 1986: 171–72; Zevallos Quiñones 1989: 96.

23. In records of the auction and division of his goods, various subjects came forward claiming part of his herds. Apparently, animals belonging to commoners had been entrusted to don García for care.

24. It is not known whether or not this is before or after Cuenca's reducciones.

25. See Lévi-Strauss 1983 on the "raw" and the "cooked."

26. In an almost contemporary case, started in 1558, over the gold and silver treasure taken from a native religious shrine, or *huaca*, the Chimú people, Mochica-speaking inhabitants of the Moche Valley near Trujillo, claimed possession of the structure and other "houses" because they had been built with their labor or that of their forbears. They had rights to the structures but not to the land on which they were built (Ramírez 1996b: chap. 5).

27. Goods left by the lords indicate that tents were also used.

28. Cock (1984) ascribes ownership of land to the curaca. I disagree, finding his statement an error of interpretation, based as it is on the fact that one generation later don García's *heir* (emphasis mine) left land to the church. That alienation

occurred after the visita de la tierra, when land titles were reviewed or issued (for a fee) if none existed.

29. Comparisons are made difficult because these two lords were of different ranks. It was normal for a lower-status lord to have fewer followers.

30. Another factor that may have skewed the numbers in don Melchior's favor is the differential rate of death in the highlands and the coast. Since contact with the Spanish was far less in the highlands than on the coast, the survival rate of don Melchior's subjects was undoubtedly higher than that of people on the coast (AGI Justicia 461: 845–46).

31. AGI Justicia 458: 1463–64; Justicia 459: 3085v–86, 3090v; Justicia 461: 853v–67v.

32. AAL Hechicerias; Duviols 1986; García Cabrera 1994; Ramírez 1979.

33. ART Compulsa, Jan. 15, 1781: 13v; Recopilación de las Leyes de los Reynos de las Indias 1681 [1973], esp. 3, 6, 2: 198–200v *bis*; Ugarte 1923: 390–91; Valdéz de la Torre 1921: 74; AGI Justicia 461: 928v.

34. Later wills, such as that of Diego Caqui of Tacna of 1588, indicate that some natives held unplanted land that they claimed as their own (see Pease 1981: 214). The idea of private landholding may have been accepted more quickly in the south due to the greater interaction between Spaniards and natives in the markets that developed as an outgrowth of mining activities. By 1598, don Diego Collin, cacique of the town of Machache in the jurisdiction of Quito, also claimed lands (Caillavet 1983: 12–22).

35. These activities may reflect (by 1574) more tribute needs than traditional Andean expectations of reciprocity and redistribution of his people.

36. See AGI Justicia 458: 1915v–16 for a copy of a petition, dated May 3, 1566, in which don García Pilco Guamán, who identified himself as the cacique principal of the *repartimiento* (here synonymous with encomienda) and Valley of Moro, complains to Dr. Cuenca about the amount of corn and wheat he is to receive from his subjects according to the then recently adjusted tribute list. He states that thirty fanegas of wheat and fifty fanegas of maize are not enough to support him, his wife, and family for one year. Cuenca then orders the 500 tribute-paying Indians of Moro to increase his allotment from communally worked fields to forty fanegas of wheat and seventy of corn annually.

37. Stern 1983; Salomon (1988: 330–31) points out that wills ran counter to Andean traditional thinking and practice: "In some respects the Spanish definition of dying and testating was, however, alien to Andean thinking. Andean thought did not dispatch the dead to another world, but put them squarely and actively among the living as personages with whom goods and alliances had to be exchanged for several generations." Instead of remaining a "fixed feature of social organization," he continues, an Indian making a will was "dissolving her ties of reciprocity with earth and the living."

38. Powers, in her study of Riobamba (1991), wrote that the same was true. See also AGI Justicia 458: 1886v–87, 1902v–93.

CHAPTER 10

Tributes to Bad Conscience: Charity, Restitution, and Inheritance in Cacique and Encomendero Testaments of Sixteenth-Century Charcas

THOMAS A. ABERCROMBIE

Nearing the end of their days, some sixteenth-century inhabitants of the Andes took stock of their lives and, calling upon the aid of priests and scribes, dictated their last wills and testaments. When they did so, they quite evidently sought to accomplish a series of interrelated ends. First and foremost, they wanted to leave behind a legally binding document, carrying out for them certain transactions that as corpses and other-worldly spirits they would be soon be unable to complete. Testamentary goals were generally (though not always) postmortem ones and were achieved in part through the transfer to others of the assets—wealth, social status, and power—that would soon become intangible to them.[1] Yet sixteenth-century wills were not only tools for carrying out practical property transfers. While it may be difficult to appreciate in these secularized times, early-modern testators regarded their wills as the means to do work on behalf of their souls, and they made their testaments into salves of conscience.[2]

Late-sixteenth-century testaments of the Audiencia de Charcas, the district of colonial Peru that is today Bolivia, share in the general features of the early-modern will as characterized by Ariès (1982) and as exhaustively studied for Spanish wills of the period by Eire (1995).[3] A set of preliminaries including an invocation of divine powers, identification of the subject of the testament, supplication, meditation on death, meditation

249

on judgment, and profession of faith establish the will-maker's adherence to the Christian faith and general bona fides on which the will's documentary power rests. Several clauses then specify where and how the body is to be buried. Once the body is commended to the earth, the will turns to matters by which the soul may be saved from eternal damnation, largely through the effects of distributing in death the property that the deceased had accumulated in life. Finally, executors are named, and witnesses join the notary in attesting to the authenticity of the document.

Preparing a will amounted to an admission of mortality. Anticipating death, testators did what they could to settle two troubling issues: the destiny of their souls and the destination of the material goods their deaths left out of their hands. Two apparently separable parts of the will, which have been termed its pious clauses and distributive clauses (Eire 1995: 20), seem then to address quite distinct issues. Matters of faith, the afterlife, and the soul seem analytically distinct from matters of property, or at least they have been so treated. Yet we would surely be mistaken to assume that the "faith" clauses were mere scribal formulas that served to complete a legal document that was "really" about material rather than spiritual concerns (see Vovelle 1973; Eire 1995: 40–44). Sixteenth-century mortals, at any rate, were counseled by handbooks on the "art of dying" and by priests who taught them that the distribution of their property, like profession of the faith and a good confession, was a requisite step in speeding their souls toward heaven.[4]

By controlling payments from their property after death through a written will, testators sought to mock the grim reaper. Through properly authorized writing, their words could be heard once their bodies were unable to speak, and their property transferred in ways that would give them more lasting and tangible life after death. But they made their payments in varying ways to forward goals that seem to contradict one another. One of these ways was expressly promoted by the church. Jesus himself had counseled his followers to "go sell what you possess and give it to the poor" (Matthew 19:21, quoted in Eire 1995: 38). Renunciation of the material world by distributing property, and especially by making donations to charity, followed straightforward Christian precepts and emulated actions of Jesus as well as those of world-renouncing saints and the mendicant orders they founded. In short, giving away property to the poor cleared a path to heaven. As a kind of "insurance policy," the will "guaranteed eternal wealth in the hereafter in exchange for premiums paid in temporal currency, that is, the pious bequests" (Eire 1995: 38, paraphrasing Ariès 1981: 190).

In another kind of postmortem payment, testators distributed most of their estate among their rightful heirs. Ever since medieval times, charity, after all, had begun at home: The legal code of Alfonso X, the *Siete Partidas,* mandated that no more than a fifth of the testator's estate go to charity, with the remaining four-fifths to be retained for heirs (Eire 1995: 236–37). Under the aegis of scriptural mandates to care for kith and kin, such customary practice underwrote testators' efforts to achieve a kind of immortality that was not expressly recognized: social life after personal death, best served by keeping the testators' estate, and hence social standing, intact rather than squandering it in charity.

So far so good. But the problem for testators was that these two goals, achieved through distinct sorts of payments, contradicted one another. Aiming to keep their estates intact to be enjoyed by their spouses, blood kin, and namesakes, passing status through the generations and across the abyss, testators placed private interests before those of humankind at large. Proprietorial litanies of bequests to heirs may have been prudent, arising from their love of kinsmen, but they had the effect of emphasizing testators' attachment to worldly goods rather than their renunciation of them. By plotting to clasp their dead hands around their treasure hoards, testators not only mocked death, they mocked the teachings of Christ. Striving to keep an estate intact and in the family was a form of post-mortem selfishness and greed, and it put testators' immortal souls at risk. The solution was to demonstrate their Christian charity, letting loose of some of their property in generous gifts to the poor. (A small percentage of testators were unwilling to risk their souls at all, choosing to donate all of their wealth to charity so as to undo lifetimes of selfish greed. Then as now, would-be heirs found such acts to be evidence of the testator's insanity.) And since a deeply contested or invalidated will was as good as none at all, and the intestate practically turned over their wealth to the Crown, church, and lawyers, most testators sought to construe an enforceable will, achieving a reasonable balance in their bequests. A brief scan of a sample of sixteenth-century wills suggests that the ideal was to keep most wealth intact for family, while dispersing some to charity and to the church. In other words, just as believing mortals had to die in order to live forever, testators had to give away their wealth, divided between two distinct channels of payment, in order to gain lineage immortality and to win "spiritual wealth" in the beyond. Through one kind of payment (alms), they supported the transit of their souls; through the other kind (inheritance), they strove to re-embody themselves in their descendants and heirs.

Here I will suggest that in the sixteenth-century Audiencia de Charcas, Indian and Spanish testators shared such concerns. Members of both groups wrote wills, but not all, or even most, soon-to-die sixteenth-century inhabitants of Peru actually produced testaments. To make a will cost money, and in the absence of substantial wealth, it was thus a waste of time. Most testators were either rich and powerful or were urban artisans and merchants who, however modest their means, had some capital to bequeath. The *protocolos notariales*, scribal books in which testaments and other contracts were recorded in colonial times, contain scarcely a contract or testament carried out by members of the farming and herding tributary indigenous majority of the population. With little more than a small herd, rights in collectively owned lands, some few items of clothing, cooking pots, tools, and tribute debts to pass along to heirs, they were not the stuff that sixteenth-century testators were made of. And besides, they had their own ways of transferring property and achieving immortality. The testaments of both Spaniards and Indians appear in the notarial books of towns like Potosí and La Plata, but always the documents came from people of means.

Here I leave aside the more numerous wills of shopkeepers and traders, jewelers and shoemakers, many of indigenous, African, or culturally mixed *casta* background, who dictated wills to scribes in those towns. Instead, I focus attention on the postmortem payments of the most privileged elites: the Spanish *encomenderos*, individuals who had been granted by Crown representatives the tributes and labor services of Indians; and the Indian caciques, the native lords whom the Crown recognized as the Indies' "natural princes," hereditary elites whose job, in part, was to coordinate delivery of their peoples' tributes and labors to the Spanish encomenderos. As privileged elites, both encomenderos and caciques were much wealthier than their respective Spanish and Indian compatriots. Their position of wealth and power was also of a heritable sort, but given that both had engaged in structured forms of exploitation of their tributary Indian charges, they also sought to make charitable amends for such sins.

In this discussion I privilege the testaments of a particular group of encomenderos and caciques who were in intimate contact with one another: All of the encomenderos I discuss are from the Audiencia de Charcas, and all were granted their Indian tributaries in 1548 by the Crown delegate (and president of the Audiencia de los Reyes in Lima), Pedro de la Gasca. The cacique wills I treat belonged to the native lords who served this group of encomenderos. The wills date from the mid-1550s to the mid-1580s, during which time the prerogatives and moral standing of both encomenderos and caciques were under attack by the Spanish Crown. Encomenderos, particularly, were charged during this period with grave moral faults, actionable by the Crown because of the specific contractual language of their grants of *encomienda* (the Indians whom the king placed under their care). As a result, all of the encomenderos of Charcas were charged in 1551 with taking excess tributes from Indians; all resorted to extraordinary testamentary acts of charity to deflect such charges. Caciques, on the other hand, were accused of exercising tyrannical powers over their Indians and were reined in by making them into paid functionaries of the Crown. Among others, Spalding (1984) and Stern (1982) have commented on the difficulty of the intermediary role played by colonial caciques. To act in their subjects' interest, they were forced to curry favor with the Spanish Crown. To increase their autonomy and power, they had to improve their positions in the colonial world. Thus caciques sought recognition as the Indies' equivalents of Castile's nobility. A collective memorial signed by many native lords of Charcas makes this goal explicit: "Given that we are principal lords of vassals . . . such as in Spain are the dukes and counts and marquises . . . we beseech your majesty . . . to grant us mercies . . . in conformity with the quality and gravity of our persons, granting to us mercies such as those which in Spain are granted to knights and hidalgos" (Espinoza Soriano 1969: 16).[5] Quickly enough, caciques learned that to earn such privileges, they had to abide by Castilian rules of nobility, succession, inheritance, and Christian standards of moral conduct in death as in life.

Given the similarity of their circumstances, it is not surprising that the testaments of encomenderos and caciques are more alike than different. As with all testaments, both serve as registers of property and its transfer and thus read in large part as a list of holdings and payments. Since the basis of encomendero and cacique wealth was their access to Indian tribute and labor not long after the Spanish invasion, their likeness extends even to use of the indigenous knotted-cord accounting devices known as *khipus*. The testaments of Spanish encomenderos and Indian caciques are also alike in other respects. Both kinds of documents evince concern for the well-being of testator souls, specifying the disposition of their mortal remains and stipulating that masses be said and sung for their souls. Both ordain a final reckoning of debts and obligations, thereby liquidating all of the outstanding social relations they had created by lending and borrowing, owing and being owed, so as to make their estate whole. From this single inviolate hoard, now a material measure of their worth as a social person, they were in a position to remake themselves once and for all as spiritual and social beings, making their mark through the specifics of their testamentary payments to charity and to their heirs.

Only in a single notable respect do encomendero wills differ from those of caciques in this group: Encomenderos repeatedly admit to having gouged their Indians for excessive tribute payments and, in restitution for such acts, make large testamentary refunds. As we shall see, such restitution payments in this period resulted from certain special contractual obligations to which encomenderos were subject. Formulated explicitly as matters of conscience of interest to the Crown, such contractual stipulations responded to a more general debate over the morality of encomienda and, indeed, of the conquest as a whole. The Crown could not tolerate gross mistreatment of Indians, failure to indoctrinate them in the True Faith, or collection of excessive tributes without scratching the veneer of legality lent to the colonial enterprise by well-known Papal Bulls. These had donated power over Indians and their tribute to the Spanish Crown and entrusted that Crown with the obligation of saving Indian souls by baptizing them into the faith. The resulting link between the Crown's secular and evangelical goals in the Indies thus snared the king's conscience in matters of his pocketbook (see Hanke 1949; Las Casas 1975; Zavala 1971, 1973).

Encomenderos exercised power over Indian souls and tributes in the king's name, and their actions lightened his pocketbook while weighing on his soul. So just as the king employed a council and confessor to safeguard his interests in this world and the next, encomenderos too were subject to paternal surveillance by ministers of the Crown and the church. And thus such intertwined fiscal and moral concerns, expressed always in terms of the link between Indian tributes and Indian souls, led in the 1550s to the prosecution by Crown officials of encomenderos in trials where caciques presented evidence of encomenderos' mistreatment of Indians and excess tribute collection, supported by evidence contained in Indian khipus. It was in this context (and while such trials dragged on into the 1570s) that encomendero wills mandating restitution payments to Indians were dictated, sometimes while the testating encomendero awaited execution at the gallows. Surviving cacique testaments also date to the period after the connection between conscience and property transfers had been made manifest in such trials, and after caciques had learned the importance of Spanish rules of noble succession (from father to first-born son) and the Christian theology of salvation. To evaluate just how freely the last will of encomendero or cacique was exercised, we must consider the moral debates and legal struggles with which both sorts of Peruvian aristocrats, native lord and encomendero, had to contend.

Encomienda, Indian Tribute, and Restitution

Spanish conquistadors are not generally regarded as men of delicate conscience. Even the most laudatory chroniclers of the Spanish invasion of "The Indies" described acts committed against Indians that are outrageous to modern sensibilities. They do so because at the time such acts were regarded as rewardable service to God and King. Almost without regard to their ruthlessness, soldierly service to the "two crowns," that of the Castilian monarch and that of Saint Peter, was a principal route by which social-climbing Spaniards might achieve honor, title, and, above all, vassals and the tributes necessary to sustain an aristocratic life, one free of the dishonoring manual labors that made men plebeians and therefore tributary vassals of king, church, or nobleman (Maravall 1984). Of course, there were rules and limits as to the proper exercise of warrior virtues that might make ordinary, plebeian men into *hijosdalgo* ("sons of something," meaning heirs of title, status, and property). The ambitions of don Quixote and Sancho Panza ran up against such limits when they practiced their quest within Castile itself, assaulting not only windmills but the king's subjects rather than the infidels and apostates who were, in those days, the legal targets of ennobling sword thrusts, since both king and pope hoped to see such people reduced to the status of proper vassals so they might be elevated to the rank of proper Christians. Conquistadors such as the Pizarros were sometimes punished for having violated such rules; entitlement to encomienda and the tributary wealth it generated were frequently subjected to the risk of cross fire in the war between silver bars and conscience.[6]

Somewhat akin to the form of Spanish lordship over vassals known as *señorío* (or so early conquistadors hoped it would be), encomienda gave to a deserving Spaniard charge of collecting tribute and labor service from Indian vassals, generally by assigning to each encomendero a native lord who was to ensure that his own subjects now served the Spaniard. By living from rents rather than by any sort of dishonoring manual labor or commerce, Spaniards who gained encomiendas became de facto aristocrats, no matter what their social status had been in Spain. In fact, many had emigrated to avoid the humble status of plebeian *pechero*, as tribute-payers were called there.[7]

The potential reward was motive for efforts not only to gain Indians in encomienda but for all-out efforts at rapid accumulation of moveable wealth; silver could be taken back to Spain and there turned into authentic and more permanent aristocratic status. Urgency of accumulation was heightened because encomienda was in flux, its permanence and long-term profitability in doubt. This was a recipe for encomendero rebellion against the Crown, and also for mistreatment of Indians.

All this was well understood by the cleric Pedro de la Gasca, sent to pacify Peru in the wake of a serious encomendero rebellion against the Spanish Crown set in motion by the New Laws of 1542, which had endeavored to limit and then end encomienda, thereby forestalling the rise of a landed aristocracy in Spain's overseas territory. After Peru's unfortunate first viceroy, Blasco Núñez Vela, arrived with the New Laws of 1542 that drastically restricted conquistadors' rights over their newly won Indian vassals, those conquistadors rebelled. Led by Gonzalo Pizarro, half-brother of Francisco Pizarro, Peru's encomenderos declared war on Viceroy Núñez Vela, defeated his forces, and put him to death. Gasca, who had been granted broad powers to pacify Peru and put an end to the secessionist threat (some of Pizarro's followers had urged him to crown himself king of Peru), managed to defeat Gonzalo Pizarro on the field of battle. To regain support for the Crown, Gasca suspended the New Laws.

Far from presiding over their dismantling, Gasca was forced to grant a record number of new encomiendas to reward those Spaniards who had rallied to the Crown. But Gasca was worried over the end results on two counts. On the one hand, he had divided and redivided native groups to increase the number of available encomiendas to satisfy social-climbing conquistadors. Unfortunately, there were far more social-climbing Spaniards in Peru than there were encomiendas to give.[8] Members of the *cabildo* (city council) of Lima warned the king of much discontent in the land over Gasca's grants. It was stirred up especially by the large number of soldiers who had been left out of accounts, particularly those passed over because of ties to the rebel Gonzalo Pizarro, who especially resented grants made to late-coming Núñez Vela loyalists.[9]

Like the encomienda grants that Francisco Pizarro had doled out to those who served him well, Gasca's grants awarded each Spanish recipient a native lord and that lord's subjects. Native lords were then expected to act as intermediaries, collecting tribute and levying the labor of their subjects on behalf of the encomendero. Encomiendas did not include title to land and, as with earlier grants, were provided at the discretion of the Crown. Encomiendas could not be bought or sold, and inheritance rights of encomienda were limited. Encomienda placed Indians "into the care of" Spaniards, enriching the latter and providing them with the rents and status of de facto nobility, but nobility was not assured as with the heritable and inalienable señorío of Spain. What is more, encomienda in Peru demanded that encomenderos care for their Indians, in particular by providing them with proper instruction in Christian doctrine. Thus encomenderos shouldered the king's duty to save Indian souls, and when they took this duty lightly, they created a burden not only for their own consciences, but for the king's.

With such matters in mind, and to protect his own conscience as well as that of the distant king, Gasca went a step further in his grants of encomienda than had Francisco Pizarro. In his 1548 encomienda grants, Gasca allowed that encomenderos, such as Hernán Vela who received the Aullagas Indians, could ask from their Indians only "moderate tributes such as they can well give" (AGI Escribanía de Cámara 497C, 23: 3r).[10] All of Gasca's grants were made in full awareness of the moral considerations that had underlain the New Laws. Although the laws were now in abeyance, Gasca chose to underline the encomendero's moral duties while shifting the burden of guilt. He therefore ordered Vela to indoctrinate his Indians "in matters of our holy Catholic faith as his majesty has commanded. And if you do not do so or you should be careless in it, it shall weigh on your conscience and not upon his majesty's or mine" (ibid.). In the last of the encomienda grants decreed by Gasca, he held all encomenderos liable to new limits he would soon place on tributes in an assessment known as a *tasa* ("Gasca al Consejo, Los Reyes, Nov. 8, 1549," *Cartas de Indias* 2: 552). Those who exceeded this amount were liable for restitution payments (Lohmann Villena 1966; Zavala 1973).[11]

To put teeth into such prophylactics of conscience, Gasca ordered an end to Indian mine labor in 1549.[12] To set tasa tribute limits, he appointed a traveling commission, heavily weighted with priests sympathetic to the anti-encomienda positions of Bartolomé de Las Casas. While this commission, which included the pro-Indian Quechua linguist and lexicographer Domingo de Santo Tomás, moved through the countryside conducting censuses and lowering tribute levels, Las Casas published in Spain his advice to priests who might hear the confessions of encomenderos, declaring that under no circumstances should they be given absolution without first renouncing their encomiendas and making restitution to Indians (see Lohmann Villena, 1966).[13]

Gasca's intention, he wrote the Crown in November of 1549, was "to do that which is so pertinent to your royal conscience; . . . thus putting the brakes on the greed and the extortions to which Spaniards have until now been accustomed to subject the natives, in order to take from them that which they have and have not, and for this subjecting them to such tortures that many of them have died and others have hung themselves out of desperation . . ." ("Gasca al Consejo, Los Reyes, 8 Nov. 1549," *Cartas de Indias* 2: 552 [my translation]).[14] It is worth remembering that as deliberations over the new tasa were under way so was the well-known debate in Valladolid between the Dominican Bartolomé de Las Casas and Juan Ginés de Sepúlveda. The ease of royal conscience and, perhaps, the moral basis of the very enterprise of the Indies were at this time in question. Thus did Gasca call upon encomendero consciences to confess their sins, now accountable to measurable monetary limits.

In a final parting salvo before returning to Spain and taking up the post of bishop of Palencia, in 1550 Gasca appointed a set of special judges, instructing them to make sure encomenderos did not exceed the new tasa, and to collect evidence of their mistreatment of Indians. To the region known as Charcas,[15] he sent one Lorenzo de Estopiñán, who formally notified encomenderos of their new tasas in Potosí, and began inquiries there among caciques, in February 1551.

Estopiñán was a zealous judge. Convening caciques from most, if not all, of the region's encomiendas, he took their testimony, and that of special Indian accountants called *khipu kamayuqs*, on excessive tributation and the abuse that made it involuntary. "Reading" from the knotted-string records called khipus, these accountants produced detailed accounts of tributes paid to Spaniards, plus information on deliveries, labor levies, and the like. Khipus had been used throughout Inka territory for a variety of mnemonic purposes, especially for keeping track of the movement of goods and services within the Inka system for generating state revenues.[16] Using such accounts, Estopiñán then brought charges against numerous encomenderos for their activities between 1548 and 1551. Since virtually every man targeted was a Gascan appointee and follower of Blasco Núñez Vela, it is probable that former Pizarro loyalists were exacting their vengeance.[17] Records of three of Estopiñán's *procesos* survive, along with a summary account by his prosecutor Diego de Ocampo of judgments against other Charcas encomenderos. The latter is summarized in table 10.1.

The list includes nearly every encomendero in Charcas. Most notable for our purposes is the mention of testamentary restitution. Compiled between 1556 and 1559, the document's account of testamentary restitution is not exhaustive: several men, most notably Lorenzo de Aldana, Alonso de Montemayor, Gómez de Solís, and Hernán Vela, apparently made out their wills in the years after the list was sent to Spain. Robles was executed in 1556 for his participation in the 1553 rebellion of Sebastián del Castillo, during which Pedro de Hinojosa died at rebel hands, intestate, in his bed. Owing to such rebel activity, spurred on by la Gasca's much-resented persecution of encomenderos, only two of these suits, against Hinojosa and Vela, had been concluded by 1559, the year of Vela's death in Spain.[18] Some encomenderos, such as Robles, who dictated his will while awaiting execution, had already made amends with their caciques.

Like the consciences of these men—whose restitution via the testament amounted essentially to out-of-court settlements, enabling them (or so they hoped) to pass on their encomiendas and the rest of their fortunes to their heirs—the king's conscience was also tied to his pocketbook. One might think that "restitution" implied repayments to Indians of what had unjustly been taken from them. But Philip II, who as prince and king took considerable interest in these cases, saw them as a means of extracting monetary payments from encomenderos to the Crown. In those years the Crown of Spain was in constant jeopardy of bankruptcy; councilors to the king thus advised him: "Item: It is convenient to command that in Peru be carried out the business done by Lorenzo de Estopiñán de Figueroa, on the excess by which the encomenderos and their retainers collected Indian tributes, which is a business of much importance and usefulness for the king, and from which might be taken more than seven hundred thousand pesos" (RAH Colección Muñoz, *Cosas del Perú*, tomo 65 [A/92]: 83r).[19]

This document also recommends that the Council of the Indies proceed to investigate private arrangements between encomenderos and caciques by which illegal substitutions were made in tributary payments, "from which another goodly amount of silver might be made for His Majesty" (ibid.).[20]

When Hernán Vela got the encomienda from Gasca in 1548, he settled two hundred Aullagas Indians in Potosí. For a few years, Vela collected the tributes the Indians brought to his houses in Potosí and La Plata. Like other encomenderos, Vela made an immense fortune in those boom years. But in March of 1551, less than three years later, Vela's fortune was under siege by Lorenzo de Estopiñán.[21] Gathering testimony from Aullagas caciques, Estopiñán accused Vela of collecting excessive tributes and of seriously abusing his Indians in Potosí, coercing them to deliver more silver "than they could well give." Vela had risked the king's conscience and would pay the price.

Indian witnesses provided detailed accounts of Vela's alleged abuses. The formal accusation seems to paraphrase Gasca's description to the

Table 10.1

Restitution Judgments against Charcas Encomenderos, 1550s

Encomendero	Encomienda	Restitution	Outcome
Lope de Mendieta (d)[a]	Chuquicota	70,000 ps	Restitution paid to theologians of Seville in Mendieta will.
Pedro & Francisco Isasaga	Colquemarca and Andamarca	50,000 ps	Still owed.
Antonio Alvarez	Orinoca	1,700 ps	Still owed.
Hernán Vela[b]	Aullagas	65,000 ps	Confirmed on appeal.
don Pedro de Portugal (d) and Diego Pantoja	Their Indians [Quillacas & Asanaques]	15,000 ps	Lawsuit brought by Indians in progress.
Lorenzo de Aldana[b]	Paría	50,000 ps	Lawsuit pending.
Gómez de Solís[b]	Tapacari	50,000 ps	Solís gave Indians 1,500 ps in goods [*menudencias*].
General Hinojosa (d)	Macha	140,000 ps	Heirs settled with Indians for 40,000 ps.
don Alonso de Montemayor[b]	Sacaca and Charcas	5,000 ps	Indians owe king 8,000 ps; king gave *provisión* to wait for their payment.
Martín de Robles (d)[a]	Chayanta	25,000 ps	Robles declared same amount in testament.
Gómes de Alvarado (d)[a]	Pocona	23,000 ps	Should collect from heirs, (brothers, including Pero Banegas in Zafra); more light in Alvarado's testament.
Pero Hernández Payagua and Pedro de Portugal (both deceased)	Poxo	25,000 ps	Lawsuit pending.

Total: 560,700 pesos

Source: RAH Col. Muñoz, Cosas del Perú Tomo 65 [A/92]: 196r–197v, from Diego de Ocampo's account of *encomendero* debts for taking excess tributes.

Note: Internal evidence dates the list to between 1556 (date of Robles's execution) and 1559 (date of Vela death and will) (Audiencia de Charcas; original charges from 1551, augmented with additional information between 1556 and 1559, soon after Robles's execution for the murder of Pedro de Hinojosa).

ᵃ Reference to testamentary restitution here.

ᵇ Reference to restitution in will elsewhere.

king of encomendero excess, while eyewitness accounts of torture at times echo passages from Las Casas's *Brevísima Relación*. According to Indian as well as Spanish witnesses, Vela had used torture and terror to guarantee delivery of the goods, labor, and silver that he demanded, and despondent Indians had committed suicide to avoid further punishment.

In the trial presided over by Estopiñán, all three of the caciques whom Gasca had placed in Vela's hands testified against Vela. Here is testimony from the cacique Cari, who details the consequences of a shortfall in his tribute deliveries to Vela:

> About two years ago . . . Hernán Vela . . . ordered a *negro* named Juan / to strip this witness, and thus naked the said Hernán Vela ordered the said negro to hang [this witness] by the feet from a roof beam of the said house, . . . and [Vela] ordered that this witness be whipped in front of him. And the said negro with a whip gave this witness many lashes, until he made the blood spurt, and after being well whipped his master ordered the negro to cure the wound with chili peppers, which the negro did and this witness promised to give him the ten marks of silver that were short so as not to be whipped further. . . . And then the judge ordered him to show these marks . . . and he found certain signs. . . ." (AGI Escribanía de Cámara 497C, 22: 15r–15v, "Memorial del pleito que tratta el señor don Rodrigo Calderón . . . con . . . el dicho Hernán Vela . . . ")²²

This and other abuses were confirmed by further witnesses, including Vela's *mayordomo* Barrientos and a parish priest. As horrifying as these accounts appear to us, the Indians' suit put far more emphasis on matters of fiscal malfeasance. This required careful accounting. And so first the Aullagas caciques, and then a series of khipu kamayuqs, were called upon by the prosecution to read their khipus into the legal record. Similar procedures were carried out by caciques and khipu kamayuqs of Sacaca and Chayanta. Accountant witnesses provide astonishing detail of the deliveries of corn, cloth, and animals (as well as many other goods and services) to

Vela's Indian-built houses in Potosí and La Plata, including a running account of the labor time and animal energy invested in building the houses and making the deliveries, and the market prices of all goods on the dates delivered. Khipu records also reveal Vela's Potosí interests. Anywhere from 170 to 200 Indians delivered a weekly quota of one mark of silver each, totaling over the period in question some 23,000 marks (one mark equaling four pesos) from mining operations alone.[23]

Apart from questioning the validity and reliability of khipus, Vela sought to strike Indian testimony altogether by questioning the reliability of Indians as witnesses. Calling them notorious drunkards and infidels who were habitual liars, he asked that all Indian testimony be discounted, and in particular that of the khipu accountant, who "was drunk as the old men who have charge of my *repartimiento*'s accounts always were" (AGI Escribanía de Cámara 497B, 16: 52r, "Autos presentados por parte de los yndios aullagas. . . ."). Again, the ploy is repeated in the Sacaca and Chayanta suits (AGI Justicia 654, "La Plata 1572. Los herederos del General Pedro de Ynojosa, difunto, con don Hernando de Zarate, y doña Luisa de Vibar, su muger, Vezinos de la ciudad de la Plata, sobre ciertos pesos").[24]

Unfortunately for Vela, first Estopiñán and then the Audiencia de Lima, to which he had appealed, found him guilty of extorting some 63,000 pesos of excess tribute during the first two and a half years that he held his encomienda. We have seen the sums adjudicated against other encomenderos of the region. Most of the accused avoided the application of a final sentence, settling out of court with their Indians by making token payments, or by revising their testaments to include some amount of restitution. But Vela refused to settle, appealing his case to the Council of the Indies back in Castile. At the same time, Vela liquidated his Peruvian assets and returned to Castile, where he invested a vast fortune in *censos* and *juros*, types of interest–bearing bonds, and in the purchase from Philip II of rights to the tributes of Castilian vassals. Accomplishing in Castile what they could not in the Indies, men like Vela converted Indian silver into permanent and heritable señoríos, lordships over Spanish townsmen.

Encomendero Restitution via Testament

A few of the accused, such as the encomendero of Tapacarí, Gómez de Solís, responded with immediate settlements that provided restitution in the hopes that suits would not be pursued later. In his will of April 1561, Solís acknowledged that, as ordered by Estopiñán, he had settled with his

Indians by returning to them the five thousand pesos that Indian khipus recorded as excessive. But his conscience was not yet at ease:

> Notwithstanding that in conformity with the above I am free of the said caciques and Indians, for the good that against their will they did for me in that time, . . . and also if I have not [given them] the religious indoctrination that was required . . . , I command that two thousand Spanish sheep and one hundred cows be purchased for the said caciques and Indians of the repartimiento de Tapacarí . . . all of which should be paid for from my estate, and in the absence of the estate, that they be bought through the mercy of my beloved wife, doña Luisa de Vivar. . . .[25]
>
> And with this it seems to me, being as indebted as I am [to the Indians], I do everything in my power to discharge my conscience, and thus I beg the said . . . Indians to seek to become wealthy with these animals and to pardon me in anything else . . . for let them and anyone else see how meager are my means. And I ask by the mercy of my beloved wife doña Luisa de Vivar to take great care to treat the Indians well, favoring them and helping them through in every way possible, because they are good Indians and have served me well.[26] (AGI Justicia 654, "La Plata 1572," 205r–205v, 206v)

Other encomenderos, such as Martín de Robles of Chayanta, signed restitution agreements only to later renege. Robles, who joined with the seditious Castillo conspiracy to again seek the autonomy that Gonzalo Pizarro had failed to win, was executed after a summary trial in Potosí in 1556. However, he did have time to make a last-minute will:

> Item: that I owe restitution to the Indians of Parinacocha, which while it has been ordered to be done has not yet been carried out, of the things that I have taken from them, 20,000 gold pesos.
>
> Item: that I owe to the Indians who I have in encomienda at present, from whom I took 25,000 pesos (a bit more) above the tasa.
>
> . . . and because my death has been ordered so suddenly, it was not possible to declare more . . . and of my declaration concerning what I owed to the Indians I was not completely certain if I had declared something more, which should be checked out with the Indians and paid from my estate. (AGI Justicia 651, 1a: 657v–659r, "La Plata año de 1571 Los yndios . . . de Chayanta con doña Juana de los Ríos").[27]

Men like Gómez de Solís and de Robles saved themselves from eternal damnation by opening up Pandora's boxes for their heirs. Alonso de Montemayor, encomendero of Sacaca, tried the same thing, as did Lope de Mendieta and Gómes de Alvarado. After his death in 1553, heirs of the fabulously wealthy Pedro de Hinojosa made their own settlement with their Indians. And in perhaps the most well-known act of encomendero restitution in Charcas, Lorenzo de Aldana donated great wealth, mainly in dairy cattle, to the Indians of his encomienda of Paría.[28] The latter made a name for themselves, still valid to this day, for the quality of their cheeses.

In spite of their efforts to resolve conflicts over restitution out of court, the heirs of Montemayor and Robles were for years tied up in costly litigation to preserve their estates from the consequence of conscience. But the man who brought down true royal wrath on his heirs' heads was Hernán Vela. After filing an appeal and refusing to settle with his Indians, Vela had returned to Spain and purchased the town of Siete Iglesias, for complex reasons which I pursue elsewhere (Abercrombie n.d.). But shortly after Vela's death in 1559, his heirs—two small children under the tutelage of Vela's widow—suffered a reversal in fortune when the Council of the Indies ruled in favor of the Indians of Aullagas, confiscated Vela's holdings in Castile, and ordered full restitution.

Vela died at the age of forty-three or forty-four in Valladolid, only a few months after finalizing his purchase (AGI Escribanía de Cámara 497 C, 22, "Memorial del Pleito. . . .").[29] His minor children, Gonzalo Vela and doña Isabel Vela, and his widow, doña Ana Gutiérrez, inherited not the estate but a massive legal tangle. But Vela had prepared a final weapon: his will.

Vela's testament made a posthumous ploy to free himself from the burdens of lawsuit and conscience. It was an act of testamentary restitution, freeing Indians of one half of the outstanding tributes since his departure for Spain. The donation would take effect, however, only if the Indians would forsake all legal actions against him.[30] Even that limited and self-interested act, however, was essentially vacuous, for Vela had already given up half of his tributes, assigning them to the king, in exchange for Crown permission to continue to hold the encomienda in absentia. No doubt his agreement with the king, signed in 1553 and renewed in 1558, involved other arrangements, too. Cash payments to the Crown might well have helped Vela to win the right to purchase a señorío and subsequent rights to Spanish tributes.

Hernán Vela's testament established three *capellanías* (chaplaincies) in the church of San Pelayo in his newly purchased seigneurial town of Siete Iglesias.[31] He was to be buried in the central chapel. Capellanías, however, were more than just tombs and altars; the amount served as capital, the income on which was to provide perpetual salaries for three priests.

These were to perform daily masses for the salvation of Vela's soul. Establishment of capellanías was fairly routine for well-to-do testators of the period in both Spain and the Indies, but Vela's stipulations went in an unusual direction.[32]

In addition to the masses for Vela, priests were perpetually to pray for the "conversaçión" of the Aullagas Indians. Whether he meant *conversión* or *conservación* (or perhaps—in accord with the demands of his encomienda title—both), it is impossible to say, but he did seem here to acknowledge some wrongdoing. Yet since the capital for the capellanías was part of the Indians' claim, Vela's posthumous charitable work on behalf of Indian souls would take effect only if the law enabled Vela's heirs to keep his ill-gotten Indian silver. In the end, they did not keep it. The chaplaincies, however, were established, and three priests hired to pray for Vela's soul.[33]

In a transatlantic transubstantiation, Indian encomienda payments had been transformed into a dramatic rise in the Vela family's social standing. At the time of his testament and death in 1559, Vela suffered the death of his physical body, but the transfer of property and status to his heirs, through which he hoped to achieve conscience-cleansing and lawsuit-erasing testamentary payments to Indians, kept his social person alive, just as priestly masses sped his soul on to paradise. For Vela, however, the testament was inadequate as an instrument of immortality. His social death came in 1663–67, when his heirs were stripped of the proceeds of the silver he had bequeathed them. Unlike Vela's physical body, his heritable social status did not die a natural death. It was killed, run through by the sword of the law, or, as the jurist Solórzano held, by the sword of God's wrath. In his compilation of the laws of the Indies, Solórzano (who had served as judge of one of the Vela heirs' later appeals) used Vela's case to illustrate the importance of encomendero restitution.

In a chapter of *Política indiana* titled "On the second duty of encomienda, and encomenderos, which is to watch over the spiritual and temporal welfare of the Indians," Solórzano argued that "the punishments established for those who have exceeded legal limits be carried out to the letter, so that bad customs should not continue, and frequent excesses should not provoke Divine ire." Solórzano then echoed scripture: "Those who through fraud hunger for what does not belong to them shall be deprived of what is theirs, . . . and thus those who take money from the miserably poor, shall call poverty unto themselves." Noting that this was what he tried to practice in the cases of encomendero excesses he had judged, Solórzano quoted the Old

Testament to sum up the outcome of the Vela case: "*You shall not afflict any widow or orphan. If you do afflict them, and they cry out to me, I will surely hear their cry; and my wrath will burn, and I will kill you with the sword, and your wives shall become widows and your children fatherless*" (Solórzano, *Política indiana* 3: chap. 26, paragraphs 30–31; emphasis in original].[34]

So much, then, for Hernán Vela's widow and orphans.[35] As the encomenderos of Charcas and their would-be heirs discovered, winning the spoils was one thing, keeping them another. The transfer of property, privilege, and power across the generations was fraught with dangers perhaps greater than those faced by the immortal soul at Saint Peter's gate. And this turns out to have been just as true for the cacique as for the encomendero.

Caciques and Testaments

Encomenderos sometimes used harsh measures to coerce their caciques to gather massive tribute payments and endure endless labors for encomendero benefit. And since the very existence of encomienda was predicated upon faults they might attribute to caciques' rule, the latter were subject to accusations of being tyrants, kinds of illegitimate princes whose authority could be legally usurped by morally superior pretenders to noble status. Caciques were hard put to keep hold of their privileged roles within indigenous society. They were forced to mediate between tributary Indians and Spaniards in the collection of tribute, which was in any case a novel business for Andeans. Before the conquest, caciques (and the Inka state) had asked for and received labor prestations of their subjects; now they were required to hand over property. Property transfers became the means by which colonial caciques now produced and maintained their social standing, not only by collecting tributes, but also by engaging in trade. In the postconquest Andes, caciques had an interest in amassing property and monetary wealth, whether to subsidize their subjects' tributes and protect them, or to enrich themselves so as to buy the perquisites of Spanish-style aristocracy. At the same time, they were now subject to Castilian norms of nobility. To prove their equivalence to Castile's noble dukes, counts, and marquises, caciques had to abide by Castilian rules of legitimacy in marriage and lineage. Increasingly, they sought private title to lands, houses, and businesses that might be passed on to their first-born legitimate sons. So to a large degree, they were required by the Spanish Crown to act in ways that their Indian subjects would indeed interpret as tyrannical. To guarantee proper transmission of their status, caciques, too, wrote wills.

At the same time, caciques had to demonstrate that they were the most upstanding of Christians, as devoted to the evangelization of their Indians as any *doctrina* priest. For they were always subject to the fatal accusation of apostasy, of having fallen back into pre-Christian idolatries. Estopiñán's proceeding against Hernán Vela suggested as much, when, in what appears to be an effort to smear the evangelizing zeal of Vela, cacique witnesses were sworn in in an exceedingly unusual way: Instead of being asked to swear the truth of their statements by making the sign of the cross, they were "sworn in giving reverence [mochando] to the sun and to the earth, according to their custom" (AGI Escribanía de Cámara 497C, 22: 10v, "Memorial del pleito. . . .").[36] We can surmise that the wily Estopiñán thereby hoped to prove the serious allegation that Vela had forsaken his duty properly to evangelize his Indians. Of course, the move also made it possible for Vela, on appeal, to argue the unreliability of infidel Indian testimony, just as he doubted the credibility of their khipus.[37]

To counterbalance the selfish and un-Christian behavior that encomenderos imputed to them, and which caciques brought on themselves through their efforts at capital accumulation and succession to office, they, too, paid attention to matters of conscience, being just as needful of cleansing Christian charity as any encomendero. As with the contrast between Lorenzo de Aldana or Gómez de Solís and the too-wily Hernán Vela, however, caciques also differed from one another in the relative weight given to charity and the degree to which they recognized illegitimate children. They differed, that is, in the balance of their post-mortem payments.

In early September of 1571, don García Mamani, cacique of Tapacarí and one-time recipient of Goméz de Solís's testamentary largesse, assembled relatives, witnesses, and priests in order to record a register of his possessions, heirs, and testamentary transfers. His will, carried out by his Spanish executors the following year, has been transcribed and published, along with the khipu-based "memorias de haciendas" that Mamani left behind, by Mercedes del Río (1990b: 107–13). Exceedingly rich in its references to types of Andean sumptuary textiles and other insignia of noble rank—such as silver plaques that were to hang on certain ritual occasions from his shirt of exquisite *cumbe* cloth, silver crowns (*pillos*), articles for large-scale *vicuña* hunts, and a pair of boots made of cordoban leather; the *memoria* and testament also list herd animals, mules and plow oxen, as well as saddles, houses, lands, and stores of wheat, maize, and *chuño* (freeze-dried potatoes). In a manner not unlike that of Spaniards, Mamani chose to divvy up his possessions unequally, favoring his legitimate son and providing smaller amounts to his six illegitimate sons. His daughters (three legitimate, five illegitimate) received the smallest amounts. Once again, in consonance with Spanish testamentary practice, nothing is given to the six women who mothered his illegitimate children.

Although written by the priest of Tapacarí, Mamani's testament is unusual in its lack of attention to Christian testamentary formulas. Charitable contributions are present but scarce. For poor Indians, he appears to give two shirts and one blanket or shawl of common wool (*abasca*), though perhaps we should assume that he meant to provide each poor Indian with this clothing. Young bulls are also to be slaughtered to feed the poor Indians, and seventy goats distributed among his *yanaconas*, "because they are in my charge, and to lighten my conscience" (del Río 1990b: 109, 111).[38] Like many Spaniards and some other caciques of the period, Mamani had control over Indians called "yanaconas," who, exempt from tribute, served the will of the native lord. As for his burial and masses for his soul, and contributions to the church, there is little to report: His body was to be buried in the church of his home town; fray Francisco Bezerra, who helped in the redaction of the will, was to be paid for saying nine masses for Mamani's soul, along with another twenty masses for which the friar would receive forty pesos should Mamani's brother succeed in collecting a debt for maize and flour he had sent to market in Potosí (112). So much for charity.

Several years later, another cacique, don Juan Colque Guarache of Quillacas and Asanaques, dictated his last will and testament to a trusted priest and city father of Potosí (see the will at the end of this chapter). Now Colque Guarache had succeeded to his father's role as *mallku* (as caciques were called in Aymara) of the Killaka people (a large-scale federation of four pre-Columbian diarchies). In the early 1570s he parlayed service to the Spanish Crown into a powerful administrative post as captain of the *mita* of Potosí. Several of Viceroy Toledo's *ordenanzas* for that city specifically mention Colque (Sarabia Viejo 1989). As a man of influence, he had made himself useful to the Crown during the civil wars, just as his father, Guarache, had done during the conquest itself. Guarache had surrendered himself to Francisco Pizarro on the outskirts of Cuzco in 1533, along with Manco Inca (Abercrombie 1998). In his *memoriales*, the son Colque Guarache proudly details his father's service to Inka emperors, as well as to the Spanish king, and refers to Huayna Capac's gift to him of the privilege of being carried in a litter like a great Inka lord on the shoulders of fifty yanaconas. Yet there are fewer feathers and other prestige symbols of Andean lordship in Colque Guarache's will than in that of the relatively more obscure Mamani. Drawn up after his death by his chosen Spanish executors in the city where he lived and worked, apparently on the basis of his orally transmitted wishes, Colque's will contains no reference to khipus, although his khipus are cited as a source on pre-Columbian religion by the chronicler known as the Anonymous Jesuit (1879: 143). And while Colque Guarache's Latin-trained son (Juan Colque El Mozo) was soon to go about his business dressed in fine silks (Capoche 1959), Colque Guarache still valued fine Andean textiles, such as the *cumbe* made by the *cumbe kamayuq* weavers in his employ. In a memorial to the king in the mid–1570s, the same man detailed the importance as emblems of status of the cumbe shirts given to his father by the Inka emperor himself (for the memorial, see Espinoza Soriano 1981; for commentary, Abercrombie 1998).

Through his duties as captain of the mita, Colque Guarache maintained a grip over the peoples of his large-scale society that other lords of the period did not, although it was precisely the services he performed for Spaniards that gave him this power. Those very services made him a virtual prisoner of the city and mining complex of Potosí. There, the pressure to conform to Spanish and Christian values was perhaps greater than anywhere else. A quintessentially colonial figure, Colque Guarache fully embodied the cultural frontier that was Spanish Peru.[39]

Already by 1567 Colque Guarache had spent money seeking the legitimation of his "natural" sons (born to his wife before their marriage) as well as their education in the Castilian king's court (Levillier 1918; Abercrombie 1986). In contrast to illegitimate children born to women other than the father's wife, "hijos naturales" were children born to a couple prior to their Christian marriage. And the Indians in Colque Guarache's service (no doubt his yanaconas, as attested in his memoriales), are rewarded simply with "what they ought to be" for their work. Colque Guarache is also stingy when it comes to his daughters. While Mamani grants even his illegitimate daughters as much as forty pesos and twenty sheep (del Río 1990b: 111–12), Colque gives to each of his three *hijas naturales* (his wife's daughters from before their marriage) the sum total of six llamas, two sets of clothing of common cloth, and a dozen Castilian sheep. Colque's illegitimate children fared less well. The only one mentioned in his testament, one Bernardo Guarache, receives not a legacy but the demand for collection from him of twenty pesos lent by Spaniards to pay the costs of his legitimation. Colque's "natural sons," on the other hand, come out quite nicely, especially his eldest son, don Juan Colque, who takes a traditional lion's share of his father's estate and also succeeds to his office. Even then, however, don Juan Colque is ordered to return to the estate a black felt hat that belonged to his father.

Colque Guarache, who as captain of the mita of Potosí was responsible for sending hundreds of forced Indian laborers into their lethal mine work every Monday, had tried to generate a positive cash flow by renting lands and, in company with a Spaniard, running his own silver mill and foundry. But he had apparently left his Indian workers unpaid, just as he had failed to pay his cumbe kamayuqs.

Like Mamani of Tapacarí (as well as Hernán Vela and other Spanish testators), Colque Guarache of Quillacas was aided by a Spanish priest in the preparation of his testament. But this priest seems to have done better by the church, for in comparison with Mamani's case (though not, perhaps, with Vela's), the transfer of property to charity and to the church is substantial. Perhaps it was the case that the weight upon Colque's conscience was heavier, as a wealthy mita captain and silverworks owner, and to be lightened needed more masses, better funeral arrangements, and larger charitable contributions. Just as likely, as an inhabitant of the Americas' premier city, and as a powerful force in both sacred and secular colonial institutions, Colque Guarache, in death as well as life, was under greater pressure to carry himself with noble bearing in a European manner. Whatever the reasons, Colque was posthumously generous to the church and the poor. Accompanied by four priests to his entombment in his urban parish church of San Bernardo, Colque's soul was whisked aloft by the heavenly music of a sung mass and the elevating words of four spoken ones, then pushed onward on the octave of his death by another eight spoken masses. Six masses in Potosí's cathedral church, another two sung masses sung on the *novena* of his death, and a further fifty masses (twenty in San Bernardo), helped to speed his soul to heaven. Unnamed persons for whom Colque worked were enjoined to pay for another fifty masses, and no doubt some of the eighty pesos sent to the church of Colque's rural hometown, Quillacas, also paid for masses for his soul. Then there were alms. Colque paid ten postmortem pesos of alms to Potosí's hospital, made small donations to two urban confraternities, and made unspecified "required and customary" testamentary donations (alms to the poor of various sorts). Finally, he gave a hundred pesos in alms to the poor.

Colque Guarache's testamentary legacies share much with those of contemporary Spaniards, in some ways outdoing them in attention to Christian charity. As an Indian, he would not have been urged to make formal restitution, as were encomenderos, but as to alms and donations he was otherwise their equal. Does that mean that Mamani was a "more Andean" cacique, revealing more cultural difference through his property transfers? Perhaps. Certainly, as del Río (1990b: 77–113) has shown, much can be learned about Andean symbolisms of power through attention to the feathers, crowns, and cloth transferred in wills like Mamani's.[40] But we must be careful not to overplay the degree of cultural difference embodied in a contractually binding document meant for Spanish law courts and archives. As to the sumptuary goods bequeathed to Mamani's heirs, remember that Spaniards also gave legacies of clothing, jewelry, and other status-marking items to their heirs—if not cumbe, then silk and brocades.

The external signs of aristocratic prerogative differed between Spain and the Andes, but so far as we can make out from Spanish and Andean wills, not much else varied significantly. Both transfer houses, silverwork, estates, and coin; both transfer debts, along with credits (debts owed by others to them). Encomenderos and caciques even share a testamentary penchant for formally recognizing and rewarding their illegitimate children. The native lords, however, not long past polygynous pre-Columbian days, may have had more of them. The fact would no doubt have irritated encomenderos, perhaps due as much to envy as to moral outrage.

Conclusion

What can we make of this perhaps unusual collection of wills, hailing from an agitated time? No doubt with a larger sample and a closer eye for detail, one might piece together a major part of the story of early-colonial Peru. It has been my more modest aim, however, to use a motley sample of encomendero and cacique wills to evaluate a more general question, one simple to phrase, but difficult to answer: Why and for what ends are testaments made? I believe that regardless of the peculiarities of wills that pay coerced restitution, aim to defraud through charity, and in general make invidious distinctions between kinsmen and non-kinsmen, inheritance and alms, testaments open a window onto the measures taken in the sixteenth century, and still today, to prolong life beyond death.

As a result of the centrality of property transfers to the well-being of the deceased in the hereafter and heirs as the departed one's substitutes, testaments are similar to the most common sort of document preserved in the books of public notaries. They are formulaic, requiring witnesses and powers of attorney and methods to protect against illegal emendations and forgeries, and they make liberal use of accounting techniques to carefully register the exact nature of the property being transferred and the precise identity of the recipients of that property and the boons owing to its transfer. As a result, wills are rich sources for understanding what was entailed in sixteenth-century notions of wealth and property, and for assessing relative wealth of testators according to the criteria of the day. Testaments also provide insight into how social relations were understood as being constituted through property transfers. Through wills, testators mapped out for us how social relationships were created, maintained, terminated, or themselves transferred, across generations and across the gap between this world and the next.

With respect to their accounting techniques, an unusual and shared feature of the native and Spanish wills considered here is the use of khipus. These accounting devices, made of a single braided cord with a series of additional cords dangling from it bearing an assortment of knots, had themselves been inherited from pre-Columbian days but were still in use in the last half of the sixteenth century. Spaniards, of course, had little use for khipus, and few if any Spaniards actually knew how to "read" them. Yet native peoples continued to use khipus for a variety of purposes. In Spanish wills, khipus made their appearance as devices on which were recorded prior transfers of property from Indians to Spaniards: khipus enter Spanish wills, as well as Spanish litigation records, precisely because such prior transfers, notably the payment of tribute, had become a burden on the king's conscience and therefore a risk to encomendero souls and legacies. The accounting record of khipus appears in Indian testaments as their own best register of property to be transferred. They appear in Spanish testaments as an index of what encomenderos, whose wealth derived from tribute payments Indians were forced to make to them, now were required (by Crown administrators) to repay to Indians. Restitution payments, figured by reference to khipu accounts, were one among many of such testaments' property transfers to non-kin, such as charitable contributions, that worked to erase the testator's past sins. Because restitution payments, like contractual debts, were also enforceable by Crown courts, paying restitution via the testament was a measure taken not only on behalf of the testator's eternal soul but also a means of guaranteeing the immortality of the testator's social identity (wealth, status, and name) through inheritance to kin. Charity worked to secure eternal life of the spirit; inheritance of social position secured by property gained the sort of immortality we call family heritage or lineage; restitution payments aimed to guarantee both outcomes.

Examining native wills alongside of Spanish ones, I have pointed to their similarities. This should surprise no one, since all such testaments were produced for the archive, written out by official notaries in the presence of priests and sometimes officers of the court, and followed established legal procedures of both church and state to ensure that the final testament would be efficacious. As legal instruments, wills were to achieve certain preordained effects. That much is clear. But to what ends did testators and other interested parties carry out their work? The testaments of both Spaniard and Indian, I suggest, invariably address two distinct but interrelated issues: the orderly transfer of property and social standing to the testator's heirs, and the salvation of the testator's soul. As it happens, in the last will and testament, eternal salvation is also brought about through the transfer of assets; specifically, by alienating such property from the testator's heirs and giving it instead to other institutions and persons, whether by paying outstanding debts, funding masses and funerary rites, donating funds to charitable organizations and religious institutions, or outright gifts to needy individuals or those whom the deceased has in some way mistreated during life. In the testament of Indian or Spaniard, self-interested protection of the departed soul and his or her surviving family members goes hand in glove with acts of charity that must appear to be selfless. The testament invariably begins with a profession of faith, affirming that one dies in order to live. It then records procedures suggesting that one gives in order to keep.

To extend recent insights of sociologist Viviana Zelicer (1994a, 1994b), the distinct sorts of payments made in testaments work to clarify, and rectify, transgressions made necessary by the threat of extinction. Through their testaments, individuals define family or lineage as a propertied corporation, shattering the illusion of everyday life that family loyalties follow from attachments of blood and love, from freely given succor rather than from business contracts. At the same time, the cutthroat and monetarized everyday business transactions with non-kin by which fortunes are amassed and preserved are transformed in the testament. Once debts are repaid and collected and the estate made whole, it is divided up between the legacy of heirs and the alienated sums given as charitable gifts and donations. As they turn kin relations into monetarized corporate transactions, testaments affirm the testators' membership in a larger human family, freely giving as an emblem of their Christian love to those not their kin. One kind of property transfer attempts to undo, or gain forgiveness for, the other, while through these channels of distinct payments the deceased struggles to rise phoenix-like from his own ashes. In this, Indian caciques and Spanish encomenderos were birds of a feather.

274 ℘ Thomas A. Abercrombie

Last Will and Testament of Don Juan Colque Guarache, Cacique
of Quillacas and Captain of the Mita of Potosí, 1584[41]
(ANB Escribanía de Cámara 1804, 193: 11–18)

/f.12r/ En el nombre de la Santísima Trinidad y de la eterna unidad
Padre Hijo y Espíritu Sancto tres personas distintas y una esencia divina
con cuya gracia todas las cosas tienen buen principio y dichoso fin amen.
Sepan quantos esta carta vieren como nos Juan Núñez Maldonado vecino
desta villa ymperial de Potosí e Dionisio Velásquez religioso de la casa
colegio de la companía del dulce nombre de Jesús desta dicha villa de un
acuerdo y conformidad en nombre y en vos y como comisarios que somos
de don Juan Colque Guarache capitan de los indios de la provincia de los
charcas y de la provincia de los orcoṡuyos y cacique principal de los
Quillacas y Azanaques y morador en esta dicha villa difunto que dios tiene
y por virtud del poder que para otorgarlo sera declarado nos dió y otorgó
ante Fernando de Medina escribano público desta dicha villa su tenor del
qual sacado de su original de que yo el presente escribano doy fe es como
se sigue—En el [page torn]
  . . . /f.12v/ y de la gloriosa virgen Santa María su madre sepan quantos esta carta vieren como yo don Juan Colque Guarache . . . provincia
de Orcosuyos y cacique principal de los Quillacas y Asanaques residente
en la villa ymperial de Potosí del Perú otorgo y conosco por esta presente
carta y digo que por quanto al presente estoy enfermo en una cama de
enfermedad grave a cuya causa al presente no puedo hacer ni ordenar mi
testamento y última voluntad por tanto en la mejor vía y forma que haya
lugar de derecho otorgo que doy todo mi poder cumplido qual de derecho se requiere y es necesario y más puede y debe valer e para más valer
fuere necesario a los señores Juan Núñez Maldonado alcalde ordinario
desta villa por Su Magestad y al Padre Velásquez de la companía del
dulce nombre de Jesús mi confesor y a cada uno y a qualquier dellos
ynsólidum especialmente para que si dios nuestro señor fuere servido de
llevarme desta presente vida de la enfermedad que al presente tengo
pueda [page torn] mi testamento /f.13r/ última y postrimera voluntad
nombrando lugar y sepultura en que mi cuerpo sea sepultado en lugar
sagrado con la pompa y según que les pareciere y descargar mi alma
según y como yo lo tengo tratado y comunicado con ellos nombrando
por mis herederos por el remaniente de mis bienes a don Juan Fernando
y don Francisco y don Miguel mis hijos naturales porque yo los nombro
e declaro por tales mejorando al dicho don Juan Colque mi hijo maior en
el tercio y quinto de todos mis bienes derechos y acciones y lo demás por

yguales partes y por Albaceas nombro al dicho Señor Juan Núñez Maldonado y Padre Velásquez a cada uno y qualquier dellos ynsólidum para que cumplan lo contenido en el testamento según que en el se contuviere en el qual quiere que hagan todas las mandas y legados que paresieren y que aquellos se cumplan guarden y executen según y como si por mi fueran fechas que para el dicho efecto apruebo y ratifico lo que hicieran y quiero y es mi voluntad que aquello sea llevado a /f.13v/ debida execución con efecto y por la presente doy por ningunos y por de ningún valor ni efecto otro qualquier testamento o poder que haya dado para testar que quiero que no valgan ni hagan fe en juicio ni fuera del salvo este poder y el testamento que otorgaren los susodichos en virtud del que quiero que valga por mi testamento última y postrimera voluntad o en aquella via y forma y manera que de derecho a lugar que es fecho en la villa de Potosí a veinte y ocho días del mes de setiembre de 1583 y lo firmó de su nombre el otorgante quien yo el escribano doy fé que conosco testigos el Padre Alonso Variana de la companía del dulce nombre de Jesús y el hermano Domingo de Vermeo e Pedro de Arjona y Pedro de Alcalá e Pedro Lópes de Aguirre residente en esta villa todo lo qual otorgo por interpretación del dicho Pedro de Alcalá ante mi Fernando de Medina escribano público e yo Luis García escribano de su magestad público y del cabildo /f.14r/ desta villa imperial de Potosí doy fé que de los registros del dicho mi oficio hize sacar este poder el qual parece aver pasado ante Fernando de Medina escribano de su magestad que lo uso por mi ausencia y hice aquí mi signo en testimonio de verdad Luis García escribano público —

En virtud del qual dicho poder suso incorporado y del usando decimos que por quanto el dicho don Juan Colque trató y comunicó con nosotros la orden de su testamento y despusición de sus bienes y descargo de su alma y consiencia y porque lo que nos toca en cumplimiento de la voluntad del dicho don juan Colque por tanto otorgamos y conosemos que hacemos y ordenamos este su testamento mandas y legados del en la forma y manera siguiente—

Primeramente queremos y mandamos que el cuerpo del dicho don Juan Colque sea sepultado como al presente lo esta en la yglesia del Señor San Bernardo desta dicha villa parroquia de los Quillacas y que de allí no sea traspasado a otra parte ningúna porque así fue su voluntad y la nuestra en su nombre —

Yten declaramos que el día de su enterramiento del dicho don Juan Colque se dixó una misa cantada /f.14v/ y quatro resadas y se pagaron la limosna dellas —

Yten declaramos que en el ochavario y honrras que hicieron al dicho don Juan Colque en la dicha yglesia donde está enterrado se le dijeron ocho misas rezadas —

Yten el día del entierro del dicho don Juan Colque acompañaron su cuerpo quatro sacerdotes los quales dijeron misa por su ánima —

Yten se gastó de sera en el entierro y onnras que se hicieron del dicho don Juan y ofrenda [ ] pesos corrientes —

Yten se dijeron seis misas por el ánima del dicho difunto en la yglesia mayor desta villa —

Yten se dijeron otras dos misas cantadas con sus vigilias el último día del novenario por el ánima del dicho difunto —

Yten mandamos se digan por el ánima del dicho don Juan cinquenta misas rezadas las veinte dellas en la dicha iglesia de Señor San Bernardo donde está enterrado las quales diga el cura de la dicha parroquia y las demás se digan por los clerigos y en las partes que paresiere a los albaceas que fueren declarados en el testamento y se de por ellas la limosna acostumbrada — /f.15r/

Yten mandamos que se de en limosna al hospital de la villa diez pesos corrientes —

Yten mandamos a la cofradía de San Salvador que a poco tiempo se fundó y se celebra su advocación en la casa colegio del nombre de Jesús de la dicha villa quatro pesos y a la del Sanctísimo Sacramento de la dicha casa seis pesos de plata corriente —

Yten mandamos a las mandas forzosas y acostumbradas que se suelen y acostumbran mandar en los otros testamentos a cada una quatro reales con que las apartamos de los bienes del dicho don Juan Colque —

Yten mandamos que se paguen de los bienes del dicho don Juan a la yglesia de los Quillacas ochenta pesos corrientes —

Yten mandamos se paguen a los indios que trabajaron en el ingenio y obra que el dicho don Juan Colque tiene en companía de Diego de Morales en la ribera desta villa todos los jornales que se les deviere por la cuenta que dello hubiere y pareciere —

Yten mandamos se paguen a Melchor Vázquez mercader cinquenta y tres pesos corrientes de mercaduría que sacó el dicho difunto de su tienda—

Yten mandamos se paguen a dos /f.15v/ cumbecamayos indios a cada uno veinte pesos corrientes por las cosas de cumbe que hicieron al dicho don Juan Colque los quales dichos yndios conoce don Juan, hijo del dicho difunto —

Yten mandamos se paguen los servicios de indios e indias que parecieren aver servido al dicho difunto lo que por ello hubiere de aver —

Yten mandamos se cobre de Diego de Morales morador en esta dicha villa todos los pesos que pareciere deber de tiempo de dos años que ha tenido a su cargo administración y cobranza del ingenio que en su companía tiene el dicho don Juan en la ribera de esta villa de que le pertenece y a de aver la mitad y para ello se tome cuentas al dicho Diego de Morales—

Yten se cobren de don Bernardo Guarache hijo del dicho don Juan Colque veinte pesos corrientes los diez dellos que le dió Alonso Franco y los otros diez yo el padre Dionisio Velásquez los quales se le dieron prestados para las cuentas de su legitimidad —

Yten se cobre de don Juan Colque hijo del dicho difunto lo que declarare deber a los bienes del dicho difunto —

Yten mandamos se cobren /f.16r/ de un platero que conoce y save su nombre don Juan hijo del dicho difunto un jarro y una tasa de plata pagandosela al platero la hechura dello lo que se le debiere porque lo tiene en su poder —

Yten mandamos se cobre del dicho don Juan Colque hijo del dicho difunto un sombrero de fieltro negro que pertenece a los bienes del dicho difunto por razón de ser suyo —

Yten mandamos se cobre de quienes deba pagar los pesos que se deben al dicho difunto por razón del salario que les pertenece por su oficio de capitán el tiempo que pareciere aver servido el dicho oficio conforme al salario que se ha señalado —

Yten mandamos se cobre de la caja de la comunidad de Asanaques y Quillacas lo que pareciere devérsele por razón del cargo de cacique principal de los dichos pueblos —

Yten mandamos se cobren de Rodrigo Arias de Vuiza quatrocientos pesos ensayados que parece el dicho difunto le dió para que los llevase a Castilla para ciertos negocios y no los ha llevado —

Yten mandamos se cobre de los indios y demás personas que estan en la chacra de Pocpo lo que /f.16v/ pareciere deber de los frutos y rentas de la dicha chacra que ha entrado en su poder del tiempo que la han tenido a su cargo la dicha chacra —

Yten mandamos se digan por el ánima del dicho difunto y de aquellas personas a quien el dicho difunto fuere en algún cargo cinquenta misas rezadas las quales se repartare las veinte y cinco de ellas en el monasterio de Señor Sancto Domingo y las trece restantes por los sacerdotes más pobres desta villa y se pague la limonsna acostumbrada —

Yten mandamos se gasten y distribuyan cien pesos corrientes en pobres y limosnas desta villa al parecer y voluntad de los albaceas del dicho difunto y por su ánima —

Yten mandamos que haya y lleve doña Beatrís Sisa Ocllo mujer del dicho don Juan Colque difunto los bienes gananciales que les perteneciere despues de pagadas las deudas del dicho difunto y sacados los bienes que el dicho don Juan Colque tenía antes y primero que contrajo matrimonio con la dicha /f.17r/ su mujer y todos los pesos que pareciere aver cobrado a su oficio y cargo de capitán y cacique principal —

Yten mandamos que la dicha doña Beatrís Sicssa Ocllo mujer del dicho don Juan traiga a cuerpo de hacienda y bienes partibles todos aquellos bienes que hubiere adquirido y ganado durante el matrimonio que entre ambos hubo y más todos los bienes que hubiere recibido del dicho difunto demás de aquellos que conforme a derecho en la calidad de sus personas le puede dar —

Yten mandamos se den a Juana Ucllama y Catalina Chichino e Ysavel Sumbi hijas del dicho don Juan Colque a cada una seis carneros de la tierra y dos pares de ropa de avasca y una docena de obejas de Castilla —

Y para pagar y cumplir este testamento mandas y cláusulas del en conformidad de la voluntad del dicho difunto como lo dispone en el dicho su poder dejamos y nombramos por sus albaceas a nos los dichos Juan Núñez Maldonado y Padre Dionisio Velásquez ynsólidum como el dicho difunto lo manda y pagado y cumplido este testamento y las mandas y cláusulas del conformandonos con la voluntad del dicho difunto por el dicho su poder dejamos y nombramos /f.17v/ por herederos del dicho don Juan Colque el don Fernando y don Franciso y don Miguel hijos naturales del dicho don Juan Colque difunto mejorando como mejoramos al dicho don Juan en el tercio y quinto de todos los dichos bienes del dicho difunto demás de lo que le perteneciere como tal heredero del dicho su padre —

Y en la forma referida hacemos y ordenamos el dicho testamento el qual queremos y mandamos se guarde y cumpla y lleve a debido efecto porque así fue la voluntad del dicho difunto e nuestra en su nombre y en testimonio dello lo otorgamos en la manera que dicha es ante el presente escribano público y testigos yuso escritos que es fecho en la villa de Potosí a veinte y un días del mes de enero año del nacimiento de Christo de mil y quinientos y ochenta y quatro y los otorgantes a los cuales yo el escribano público yuso escrito doy fe que conosco lo firmaron de sus nombres en este registro siendo a todo ella presentes por testigos Hernando Matheos Toribio de Sevicos y Bartolomé de Vitoria Francisco Guillermo y Matheo de Almonasi residente en esta villa Juan Núñez Maldonado Padre Dionisio Velásquez ante mi Luis García escribano público y del cabildo —

❦

[Power of Attorney]

In the name of the Holy Trinity and the eternal unity, Father, Son, and Holy Spirit, three distinct persons and one divine essence through whose grace all things have a good beginning and proper end, amen. . . . Know all who see this letter that I, don Juan Colque Guarache [captain general] . . . of the province of Orcosuyos and cacique principal of the Quillacas and Asanaques, resident in the Imperial Villa of Potosí of Peru, grant and recognize by this present letter and say that since at present I am sick in bed of a grave illness, because of which at present I cannot make or order my last will and testament, I therefore in the best manner and form that the law allows do grant and give all my power . . . to Juan Núñez Maldonado *alcalde ordinario* of this Villa by His Majesty, and to Father Velásquez of the Company of the Sweet Name of Jesus, my confessor . . . so that if God Our Lord should be served to carry me from this present life through the sickness I presently have . . . may [order] my last will and testament /f.13r/ naming the place and tomb where my body shall be buried in a sacred place with the pomp and in the manner they see fit, and to lighten my soul in accord with what I have arranged and communicated with them, naming as my heirs for the remainder of my goods don Juan Fernando and don Francisco and don Miguel my natural sons because I named and declared them for such, improving for the said don Juan Colque my eldest son by the third and fifth of all my goods, rights, and shares, and to the others in equal parts. As executors I name the said lord Juan Núñez Maldonado and Father Velásquez . . . and wish them to carry out all the donations and legacies as they see fit. . . . In the Villa of Potosí, on the 28th day of the month of September of 1583, and the declarant signed his name, of which I the scribe give faith. . . . Through the interpretation of the said Pedro de Alcalá, before me Fernando de Medina public scribe, and I Luis García His Majesty's public scribe and scribe of the cabildo /f.14r/ of this Imperial Villa of Potosí.

[Testament]

By virtue of the said power incorporated above, and using it, we say that because the said don Juan Colque treated and communicated with us the order of his testament and the disposition of his goods and the discharge of his conscience . . . we make and order this his testament, donations, and legacies in the following form and manner:

Firstly we wish and command that the body of the said don Juan Colque be entombed as it now is in the church of the Lord Saint Bernard in this said Villa, of the parish of the Quillacas, and that it not be moved to any other place because that was his will, and ours in his name.

Item: We declare that the day the said don Juan Colque was buried, one mass was sung /f.14v/ and four prayed, and the alms for them were paid.

Item: We declare that on the octave and honors carried out for the said don Juan Colque in the said church where he is buried, eight masses were prayed for him.

Item: The day of the said don Juan Colque's burial four priests accompanied his body, and said mass for his soul.

Item: _____ [blank in original] common pesos were spent on wax in the burial and honors carried out for the said don Juan, and the offering.

Item: Six masses were said for the soul of the said deceased in the great church of this Villa.

Item: Another two masses were sung, with their vigils, the last day of the novena for the soul of the said deceased.

Item: We command that for the soul of the said don Juan fifty masses be said, twenty of them in the church of Lord Saint Bernard where he is buried, which shall be said by the curate of the said parish, and the rest shall be said by clerics in the places deemed appropriate by the executors of his testament, and the customary alms shall be given for them.

/f.15r/ Item: We order payment to the hospital of the Villa of ten common pesos for alms.

Item: We order [payment] to the confraternity of Saint Savior, recently founded, whose advocation is celebrated in the Collegial House of the Name of Jesus of the said Villa, four pesos. And [the confraternity] of the Holy Sacrament of the said House, six pesos of common silver.

Item: We order the required and customary donations that are usually and customarily ordered in other testaments, to each one four reales, set apart from the said don Juan Colque's goods.

Item: We order payment to the church of the Quillacas of eighty common pesos from the goods of the said don Juan.

Item: We order payment to the Indians who worked in the mill and works that don Juan Colque owned in the *ribera* [milling center of Potosí], in company with Diego de Morales, of all the wages that were owing to them according to the accounts which may exist and appear.

Item: We order payment of fifty-three common pesos to Melchor Vázquez, merchant, for the merchandise that the deceased took from his shop.

Item: We command that two /f.15v/ Indian *cumbe camayos* be paid, to each one twenty common pesos, for the pieces of *cumbe* [cloth] they made for the said don Juan Colque. Don Juan, son of the deceased, knows the said Indians.

Item: We command that the services of the male and female Indians who apparently served the said deceased, be paid what they ought to be for it.

Item: We command that from Diego de Morales, *morador* of this said Villa [lodged there], all the pesos be collected, which it appears he owed for the period of two years that he had in his charge the administration and collection in the mill that he held in company with don Juan, in the ribera of this Villa, of which half belongs to him, and for this accounts be taken from the said Diego de Morales.

Item: Collect from don Bernardo Guarache, son of the said don Juan Colque, twenty common pesos, ten of them given to him by Alonso Franco, and the other ten, I Father Dionisio Velásquez, which were given to him as a loan for the costs of his legitimation.

Item: Collect from don Juan Colque, son of the said deceased, that which I shall declare he owes to the goods of the said deceased.

Item: We order collection from /f.16r/ a silverworker who don Juan, son of the deceased, knows and can name, of a jar and a cup of silver, paying the silverworker for the making of them that which is owing, because he has them in his power.

Item: We order the collection from the said don Juan Colque, son of the said deceased, a black felt hat, which belongs to the goods of the said deceased because it was his.

Item: We order the collection from those who should pay the pesos owing to the said deceased for reason of the salary belonging to him for his office of captain, during the time it appears he served in the said office, according to the salary that has been set.

Item: We order collection from the community chest of the Asanaques and Quillacas, that which is owing to him by virtue of his office of cacique principal of the said peoples.

Item: We order collection from Rodrigo Arias de Vuiza, four hundred assayed pesos that the said deceased apparently gave him to carry to Castile for certain matters, and which he has not taken.

Item: We order collection from the Indians and other persons who are in the *chacra* [fields] of Pocpo, that which /f.16v/ it seems they owe in fruits and rents of the said fields, which have entered into their power from the time they have had charge of the said fields.

Item: We command those persons to whom the said deceased held some charge, have fifty masses said for the soul of the said deceased, which shall be divided, twenty-five of them in the monastery of Saint Dominic and the thirteen remaining [*sic*] for the poorest priests of this Villa, paying the accustomed alms.

Item: We order the expenditure and distribution of one hundred common pesos to the poor and alms of this Villa, according to the decision and will of the executors of the said deceased, for his soul.

Item: We command that doña Beatríz Sisa Ocllo, woman of the said deceased don Juan Colque, have and take the gains on goods that pertain to her after paying the debts of the said deceased, and removing the goods that the said don Juan Colque had before contracting matrimony with the said /f.17r/ his wife, and all the pesos that appear to have been earned from his office and charge of captain and cacique principal.

Item: We command that the said doña Beatríz Sicsa Ocllo, wife of the said don Juan, bring from the properties and partible goods all those goods that had been acquired and earned during the matrimony between them, and also the goods that she had received from the said deceased beyond those which rightfully according to the quality of their persons she can be given.

Item: We command that to each of the daughters of the said don Juan Colque, Juana Ucllama, Catalina Chichino, and Isabel Sumbi, shall be given six sheep of the land [llamas], two pairs of clothing of common cloth, and one dozen Castilian sheep.

And to pay and fulfill this testament and its donations and clauses in conformity with the will of the said deceased as established in the said power [of attorney], we provide and name as his executors we, the said Juan Núñez Maldonado and Father Dionisio Velásquez, together, as the said deceased ordered, and when this testament is paid and fulfilled along with its donations and clauses, conforming ourselves to the will of the said deceased through the power [of attorney], we leave and name /f.17v/ as heirs of the said don Juan Colque, don Fernando, don Francisco, and don Miguel, natural sons of the said don Juan Colque deceased, improving as we improve to the said don Juan by the third and fifth of all the said goods of the deceased, apart from that which pertains to him as his father's heir.

. . . . Done in the Villa of Potosí on the 21st day of the month of January, year of the birth of Christ one thousand five hundred and eighty four. And the deponents, who I the below-signed public scribe give faith that I know, signed their names in this register, being for all of it present as witnesses Hernando Matheos, Toribio de Sevicos, Bartolomé de Vitoria, Francisco Guillermo, and Matheo de Almonasi, resident in this Villa. Juan Núñez Maldonado and Father Dionisio Velásquez, before me, Luis García, public scribe and scribe of the town council.

Notes

My thanks to Susan Kellogg and Matthew Restall for their invitation to contribute to this volume, and for their helpful editorial suggestions. Two anonymous reviewers also made suggestions that have aided revision. Sections on Hernán Vela and his will were developed for presentation at a 1993 conference organized by Thérèse Bouysse-Cassagne, held in memory of Thierry Saignes. This work is dedicated to him.

1. Then, as now, some wills were written far in advance of death. Announcing future renunciation of property, and future pious bequests to charity, could relieve testators of potential guilt for enjoying their wealth in life.

2. Some testators made this very clear, as did one inhabitant of Madrid in 1584: "In order to enjoy the eternal glory for which we have been created . . . it is necessary for me first to dispose of all the belongings which God saw fit to give me in this life, so that when He deigns it proper to take me from it, I may be able to discharge my conscience" (Archivo Histórico de Protocolos de Madrid [1015.289], translated and quoted in Eire 1995: 37).

3. Eire's massive work, *From Madrid to Purgatory: The Art and Craft of Dying in Sixteenth-Century Spain* (1995), based on analysis of sixteen hundred wills from the Archivo Histórico de Protocolos de Madrid, surveys changes in testament writing between the 1520s and the 1590s, giving special consideration to the impact of the Council of Trent (1563), with its orthodoxy-promoting reforms that inaugurated the Counter Reformation. A model of how to write social and cultural history undergirded by the kind of serial archival work usually associated with economic history, Eire's work came to my attention too late to fully take his insights into account here.

4. Numerous *Ars Moriendi* were published during the sixteenth century. Eire (1995: 24–34) draws especially on those of Erasmus (1534), Venegas (1536), Medina (1555), Polanco (1578), and Orozco (1583).

5. The Spanish original: ". . . Porque siendo nosotros como somos señores principales de vasallos . . . como en España los duques y condes y marqueses . . . . Suplicamos a Vuestra Majestad sea seruido de mandarlo remediar haciéndonos mercedes . . . conforme a la calidad y grauedad de nuestras personas y haciéndonos mercedes como a los caballeros y hijosdalgo, como se hacen en España."

On pre- and post-invasion roles of caciques vis-à-vis tribute collection, and the singular importance of information provided by caciques who had been old enough in pre-invasion times to remember such things, see Murra 1968. The pivotal role of caciques is also examined in Choque Canqui 1979, Murra 1977, Ramírez 1987, Rivera Cusicanqui 1978, and Saignes 1987.

6. On the nature of *hidalguía* and old-regime Spanish values see Góngora 1975; Leonard 1992; Lockhart 1972; and Maravall 1984, 1987.

7. On the struggle amongst hidalgos and pecheros in Castilian towns, see Haliczer 1981; Nader 1990; and Thompson 1979. Señorío is treated in the preceding, and also in Guilarte 1987.

8. On the Peruvian civil wars, see Gutiérrez de Santa Clara 1963 and Góngora 1975. La Gasca's life is profiled in Calvete de Estrella 1965.

9. See "Carta del cabildo de la ciudad de Los Reyes al Emperador don Carlos, participandole la situación en que quedaba el Perú á la salida del licenciado Gasca, por causa del segundo repartimiento de encomiendas. Los Reyes, 11 de agosto de 1550" (*Cartas de Indias* 2: 563). Gasca treats the same matter in "Gasca al Consejo, Los Reyes, 8 Nov. 1549" (2: 557).

10. The full text, after a description of the services to the Crown that merited the grant, reads as follows:

> . . . os encomiendo e depossito en el término e juridiçión de la Villa de Plata y Provinçia de los Charcas todo el repartimiento de yndios con sus caçiques y prinçipales e yndios e pueblos mitimaes a ellos sujetos . . . en los Aullagas e con sus estançias e chacaras de maiz e coca . . . para que os sirbáis dellos comforme a las ordenanças reales e con que dexéis a los caçiques sus mugeres e hijos e yndios de su seruiçio e con que los dotrinéis y agáis dotrinar en las cosas de nuestra santa fee católica como su magestad lo tiene mandado e si no lo hiziéredes en ello u uviere algun descuido cargue sobre buestra conçiençia e no sobre la de su magestad e mia que en su real nombre vos encargo e mando y que a ellos y a los demás yndios a ellos sujetos los tratéis bien y procuréis su conservaçion pidiéndoles tributos moderados /3bis/ y tales que vuenamente los puedan dar con aperzevimiento que si en ello ezediécedes allende de ser penado se vos mandar a tomar la demasía en parte de pago para lo que adelante oviéredes de aver comforme a las tasaçiones que de los tales tributos que huvieron de dar los dichos yndios. . . .

11. A handful of studies have remarked on restitution by Spaniards to Indians, acts which in my judgment were generally carried out postmortem through the use of testaments. Are restitution payments clear evidence of active Spanish conscience, giving the lie to Black Legend accounts of Spanish moral turpitude? It is not my intention to join the old and stale "Black Legend"/"White Legend" debate, but conscience in the sixteenth century, as today, was measured on heavenly scales after death, just as the state was asserting control over the transmission of heritable estate. Charity, including encomendero restitution, aimed not only to safeguard immortal souls, but also to make the testator's wealth and status immortal by transferring it to the heirs.

12. In July of 1549, Gasca prohibited the use of Indians in mines (they were to be replaced by African slaves). Gasca argued that the rigors of Potosí's mining regime imposed undue hardship. In response, the justicia mayor of Potosí, Juan Polo Ondegardo, gathered up every cacique in that mining center to contradict Gasca. Soon after, Charcas encomenderos produced yet another memorial to the same effect (AGI Justicia 667 "Potosí, 8 mayo 1550. Suplicación e ynformación. . . .").

13. The tasa commission, comprised of Lima's Archbishop Loaysa, fray Domingo de Santo Tomás, fray Tomás de San Martín, and the Oidor Hernando de Santillán, drastically reduced the amounts that encomenderos could take from their Indians, and more strictly enjoined Spaniards to do their Christian duty. The *confesionario* is printed in Las Casas 1965 [1552–53], 2:853–914.

14. The Spanish original: " . . . por hazer cosa en que tanto va á su Real consçiençia; y dado que por ser el freno de la codiçia y de las estorsiones que los españoles á los naturales hasta aquí han acostumbrado á hazer, para sacalles lo que

tenían y no tenían, dandoles sobrello tantos tormentos, que á muchos dellos han muerto y otros se han ahorcado de desesperados. . . .''

15. The Audiencia de Charcas, based in the City of Silver (La Plata, modern Sucre) had not yet been created, but these encomiendas correspond to the region that caciques called Charcas, in contradistinction to the area just to the north that they called the land of the Qullas. See Barnadas 1973.

16. In the Charcas region, khipus were used side by side with small stones on the ground. The Sacaca *pleito* provides the best description of these khipu depositions (AGI Justicia 653: 261v–262r, "La Plata 1579. Los yndios del repartimiento de Sacaca. . . ."). Use of khipus during the colonial period is attested in Abercrombie 1998; Cummins 1994; Murra 1975; and Urton 1994.

17. One may conclude this from Hernán Vela's claim that the Spanish witnesses against him were avenging themselves for his own denunciations of their former sympathies for Gonzalo Pizarro.

18. The Spanish original:

—107—Asi mesmo ay muchos proçesos hechos por Lorenço de Estupiñan de Figueroa con comisión que se le dió de los tributos que se sigue que los vezinos lleuaron de los yndios de su encomienda, y malos tratamientos que les hizieron y por causa de las alteraçiones pasadas no se an determinado syno solamente dos en que fueron condenados los encomenderos que fueron el General Hinojosa en çiento y veinte mill pesos por los quales se compusieron los herederos con los yndios en quarenta myll, y Hernan Vela que murio en esta tierra en sesenta mill. Su Magestad provea que se acaben y concluyan a lo que fuere seruido. (Apuntamientos para el buen gouierno y asiento del Pirú [point 107 out of 178 points]: 38v. In RAH Col. Muñoz, Cosas del Perú, tomo 65 [A/92]: 23r–50v.)

19. The Spanish original: "Yten converna proveer que en el Perú se usan los negoçios que hizo Lorenço de Estopiñán de Figueroa sobre el exçesso que huuo por los encomenderos y sus criados en la cobrança de los tributos de los yndios que es negoçio de mucha ynportançia y provecho para el rrey y de que se podría sacar mas de seteçientos mill pesos."

20. The Spanish original:

Asimesmo se podría mandar hazer ynformaçión contra los encomenderos y sus mayordomos y criados açerca de las comutaçiones que an hecho con los yndios de su encomienda desta manera que los tributos en que los yndios estauan tasados que no les hera prouechoso rreçibir los conçertauan con los caçiques e yndios que se los pagasen en ropa o en texelles ropa o en carneros o en harrieros o otra cosa de manera que se venía a conbertir el negoçio en provecho de encomendero y daño de los yndios estando proybido por çédula del rrey de que se podría hacer otra buen parte de plata para su magestad.

21. Ironically, Estopiñán shortly later defended the use of Indians in Potosí's mines to the Council of the Indies, claiming that they were well treated by their encomenderos and benefited from their mining experience (AGI Justicia 1134, Apr. 18, 1551, "Ynformacion hecha por el Señor don Lorenzo de Estopiñan y

Figueroa sobre quan probechoso les es a los caciques e indios estar en Potosí,"
13 fols.).
    22. The Spanish original:

> . . . Puede haver dos años poco mas o menos . . . Hernán Vela . . .
> mandó a un negro que se llamava Juan /15v/ y le mando que desnudase al
> testi[g]o y así desnudo el dicho Hernán Vela mandó al dicho negro que le
> colgasse por los pies de un palo del techo de la dicha casa . . . i mandó que
> delante del lo azotasen y el dicho negro con un azote dió muchos açotes al
> testi[g]o hasta que le hiço saltar la sangre y despues de bien açotado el
> dicho su amo mandó al negro que con agi le curase los açotes lo qual el
> dicho negro hiço y que el testi[g]o le prometió que le daría los 10 marcos
> de plata que faltavan no le açotó más. . . . I luego el dicho juez mandóle
> muestre las señales de acotes i ataduras hiço muestra dellas i se le allaron
> çiertas señales. . . .

    23. A second khipu record revealed only 17,128 marks, the difference being
accounted for by Vela as evidence of khipu unreliability, and by the prosecutor as a
result of the first khipu including payments made to the previous encomendero
(AGI Escribanía de Cámara 497C, 22: 45r, "Memorial del pleito . . ."). When Vela
used the discrepancy to question the validity of khipus altogether, the prosecutor
Gaspar de Ocampo countered that "he did not [prove it], because the question
they had been asked was what they had given since the battle of Jaquijoagana [sic]
and they put in the first kipo what they had given to Pedro de Hermossa [sic] to
whom they were encomendado before, until Hernán Vela took possession. . . ."
(46v, my translation).
    24. As was also common practice, Vela also sought to disqualify the Spaniards
as witnesses against him, alleging that all were his mortal enemies. Some, he said,
hated him for having denounced them as sympathizers of Gonzalo Pizarro, while
in other cases the cause was more personal, such as the priest whom Vela had publicly called "puto judío moro" (AGI Escribanía de Cámara 497C, 22: 30v–31r).
    25. The Spanish original:

> . . . y no ubstante que conforme a esto yo estoi libre de los dichos
> caçiques e yndios por lo bien que me ha . . . servido y servieron en aquel
> tiempo e sin voluntad y así lo quiero y mando que aunque los dichos
> caçiques e yndios que estan pagados por este conçierto que así por lo que
> me sirvieron y dieron . . . y asimismo por si no le tenido la dotrina tan
> sufisiente como hera menester . . . mando que se les conpre a los dichos
> caçiques e yndios del repartimiento de Tapacarí . . . dos mill ovejas de
> Castilla y çien vacas todo lo qual mando se conpren de los dichos mis
> bienes y no aviendo de los dichos mis bienes de que se comprar pido por
> merçed a mi amada y querida muger doña Luisa de Bivar. . . .

    26. The Spanish original:

> . . . . y con esto me paresçe estando tan adeudado como estoi que hago
> todo lo que es en mi para descargo de mi consençia y así rruego a los dichos
> caçiques prinçipales e yndios procuren de se hazer ricos con estos ganados y

me perdonen si alguna otra cosa [. . .] pues veen ellos e todos lo poco que de presente puedo y pido por merçed ami querida muger doña Luisa de Bivar tenga grand quenta con el buen tratamiento de los dichos yndios favoresiéndoles en todo y sobre llevándoles en lo que pudiere pues son buenos yndios y me an servido bien. . . .

Gómez de Solís goes on to order payments to a long list of Indians to whom he felt indebted, including not only those who worked for him in Potosí, but also Indians as far away as La Paz, Lima, and Quito whom he felt he had oppressed.

27. The Spanish original:

. . . Yten que deve a los yndios de Parinacocha de restituçiones que le an mandado hazer y no las an hecho de cosas que les ha tomado veinte mill pesos de oro—yten deve a los yndios de Machaca que tubo encomienda dos mill pesos de buen oro—yten que deve a los yndios que al presente tiene en encomienda que les ha llevado demás de la tasa veinte y çinco mill pesos poco más—/ todas las quales dichas deudas dixo de ver a las dichas personas e que por ser la muerte que se le mandavan dar tan repentinamente no tenía lugar declarar más pero que si alguna persona viniese declarando y pidiendo con juramento que le devía algunos pesos de oro se le pagasen de su ha /659r/ zienda e que en lo que avía declarado que devía a los yndios no estava bien çierto si avía declarado alguna cosa más que se averiguase con ellos y se pagase de su hazienda.

Using this will, the caciques of Chayanta sought (unsuccessfully) to collect, appealing to the audiencia and presenting the khipu accounts they had prepared for Estopiñán in 1551.

28. Aldana's donation dates to 1557, during a period when Estopiñán's charges were again pursued with renewed fervor. Like other donations and acts of restitution, it was at least in part coerced. In 1592, the Indians of Paría held a mill in Arque, three ranches in Cliza with six thousand cows producing six thousand cheeses annually, three highland ranches with eleven thousand Spanish sheep producing two thousand cheeses per year, and two inns. The donation is in ANB Escrituras Coloniales 1624, no. 13; for the worth of the donation and further information, see del Río 1990a: 401–2).

29. On Aug. 23, 1559, doña Ana Gutiérrez became *tutora* of her children, stating that "Hernán Vela señor de la Villa de Siete Iglesias . . . era falleçido e pasado desta presente vida podrá aber veynte dias poco más o menos. . . ." At the time of his death, Vela's son Gonzalo was three years old, and doña Isabel eight months (AGI Escribanía de Cámara 497B, 4: 77v).

30. The will also offered the promise of a large sum of cash to his mestizo son, provided the latter came personally to Spain to collect it. Since it seems that no effort was made in Peru to inform his son of this provision, this act too seems rather empty (AGI Escribanía de Cámara 497B, 11: 11v).

31. Vela's death was sudden, and he did not, apparently, complete his own will. Instead, two priests came forward claiming full knowledge of Vela's true last will. Apart from the chaplaincies and the usual stipulations about the inheritance of Vela's estate, they also provided large payments to themselves.

32. On the centrality of charity to Spanish notions of Christian conduct, see Flynn 1989. Flynn also provides the fullest account of Spanish confraternities, frequent legates in Spanish wills and guardians of their members' souls. On confraternities in Peru, see Celestino and Meyers 1981.

33. In 1565, Philip II ordered the person who held Vela's embargoed estate to pay the three chaplains for more than a year's worth of unpaid prayers (AGI Indiferente 425, 24: 250v–51v).

34. The original text reads:

> . . . lo que se ha de procurar es . . . que se executen irremisiblemente las penas, que están puestas á los que excedieren de lo ordenado; porque con esto . . . no pasen adelante las malas costumbres, no provoquen la ira Divina los frequentes excesos, y sean privados de lo proprio los que con fraude apetecieren lo ageno. . . . y llaman así la pobreza quando se valen de dinero de los que miserablemente pasan en ella, y que quien puede socorrer los hambrientos, los mata quando no los sustenta.
>
> . . . .y del Exodo [Exod. c. 22], en que dice: *No hagais agravio á las viudas, y pupilos; si se los hiciéredes clamarán a Mí, y Yo oiré su clamor, y se indignará mi furor, y os pasaré á cuchillo, y dispondre que paguéis el Talion, dexando vuestras mugeres viudas, y vuestros hijos pupilos.*

Solórzano served as oidor in the Audiencia de Lima from 1610 to 1626, becoming on his return to Spain fiscal in the Consejo de Indias on June 7, 1627, a post that he vacated Oct. 18, 1629, on being named Consejero de Indias (Malagón and Ots Capdequí 1965: 15, 30). The quotation from Exodus is from the ordinances that God commanded Moses to set before the Israelites. Given just after the ten commandments, the ordinances largely treat the restitution due to aggrieved parties in the case of a wide range of sinful behavior. Notwithstanding Solórzano's decision in favor of the Aullagas Indians, this chapter of the *Política indiana* continues with doubts about the legal admissibility of evidence taken from khipus, with specific reference to the case brought by the Indians of Sacaca against their encomendero "don Alonso de Sotomayor" [*sic* for Montemayor]. He voiced no doubts over crucial khipu evidence in the Vela case.

35. Though it took more than seventy-five years for God's wrath upon the Vela family to be completely ratified by the Council of the Indies, the principal case brought by Indians against Vela was concluded during the eventful 1560s. The Indians' attorney claimed to have sent the first payment on restitution to Aullagas in the fleet of 1567. Ironically, that payment consisted almost entirely of back tributes that the commoners of Siete Iglesias had owed to Hernán Vela's estate from the time of his death to the town's sale at Crown auction. By 1588, Hernán's children in Spain, Gonzalo and doña Isabel Vela, had died without children; the estate passed back to their mother, doña Ana Gutiérrez (who had acted as their "tutor y curadora") and thence to doña Ana's siblings, nieces, and nephews, and their children (AGI Escribanía de Cámara 844A: 4r–6r, La Plata Año 1583, "Lucas de Murga Menchaca. . ."). Gonzalo Vela and doña Isabel Vela both died before their mother. Doña Ana herself died in 1589, leaving to her sisters- and brothers-in-law "todas mis vienes i rentas así de la haçienda que tengo en España y contra el dicho don Pedro de Castro y Quiñones de ciertos maravedizes

que en su poder estan envargados e de lo de las indias" (10r). Hope of another reversal of fortune remained alive.

36. The Spanish original: " . . . y haviendo jurado mochando al sol y a la tierra segun su costumbre y por lengua de Juan Indiano ladino natural del Valle de Xauxa. . . ." To "mochar" apparently referred to an honorific gesture—such as blowing words to a deity—by which sacred places and beings were customarily honored.

37. Vela countered by producing a priest who swore to have indoctrinated the Aullagas, but his own arguments concerning Indian "infidelity" spoke to the contrary. Yet the fiscal's swearing-in strategy also gave Vela a ready-made objection: The testimony of non-Christians could not be trusted.

38. The Spanish original: "–Yten declaro que tengo setenta cabecas de cabras las quales mando se reparten entre mis yanaconas por lo.que les soy a cargo y por descargo de mi consciencia."

39. On the mita of Potosí, see Bakewell 1984.

40. On the Andean symbolism of power, see also Martínez Cereceda 1995; Pease 1992; and Platt 1987b. The significance of cloth, especially *cumbe*, is detailed in Murra 1989.

41. ANB Escribanía de Cámara 1804, 193: 11–18 (will dated Jan. 12, 1584): "Expediente seguido en la villa de Potosí por el testamento hecho de don Juan Choquetilla Colque Guarachi en el año de 1707 por la india Antonia Copatite Colqueguarachi, indígena principal de los Quillacas, en autos con doña Narcisa Choquetilla sobre derecho al cacicazgo de Quillacas." The complete 269-folio expediente is badly deteriorated and missing its first page.

Conclusion

Susan Kellogg and Matthew Restall

In colonial Mesoamerica and the Andes, a last will and testament was often far more than the mere listing of bequests by the dying to their relatives—as the diverse methods, insights, and emphases of the preceding ten chapters have illustrated. In these final pages we offer a brief summary of these chapters within an outline of a thematic comparison, leaving readers to explore further, according to their particular interests, the ways in which the approaches and conclusions of the contributing authors differ or coincide, support or contradict each other (for a sequential summary of the chapters, the volume's structure, and the broader historiographical context, see the introduction).

The fact that Nahuatl is the best-represented language among extant colonial Mesoamerican notarial documents—wills included—is reflected in the use of Nahua testaments by four of the contributing authors in this book. However, each studies a different set of samples for different purposes. Cline's focus on fray Alonso de Molina's model Nahuatl will permits some examination of native and Spanish antecedents to the phenomenon of will-making in the context of sixteenth-century central Mexico (also see Kellogg's, Terraciano's, and Hill's references to the Molina model). This treatment complements the use by both Kellogg and Wood of Nahuatl-language wills to examine changes in, and conflicts over, the rights of individuals and groups within indigenous society.

Kellogg's emphasis, however, is on gender and the impact of codified legal practices (primarily testaments) upon both elite and non-elite Mexica women in sixteenth- and seventeenth-century Mexico City. She finds that access to legal literacy did not strengthen indigenous women's position within colonial society. Wood, on the other hand, shows that the

Nahua elite in the colonial Tolucan community of San Bartolomé Capulhuac sought to maximize the advantage of—even as they fought over—the benefits accruing to their position as an economic, political, and cultural bridge between the Spanish community and native commoners. Through the colonial period, traditional privileges and social stratification, individual and community rights, were both maintained and contested.

Horn's treatment of Nahua testaments is different still; she uses them as an entrée into the economic history of late-sixteenth-century Coyoacan, an indigenous community and microregion to the immediate south of Mexico City, stressing the increasingly complex nature of economic relations between the local Nahua ruling class and Spaniards. The fact that testaments make arrangements for the distribution of material property means they are an obvious medium for the study of economic history and socioeconomic relations. In complement to Horn's study is Hill's analysis of Cakchiquel Maya wills from highland Guatemala. Hill emphasizes the adoption of the testamentary genre by Cakchiquel kinship groups (which he terms "family corporations") as a mechanism for consolidating and defending agricultural enterprises. Land plays a critical role in all collections of indigenous testaments in Spanish America; Cakchiquel wills, like those of the Andean caciques (community rulers) studied by Ramírez, expose the links between land use, cultural change, and the colonial experience.

Hill's theme of the flourishing and decline of a body of testaments as representative of the rise and fall of an indigenous economic and social phenomenon is paralleled by Powers's study. She analyzes more than a century and a half of testaments by the Duchisela dynasty of the Riobamba region (in what is now Ecuador), demonstrating not only how such sources can offer lush family histories but also ways in which they can illuminate questions of identity, legitimacy, and political structure in indigenous communities. By exposing the incredible levels of political and interpersonal conflict that might be reached within family and kin groups as indigenous individuals jockeyed for position in the colonial hierarchy, Powers vividly illustrates regional political dynamics as well as demonstrates the utility of theoretical sophistication in textual analysis.

The topic of culture change—and the insights that native wills offer into change within indigenous cultures during the period of Spanish colonial rule—is a major theme of this volume. Horn, for example, argues that the development in Coyoacan of the local early-colonial economy by representatives of both settler and indigenous communities became an "important avenue of cultural transformation" as Spanish-dominated enterprises gradually overshadowed a subsistence- and tribute-oriented Nahua economy. Abercrombie is also concerned with cultural contrasts and exchanges between Spaniards and natives. Focusing on mid- to late-sixteenth-century elite wills, Abercrombie analyzes the strategies testators used to meet often conflicting spiritual, material, and political obligations. The deep engagement of these testators in the great political matters of their day, especially the politics of *encomienda*, made for the creation of documents that (like those used by Wood, Hill, Powers, and Ramírez) shed light on the economic and political tensions of a particular time and place; Abercrombie's analysis shows how individuals struggled to meet varied and conflicting demands.

Ramírez, in her study of native wills from sixteenth-century northern Peru, suggests that in the Andes the dynamic between economic change and culture change featured a conflict between native and Spanish conceptions of wealth—with the wills of local Andean rulers revealing the gradual triumph of the latter. Changes in material culture are also among the concerns of Restall's comparison of three sample wills dictated by Yucatec Maya testators in the seventeenth, eighteenth, and nineteenth centuries. Using the larger body of Maya-language wills from the colonial period as a backdrop, Restall argues that while wills do to some extent illustrate a gradual acculturation toward the Hispanic world, they also reveal a more complex adaptive process of interculturation. Culture change did not necessarily mean Hispanization; colonial-era Mayas were comfortably engaged in a constant intercourse between coexisting cultural systems.

Kellogg, however, suggests that wills themselves were an instrument of cultural change, being part of the shift in the cultures of legal practices and gender structures. Terraciano's focus is on changes in the Ñudzahui (Mixtec) culture of expression, as reflected in wills, with written records assuming the role played by oral and pictorial traditions before the conquest. He pays particular attention to opening religious formulas, an aspect of testaments often viewed as formulaic by other scholars (such as Restall, with respect to the Yucatec Mayas). Terraciano argues that, at least with respect to Ñudzahui society, individual testators expressed personal piety through variations in these opening phrases.

Related to the theme of culture change is the comparative context of other genres of documentation. Various aspects of this context are explored in the volume's chapters: Cline analyzes the Molina model Nahua will; Wood gives comparative treatment to wills and the important genre of primordial titles; Terraciano elucidates the broader context of Ñudzahui (Mixtec) writing in the colonial period; Restall compares wills by Mayas written in Yucatec to one written in Spanish (an intraregional complement to the interregional comparison offered by the chapters studying the native-language wills of Mesoamericans and the chapters on the Spanish-language wills of Andeans); and Abercrombie draws specific comparisons between the testaments of Spanish *encomenderos* and Andean caciques.

The combination of these various comparisons helps situate testaments as a historical genre and illustrates further dimensions to their utility as historical sources. The authors of this volume not only explore the context of related genres. To mention just a few of the threads that run between the chapters: some look in detail at two or three wills as illustrative of patterns gleaned from a broader corpus (Kellogg, Restall, Powers, Abercrombie); most pay particular attention to the literary expressiveness of the testamentary genre (Cline, Kellogg, Wood, Terraciano, Restall, Powers); some examine the evolution of material culture (Horn, Restall, Ramírez), and others that of gender or class relations (Kellogg, Powers).

Some chapters are especially concerned with regional economic or political transformation (Hill, Horn, Wood), but all the studies of the volume contain a regional emphasis of some kind. As a result, various contrasting regional patterns can be detected. One such pattern, for example, is that of the differences in the nature of group identities and relative affiliations. While the willingness and ability of indigenous elites to promote their interest—in family and/or class terms—is evident from Toluca to Charcas, the role of the municipal community seems to be somewhat stronger in colonial Mesoamerica than in the Andes. This greater role is perhaps reflective of the greater urbanization of pre-Hispanic Mesoamerica and the more dispersed settlement patterns and patterns of vertical integration of the Andes.

Another difference, also likely reflective of indigenous patterns and practices in written expression of the pre-Hispanic era, is the development of colonial alphabetic writing in Mesoamerica. Native Andeans, when expressing themselves through the written word, did so in Spanish. But as both Powers and Ramírez show, the use of Spanish did not stop elites from bringing their own cultural assumptions to bear on the description of property and social relations and how these relations might influence the flows of property after death. Within Mesoamerica, the indigenous communities of the southern regions experienced a less intense intrusion of Spaniards, and this is reflected in the level, pace, and types of culture change relative to central Mexico.

In his contribution to this book, Abercrombie evokes an image of the indigenous testator not as an agent of cultural transformation, but as a phoenix, empowered by his or her written will to rise from the funeral ashes and enjoy a form of posthumous economic and social life in the community. This volume is an attempt to grant those wishes of immortality, in ways they could not possibly have foreseen, to native men and women of colonial Mesoamerica and the Andes.

Bibliography

Archival Sources and Other Source Abbreviations

AAL	Archivo Arzobispal de Lima (Lima, Peru)
AGCA	Archivo General de Centro América (Guatemala City, Guatemala)
AGEY	Archivo General del Estado de Yucatán (Mérida, Mexico)
AGI	Archivo General de las Indias (Seville, Spain)
AGN	Archivo General de la Nación (Mexico City, Mexico)
AJT	Archivo Judicial de Teposcolula (Oaxaca, Mexico)
AN	Archivo de Notarías del Departamento del Distrito Federal (Mexico City, Mexico)
ANB	Archivo Nacional de Bolivia (Sucre/La Plata, Bolivia)
ANEY	Archivo Notarial del Estado de Yucatán (Mérida, Mexico)
ANQ	Archivo Nacional de Quito (Quito, Ecuador)
ART	Archivo Regional de Trujillo (now, Archivo Departamental de la Libertad) (Trujillo, Peru)
BC	*Beyond the Codices* (Anderson, Berdan, and Lockhart 1976)
BL	The Bancroft Library (University of California, Berkeley)
BNM	Biblioteca Nacional (Madrid, Spain)
BNP	Bibliothèque National de Paris (Paris, France)
CCA	Colección Carrillo y Ancona, Centro de Apoyo a la Investigación Histórica de Yucatán (Mérida, Mexico)
CDC	*Colección de documentos sobre Coyoacán* (Carrasco and Monjarás-Ruiz 1976, 1978)
DT	Documentos de Tekanto (in ANEY)
FHT	*Fuentes para la historia del trabajo en Nueva España* (Zavala and Costelo 1939–46)
GSU	Genealogical Society of Utah (Salt Lake City, Utah)
LC	Libro de Cacalchen (in TULAL)
MNAH-AH	Museo Nacional de Antropología e Historia, Archivo Histórico (Mexico City, Mexico)
NL	Newberry Library (Chicago, Illinois)
RAH	Real Academia de Historia (Madrid, Spain)
TE	*Titles of Ebtun* (Roys 1939)
TI	Testaments of Ixil (Restall 1995a)
TULAL	Tulane University, Latin American Library, Rare Manuscript Collection (New Orleans, Louisiana)

Published Sources

Abercrombie, Thomas A. 1986. The politics of sacrifice: An Aymara cosmology in action. Ph.D. diss., University of Chicago.

———. 1998. *Pathways of memory and power: Ethnography and history among an Andean People.* Madison: University of Wisconsin Press.

———. n.d. Vassals' liberty and lords' consciences on trial. Unpublished ms.

Alchon, Suzanne. 1991. *Native society and disease in colonial Ecuador.* Cambridge: Cambridge University Press.

Alvarado, fray Francisco de. 1962 [1593]. *Vocabulario en lengua mixteca.* Ed. Wigberto Jiménez Moreno. Mexico City: Instituto Nacional Indigenista.

Anders, Ferdinand, Maarten Jansen, and Luis Reyes García. 1992. *Origen e historia de los reyes mixtecos: Libro explicativo del llamado Códice Vindobonensis Mexicanus I.* Mexico City: Fondo de Cultura Económica.

Anderson, Arthur (J.O.), Frances Berdan, and James Lockhart, eds. 1976. *Beyond the codices: The Nahua view of colonial Mexico.* Berkeley: University of California Press.

Anderson, Benedict. 1991 [1983]. *Imagined communities: Reflections on the origin and spread of nationalism.* London: Verso.

Anonymous. 1921–26 [1583]. *Relación anónima sobre el modo de gobernar de los Incas.* In *Gobernantes del Perú, cartas y papeles, siglo XVI,* vol. 9, ed. Roberto Levillier. Madrid: Imprenta de Juan Pueyo.

Anonymous Jesuit. 1879 [ca. 1590]. Relación de las costumbres antiguas de los naturales del Pirú. In *Tres relaciones de antiguedades peruanas.* Madrid: Imprenta y Fundición de M. Tello.

Ariès, Philippe. 1982. *The hour of our death.* Trans. Helen Weaver. New York: Vintage Books.

Arrom, Silvia. 1985. *The women of Mexico City, 1790–1857.* Stanford, Calif.: Stanford University Press.

Assadourian, Carlos Sempat. 1982. *El sistema de la economía colonial: Mercado interno, regiones, y espacio económico.* Lima: Instituto de Estudios Peruanos.

Bakewell, Peter J. 1984. *Miners of the red mountain: Indian labor in Potosí, 1545–1650.* Albuquerque: University of New Mexico Press.

Barnadas, Josep M. 1973. *Charcas: Orígenes históricos de una sociedad colonial (1535–1565).* La Paz: Centro de Investigación y Promoción del Campesinado.

———. 1984. The Catholic Church in colonial Spanish America. In *Cambridge History of Latin America,* ed. Leslie Bethell. Cambridge: Cambridge University Press.

Barrett, Ward. 1970. *The sugar hacienda of the Marqueses del Valle.* Minneapolis: University of Minnesota Press.

Berdan, Frances. 1982. *The Aztecs of Central Mexico: An imperial society.* New York: Holt, Rinehart and Winston.

———. 1986. Enterprise and empire in Aztec and early colonial Mexico. In *Research in Economic Anthropology (A Research Annual, Supplement 2): Economic Aspects of Prehispanic Highland Mexico,* ed. Barry L. Isaac. Westport, Conn.: JAI Press.

Betanzos, Juan de. 1987 [1551]. *Suma y narración de los Incas*. Madrid: Atlas.
Birkett, Jennifer. 1984. "A mere matter of business": Marriage, divorce, and the French Revolution. In *Marriage and property: Women and marital customs in history*, ed. Elizabeth M. Craik. Aberdeen, U.K.: Aberdeen University Press.
Boone, Elizabeth Hill, and Walter D. Mignolo, eds. 1994. *Writing without words: Alternative literacies in Mesoamerica and the Andes*. Durham: Duke University Press.
Borah, Woodrow. 1983. *Justice by insurance: The General Indian Court of colonial Mexico and the legal aides of the half-real*. Berkeley: University of California Press.
Borchart de Moreno, Christiana. 1989. Origen y conformación de la hacienda colonial. In *Nueva historia del Ecuador*, vol. 4, ed. Enrique Ayala Mora. Quito: Grijalbo.
Brüning, Enrique. 1922–23. *Estudios monográficos del Departamento de Lambayeque*. Chiclayo, Peru: D. Mendoza.
Burgos Guevara, Hugo. 1975. El guaman, el puma, y el amaru. Ph.D. diss., University of Illinois.
Burkhart, Louise. 1989. *The slippery earth: Nahua-Christian moral dialogue in sixteenth-century Mexico*. Tucson: University of Arizona Press.
———. 1996. *Holy Wednesday: A Nahua drama from early colonial Mexico*. Philadelphia: University of Pennsylvania Press.
———. 1997. Mexica women on the homefront: Housework and religion in Aztec Mexico. In *Indian women of early Mexico*, ed. Susan Schroeder, Stephanie Wood, and Robert Haskett. Norman: University of Oklahoma Press.
Burkitt, Eleanor. 1978. Indian women and white society: The case of sixteenth-century Peru. In *Latin American women: Historical perspectives*, ed. Asunción Lavrin. Westport, Conn.: Greenwood Press.
Burkitt, Robert. 1905. A Kekchi will of the sixteenth century. *American Anthropologist* 7: 271–94.
Burns, Robert I. 1996. *Jews in the notarial culture: Latinate wills in Mediterranean Spain 1250–1350*. Berkeley: University of California Press.
Cabello de Balboa, Miguel. 1951 [1586]. *Miscelánea antártica*. Lima: Instituto de Etnología de la Universidad Nacional Mayor de San Marcos.
Caillavet, Chantal. 1983. Ethno-histoire equatorienne: Un testament indien inedit du XVIᵉ siecle. *Cahiers du monde hispanique et luso-brésilien* 41: 5–23.
Calvete de Estrella, Juan. 1965. *Vida de don Pedro de la Gasca. Biblioteca de Autores Españoles*, vol. 168, *Crónicas del Perú*, vol. 5. Madrid: Ediciones Atlas.
Capoche, Luis. 1959 [1585]. *Relación general de la villa imperial de Potosí*. Vol. 12, *Biblioteca de Autores Españoles*. Madrid: Ediciones Atlas.
Carmack, Robert M. 1978. *Quichean civilization: The ethnohistoric, ethnographic, and archaeological sources*. Berkeley: University of California Press.
Carmagnani, Marcello. 1988. *El regreso de los dioses: El proceso de reconstitución de la identidad étnica en Oaxaca, siglos XVII y XVIII*. Mexico City: Fondo de Cultura Económica.

Carrasco, Pedro. 1964. Family structure of sixteenth-century Tepoztlan. In *Process and pattern in culture: Essays in honor of Julian H. Steward*, ed. Robert A. Manners. Chicago: Aldine.

————. 1972. La casa y la hacienda de un señor tlalhuica. *Estudios de Cultura Náhuatl* 10: 225–44.

————. 1976. The joint family in ancient Mexico: The case of Molotlá. In *Essays on Mexican kinship*, ed. Hugo G. Nutini, Pedro Carrasco, and James M. Taggart. Pittsburgh: University of Pittsburgh Press.

————. 1984. Royal marriages in ancient Mexico. In *Explorations in ethnohistory: Indians of Central Mexico in the sixteenth century*, ed. H. R. Harvey and Hanns J. Prem. Albuquerque: University of New Mexico Press.

————. 1997. Indian-Spanish marriages in the first century of the colony. In *Indian women of early Mexico*, ed. Susan Schroeder, Stephanie Wood, and Robert Haskett. Norman: University of Oklahoma Press.

Carrasco, Pedro, and Jesús Monjarás-Ruiz. 1976, 1978. *Colección de documentos sobre Coyoacán*. 2 vols. Mexico City: SEP, Instituto Nacional de Antropología e Historia, Centro de Investigaciones Superiores.

Carrera Andrade, Jorge. 1963. *El fabuloso reino de Quito*. Quito: Casa de la Cultura Ecuatoriana.

Cartas de Indias. 1974. *Cartas de Indias*. 2 vols. *Biblioteca de Autores Españoles*, vols. 264–65. Madrid: Ediciones Atlas.

Carter, William E. 1968. Secular reinforcement in Aymara death ritual. *American Anthropologist* 70: 238–63.

Celestino, Olina, and Albert Meyers. 1981. *Las cofradías en el Perú: Región central*. Frankfurt/Main: Verlag Klaus Dieter Vervuert.

Chance, John. 1989. *Conquest of the Sierra: Spaniards and Indians in colonial Oaxaca*. Norman: University of Oklahoma Press.

————. 1994. Indian elites in late colonial Mesoamerica. In *Caciques and their people: A volume in honor of Ronald Spores*, ed. Joyce Marcus and Judith Francis Zeitlin. Ann Arbor, Mich.: Museum of Anthropology, University of Michigan.

Chaunu, Pierre. 1978. *La Mort a Paris: XVIᵉ, XVIIᵉ, et XVIIIᵉ siecles*. Paris: Fayard.

Chevalier, Francois. 1963 [1952]. *Land and society in colonial Mexico: The great hacienda*. Trans. Alvin Eustis. Berkeley: University of California Press.

Choque Canqui, Roberto. 1979. Las haciendas de los caciques "Guarachi" en el Alto Perú. *America Indígena* 4: 733–48.

————. 1993. *Sociedad y economía colonial en el sur andino*. La Paz: Hisbol.

Christian, William. 1981. *Local religion in sixteenth-century Spain*. Princeton: Princeton University Press.

Cieza de León, Pedro de. 1984 [1553]. *Crónica del Perú: Primera parte*. Lima: Pontificia Universidad Católica del Perú.

————. 1964 [1864]. *The travels of Pedro de Cieza de León*. Trans. Clements B. Markham. New York: Burt Franklin.

Clendinnen, Inga. 1987. *Ambivalent conquests: Maya and Spaniards in Yucatan, 1517–1570*. Cambridge: Cambridge University Press.

Cline, S. L. 1981. Culhuacan 1572–1599: An investigation through Mexican Indian testaments. Ph.D. diss., UCLA.

———. 1984. Land tenure and land inheritance in late sixteenth-century Culhuacan. In *Explorations in ethnohistory: Indians of Central Mexico in the sixteenth century*, ed. H. R. Harvey and Hanns J. Prem. Albuquerque: University of New Mexico Press.

———. 1986. *Colonial Culhuacan, 1580–1600: A social history of an Aztec town*. Albuquerque: University of New Mexico Press.

———. 1991. A *Cacicazgo* in the seventeenth century: The case of Xochimilco. In *Land and politics in the Valley of Mexico: A two-thousand-year perspective*, ed. H. R. Harvey. Albuquerque: University of New Mexico Press.

———. 1993a. *The book of tributes: Early sixteenth-century Nahuatl censuses from Morelos*. Los Angeles: UCLA Latin America Center Publications.

———. 1993b. The spiritual conquest reexamined: Baptism and church marriage in early sixteenth-century Mexico. *Hispanic American Historical Review* 73: 453–80.

Cline, S. L., and Miguel León-Portilla, eds. 1984. *The testaments of Culhuacan*. Los Angeles: UCLA Latin America Center Publications.

Cobo, Father Bernabé. 1956 [1653]. *Obras del Padre Bernabé Cobo* (*Historia del Nuevo Mundo*). 2 vols. *Biblioteca de autores españoles*. Madrid: Ediciones Atlas.

Cock, Guillermo. 1984. Poder y riqueza de un Hatun Curaca del Valle del Jequetepeque en el siglo XVI. *Historia y Cultura* 17: 133–35.

———. 1986. Power and wealth in the Jequetepeque Valley during the sixteenth century. In *The Pacatnamu Papers*, vol. 1, ed. Christopher B. Donnan and Guillermo Cock. Los Angeles: Museum of Cultural Anthropology, University of California, Los Angeles.

Códice de Métepec. 1992. *Códice de Métepec: Estado de México*. Métepec: H. Ayuntamiento Constitucional de Métepec, Mexico.

Collier, George A., with Elizabeth Lowery Quaratiello. 1994. *Basta! Land and the Zapatista rebellion in Chiapas*. Oakland, Calif.: Institute for Food and Development Policy.

Comaroff, Jean, and John Comaroff. 1992. *Ethnography and the historical imagination*. Boulder, Colo.: Westview Press.

Connerton, Paul. 1989. *How societies remember*. Cambridge: Cambridge University Press.

Conrad, Geoffry W., and Arthur A. Demarest. 1984. *Religion and empire: The dynamics of Aztec and Inca expansionism*. Cambridge: Cambridge University Press.

Cook, Noble David. 1981. *Demographic collapse: Indian Peru, 1520–1620*. Cambridge: Cambridge University Press.

———. ed. 1975. *Tasa de la visita general de Francisco de Toledo*. Lima: Universidad Nacional Mayor de San Marcos.

Cook, Sherburne F., and Woodrow Borah. 1968. *The population of the Mixteca Alta, 1520–1960*. University of California Publications, Ibero-Americana, vol. 50. Berkeley and Los Angeles: University of California Press.

Cope, R. Douglas. 1994. *The limits of racial domination: Plebian society in colonial Mexico City, 1660–1720*. Madison: University of Wisconsin Press.

Costales, Piedad, and Alfredo Costales. 1992. *La real familia Duchisela*. Valencia: Estudios Ediciones y Medios.

Crider, John. Forthcoming. Between frontier and empire: Negotiation, migration, and memory among the Otomí of colonial Mexico, 1550–1725. Ph.D. diss., Tulane University.

Cummins, Tom. 1994. Representation in the sixteenth century and the colonial image of the Inca. In *Writing without words: Alternative literacies in Mesoamerica and the Andes*, ed. Elizabeth Hill Boone and Walter D. Mignolo. Durham: Duke University Press.

Dávila Padilla, Agustín. 1955 [1596]. *Historia de la fundación y discurso de la provincia de Santiago de México de la Orden de Predicadores*. Mexico City: Editorial Academia Literia.

del Busto D., José Antonio. 1959. El Capitán Melchor Verdugo, *Encomendero* de Cajamarca. *Revista Histórica* 24: 318–83.

del Río, Mercedes. 1990a. La tributación indígena en el repartimiento de Paria (siglo XVI). *Revista de Indias* 50: 397–429.

———. 1990b. Simbolismo y poder en Tapacarí. *Revista Andina* 1: 77–113.

Delumeau, Jean. 1990. *Sin and fear: The emergence of a Western guilt culture, thirteenth–eighteenth centuries*. Trans. Eric Nicholson. New York: St. Martin's Press.

Díaz Rementería, Carlos J. 1977. *El cacique en el virreinato del Peru: Estudio histórico-jurídico*. Sevilla: Universidad de Sevilla.

Dibble, Charles. 1971. Writing in Central Mexico. In *Archaeology of northern Mesoamerica*, ed. Gordon Ekholm and Ignacio Bernal, vol. 10 of *Handbook of Middle American Indians*. Austin: University of Texas Press.

Ditz, Toby L. *Property and kinship: Inheritance in early Connecticut, 1750–1820*. Princeton, N.J.: Princeton University Press.

Durán, fray Diego. 1971 [1581]. *Book of the gods and rites and the ancient calendar*, trans. and ed. Fernando Horcasitas and Doris Heyden. Norman: University of Oklahoma Press.

Durand-Forest, Jacqueline. 1962. Testament d'une indienne de Tlatelolco. *Journal de la Société des Américanistes* 52: 129–58.

Duviols, Pierre. 1986. *Cultura andina y represión*. Cuzco: Centro de Estudios Rurales Andinos "Bartolomé de Las Casas."

Edmonson, Munro S. 1964. Historia de las tierras altas Mayas según los documentos indígenas. In *Desarollo cultural de los Maya*, ed. Evon Z. Vogt and Alberto Ruz L. Mexico City: UNAM.

Edmonson, Munro S., and Victoria R. Bricker. 1985. Yucatecan Mayan literature. In *Supplement to the Handbook of Middle American Indians*, vol. 3 (Literatures), ed. Munro S. Edmonson, with the assistance of Patricia A. Andrews. Austin: University of Texas Press.

Eire, Carlos M. N. 1995. *From Madrid to purgatory: The art and craft of dying in sixteenth-century Spain*. Cambridge: Cambridge University Press.

Elliott, John H. 1970. *The old world and the new, 1492–1650*. Cambridge: Cambridge University Press.

Eno Belinga, Samuel M. 1995. Wealth in people as wealth in knowledge: Accumulation and composition in equatorial Africa. *Journal of African History* 36: 91–120.

Erasmus, Desiderius. 1969 [1534]. *De praeparatione ad mortem.* In *Opera omnia desiderii Erasmi Roterodami,* ordinus 5, vol. 1. Amsterdam: North-Holland Publishing Co.

Espinoza Soriano, Waldemar. 1967. El primer informe etnológico sobre Cajamarca, año de 1540. *Revista Peruana de Cultura* 11–12: 1–37.

———. 1969. El "memorial" de Charcas: "Crónica" inédita de 1582. *Cantatu: Revista de la Universidad Nacional de Educación* (Chosica, Peru).

———. 1981. El reino Aymara de Quillaca-Asanaque, siglos XV y XVI. *Revista del Museo Nacional* (Lima) 45: 175–274.

Fabian, Johannes. 1983. *Time and the other: How anthropology makes its object.* New York: Columbia University Press.

Farriss, Nancy M. 1984. *Maya society under colonial rule: The collective enterprise of survival.* Princeton, N.J.: Princeton University Press.

Field, Les W. 1992. Who are the Indians? Reconceptualizing indigenous identity, resistance, and the role of social science in Latin America. *Latin American Research Review* 29: 237–48.

Flynn, Maureen. 1989. *Sacred charity: Confraternities and social welfare in Spain, 1400–1700.* Ithaca, N.Y.: Cornell University Press.

Fox, Robin Lane. 1986. *Pagans and Christians.* Harmondsworth, U.K., and New York: Viking.

Gage, Thomas. 1958 [1648]. *Travels in the New World.* Ed. J. E. S. Thompson. Norman: University of Oklahoma Press.

García, fray Gregorio. 1981 [1607]. *Orígen de los indios de el Nuevo Mundo.* Mexico City: Fondo de Cultura Económica.

García Bernal, Manuela Cristina. 1972. *La sociedad de Yucatán, 1700–1750.* Sevilla: Escuela de Estudios Hispano-Americanos.

García Cabrera, Juan Carlos. 1994. *Ofensas a dios: Pleitos e injurias: Causas de idólatrias y hechicerías: Cajatambo, siglos XVII–XIX.* Cuzco: Centro de Estudios Regionales Andinos "Bartolomé de las Casas."

Geertz, Clifford. 1988. *Works and lives: The anthropologist as author.* Stanford, Calif.: Stanford University Press.

Gerhard, Peter. 1993. *A guide to the historical geography of New Spain.* Rev. ed. Norman: University of Oklahoma Press.

Gibson, Charles. 1952. *Tlaxcala in the sixteenth century.* New Haven, Conn.: Yale University Press.

———. 1964. *The Aztecs under Spanish rule: A history of the Indians in the Valley of Mexico, 1519–1810.* Stanford, Calif.: Stanford University Press.

Glave, Luis Miguel. 1989. *Trajinantes: Caminos indígenas en la sociedad colonial, siglos XVI y XVII.* Lima: Instituto de Apoyo Agrario.

Góngora, Mario. 1975. *Studies in the colonial history of Spanish America.* Trans. Richard Southern. Cambridge: Cambridge University Press.

González Echevarría, Roberto. 1990. *Myth and archive: A theory of Latin American narrative.* Cambridge: Cambridge University Press.

Goody, Jack. 1973. Strategies of heirship. *Comparative Studies in Society and History* 15: 3–20.

———. 1983. *The development of the family and marriage in Europe.* Cambridge: Cambridge University Press.

———. 1986. *The logic of writing and the organization of the state.* Cambridge: Cambridge University Pess.

———. 1987. *The interface between the written and the oral.* Cambridge: Cambridge University Press.

———, ed. 1968. *Literacy in traditional societies.* Cambridge: Cambridge University Press.

Goody, Jack, Joan Thirsk, and E. P. Thompson. 1976. *Family and inheritance: Rural society in western Europe, 1200–1800.* Cambridge: Cambridge University Press.

Goody, Jack, and Ian Watt. 1963. The consequences of literacy. *Comparative Studies in Society and History* 5: 304–45.

Greenleaf, Richard. 1961. *Zumárraga and the Mexican Inquisition, 1536–1543.* Washington D.C.: Academy of American Franciscan History.

Gruzinski, Serge. 1988. *La colonisation de l'imaginaire: Sociétés indigénes et occidentalisation dans le Mexique espagnal, XVIᵉ–XVIIIᵉ siécle.* Paris: Gallimard.

———. 1992. *Painting the conquest: The Mexican Indians and the European conquest.* Paris: UNESCO/Flammarion.

———. 1993. *The conquest of Mexico: The incorporation of Indian societies into the Western world, sixteenth through eighteenth centuries.* Trans. Eileen Corrigan. Cambridge, England: Polity Press.

Guamán Poma de Ayala, Felipe. 1980 [1615]. *Nueva crónica y buen gobierno.* Ed. John V. Murra and Rolena Adorno. 3 vols. Mexico City: Siglo Veintiuno.

Guevara-Gil, Armando, and Frank Salomon. 1994. A personal visit: colonial political ritual and the making of Indians in the Andes. *Colonial Latin American Review* 3: 3–36.

Guha, Ranajit. 1987. Chandra's death. In *Subaltern Studies V: Writings on South Asian History,* ed. Ranajit Guha. Oxford: Oxford University Press.

Guilarte, Alfonso María. 1987. *El régimen señorial en el siglo XVI.* 2d ed. Valladolid, Spain: Universidad de Valladolid.

Gutiérrez de Santa Clara, Pedro. 1963. *Historia de las guerras civiles del Peru.* Vol. 165 of *Biblioteca de Autores Españoles: Crónicas del Perú,* vols. 2–4. Madrid: Ediciones Atlas.

Gutiérrez Flores, fray Pedro. 1964 [1574]. Padrón de los mil indios ricos de la Provincia de Chucuito en el año 1574. In *Visita hecha a la Provincia de Chucuito por Garcí Diez de San Miguel en el año 1567.* Lima: Casa de la Cultura del Perú.

Guyer, Jane I. 1995. Wealth in people, wealth in things. Introduction. *Journal of African History* 36: 83–90.

Haliczer, Stephen. 1981. *The Comuneros of Castile: The forging of a revolution, 1475–1521.* Madison: University of Wisconsin Press.

Hampe Martínez, Teodor. 1986–87. Notas sobre población y tributo indígena en Cajamarca (primera mitad del siglo XVIII). *Boletín del Instituto Riva-Agüero* 14: 65–81.

Hanke, Lewis. 1949. *The Spanish struggle for justice in the conquest of America.* Philadelphia: University of Pennsylvania Press.

Hanks, William F. 1986. Authenticity and ambivalence in the text: A colonial Maya case. *American Ethnologist* 13: 721–44.

Harvey, H. R. 1986. Techialoyan codices: Seventeenth-century Indian land titles in Central Mexico. In *Supplement to the Handbook of Middle American Indians*, vol. 4 (*Ethnohistory*), ed. Ronald Spores. Austin: University of Texas Press.

Haskett, Robert. 1991. *Indigenous rulers: An ethnohistory of town government in colonial Cuernavaca*. Albuquerque: University of New Mexico Press.

———. 1992. Visions of municipal glory undimmed: The Nahuatl town histories of colonial Cuernavaca. *Colonial Latin American Historical Review* 1: 1–36.

———. 1996. Paper shields: The ideology of coats of arms in primordial titles. *Ethnohistory* 43: 99–127.

Hassig, Ross. 1985. *Trade, tribute, and transportation: The sixteenth-century political economy of the Valley of Mexico*. Norman: University of Oklahoma Press.

Hernández, fray Benito. 1567. *Doctrina en lengua misteca*. Mexico City: Pedro Ocharte.

Hernández Rodríguez, Rosaura. 1954. El valle de Toluca, su historia: Epoca prehispánica y siglo XVI. Master's thesis, Universidad Nacional Autónoma de México.

———. 1966. Los pueblos prehispánicos del Valle de Toluca. *Estudios de Cultura Náhuatl* 6: 219–25.

Hill, Robert M. II. 1984. Chinamit and Molab: Late postclassic highland Maya precursors to the closed corporate community. *Estudios de Cultura Maya* 15: 301–27.

———. 1986. Manteniendo el culto a los santos: Aspectos financieros de las instituciones religiosas Mayas en el altiplano colonial. *Mesoamerica* 11: 61–77.

———. 1989. *The Pirir papers and other colonial period Cakchiquel-Maya testamentos*. Vanderbilt University Publications in Anthropology, no. 37. Nashville, Tenn.: Vanderbilt University.

———. 1991. The social uses of writing among the colonial Cakchiquel Maya: Nativism, resistance, and innovation. In *Columbian consequences*, vol. 3, ed. David Hurst Thomas. Washington, D.C.: Smithsonian Institution Press.

———. 1992. *Colonial Cakchiquels: Highland Maya adaptations to Spanish rule, 1600–1700*. New York: Harcourt Brace Jovanovich.

Hill, Robert M. II, and John Monaghan. 1987. *Continuities in highland Maya social organization: Ethnohistory in Sacapulas, Guatemala*. Philadelphia: University of Pennsylvania Press.

Hinze, Eike, Claudine Hatau, and Marie-Luise Heimann-Koenen. 1983. *Aztekischer Zensus: Zurindianischen Wirtshaft und Gesellschaft im Marquesado um 1540: Aus dem "Libro de Tributos" (Col. ant. ms. 551) im Archivo Historico, Mexico*. Hannover: Verlag für Ethnologie.

Horn, Rebecca. 1989. Postconquest Coyoacan: Aspects of indigenous sociopolitical and economic organization in Central Mexico, 1550–1650. Ph.D. diss., UCLA.

———. 1997a. Gender and social identity: Nahua naming patterns in post-conquest Central Mexico. In *Indian women of early Mexico*, ed. Susan Schroeder, Stephanie Wood, and Robert Haskett. Norman: University of Oklahoma Press.

————. 1997b. *Postconquest Coyoacan: Nahua-Spanish relations in Central Mexico, 1519–1650.* Stanford, Calif.: Stanford University Press.

Huertas Vallejos, Lorenzo. 1987 [1578]. *Ecología e historia: Probanzas de indios y españoles referentes a las castatróficas lluvias de 1578, en los corregimientos de Trujillo y Saña.* Chiclayo, Perú: CES Solidaridad.

Hunt, Marta Espejo-Ponce. 1974. Colonial Yucatán: Town and region in the seventeenth century. Ph.D. diss., UCLA.

Hunt, Marta Espejo-Ponce, and Matthew Restall. 1997. Work, marriage, and status: Maya women of colonial Yucatán. In *Indian women of early Mexico*, ed. Susan Schroeder, Stephanie Wood, and Robert Haskett. Norman: University of Oklahoma Press.

Jurado Noboa, Fernando. 1990. *Sancho Hacho: Orígenes de la formación mestiza ecuatoriana.* Quito: CEDECO/Abya-Yala.

Kanter, Deborah. 1995. Native female land tenure and its decline in Mexico, 1750–1900. *Ethnohistory* 42: 607–16.

Karttunen, Frances. 1982. Nahua literacy. In *The Inca and Aztec States, 1400–1800*, ed. George Collier, Renato Rosaldo, John Wirth. New York: Academic Press.

————. 1985. *Nahuatl and Maya in contact with Spanish.* Austin: Department of Linguistics and Center for Cognitive Science, University of Texas.

Karttunen, Frances, and James Lockhart. 1976. *Nahuatl in the middle years: Language contact phenomena in texts of the colonial period.* University of California Publications in Linguistics, no. 85. Berkeley: University of California.

Keen, Benjamin. 1985. Main currents in United States writings on colonial Spanish America, 1884–1984. *Hispanic American Historical Review* 65: 657–82.

Keith, Robert G. 1971. *Encomienda, hacienda*, and *corregimiento* in Spanish America: A structural analysis. *Hispanic American Historical Review* 51: 431–46.

————. 1976. *Conquest and agrarian change: Emergence of the hacienda system on the Peruvian coast.* Cambridge, Mass.: Harvard University Press.

Kellogg, Susan. 1980. Social organization in early colonial Tenochtitlan-Tlatelolco. Ph.D. diss., University of Rochester.

————. 1986. Aztec inheritance in sixteenth-century Mexico City: Colonial patterns, pre-Hispanic influences. *Ethnohistory* 33: 313–30.

————. 1991. Histories for anthropology: Ten years of historical research and writing by anthropologists, 1980–1990. *Social Science History* 15: 417–55.

————. 1995a. *Law and the transformation of Aztec culture, 1500–1700.* Norman: University of Oklahoma Press.

————. 1995b. The woman's room: Some aspects of gender relations in Tenochtitlan in the late pre-Hispanic period. *Ethnohistory* 42: 563–76.

————. 1997. From parallel and equivalent to separate but unequal: Tenochca Mexica women, 1500–1700. In *Indian women of early Mexico*, ed. Susan Schroeder, Stephanie Wood, and Robert Haskett. Norman: University of Oklahoma Press.

Kettle, Ann J. 1984. "My wife shall have it": Marriage and property in the wills and testaments of later mediaeval England. In *Marriage and property: Women and marital customs in history*, ed. Elizabeth M. Craik. Aberdeen, Scotland: Aberdeen University Press.

King, Mark. 1990. Poetics and metaphor in Mixtec writing. *Ancient Mesoamerica* 1: 141–51.

Klor de Alva, J. Jorge. 1982. Spiritual conflict and accommodation in New Spain: Toward a typology of Aztec responses to Christianity. In *The Inca and Aztec states, 1400–1800: Anthropology and History*, ed. George A. Collier, Renato I. Rosaldo, and John D. Wirth. New York: Academic Press.

———. 1992. Introduction to *The Aztec image of self and society: An introduction to Nahua culture*, ed. Miguel León-Portilla. Salt Lake City: University of Utah Press.

Krech III, Shepherd. 1991. The state of ethnohistory. In *Annual Review of Anthropology*, vol. 20, ed. Bernard Siegel, Alan Beals, and Stephen Tyler. Palo Alto, Calif.: Annual Reviews.

Larson, Brooke. 1988. *Colonialism and agrarian transformation in Bolivia: Cochabamba, 1500–1900.* Princeton, N.J.: Princeton University Press.

Larson, Brooke, and Olivia Harris, with Enrique Tandeter, eds. 1995. *Ethnicity, markets, and migration in the Andes: At the crossroads of history and anthropology.* Durham, N.C.: Duke University Press.

Las Casas, Bartolome de. 1965 [ca. 1552–53]. *Tratados de Fray Bartolomé de las Casas.* 2 vols. Mexico City: Fondo de Cultura Económica.

———. 1975 [ca. 1536]. *Del único modo de atraer a todos los pueblos a la verdadera religion.* Mexico City: Fondo de Cultura Económica.

Lavrin, Asunción, and Edith B. Couturier. 1979. Dowries and wills: A view of women's socioeconomic role in colonial Guadalajara and Puebla, 1640–1790. *Hispanic American Historical Review* 59: 280–304.

León, Martín de. 1611. *Camino del cielo.* Mexico City: Emprenta de Diego López Davalos.

Leonard, Irving. 1992 [1949]. *Books of the brave: Being an account of books and of men in the Spanish conquest and settlement of the sixteenth-century New World.* Berkeley: University of California Press.

León-Portilla, Miguel. 1976. El libro de testamentos indígenas de Culhuacan. *Estudios de Cultura Náhuatl* 12: 11–31.

———, ed. 1992. *The Aztec image of self and society: An introduction to Nahua culture.* Salt Lake City: University of Utah Press.

Levillier, Roberto D., ed. 1918. *La audiencia de Charcas: Correspondencia de presidentes y oidores, documentos del Archivo de Indias.* Vol. 1, 1561–79. Madrid: Imprenta de Juan Pueyo.

———, ed. 1929. *Ordenanzas de don Francisco de Toledo, virrey del Perú, 1569–1581.* Madrid: Imprenta de Juan Pueyo.

Lévi-Strauss, Claude. 1983 [1969]. *The raw and the cooked.* Chicago: University of Chicago Press.

Lewin, Linda. 1992. Natural and spurious children in Brazilian inheritance law from colony to empire: A methodological essay. *The Americas* 48: 351–96.

Lockhart, James. 1968. *Spanish Peru, 1532–1560: A colonial society.* Madison: University of Wisconsin Press.

———. 1972. *The men of Cajamarca: A social and biographical study of the first conquerors of Peru.* Austin: University of Texas Press.

———. 1976. Capital and province, Spaniard and Indian: The example of late sixteenth-century Toluca. In *Provinces of early Mexico: Variants of Spanish American regional evolution,* ed. Ida Altman and James Lockhart. Los Angeles: UCLA Latin American Center Publications.

———. 1982. Views of corporate self and history in some Valley of Mexico towns, seventeenth and eighteenth centuries. In *The Inca and Aztec states, 1400–1800,* ed. George Collier, Renato Rosaldo, and John Wirth. New York: Academic Press.

———. 1991a. *Nahuas and Spaniards: Postconquest Central Mexican history and philology.* Stanford and Los Angeles: Stanford University Press and UCLA Latin America Center Publications.

———. 1991b. Views of corporate self and history in some Valley of Mexico towns, seventeenth and eighteenth centuries. In *Nahuas and Spaniards: Postconquest Central Mexican history and philology.* Stanford and Los Angeles: Stanford University Press and UCLA Latin America Center Publications.

———. 1992. *The Nahuas after the conquest: A social and cultural history of the Indians of central Mexico, sixteenth through eighteenth centuries.* Stanford, Calif.: Stanford University Press.

———. 1994. Sightings: Initial Nahua reactions to Spanish culture. In *Implicit understandings: Observing, reporting, and reflecting on the encounters between Europeans and other peoples in the early modern era,* ed. Stuart B. Schwartz. Cambridge: Cambridge University Press.

Loera y Chávez, Margarita. 1977. *Calimaya y Tepemaxalco: Tenencia y transmisión hereditaria de la tierra en dos comunidades indígenas (época colonial).* Mexico City: Departmento de Investigaciones Historicas del Instituto Nacional de Antropología e Historia.

Lohmann Villena, Guillermo. 1966. La · restitución por corregidores y encomenderos: Un aspecto de la incidencia lascasiana en el Perú. *Anuario de Estudios Americanos* 23: 21–89.

López de Gómara, Francisco. 1943 [1552]. *Historia de la conquista de México.* Mexico City: Editorial Robredo.

Malagón, Javier, and José M. Ots Capdequí. 1965. *Solórzano y la Política indiana.* Mexico City: Fondo de Cultura Económica.

Maravall, José Antonio. 1984. Trabajo y exclusión: El trabajador manual en el sistema social de la primera modernidad. In *Estudios de historia del pensamiento español.* Vol. 2. Madrid: Ediciones Cultural Hispánica.

———. 1987. *Culture of the baroque: Analysis of a historical structure.* Trans. Terry Cochran. Minneapolis: University of Minnesota Press.

Marcus, Joyce. 1992. *Mesoamerican writing systems: Propaganda, myth, and history in four ancient civilizations.* Princeton, N.J.: Princeton University Press.

Markov, Gretchen. 1983. The legal status of Indians under Spanish rule. Ph.D. diss., University of Rochester.

Martin, Cheryl English. 1985. *Rural society in colonial Morelos.* Albuquerque: University of New Mexico Press.

Martínez Cereceda, José Luis. 1988. Kurakas, rituales, e insignias: Una proposición. *Histórica* 12: 61–74.

————. 1995. *Autoridades en los Andes: Los atributos del señor.* Lima: Pontificia Universidad Católica del Perú, Fondo Editorial.

Matienzo, Juan de. 1967 [1567]. *Gobierno del Perú (1567).* Paris: L'Institut Francais d'Etudes Andines.

Máynez, Pilar, Paciano Blancas, and Francisco Morales. 1995. Títulos sobre la fundación de Coatepec de las Bateas. *Estudios de Cultural Náhuatl* 25: 263–319.

McLeod, Murdo. 1973. *Spanish Central America: A socioeconomic history, 1520–1720.* Berkeley: University of California Press.

Medina, Pedro de. 1944 [1555]. *Libro de grandezas y cosas memorables de España. Libro de la verdad.* In *Obras de Pedro de Medina,* ed. Angel González Palencia. Vol. 1 of *Clásicos Españoles.* Madrid: Consejo Superior de Investigaciones Científicas.

Menegus Bornemann, Margarita. 1991. *Del Señorío a la República de indios: El caso de Toluca: 1500–1600.* Madrid: Ministerio de Agricultura, Pesca, y Alimentación, Secretaría General Técnica.

Mignolo, Walter D. 1994. Signs and their transmission: The question of the book in the New World. In *Writing without words: Alternative literacies in Mesoamerica and the Andes,* ed. Elizabeth Hill Boone and Walter D. Mignolo. Durham, N.C.: Duke University Press.

————. 1995. *The darker side of the European Renaissance: Literacy, territoriality, and colonization.* Ann Arbor: University of Michigan Press.

Mintz, Sidney W. 1974. *Caribbean transformations.* Chicago: Aldine.

Molina, fray Alonso de. 1565. *Confesionario mayor, en lengua mexicana y castellana.* Mexico City: Antonio de Espinosa.

————. 1984a [1569]. *Confesionario mayor en la lengua mexicana y castellana,* ed. Roberto Moreno. Mexico City: UNAM.

————. 1984b [1565]. *Confesionario mayor en la lengua mexicana y castellana.* In *Monumenta Catechetica Hispanoamericana (siglos XVI–XVIII),* ed. Juan Guillermo Durán. Buenos Aires: Facultad de Teología de la Pontificia Universidad Católica Argentina "Santa María de los Buenos Aires."

Monaghan, John. 1990. Performance and the structure of Mixtec codices. *Ancient Mesoamerica* 1: 133–40.

————. 1995. *The covenants with earth and rain: Exchange, sacrifice, and revelation in Mixtec sociality.* Norman: University of Oklahoma Press.

Moreno Yánez, Segundo. 1983. "Formaciones políticas tribales y señoríos étnicos. In *Nueva historia del Ecuador,* vol. 2, ed. Enrique Ayala Mora. Quito: Grijalbo.

————. 1985. *Sublevaciones indígenas en la Audiencia de Quito.* Quito: Pontificia Universidad Católica del Ecuador.

Mörner, Magnus. 1966. La infiltración mestiza en los cacicazgos cabildos de indios, siglos XVI–XVIII. In *Actas y memorias,* vol. 2, Congreso Internacional de Americanistas, XXXVI (Seville, 1964). Sevilla: ECESA.

Morris, Craig, and Idilio Santillana. 1997. Chincha and Huánuco: Contrasts in the exercise of power. Paper presented at a symposium entitled "Variations in the Expression of Inka Power." Washington, D.C.: Dumbarton Oaks.

Motolinía, fray Toribio de Benavente. 1971 [1541]. *Memoriales o libro de las cosas de la Nueva España.* Mexico City: UNAM.

Münch, Guido. 1976. *El cacicazgo de San Juan Teotihuacan durante la colonia, 1521–1821.* Mexico City: SEP, Instituto Nacional de Antropología e Historia, Centro de Investigaciones Superiores.

———. 1980. Tenencia de la tierra y organización social en Oaxaca durante la colonia. *Anales de Antropología* 17: 159–83.

Murra, John V. 1968. An Aymara kingdom in 1567. *Ethnohistory* 15: 115–51.

———. 1970. Current research and prospects in Andean ethnohistory. *Latin American Research Review* 61: 3–36.

———. 1975. Las etno-categorías de un *khipu* estatal. In *Formaciones económicas y politicias del mundo andino.* Lima: Instituto de Estudios Peruanos.

———. 1977. La correspondencia entre un "capitán de la mita" y su apoderado en Potosí. *Historia y Cultura* (La Paz) 3: 45–58.

———. 1989. Cloth and its functions in the Inka state. In *Cloth and human experience,* ed. Annette B. Weiner and Jane Schneider. Washington, D.C.: Smithsonian Institution Press.

Nader, Helen. 1990. *Liberty in abolutist Spain: The Hapsburg sale of towns, 1516–1700.* Baltimore: Johns Hopkins University Press.

Nalle, Sara T. 1989. Literacy and culture in early modern Castile. *Past and Present* 125: 65–96.

———. 1992. *God in La Mancha: Religious reform and the people of Cuenca, 1500–1650.* Baltimore: Johns Hopkins University Press.

Namala, Doris. 1995. Native voices: A textual analysis of seventeenth- and eighteenth-century Nahuatl testaments from Coyoacan (Mexico). Master's thesis, University of Utah.

Nutini, Hugo. 1965. Polygyny in a Tlaxcalan community. *Ethnology* 4: 123–47.

Oberem, Udo. 1993. *Sancho Hacho: Un cacique mayor del siglo XVI.* Quito: CEDECO/Abya-Yala.

Offutt, Leslie S. 1992. Levels of acculturation in northeastern New Spain: San Esteban testaments of the seventeenth and eighteenth centuries. *Estudios de Cultura Náhuatl* 22: 409–43.

Ohnuki-Tierney, Emiko, ed. 1990. *Culture through time: Anthropological approaches.* Stanford, Calif.: Stanford Unversity Press.

Ong, Walter J. 1982. *Orality and literacy: The technologizing of the word.* London: Methuen.

Orozco, Alonso B. 1921 [1583]. *Victoria de la muerte.* Madrid: Gil-Blas.

Ortiz, Fernando. 1947. *Cuban counterpoint: Tobacco and sugar.* New York: Knopf.

Patch, Robert W. 1993. *Maya and Spaniard in Yucatan, 1648–1812.* Stanford, Calif.: Stanford University Press.

Pease G.Y., Franklin. 1981. Las relaciones entre las tierras altas y la costa del sur del Perú: Fuentes documentales. In *Estudios etnográficos del Perú meridional,* ed. Shozo Masuda. Tokyo: University of Tokyo.

————. 1988. Curacas coloniales: Riqueza y actitudes. *Revista de Indias* 48: 87–107.

————. 1992. *Curacas: Reciprocidad y riqueza.* Lima: Pontificia Universidad Católica del Perú, Fondo Editorial.

Peñafiel Ramón, Antonio. 1987. *Testamento y buena muerte: Un estudio de mentalidades en la Murcia del siglo XVIII.* Murcia, Spain: Academía Alfonso X El Sabio.

Pérez, Aquiles. 1969. *Los Puruhuayes.* Vol. 1. Quito: Casa de la Cultura Ecuatoriana.

Platt, Tristan. 1978. Acerca del sistema tributario pre-toledano en el Alto Perú. *Avances* (La Paz): 33–46.

————. 1987a. The Andean soldiers of Christ: Confraternity organization, the mass of the sun, and regenerative warfare in rural Potosí (18th–20th centuries). *Journal de la Société des Américanistes* 73: 157–75.

————. 1987b. Entre xh'awxa y muxsa: Para una historia del pensamiento político Aymara. In *Tres reflexiones sobre el pensamiento andino,* ed. Thérèse Bouysse-Cassagne et al. La Paz: HISBOL.

Polanco, Juan de, S.J. 1578. *Regla y orden para ayudar a bien morir a los que se parten de esta vida.* Zaragoza.

Poole, Stafford. 1995. *Our Lady of Guadalupe: The origins and sources of a Mexican national symbol, 1531–1797.* Tucson: University of Arizona Press.

Powers, Karen. 1991. Resilient lords and Indian vagabonds: Wealth, migration, and reproductive transformation of Quito's chiefdoms. *Ethnohistory* 38: 225–49.

Powers, Karen Vieira. 1995. *Andean journeys: Migration, ethnogenesis, and the state in colonial Quito.* Albuquerque: University of New Mexico Press.

Prior, Mary. 1990. Wives and wills, 1558–1700. In *English rural society, 1500–1800: Essays in honor of Joan Thirsk,* ed. John Chartres and David Hey. Cambridge: Cambridge University Press.

Quezada Ramírez, María Noemí. 1972. *Los matlatzincas, época prehispánica y época colonial hasta 1650.* Mexico City: Instituto Nacional de Antropología e Historia.

Ramírez, Susan. 1979. Chérrepe en 1572: Un análisis de la visita general del Virrey Francisco de Toledo. *Historia y cultura* 11: 79–121.

————. 1982. Retainers of the lords or merchants: A case of mistaken identity? In *El hombre y su ambiente en los Andes centrales,* ed. Luis Millones and Hiroyasu Tomoeda. Osaka: National Museum of Ethnology.

————. 1986. *Provincial patriarchs: Land tenure and the economics of power in colonial Peru.* Albuquerque: University of New Mexico.

————. 1987. The *Dueño de Indios:* Thoughts on the consequences of the shifting base of power of the "*Curacas de los viejos antiguos*" under the Spanish in sixteenth-century Peru. *Hispanic American Historical Review* 67: 575–610.

————. 1995. De pescadores y agricultores: Una historia local de la gente del Valle de Chicama antes de 1565. *Boletín del Instituto de Estudios Andinos* 24: 245–79.

————. 1996a. To feed and be fed: Curacas, community, and cosmology. Paper presented at the conference entitled "Making Sense of the World:

Perceptions of Change in Mesoamerica and the Andes," a Bilingual CEDLA Workshop, Amsterdam.

———. 1996b. *The world upside down: Cross-cultural contact and conflict in sixteenth-century Peru.* Stanford, Calif.: Stanford University Press.

———. 1997. Un mercader . . . es un pescador: Reflexiones sobre las relaciones económicas y los multiples roles de los indios americanos en el Perú del siglo XVI. In *Arqueología, antropología, e historia en los Andes: Homenaje a María Rostworowski,* ed. Rafeal Varón Gabai and Javier Flores Espinoza. Lima: Instituto de Estudios Peruanos and Banco Central de Reserva del Perú.

Ramón, Galo. 1987. *La resistencia andina: Cayambe, 1500–1800.* Quito: Centro Andino de Acción Popular.

Rappaport, Joanne. 1990. *The politics of memory: Native historical interpretation in the Colombian Andes.* Cambridge: Cambridge University Press.

———. 1994a. *Cumbe reborn: An Andean ethnography of history.* Chicago: University of Chicago Press.

———. 1994b. Object and alphabet: Andean Indians and documents in the colonial period. In *Writing without words: Alternative literacies in Mesoamerica and the Andes,* ed. Elizabeth Hill Boone and Walter D. Mignolo. Durham: Duke University Press.

Rappaport, Joanne, and Tom Cummins. 1994. Literacy and power in colonial Latin America. In *Social construction of the past: Representation as power,* ed. George Clement Bond and Angela Gilliam. New York: Routledge.

Real Academia Española. 1832. *Diccionario de la lengua Castellana.* 7th ed. Madrid: La Imprenta Real.

Recinos, Adrian. 1950. *Memorial de Sololá/Anales de los Cakchiquels.* Mexico City: Fondo de Cultural Económica.

Recopilación. 1973 [1681]. *Recopilación de leyes de los reynos de las indias.* Madrid: Ediciones Cultura Hispánica.

Remy S., Pilar. 1983. Tasas tributarias pre-toledanas de la provincia de Cajamarca. *Historia y cultura* 16: 67–82.

———. 1986. Organización y cambios en el Reino de Cuismancu, 1540–70. In *Historia de Cajamarca,* vol. 2, compiled by Fernando Silva Santisteban, Waldemar Espinoza Soriano, and Rogger Ravines. Cajamarca: Instituto Nacional de Cultura.

Restall, Matthew. 1991. Yaxkukul revisted: Dating and categorizing a controversial Maya land document. *UCLA Historical Journal* 11: 122–30.

———. 1994. "The document shall be seen": Yucatec Maya literacy. In *Chipping away on earth: Studies in prehispanic and colonial Mexico in honor of Arthur J. O. Anderson and Charles E. Dibble,* ed. Eloise Quiñones Keber, with the assistance of Susan Schroeder and Fredric Hicks. Lancaster, Calif.: Labyrinthos.

———. 1995a. "He wished it in vain": Subordination and resistance among Maya women in post-conquest Yucatan. *Ethnohistory* 42: 577–94.

———. 1995b. *Life and death in a Maya community: The Ixil testaments of the 1760s.* Lancaster, Calif.: Labyrinthos.

———. 1997a. Heirs to the hieroglyphs: Indigenous writing in colonial Mesoamerica. *The Americas* 54: 239–67.

———. 1997b. *The Maya world: Yucatec culture and society, 1550– 1850.* Stanford, Calif.: Stanford University Press.

———. 1998. *Maya conquistador.* Boston: Beacon Press.

Reyes, fray Antonio de los. 1976 [1593]. *Arte en lengua mixteca.* Vanderbilt University Publications in Anthropology, no. 14. Nashville, Tenn.: Vanderbilt University.

Ricard, Robert. 1966. *The spiritual conquest of Mexico: An essay on the apostolate and the evangelizing methods of the Mendicant orders in New Spain: 1523–72.* Trans. Lesley Byrd Simpson. Berkeley: University of California Press.

Rivera Cusicanqui, Silvia. 1978. El mallku y la sociedad colonial en el siglo XVII: El caso de Jesús de Machaca. *Avances* (Revista Boliviana de Estudios Históricos y Sociales, La Paz) 1: 7–27.

Robertson, Donald. 1966. The Mixtec religious manuscripts. In *Ancient Oaxaca,* ed. John Paddock. Stanford, Calif.: Stanford University Press.

Rostworowski de Diez Canseco, María. 1966. Visitas de indios en el siglo XVI. *Cahiers du monde hispanique et luso-brésilien* 7: 85–92.

———. 1977. Mercaderes del Valle de Chincha en la época prehispanica: Un documento y unos comentarios. In *Etnia y Sociedad.* Lima: Instituto de Estudios Peruanos.

Rostworowski de Diez Canseco, María, and Pilar Remy. 1992. *Las visitas a Cajamarca 1571–72/1578: Documentos.* Lima: Instituto de Estudios Peruanos.

Roys, Ralph L. 1939. *The titles of Ebtun.* Washington, D.C.: Carnegie Institution.

Rugeley, Terry. 1996. *Yucatan's Maya peasantry and the origins of the Caste War, 1800–1847.* Austin: University of Texas Press.

Ruíz de Alarcón, Hernando. 1984 [1629]. *Treatise on the heathen superstitions that today live among the Indians native to this New Spain, 1629.* Trans. and ed. J. Richard Andrews and Ross Hassig. Norman: University of Oklahoma Press.

Sahagún, fray Bernardino de. 1950–82 [1569]. *The Florentine Codex: General history of the things of New Spain.* Trans. and ed. Arthur J. O. Anderson and Charles E. Dibble. No. 14, 13 parts. Salt Lake City: School of American Research and University of Utah Press.

Saignes, Thierry. 1985. *Caciques, tribute, and migration in the southern Andes: Indian society and the seventeenth-century colonial order.* Trans. Paul Garner. London: University of London.

———. 1987. De la borrachera al retrato: Los caciques andinos entre dos legitimadades (Charcas). *Revista Andina* 5: 139–70.

Salmon, Marylynn. 1986. *Women and the law of property in early America.* Chapel Hill: University of North Carolina Press.

Salomon, Frank. 1986. *Native lords of Quito in the age of the Incas: The political economy of north-Andean chiefdoms.* Cambridge: Cambridge University Press.

———. 1988. Indian women of early colonial Quito as seen through their testaments. *The Americas* 44: 325–42.

Sandweiss, Daniel H. 1992. *The archaeology of Chincha fishermen: Specialization and status in Inka Peru.* Pittsburgh: Carnegie Musuem of Natural History.

Santillán, Licenciado Fernando de. 1927. Relación. In *Historia de los Incas y relación de su gobierno*, ed. Horacio H. Urteaga. Lima: Imprenta y Librería Sanmarti y Ca.

Sarabia Viejo, María. 1978. *Don Luis de Velasco: Virrey de Nueva España, 1550–1564.* Sevilla: Escuela de Estudios Hispano-Americanos de Sevilla.

———, ed. 1986–89. *Francisco de Toledo: Disposiciones gubernativas para el virreinato del Perú, 1569–1574.* 2 vols. Sevilla: Escuela de Estudios Hispano-Americanos, Consejo Superior de Investigaciones Científicas, Monte de Piedad y Caja de Ahorros de Sevilla.

Schroeder, Susan. 1991. *Chimalpahin and the kingdoms of Chalco.* Tucson: University of Arizona Press.

Seed, Patricia. 1988. *To love, honor, and obey in colonial Mexico: Conflicts over marriage choice, 1574–1821.* Stanford, Calif.: Stanford University Press.

Sell, Barry. 1993. Friars, Nahuas, and books: Language and expression in colonial Nahuatl publications. Ph.D. diss., UCLA.

———. n.d. The spiritual mothers of Tula and other episodes in the life of an indigenous confraternity. Unpublished ms.

Shammas, Carole, Marylynn Salmon, and Michael Dahlin. 1987. *Inheritance in America: From colonial times to present.* New Brunswick, N.J.: Rutgers University Press.

Siete Partidas. 1974 [1555]. *Las siete partidas del rey don Alonso el nono, nueuamente glosadas por el Licenciado Gregorio López del Consejo Real de Indias de su Magestad.* 3 vols. Madrid: Imprenta Nacional del Boletín del Estado.

Silva Santisteban, Fernando. 1982. El reino de Cuismanco. *Revista del Museo Nacional (Lima).* 46: 293–315.

Silverblatt, Irene. 1987. *Moon, sun, and witches: Gender ideologies and class in Inca and colonial Peru.* Princeton, N.J.: Princeton University Press.

Smith, Mary Elizabeth. 1973. *Picture writing from ancient southern Mexico: Mixtec place signs and maps.* Norman: University of Oklahoma Press.

Solórzano y Pereyra, Juan de. 1972 [1647]. 5 vols. In *Biblioteca de Autores Españoles*, vols. 252–56. Madrid: Companía Iberoamericana de Publicaciones.

Sousa, Lisa M. 1998. Women in native societies and cultures of colonial Mexico. Ph.D. diss., UCLA.

Spalding, Karen. 1984. *Huarochirí: An Andean society under Inca and Spanish rule.* Stanford, Calif.: Stanford University Press.

Spores, Ronald. 1964. The genealogy of Tlazultepec: A sixteenth-century Mixtec manuscript. *Southwestern Journal of Anthropology* 20: 15–31.

———. 1967. *Mixtec kings and their people.* Norman: University of Oklahoma Press.

———. 1997. Mixteca cacicas: Status, wealth, and the political accommodations of the native elite women in early colonial Oaxaca. In *Indian women of early Mexico*, ed. Susan Schroeder, Stephanie Wood, and Robert Haskett. Norman: University of Oklahoma Press.

Starr, Fredrick. 1898. *The Mapa de Cuauhtlantzinco or Códice Campos.* Chicago: University of Chicago Press.

Stern, Steve J. 1982. *Peru's Indian peoples and the challenge of the Spanish conquest: Huamanga to 1640*. Madison: University of Wisconsin Press.

———. 1983. The struggle for solidarity: Class, culture, and community in highland Indian America. *Radical History Review* 27: 21–45.

———. 1988. Feudalism, capitalism, and the world-system in the perspective of Latin America and the Caribbean. *American Historical Review* 93: 829–72.

Swanson, R. N. 1995. *Religion and devotion in Europe, c. 1215–c. 1515*. Cambridge: Cambridge University Press.

Taylor, William B. 1972. *Landlord and peasant in colonial Oaxaca*. Stanford, Calif.: Stanford University Press.

———. 1979. *Drinking, homicide, and rebellion in colonial Mexican villages*. Stanford, Calif.: Stanford University Press.

———. 1987. The Virgin of Guadalupe in New Spain: An inquiry into the social history of Marian devotion. *American Ethnologist* 14: 9–33.

———. 1996. *Magistrates of the sacred: Priests and parishioners in eighteenth-century Mexico*. Stanford, Calif.: Stanford University Press.

Terraciano, Kevin. 1994. Ñudzahui history: Mixtec writing and culture in colonial Oaxaca. Ph.D. diss., UCLA.

Terraciano, Kevin, and Lisa M. Sousa. 1992. The "Original Conquest" of Oaxaca: Mixtec and Nahua history and myth. *UCLA Historical Journal* 12: 29–90.

Thompson, I. A. A. 1979. The purchase of nobility in Castile, 1552–1700. *Journal of European Economic History* 8: 313–60.

Thompson, Philip C. 1978. Tekanto in the eighteenth century. Ph.D. diss., Tulane University.

Tutino, John. 1983. Power, class, and family: Men and women in the Mexican elite, 1750–1810. *The Americas* 39: 359–82.

Ugarte, Cesar A. 1923. Los antecedentes históricas del régimen agrario peruano. *Revista Universitaria* 1: 318–98.

Urteaga, Horacio H. 1919. *El Perú: Bocetos históricos*. 2 vols. Lima: Casa Editora E. Rosay.

Urton, Gary. 1994. A new twist in an old yarn: Variation in knot directionality in the Inka khipus. *Baessler-Archiv Beitrage Zur Völkerkunde*, Neue Folge, 42: 271–305.

Valdéz de la Torre, Carlos. 1921. *Evolución de las comunidades de indígenas*. Lima: Editorial Evforion.

Velasco, Juan de. 1979 [1789]. *Historia del reino de Quito en la America Meridional*. 3 vols. Quito: Editorial Casa de la Cultural Ecuatoriana.

Venegas, Alejo de. 1911 [1536]. *Agonía del tránsito de la muerte: Con avisos y consuelos que cerca della son provechosos*. In *Escritores misticos españoles*, vol. 1, ed. Miguel Mir (*Nueva Biblioteca de Autores Españoles*, vol. 16). Madrid: Bailly-Bailliere.

Villanueva Urteaga, Horació. 1975. *Cajamarca: Apuntes para su historia*. Cuzco: Editorial Garcilaso.

Vovelle, Michel. 1973. *Piété baroque et déchristianisation en Provence au XVIIIᵉ: Les attitudes devant le mort d'aprés les clauses des testaments*. Paris: Plon.

———. 1978. *Piété baroque et déchristianisation en Provence au XVIIIᵉ siécle*. Edition abregée. Paris: Editions du Seuil.

————. 1990. *Ideologies and mentalities.* Trans. Eamon O'Flaherty. Chicago: University of Chicago Press.

Wightman, Ann M. 1990. *Indigenous migration and social change: The forasteros of Cuzco, 1570–1720.* Durham: University of North Carolina Press.

Wood, Stephanie. 1984. Corporate adjustments in colonial Mexican Indian towns: Toluca region, 1550–1810. Ph.D. diss., UCLA.

————. 1991a. Adopted saints: Christian images in Nahua testaments of late colonial Toluca. *The Americas* 42: 259–94.

————. 1991b. The cosmic conquest: Late-colonial views of the sword and cross in Central Mexican *títulos. Ethnohistory* 38: 176–91.

————. 1992. The evolution of the Indian corporation of the Toluca region, 1550–1810. *Estudios de Cultura Náhuatl* 22: 381–407.

————. 1994. La mujer Nahua rural bajo la colonización española: El Valle de Toluca durante la época colonial tardía/Rural Nahua women under Spanish colonization: The late-colonial Toluca Valley. In *Mesoamerican and Chicano art, culture, and identity/El arte, la cultura, y la identidad mesoamericana y chicana*, ed. Robert C. Dash. *Willamette Journal of the Liberal Arts*, Supplemental Series, no. 6. Salem, Ore.: Willamette University.

————. 1997a. Matters of life and death: Nahuatl testaments of rural women, 1589–1801. In *Native women of early Mexico*, ed. Susan Schroeder, Stephanie Wood, and Robert Haskett. Norman: University of Oklahoma Press.

————. 1997b. The social versus legal context of Nahua *títulos.* In *Native traditions in the postconquest world*, ed. Elizabeth Hill Boone and Tom Cummins. Washington, D.C.: Dumbarton Oaks.

Ximénez, Francisco. 1929–31. *Historia de la provincia de San Vicente de Chiapa y Guatemala.* 3 vols. Guatemala City: Sociedad de Geografía e Historia.

Zavala, Silvio. 1971. *Las instituciones jurídicas en la conquista de América.* 2d ed. Mexico City: Editorial Porrúa.

————. 1973. *La encomienda indiana.* 2d ed. Mexico City: Editorial Porrúa.

————. 1984. *Tributos y servicios personales de indios para Hernán Cortés y su familia: Extractos de documentos del siglos XVI.* Mexico City: Archivo General de la Nación.

Zavala, Silvio, and María Costelo, eds. 1939–46. *Fuentes para la historia del trabajo en Nueva España.* 8 vols. Mexico City: Fondo de Cultural Económica.

Zelicer, Viviana A. The creation of domestic currencies. *American Economic Review* 84: 138–42.

————. 1994b. *The social meaning of money.* New York: Basic Books.

Zevallos Quiñones, Jorge. 1989. *Los cacicazgos de Lambayeque.* Trujillo, Peru: Gráfica Cuarto.

Zulawski, Ann. 1990. Social differentiation, gender, and ethnicity: Urban Indian women in colonial Bolivia, 1640–1725. *Latin American Research Review* 25: 93–114.

————. 1994. *They eat from their labor: Work and social change in colonial Bolivia.* Pittsburgh: University of Pittsburgh Press.

Contributors

Thomas A. Abercrombie is Associate Professor of Anthropology at New York University. His new book, *Pathways of Memory and Power: Ethnography and History among an Andean People*, provides parallel histories about and by a community of Aymara-speaking llama herders of the Bolivian highlands from the Spanish invasion to the 1990s. He is currently writing a book on the genesis and pageantry of the "mestizo-cholo" interculture in the cities of Oruro and Potosí from the early colony to the present, as well as researching other projects comparing aspects of Castilian and Bolivian social history.

Sarah Cline is Professor of History and Religious Studies at the University of California, Santa Barbara. She has served as contributing editor of the *Mesoamerican Ethnohistory* section of the *Handbook of Latin American Studies*, has published extensively on Mexican social and cultural history, and is currently focusing on religion in Latin America.

Robert M. Hill II is Professor of Anthropology at Tulane University. His many publications in the field of highland Maya ethnohistory include *The Traditional Pottery of Guatemala* (with R. E. Reina), *Continuities in Highland Maya Social Organization: Ethnohistory in Sacapulas, Guatemala* (with John Monaghan), *The Pirir Papers*, and *Colonial Cakchiquels: Highland Maya Adaptations to Spanish Rule, 1600–1700*.

Rebecca Horn is Associate Professor of History at the University of Utah. Her book *Postconquest Coyoacan: Nahua-Spanish Relations in Central Mexico, 1519–1650*, was recently published by Stanford University Press.

Susan Kellogg is Associate Professor of History at the University of Houston. Her book *Law and the Transformation of Aztec Culture,*

1500–1700, won honorable mention for the Howard Francis Cline Prize (1997) for the most significant contribution to the history of indigenous peoples in Latin America. She is currently working on a history of indigenous women in Latin America and conducting research on "women of color" in and around mid-colonial Mexico City.

Karen Vieira Powers is Associate Professor of Comparative Colonization in the Department of History at Northern Arizona University. Her principal research interests are in ethnogenesis, cultural reconstitution, and gender relations in the Andes. Her book *Andean Journeys: Migration, Ethnogenesis and the State in Colonial Quito* won the Howard Francis Cline Prize (1997) for the most significant contribution to the history of indigenous peoples in Latin America.

Susan E. Ramírez is Professor of Latin American History at DePaul University in Chicago. She has published two books: *Provincial Patriarchs: Land Tenure and the Economics of Power in Colonial Peru* and *The World Upside Down: Cross Cultural Contact and Conflict in Sixteenth-Century Peru*. (Honorable mention, Bolton Prize, 1997.) She is currently writing a book on cosmology and legitimacy in the Andes.

Matthew Restall is Associate Professor of History at Pennsylvania State University. His publications include *The Maya World: Yucatec Culture and Society, 1550–1850, Life and Death in a Maya Community: The Ixil Testaments of the 1760s*, and *Maya Conquistador*. He is currently writing another book on the social history of colonial Yucatan.

Kevin Terraciano is Assistant Professor of History at the University of California, Los Angeles. His publications on the ethnohistory of colonial Mesoamerica will include a forthcoming book on the social and cultural history of the Mixtecs of colonial Oaxaca, based primarily on Mixtec-language sources.

Stephanie Wood is a co-editor of *Indian Women of Early Mexico* and contributing editor of the *Mesoamerican Ethnohistory* section of the *Handbook of Latin American Studies*. She has authored numerous articles and teaches in the Department of History at the University of Oregon.

Index

212n.46–47, 227, 230, 247–48n.28;
títulos and ownership of, 86–87; in will
of Melchora de Santiago, 45; wills as
source of information on tenure, 107n.8.
See also Cacicazgo
Language: evidence of individual religious
beliefs in wills and, 24–25; expressions
of piety in Ñudzahui testaments and,
115–38; native notaries and indigenous,
18; testaments as ethnohistorical source
on Spanish and indigenous, 4;
testaments as genre of indigenous document, 14. *See also* Nahuatl language;
Ñudzahui; Spanish and Spain; Writing
Larson, Brooke, 6
Lavrin, Asunción, 30n.2
Law and legal system: gender and property
litigation in Mexico City, 50, 57n.15;
marriage and property rights of women
in Mexico City, 53; Maya wills from
Guatemala and, 164; north Andean
lawsuits over cacicazgos and
landownership, 208n.3; Ñudzahui
pictorial writing and, 119–20;
procedural problems and fraud in,
110–11n.37; wills and lawsuits over
property, 38; wills as religious
documents in European context, 16
Legitimacy: caciques in Andes and, 266,
268, 269–70, 271; caciques and testaments in Capuluac, 95; Church and
concepts of family structure, 22–23;
rulers and wills from north Andes,
183–208
Lienzo of Nativitas, 119
Lima (Peru), 256, 262
Literacy: concept of "legal literacy," 10n.3;
indigenous notaries and, 17–18; indigenous women in central Mexico and,
31n.16; of Nahuatl speakers in Mexico,
15
Lliufa y Nitibron, Doña Juana, 191, 192,
193, 202
Lobato, Don Estebán, 201
Lockhart, James, 5–6, 7, 30n.3, 80n.1,
80n.3, 87, 106n.3, 140n.19–20, 142,
160n.1–2, 160n.6, 161n.11, 216
Lopes, Doña Antonia, 203
López, Diego, 164, 168, 169
López, Doña María, 122–23, 124
López de Gómara, Francisco, 21–22
Luján, Rafael de, 168, 178n.3

Maguey cactus, 74, 77
Mahuito, Joséph, 43, 47, 52, 54–56,
58n.24
Malcaden (Peru), 221
Mamani, Don García, 267–68, 270, 271
Manco Inca, 268
María, Nicolasa, 122
Markets: Nahua traders and ties with local
Spanish in Coyoacan, 71–73, 76–77.
See also Commerce; Trade
Marriage: Church's view of as sacrament,
22–23, 32n.21; indigenous rulers and
consolidation of power in north Andes,
202–203, 213n.61; interracial among
indigenous elite in north Andes,
209n.6; property rights of women in
Mexico City, 53; rival families and
indigenous rulership in Capuluac, 96.
See also Polygyny
Martina, Angelina, 52, 53, 57–58n.17–18
Mata, Juan de, 221
Matlatzincas (ethnic group), 88, 90, 92
Matu, Pasquala, 145
Maxa Paico, Don Pedro, 226
Maya: acculturation and indigenous testa-
ments from Yucatan, 141–60;
community and individual variations in
formulas for wills, 139n.18; land, family,
and community in Cakchiquel testaments
from highland Guatemala, 163–78
Mendez, Diego, 162n.20
Mendieta, Lope de, 263–64
Mendoza, Don Antonio de, 89, 92, 93,
108n.19, 109n.28
Menegus Bornemann, Margarita, 91, 92
Mestizos: caciques in Capuluac and, 95,
109n.28; indigenous rulers in north
Andes and, 185, 197, 202, 209n.6–7;
trade in Coyoacan and, 77
Metepec (Mexico), 91, 99
Mexico: caciques and community interests
in central, 85–105; gender differences
in indigenous testaments from Mexico
City, 37–56; recent historiography of
colonial era, 5–6; testaments and
interethnic ties among traders in
Coyoacan, 59–80; themes of wills from
Andes compared to, 291–95
Mexico City, 37–56, 63, 73
Miguel, Don Agustín, 92, 93, 94, 95–96,
97–98, 99–100, 104–105, 110n.30
Miguel, Don Bartolomé, 85–105